GLORIES OF MARWAR

AND

THE GLORIES RATHORES

GLORIES OF MARWAR

AND

THE GLORIES RATHORES

PANDIT BISHESHWAR NATH REU

GYAN

Published by

Gyan Publishing House
5, Ansari Road
Daryaganj, New Delhi-110002
Phone: 011-47034999, 9811692060
E-mail: books@gyanbooks.com

Distribution Network
gyanbooks.com
India, USA, Canada, UK, Australia

ISBN: 978-93-6920-334-5 (PB)

First Published, 1943

2nd Impression 2025

Printed at: Gyan Press, Delhi.

GLORIES OF MARWAR AND THE GLORIES RATHORES
Author: PANDIT BISHESHWAR NATH REU

GLORIES OF MARWAR

&

THE GLORIOUS RATHORS.

GLORIES OF MARWAR
&
THE GLORIOUS RATHORS.

By

MAHAMAHOPADHYAYA

PANDIT BISHESHWAR NATH REU

SAHITYACHARYA

Superintendent,

Archaeological Department and Sumer Public Library,

JODHPUR

(Member Historical Records Commission)

JODHPUR

ARCHAEOLOGICAL DEPARTMENT

1943.

Air Commodore His Highness Raj Rajeshwar Saramad Raja-i-Hind Maharajadhiraj Shri Sir UMAID SINGHJI Sahab Bahadur, G.C.S.I., G.C.I.E., K.C.V.O., A.D.C., LL.D. of Jodhpur.

PREFACE

This book contains a brief history of Marwar and its illustrious rulers. In the appendices are given those articles, which were published in various research journals or read at the various conferences held from time to time at different places.

The information as to when and where these articles were published or read is also given in the beginning of each of the articles. Some of these articles are, truly speaking, reproduction of the original correspondence, which passed between the Rathor rulers and their officials or contemporary rulers. They throw new light not only on the history of Marwar, but also on the history of India.

Some of these articles have been appreciated by eminent scholars like Dr. D. R. Bhandarkar, Sir Jadunath Sarkar, etc. and some of them requested me to publish them in a book form for the easy access to the scholars.

In compliance to their wishes I have compiled this volume and the references to the articles at their proper places in the brief history will, I trust, prove useful to the scholars interested in the Rajput history.

As the articles were published in different journals and in the proceedings of the various conferences at different dates, so the spelling of proper names vary at places. Further owing to the absence of the letter S, Sh is used for both श and ष

I hope the readers will kindly excuse the author for the long errata which is due to unavoidable circumstances.

Further I may add that though this volume was sent for publication in 1940 A. D., yet the press took an unexpected long time in its printing.

Archaeological Department
Jodhpur.
4th June, 1943.

BISHESHWAR NATH REU,

FOREWORD.

by

Bada Maharaj-Kumar Shri Hanwant Singhji Sahib
Heir Apparent of Jodhpur.

THE PALACE,
JODHPUR,
RAJPUTANA.

Mahamahopadhyaya Pandit Bisheshwar Nath Reu has already published "the History of the Rashtrakutas" and "the History of Marwar". The former work traces the History of the Rashtrakutas (Rathors) from the earliest times to the migration of Rao Sihaji to Marwar, while the latter, apart from the brief history of the early ruling dynasties of Marwar, deals with the history of the Rathors from Rao Sihaji up to the present time.

This volume entitled "Glories of Marwar and the Glorious Rathors" is Mr. Reu's latest production and in addition to a brief history of Marwar contains a number of his articles, based on original researches, which the author has read at various historical conferences from time to time.

Mr. Reu has done a great service to the State by his exhaustive and patient labour in the field of historical research and we owe him a deep debt of gratitude.

"Histories make men wise"-and I hope that this book will be read widely, not only for its own absorbing interest, but for the knowledge which it contains. The story of Marwar is full of romance—tales of gloomy failure and of glittering success.

It is by a study of these events that we can acquire much wisdom—and perhaps even inspiration—to help guide us in the planning of an ever more prosperous and happy future for our beloved Homeland.

I therefore commend this book to all those who are interested in Marwar—its Past—its Present and its Future.

12th May, 1943. HANWANT SINGH.

CONTENTS.

(D)

(APPENDIX A)

(APPENDIX B)

(Its first part has been summarized and published in the proceedings of the IV History Congress, held at Lahore, in December 1940 A D under the heading "Maharaja Jaswantsingh of Jodhpur at the battle of Dharmat," pp 269-271)

(Published in the proceedings of the XVIII Historical Records Commission, held at Mysore in December 1941 A D., pp 328-331)

(Read at the XIX Historical Records Commission, held at Trivandrum, in December 1942, A D and published in its proceedings, pp 146-148)

(APPENDIX C)

(APPENDIX D.)

ILLUSTRATIONS

GLORIES OF MARWAR
AND THE
GLORIOUS RATHORS

Marwar

The Western part of Rajputana, the land of the Rajputs[1] (App. A. 1, pp. 1-15), now known as Marwar, is bounded on the north by Bikaner, on the north-east by Shaikhawati (Jaipur), on the east by Jaipur, Kishangarh and Ajmer, on the south-east by Ajmer, Merwara and Udaipur (Mewar), on the south by Sirohi and Palanpur, on the south-west by the Rann of Cutch, on the west by Thar-Parkar and Sindh and on the north-west by Jaisalmer.

It lies between latitude 24'36' and 27'42' N. and longitude 70'6' and 75'24' E. Its greatest length from north-east to south-west is 320 miles and the breadth from north to south is 170 miles and it covers an area of 36,071 sq. miles.

It is not only the largest state in Rajputana in point of size, but of all the other states in India excepting Hyderabad (Deccan), Kashmir and Kelat (Baluchistan).

According to 'Rāmāyana,' a Hindu epic, Rāma, while on his way to invade Lankā (Ceylon) threw his arrow on this part of the land which was then submerged under the sea. This arrow was drawn to threaten the sea god for passage and due to the upheavels (caused by it) this land emerged out of water and was blessed by Rāma. From this narrative we can infer that owing to the natural forces, the sea receded from this part of the land, and the Āryans began to migrate to this part of the country.

At the time of 'Mahābhārata,' (the Great War fought between Pāndavas and Kauravas), the northern part of Marwar, together with the territory comprising the present Bikaner State, was known as Jāngal, and was under the suzerainty of the Kauravas.

[1] Appendix D 4., pp 235-240.

A pillar inscription of Ashōka found at Bairat in the Jaipur State also leads us to the conclusion that probably Marwar was at that time included in the Mauryan Empire.

Ashoka.

Kushān kings ruled over India from 40 to 226 A. D. and the mightiest among them was Kanishka, who conquered the whole of the north-western India up to the Vindhya hills in the south. Therefore a part of Marwar might also have been under his sway.

Kushans

About 119 A. D. Nahapān, the well known western satrap, ruled over Gujrat, Kathiawar, Cutch, etc., hence it is just possible that the Southern portion of Marwar was also under his rule.

Western Satraps

According to the Junagarh inscription of Shak era 72 (150 A. D.) Western satrap Rudradāman ruled over Northern Gujrat, Marwar, Cutch, and Sindh.

Chandragupta II, better known as Vikramāditya, overthrew the Kingdom of the Western Kshatraps (satraps) about 388 A. D. An inscription, dated 289 of the Gupta era (609 A. D.), was found in the temple of the goddess Dadhimatī situated near Goth and Manglod villages of Marwar. The Toran pillars in the ruined fort of Mandōr, the old capital of Marwar, had an inscription in Gupta script, which has now peeled out. A big earthen pot excavated there also bears the name of the potter in the same script. All these facts lead us to the belief that certain parts of this country were also held by the Gupta Emperors.

Guptas.

In 470 A. D. the Huns invaded the Gupta Empire and conquered its Western portion which might have included some parts of Marwar also.

Huns.

About 388 A. D., when the kingdom of the Western Kshatraps was overthrown, some portion of Marwar was captured by the Gurjaras, and in course of time its Eastern part (all along from the north to the south) came to be called as Gurjaratrā (Gurjar or Gujrat). From the copper grant of Pratihār Bhōjadēv, dated

Gurjaras.

844 A. D., it is learnt that the village Siva (of Dīdwānā Dist.) was at that time included in the Gurjar Province. Bhīnmāl, a district town of Marwar, was also for some time the capital of Gujrat.

Chavaras

In 628 A. D. when Brahmagupta, a resident of Bhīnmāl, wrote his famous book on astronomy called 'Brahmasphutasiddhānta', Chāvarā Vyāghramukh ruled over the town. The famous Sanskrit poet Māgh of Bhīnmāl, who wrote the well-known poem 'Shishupālavadha,' writes in his family narrative that his grandfather was the minister of king Varmalāt. From an inscription of Varmalāt, dated 625 A. D., found at Vasantgarh, (in Sirohi State), it is found that there is a difference of only three years between the composition of 'Brahmasphuta Siddhānta' and this inscription, hence Varmalāt was either the father of Vyāghramukh, or it was his own second name. This leads us to the belief that after Gurjaras, the Southern part of Marwar passed to the Chāvarās. But in the reign of Khalīfā Hasham, the armies of Junaid—the governor of Sindh, invaded certain parts of Marwar, before the year 739 A. D. This invasion weakened the power of the Chāvarās, and soon after their kingdom was conquered by Parihārs.

Pratihars

From the inscriptions of Parihārs found in Marwar, it is learnt that the sons of Parihār Harishchandra conquered Mandōr about 613 A. D. and his great-grandson Nāgbhat established his capital at Mērtā.

Jinasēn, a Jain writer, who wrote 'Harivamsha Purana' in 783 A. D. gives the name of the ruler of the Western part of Marwar as Parihār Vatsarāj. His (Vatsarāj's) son Nāgabhat I, who is said to have built the ghāts (steps) at Pushakar, shifted his capital from Bhīnmāl to Kanauj in about 815 A. D. These Parihārs ruled at Mandōr up to

Chohans

about 1143 A. D. when Chauhān Rāyapāl of Nādōle took possession of it, as is evident from the fragmentary inscription of Sahajpāl found at Mandōr.

These Chauhāns ruled there up to 1227 A. D. when Shamsuddīn Altamash overthrew them, but soon after the Parihars drove the Mohamedans away and recovered their old capital. In 1294 A.D. Jalāluddīn Firōz Shāh Khilji invaded Mandōr and conquered it.

Shamsuddin Altamash

Pratihars.

Jalaluddin Firoz

Once again in 1395 A. D. the Parihārs re-took Maṇḍōr from the Mohamedans and considering themselves not strong enough to retain it gave it over to Rāthōr Rao Chūndā in dowry.

Pratihars.

About 686 A. D. Chauhan Vāsudev, coming from Ahichchhatrapur, established his government at Sāmbhar, and thus his descendants came to be known as 'Shākambharīshvara' or 'Sāmbharī Rāj' and their territorial possessions, including Nāgaur, were called 'Sapādalakhsha' or 'Savālakh'. About 1108 A. D. they shifted their capital to Ajmer and ruled there till about 1194 A. D., when the Mohamedans took possession of it from them.

Chauhans.

About 960 A.D. a branch of the Chauhāns established its sway over Nāḍole, which in 1021 A.D. was forced to accept the surzerainty of the Solankis, but in about 1202 A.D. they (Chauhans) were completely wiped out by Kutubuddīn.

In 1161 A. D. another branch of the Chauhāns established its rule over Jālore, where it continued ruling till it was ousted by Rāthōṛ Rāo Raṇmal, son of Rāo Chūṇḍā, about 1425 A. D.

From an inscription (App. C. 3, pp. 211-214) of Paramār Sōmēshvar, a feudatory of Chalukya (Sōlanki) Kumārapāl, dated 1161 A. D., found at Kirādū, it is known that Paramār also ruled over some parts of Marwar. From the time of Krishnarāj II (whose inscriptions dated 1060 and 1067 A. D. found at Bhīnmāl,) they were divided into two branches, one of which established its seat of Government at Abū[1] (App. C. 1, pp. 205-207) and the other at Kirādu. For some time Gōdwād also remained under the rule of the first branch, while the second one was the feudatory of the Sōlankīs.

Paramars

1 Appendices D. 2, pp. 226-228, D 3, pp 229-231; and (Malwa) D. 1, pp. 223-225.

For some time Paramārs also ruled at Jalore (App. C 2, pp. 208-210) as well as at Rol (in Nagāur District).

It is learnt from an inscription, dated 1013 A. D., found at Pokaran, that at that time it was under the rule of the Paramārs while another inscription of a somewhat earlier period gives the names of its Guhil rulers.

Solankis

Sōlankī Mūlarāj subdued the Paramārs of Sānchōre before the year 994 A. D. and Sōlankī Bhīmadêva I subjugated the Chauhāns of Nādōle in about 1021 A. D. The Sāmbhar inscription (App. C. 5, pp.217-221) of Sōlankī Jayasimha, who ruled between 1093 and 1142 A.D., also goes to show that he was the ruler of Sāmbhar.

An inscription of Sōlankī Kumārapāl, datad 1153 A.D., found at Pālī, shows that at that time the town of Pālī was under his sway and that his feudatory Bāharadēv ruled at the place.

We also learn from the inscription (App. C. 4, pp. 215-216) of 1178 A. D. found at Kīrādu that Chauhān Madanabrahmadēv, a feudatory of Sōlankī Bhīmadēv II ruled there at that time.

For some time Desuri also remained under these Sōlankī rulers.

Nāgvamshīs

The chronicles show that Nāgvamshīs also ruled at Mandōr and Nāgaur, and it is believed that the word 'Nāg' found in the names of the places, such as Nāgkund, Nāgādarī, Nāgaur and Nāgānā also supports the above fact.

Johyās, Dahiyas and Gaurs

In a similar way the rule of the Jōhiyās (Yaudhēyas) Dahiyās, and Gaur Rajputs over the parts of Marwar is also substantiated. Johiyās ruled over its Northern-most part adjoining Bikaner while Dahiyās ruled near Parbatsar. Both of them were feudatories of the Chauhāns. Gaurs ruled in Godwāḍ and Gōrāvātī (Mārōth), which seem to bear these names after them.

Indas, Parihars & Rathors

It has already been mentioned that in about 1395 A.D. the Īndās, a branch of Parihārs, finding themselves unable to defend the fort of Mandōr, from the onslaughts of the Mohamedans gave it over to Rāṭhōr Rāo Chūndā in dowry. These Rāṭhōṛs or Rashtrakūtas originally belonged to the Punjab, whence they migrated to the south and in course of time established their Kingdom in the Deccan[1].

Rashtrakutas of the Deccan

From a copper grant found at Miraj, it is learnt that Sōlankī Jayasimha defeated the Rashṭrakūṭa King Indra, and re-established the kingdom of Vallabharāj (Sōlankīs). But in the time of Sōlankī Kīrtivarman II the Rashtrakūtas recovered their lost kingdom.

On this evidence it is concluded that for the first time when the Rāshtrakūtas were the rulers of the Deccan in the early part of the sixth century A.D., Sōlankī Jayasimha defeated them and established a Chalukya-Kingdom there. But some time between 747 and 753 A.D. Dantidurga II, a Rāshtrakūta King, overthrew the Sōlankīs and re-established his own kingdom, which lasted till about 982 A. D. and nearly the whole of the Deccan, including the present territories of Mysore (App. A. 2, pp. 16-20.), Hyderabad (Deccan) (App. A.3, pp. 21-28), Trivendram and Cochin came under the direct or indirect rule of these Rāshtrakūtas.

As regards their Vamsha one may draw his conclusion from the following:—

In the coins of Krishnarāj I, who built the world famous Shiva temple, known as 'Kailas Bhavan', in the Ellora caves situated in the present Nizam's dominions, he is styled as:—

" परममाहेश्वर महादित्यपादानुध्यात श्रीकृष्णराज "

(i.e. Krishnārāj the staunch shaivite and son or descendant of the great sun).

Similarly in a copper plate of Govindarāj III, dated 808 A. D., the following verse is found.

" यस्मिन्सर्वगुणाश्रये क्षितिपतौ श्रीराष्ट्रकूटान्वयो
जाते यादववंशवन्मधुरिपावासीदलङ्घ्यः परैः । "

i. e. by the birth of this virtuous king the Rashtrakūta dynasty become as invincible as the Yādav dynasty by the birth of Shri Krishṇa.

---

1 See my book "History of the Rashtrakutas" (English edition) published by the Archaeological Department, Government of Jodhpur for the detailed history of the Rashtrakutas of the Deccan Lat (Gujrat) etc. and the Gahadavals of Kanauj

'The History of the Gahadavals of Kanauj from about V. S 1125 to about V S 1280 (1223 A D)", written by me, also appeared in the Journal of the Royal Asiatic Society of Great Britain and Ireland, London in January 1932, pp. 1—21.

It is quite clear from the above that uptill then the Rāshtrakūta dynasty was considered as quite distinct from the Yādav dynasty. But later on, the composer of the verses in the copper grant of Amōghavarsha I, dated 860 A.D., being unable to follow the analogy of the above mentioned verse, mentioned the Rāshtrakūtas as Yādavs, and out of 75 inscriptions and copper grants of the Rāshtrakūta kings of the Deccan and Gujrāt, the scribes of only eight followed in committing this mistake. Moreover, as the present Rāshtrakūtas too claim to be Sūryavamshis, it can be inferred that it was only the mistake of the later eight writers, who mentioned them as belonging to Yādav family.

The early Arab historians of India describe some of these Rāshtrakūtas as great and powerful kings. They were men of great learning and always patronised men of letters. To illusrate their generosity, a couplet is re-produced here from the copper grant of Dantivarman (Dantidurga) II dated 753 A. D.

"मात्रिभक्ति. प्रतिग्रामं ग्रामलक्षचतुष्टयम् (ये?)
ददत्याभूप्रदानानि यस्यमात्रा प्रकाशिता ।"

i. e. His (Dantivarman's) mother, by granting lands in charity in all the 4,00,000 villages of his kingdom, testified to his reverence in which he held his mother.

There were about 19 Rāshtrakuta kings of this dynasty.

Rashtrakutas of Lāt

Dantivarman (Dantidurga) II, the sixth in order, after overthrowing the Chālukya rule in the Deccan, made Karkaraj II, one of his relatives, the king of the Lāt (Central and Southern part of Gujrat) We know only four names of this branch from the copper grant of this Karkaraj II. After him about 808 A D. Govindaraj III, the tenth king of the Deccan, made over the aforesaid province of Lāt (Gujrāt) to his younger brother Indrarāj, who was the founder of the second branch of the Rāshtrakūtas of Lāt.

There were in all eight kings in this branch, who ruled over Gujrāt. Somewhere bĕtween 808 and 910 A D. Krishnarāj II, the twelfth king of the Deccan branch annexed the kingdom of Lāt (Gujrāt) from Krishnarāj, the eighth ruler of that line.

Besides this Karkarāj, the second ruler of this second branch of the Rāshtrakūtas of Lāt (Southern and Central Gujrāt), gave away the village Vatapadraka (the modern Baroda) in charity as is evident from his copper grant dated 812 A. D.

Four names of the first branch and fourteen names of the second branch of the Raṭṭas (Rāshṭrakūṭas), who ruled at Saundatti (Kuntal in the Belgaum Dist.), from 875 A.D. to 1229 A.D., four names of the early Rāshtrakūṭas of Hastikuṇḍi (Hathuṇḍī, Jodhpur State), who ruled from 893 A.D. to 997 A. D. and four names of the Rāthōrs of Dhanōp (Shāhpurā, Rājpūtānā), who ruled there about 1006 A. D. are also found in their records besides the short account given above.

Rashtrakutas of other places

Further some more grants of the Rāshṭrakuṭas are found, of which the first is of Abhimanyu, who flourished in the sixth century A. D. at Mānpur (perhaps in Mālwā). The second and the third of 631 and 709 A. D. respectively, from Multaī (Bētūl district in C. P.), the fourth an inscription, dated 861 A. D. from the Bhopal State, while the fifth from Bōdhagayā. All these are clear evidences that these miscellaneous Rāshtrakūta rulers ruled at these places as well.

Let us now turn to the Gāhadavāls of Kanauj, who in our considered opinion, is only a branch of the Rāshtrakūtas (App. A. 5, 6, and 7, pp. 37-53) and who appear to have assumed this surname on account of their connection with Gādhipur (Kanauj). The Rāthor rulers of Jodhpur, the premier State among all the States held by Rāthors, consider themselves to be the descendants of Jayachandra, the well-known king of Kanauj. The learned author of 'Aīn-e-Akbarī', also supports this fact, and we too have dwelt on this point at length in our "History of the Rāshtrakūṭas (Rāthors)' and have discussed there from every point of view that the Rāshtrakutas of Badāyūn, of the Lakhanapāl inscription (of about 1201 A. D.), belonged to the younger branch of Chandra, who first ruled at Badāyūn and then conquered Kanauj. His eldest son Madanapāl became king of Kanauj while his younger son Vigrahapāl or his descendants got Badāyūn in 'Jāgīr'. The members of the Badāyūn family continued to be called as Rāshtrakūtas, while those of the Kanauj family, in course of time, came to be known as Gāhaḍavāls, after their association with Gādhipur (Kanauj)

Gahadavals of Kanauj.

This last surname is found only in copper grants, dated 1104, 1105 and 1109 A. D. (1161, 1162 & 1166 V. S respectively) of the prince—regent Govindachandra as well as in the inscription of his queen Kumāradēvı

There were in all only eight kings of the Gāhadavāl dynasty at Kanauj, including Harishchandra, son and successor of Jayachandra, who ruled from 1194 to 1196 A.D. Some of these kings were very powerful, generous and great patrons of learning.

Govindachandra, the fifth king of this line, levied 'Turushkadanda,' a tax similar to 'Jaziā' on the Mohamedans. Out of the numerous copper grants discovered of their (Gāhadavāl's) time no less than forty-two speak of the munificence of this Govindachandra alone. Shrīharsha, the author of "Naishadhīya Charita", a well-known Sanskrit poem as well as 'Dvirūpa kōsha', composed his works under the patronage of king Jayachandra, who was the last powerful Hindu king of Kanauȷ.

His quarrel with the Chauhān ruler Prithvīrāj, for the abduction of his daughter, during the performance of his 'Rāȷasūya' sacrifice, and his inviting Shahābuddīn Ghōrī to invade India, is only the invention of the fertile brain of the learned author of "Raso" (App. A.4, pp. 29-34 and History of the Rāshtrakūtas" by the author, pp. 134 to 141).

When Jayachandra died in 1194 A. D., while fighting against Shahābuddīn Ghōrī, his son Harishchandra came to the throne, and ruled the country around Kanauj. But owing to the invasion of Shamsuddīn Altamash, this part of the territory also slīpped out of his hands and his (Harishchandra's) descendants migrated towards Mahui, via Khōr (Shamsābād) and Mōdhā and settled there.

(1) Rāo Sīhā

It is just probable that like his father's (Jayachandra's) well-known title of 'Dalapangula' 'Varadāyīsēn' might have also been the title of Harıshchandra or that it (Vardāyīsēn) was the name of his (Harischandra's) younger brother, whose sons Sētarām and Sīhā went towards Khōr and thence to Mahui. Some-time after Rāo Sīhā built a residence for himself on the banks of the river Kālī, which is as yet known as "Sīhā Rāo-kā-khēḍā". But when the Mohamedans invaded this place also, Sētarām and Sīhā were obliged to migrate towards Marwar and reached there in about 1212 A. D.

According to the chronicles, Rāo Sīhā was the son of Sētarām and grandson of Vardāyisēn. If it is so, then it can only be presumed that Sētarām might have adopted his younger brother Sīhā as his son. Without this presumption we are unable to arrange the genealogy of the early eleven Rāṭhoṛ rulers of Marwar.[1]

As already stated, Rāo Sīhā reached Marwar in 1212 A. D. and at the outset established his sway over Pāli, a prosperous town, about forty miles to the south south-east of Jodhpur. He ended his adventurous career at Bīthu (about six miles from Pālī) in 1273 A. D. while fighting against the Mohamedans.

Col Todd, in his 'Annals and Antiquities of Rājasthān,' writes that Rāo Sīhā took possession of Pāli, after treacherously massacring the Pallīvāl Brahmans of the town. But this is not so. The town was then under the rule of the Sōlankīs and not under the Pallīvāls (App. B. I, pp. 55-57).

Rāo Sīhā had three sons.

(2) Rāo Āsthān

Rāo Asthān, the eldest, succeeded his father and after putting to the sword the Gohil Rājpūts added their principality of Khēr to his parental possessions. It is this town of Khēṛ which gives its name to his descendants known as "Khērēchās".

Some time later Rāo Asthān also killed Sāmaliā Sodh, the ruler of Īdar, and granted this province to his younger brother Sōnag, whose descendants were styled as Īdariā Rāthoṛs after the name of Īdar.

(1) For detailed history of the Rathor Rulers of Marwar see my मारवाड़ का इतिहास भाग १-२, published by the Archæological Department, Government of Jodhpur, Jodhpur.

His third brother Aj captured Ōkhāmandal (near Dwārkā) and as he himself beheaded Chāvarā Bhōjarāj, the then ruler of the place, his descendants came to be known as 'Vādhēls.'

Rāo Āsthān met his death at Pālī while repulsing the attack of the army of Fīrōzshah II in 1292 A. D.

(3) Rāo Dhūhar

His eldest son Rāo Dhūhar, who succeeded him further extended his possessions by bringing one hundred and forty new neighbouring villages under his sway. By defeating the Parihārs, he took Mandōr also, but shortly afterwards the Parihārs re-captured it. He was killed in a battle with the Parihārs in 1309 A.D., which was fought at a place lying between the villages of Thōb and Tirsingarī.

The temple of the goddess Nāganēchiyān at Nāgānā is said to have been built by this Rāo.

(4) Rāo Rāyapāl

His eldest son, Rāo Rāyapāl succeeded him. He avenged the death of his father by defeating the Parihārs of Mandōr and took possession of the said town, though he could retain it for a short period only. He inflicted a crushing defeat on the Panvārs (Paramārs) as well, and thus annexed the whole of Mahēwā, which at present is called Mallānī. He also avenged the death of his cousin Pābū, (who even upto this day is worshipped as a deified warrior) by killing Phararā, a Bhātī Rājpūt, and annexed his eighty-four villages in his own territory.

Once in a severe famine he opened all his granaries to his subjects free and thus earned the epithet of 'Mahīrēlan' or God Indra.

(5) Rāo Kanapāl

Rāo Kanapāl, the eldest among his sons, succeeded him. His heir-apparent Bhīm once defeated the Bhātīs of Jaisalmer, and demarcated the river 'Kāk' as the boundary line between Mahēvā and their territory, but a short time after he was slain in another attack of the Bhātīs.

Soon after this occurrence Rao Kanapāl himself started to take revenge on them. But he met with a surprise attack of the combined armies of the Bhāṭīs and the Mohamedans in his way and was killed in the battle which ensued.

(6) Rāo Jālanasī

His second son and successor Rāo Jālanasī defeated the Sōdhā Rājpūts of Umarkōt (now in the Sindh province). As the Mohamedan governor of Multān had assisted the Bhātīs of Jaisalmer in killing his father, he marched up to that city as well and avenged his father's death. He also defeated the Solankis of Bhīnmāl and killing Hājī Malik of the Sarāī clan took revenge of his uncle's death. He met his death in or about 1328 A. D., while encountering the combined armies of the Bhāṭīs and the Mohamedans.

(7) Rāo Chhāḍā

Rāo Jālanasī was succeeded by his eldest son Rāo Chhādā, who defeated the Sōdhās of Umarkōṭ and the Bhātīs of Jaisalmer. He also plundered Sojat, Bhīnmāl and Jālore, but while resting at the village Rāmā, on his way back from Jālore, he was attacked unawares by the combined forces of the Sōnagarā and Dēvara Chauhāns and was killed in 1344 A. D.

(8) Rāo Tīdā

Rāo Tīdā, the eldest son and successor of Rāo Chhādā, in order to avenge the death of his sire, defeated the Sōnagarās of Bhīnmāl; and took possession of their town. He also punished the Dēvaṛās, the Bhātīs of Lōdravā, the Bālēchās (a branch of the Chauhāns) and the Sōlankīs.

He died in 1357 A.D. while defending Siwānā against the Mohamedan army.

This Rāo had three sons, namely, Kānhaṛadēv[1], Tribhuvansī[2] and Salkhā.

---

1. (9) Kānhaṛadēv succeeded his father. Though he was soon deprived off his territory by the Mohamedan army returning from Siwānā, he re-captured it and ruled there until his death.

2. (10) Rāo Tribhuvansī succeeded his elder brother, but was soon attacked by his nephew Rāwal Mallināth, the son of Rāo Salkhā, and died of his wounds.

(9) Rāo Salkhā

Rāo Salkhā, the third son of Rāo Tīdā, was given a village in Jagir by his eldest brother Rāo Kānhadadēv, which afterwards came to be known as Salkhāvāsanī. When the Mohamedans deprived his eldest brother of his territories, Rāo Salkhā seized a part of Mahēwā and established his rule there. He resided at Bhiradkōt, and after defeating the Chauhāns plunderd Bhīnmāl. He was killed in a surprise attack by the Mohamedans in or about 1374 A. D.

He had four sons, Mallināth[1]. Jaitmāl, Bīram and Shōbhit.

(10) Rāo Bīram

Rāo Bīram who was the third son of Rāo Salkhā got Khēr or Bhiradkot in 'Jāgīr'. But by helping Jōhiyā Dalā he incurred the displeasure of his eldest brother Rāval Mallināth, and was forced to migrate to Johiyāvātī, by way of Sētrāvā, Chūntīsarā and Jānglū, where he was killed in 1383 A. D. while fighting against the Jōhiyās.

(11) Rāo Chūndā.

Rāo Chūndā, the second son of Rāo Bīram, was only six years old at his father's death. He was given the village Sālōri in 'Jāgīr' by his uncle Mallināth. In course of time he gathered a band of trusted warriors around him and received Mandōr in dowry in 1395 A. D. from the Īndās (a branch of the Parihārs), who were not strong enough to hold it (Mandōr) against the Mohamedans.

Owing to the decline of the Tughlaq dynasty at Delhi, he (Rāo Chūndā) soon gathered enough strength and defended the fort of Mandōr fully well, at the time of an attack by Zafar Khān, the governor of Gujrat, in 1396 A.D. He also killed Kōtēchā Rāthōr Bhān, inflicted a crushing defeat on Khōkhar, in 1399 A. D., and annexed Nāgaur.

He also subdued Khātū, Dīdwānā, Sāmbhar and Ajmer, all of which were then under the Mohamedan rule, and wrested Nāḍole also from the Chauhāns.

---

1. (11) Rāval Mallināth, on the death of Rāo Salkhā his father, went to live with his uncle Rāo Kānhaṛadēv, but when on Rāo Kānhaṛadēv's death, he was succeeded by Rāo Tribhuvanasī, Rāval Mallināth took possession of the town of Khēṛ with the help of the Mohamedan army He was a brave warrior Once he defeated thirteen divisions of the Mohamedan army, which attacked him. He died in 1399 A. D. and was succeeded by his oldest son Jagamāl.

In 1408 A. D. Shamsakhān, with the help of his brother Muzaffar Shāh I of Gujrāt, took Nāgaur and Rāo Chūṇḍā was obliged to return to Maṇḍōr, but after the death of Shamsakhān he re-captured it in 1421 A. D. from his son Firōzkhān.

In 1411 A. D. he took Phalōdī from his own brother Jai Singh, who had ignored to respond to his request for help at the time of his invading Didwānā and Sāmbhar.

When Rāo Chūṇḍā was busy conquering one district after another, the combined armies of the Bhātīs and the Sānkhalās aided by Salīm, the governor of Multān, invaded Nāgaur and there Rāo Chūṇḍā was treacherously murdered by them in 1424 A. D. at the age of fortysix.

It was Rāo Chūndā who in fact established the Rāthōṛ rule in Mārwār on a firm footing. There is a saying common in this land which runs "मालारा मढ़े ने बीरम रा गढ़े". i. e. the descendants of Mallināth dwell in hamlets while those of Bīram live in forts.

According to the wish of Rāo Chūṇḍā, his sixth son

(12) Rāo Kānhā

Rāo Kānhā succeeded him. He slew the rebellious Punapāl Sānkhalā of Jāngalū and annexed his territory to his own. But on the other hand Nāgaur again went out of his hands and was taken possession of by Khanzādā Fīrōz, the son of Shamsakhan.

He died after a short reign of eleven months only.

(13) Rāo Sattā.

His elder brother Rāo Sattā, second son of Rāo Chūṇḍā, succeeded him, but was overthrown in 1427 A. D. by his elder brother Rāo Ranamal.

Rāo Raṇamal was the eldest son of Rāo Chūṇḍā, who

(14) Rāo Ranamal.

had waived his rights to the throne in favour of his brother Rāo Kānhā to carry out the wish of his father. He left his native abode in 1408 A. D. and proceeded towards Mēwār by the way of Jojāwar and Dhaṇlā. On his reaching there Mahārānā Lākhā received him with honour and bestowed a 'Jāgīr' on him for his maintenance. Soon afterwards Rāo Raṇamal led the army of the Mahārāṇā and brought Ajmer under the sway of the Mēwār ruler.

At the request of Rājakumār Chūndā, the eldest son of Mahārānā Lākhā, he married his sister Hansābāī to the Mahārānā on condition that the latter's son, if she gave birth to any, was to succeed to the throne of Mēwār.

As this condition was also agreed on by Rājakumār Chūndā, so on the death of Maharana Lākhā, in about 1420 A. D., Mahārānā Mōkal, the son born of Hansābāī, ascended the throne of Mēwār, at the age of about ten years only.

During the minority of Maharana Mōkal, the administration of Mēwār was first entrusted to Rāvat Chūndā, but Hansābāī very soon discovered that he was not to be relied upon, so she handed it over to her brother Ranamal, who managed the affairs of Mēwār during the minority of the Mahārānā and Rāvat Chūndā then proceeded to Māṇḍū (App. B. 20, pp. 183-184).

Ranamal avenged the death of his father by having Salīm killed and the Bhātīs punished. He wrested Nādōle from the Sōnagarās, Jaitāran from the Sīndhals and Sōjat from the Huls and appointed his elder son Akhairāj governor of the last named town.

In 1427 A. D. his own brother Ranadhīr, persuaded him to take possession of Mandōr on the grounds that he (Ranamal) had waived his right to the throne in favour of Rāo Kānhā only and in case of the latter failing to leave any male issue after him he himself and not Rāo Sattā was the only rightful claimant to the throne of Mandōr This argument convinced him and he invaded Mandōr with the help of the Mēwār army and un-seated Sattā. He also helped Mahārānā Mōkal, in his invasions of Nāgaur, Jālore, Sāmbhar, Jahāzpur etc. as well as in his battle against Mohammad (the son of Ahmadshāh of Gujrāt).

Thereafter he went on a pilgrimage to the holy Ganges and Gayā. He ruled over Mandōr, Pāli, Sōjat, Jaitāran and Nādōle, and also inflicted defeat on Hasanakhān of Jālore.

In 1433 A. D. two of the conspirators of Mēwār were successful in assasinating Mahārānā Mōkal and as his heir

Kumbhā was then only 6 years of age, Rāo Raṇamal was again called to guide the destinies of Mēwār. Soon reaching there and after overcoming great many difficulties he brought all the affairs to a settled condition. As Mahamūd Khiljī I, the Sultan of Māṇḍū has given refuge to one of assassins of Mōkal, at the hint of Rāvat Chūṇḍā, Ranamal attacked him in 1437 A. D. and gave him a crushing defeat. He also successfully led the armies of Mewār against Sārangpur (Mālwā), Nāgaur, Gāgaraun, Narāṇā (Jaipur) and Ajmer. But in spite of all these services, rendered by him, this saviour of Mēwār was treacherously murdered, while asleep in 1438 A. D, by the evil doers of Mēwār (App. B. 20, pp. 184-185).

(15) Rāo Jōdhā

When this dreadful news of the tragic end of Rāo Raṇamal reached his second son Rāo Jōdhā, he immediately quitted Chittōr for Mārwār with all his retinue. But Rāvat Chūndā, the uncle of Mahārānā Kumbhā, started on his pursuit with the Mēwār army. In the pitched battles fought in the way between the pursuers and the pursued, Rāo Jōdhā lost almost all of his seven hundred brave Rājpūts, but he himself was fortunate enough to escape death and reach Mārwār with only seven warriors. Thereafter he went to Kāhunī (in Jāngalū) by way of Sōjat and Mandōr and began to enlist men and gather material.

In the meantime Rāvat Chūndā, the commander of the Mēwār army, occupied Māṇḍōr and Sōjat, and posted his garrisons at strategic points. However, in fifteen years' time, Rāo Jōdhā was able to collect sufficient men and money and then drove away the intruders and re-captured Maṇḍōr, his ancestral capital, in 1453 A. D.

As it was due to his efforts only that the throne of Māṇḍōr was again taken possession of, so his elder brother Akhairāj renounced his claim for it and acknowledged his supremacy. After getting a firm footing at Mandōr, Rāo Jōdhā captured Sōjat and presented the 'Jāgīr' of Bagrī to his elder brother. When in course of time he felt himself strong enough to avenge his father's tragic death, he attacked Chittōr, set fire to the gate of this world famous fort, and plundered Mēwār.

This invasion of Rāo Jōdhā compelled the Mahārānā to launch a counter invasion of Mārwār. But when both the armies of Mēwār and Mārwār came face to face at Nādōle (in Gōḍwād district), Maharānā Kumbhā, who was then apprehensive of an invasion by the Sultān of Mālwā, negotiated a treaty with Rāo Jōdhā, and fixed the boundaries of Mēwār and Mārwār.

After this settlement, Rāo Jōdhā performed his coronation ceremony in 1458 A. D. at Maṇdōr. In the following year, on May 12th, 1459 A.D., he laid the foundation of a new fort and also laid out a new city some six miles to the south of Mandōr and named it Jodhpur after his own name.

At his command, his sons Barsingh and Dūdā annexed Mērtā as well as its 360 villages in 1461 A. D., which were at that time under the rule of the Mohamedan governor of Ajmer.

He proceeded on a pilgrimage to Gayā and persuaded King Husainshāh of Jaunpur to repeal the tax levied on the pilgrims there. He also visited Kāshī, the sacred place of pilgrimage for the Hindus.

In 1465 A. D. his fifth son Bīkā went towards Jāngalū and by and by carved out a new state for himself which is now known as Bikaner.

In 1466 A. D. Rāo Jōdhā annexed Chhāpar-Drōnpur, but returned it back to Mēghā on his submission. The following year he seized Nāgaur and Fatankhān, the then ruler of the place, was obliged to flee away towards Jhūnjhanū.

In 1468 Mahārānā Udayasingh, after killing his own father Mahārānā Kumbhā, usurped the throne of Mēwār, and gave Ajmer and Sāṁbhar to Rāo Jōdhā as a bribe to keep the latter aloof from meddling in the internal affairs of Mēwār.

In 1474 A. D. Rāo Jōdhā re-took Chhāpar-Drōnpur because Bairasal, the son of Mēghā, was thought incompetent to keep a proper control over his province.

He again invaded Fatankhān and razed Fatehpur to the ground. He also defeated the combined forces of King Behalōl of Delhi and Husainshāh of Jaunpur, which were sent to aid Bairsāl and his younger brother Narbad against him. He soon crushed the bands of the freebooters, who roamed under the leadership of Usmānkhān of Jālore and Rāval Lākhā of Sirōhī.

In 1486 he repulsed the invading army of Rājā Chandrasēn of Āmbēr at the battle of Sāmbhar.

The following year he helped his son Bīka in avenging the death of his (Bīkā's) uncle Kāndhal in an expedition against Sārangakhān of Hissar. On his return from this expedition Rāo Jōdha acknowledged Bīkā as an independent ruler of Bīkānēr and gave him a promise of sending him all the paraphernalia of royalty.

In the same year his army defeated Rāval Dēvīdās of Jaisalmēr and re-occupied Shiv.

He died in 1489 A. D. after bringing Māṇdōr, (Jōdhpur), Mērtā, Phalōdī, Pokaran, Mahēwā, Bhādrājūn, Sojat, some portion of Gōḍwāḍ, Jaitāran, Shiv, Siwānā, Sāmbhar, Ajmer and a large part of Nāgaur under his rule. Bīkānēr and Chhāpar-Drōṇpur were in the possession of his sons Bīkā and Bīdā respectively. Thus the boundary of their combined territories extended from the Aravalli in the south to Hissār in the north, and in the west it touched the borders of the Jaisalmēr State.

As Nīmbā, his eldest son, died in his own life time and his second son Jōgā was considered unfit to occupy the throne. his third son Rāo Sātal succeeded him.

(16) Rāo Sātal

He (Rāo Sātal) received the province of Kuṇḍal, situated near Phalōdi, as a gift from Bhāti Dēvīdās his father-in-law.

He died of wounds in 1492 A. D. after routing the army of Mallūkhān (Malik Yūsuf), the governor of Ajmer, at the battle of Kōsānā.

(17) Rāo Sūjā

Rāo Sātal intended to adopt Narā, the third son of Sūjā, his younger brother, but Sūjā on his part satisfied Narā with the grant of the 'Jāgīr' of Phalōdī and himself ascended the gaddī.

But Narā was murdered by the Pokaranā Rāthōrs with the assistance of the Rāthōrs of Bāhadmēr. To avenge his death Rāo Sūjā invaded the territories of both the miscreants and plundered Bāhadmēr, Kōtarā, etc.

In the meantime Rāo Bīkā, who was given a promise by Rāo Jōdhā of having the paraphernalia of Royalty, recognising his independence, instigated by Barjāng (son of Rāthōr Bhīm), invaded Mārwār, but the nobles affected a compromise between the two brothers before any blood was shed on either side, and Bīkā returned to his capital with the promised articles of Royalty.

At Rāo Sūjā's command, his son Shēkhā subdued the Sīndhals of Rāipur, and also forced the Sīndhals of Chānōd to acknowledge his suzerainty.

Rāo Sūjā breathed his last in 1515 A. D. at the age of 76 years.

Rāo Sūjā had promised his eldest son Rājakumār Bāghā, while the latter was on his death-bed, to name (Bāghā's) eldest son Bīram as the heir-apparent to the throne. But when the time for the installation ceremony approached the nobles, assembled at the fort to witness the ceremony, got displeased on a trifling matter and leagued against him (Bīram), and calling Gāngā, his younger brother, from Mēwār (who had gone to assist Mahārānā Sāngā against the Sultān of Gujrāt about the Īdar affairs) duly installed him on the throne of Mārwār.

(18) Rāo Gāngā

In 1517 A. D. Rāo Gāngā went to help the Mahārānā a second time against Muzaffarshāh II of Gujrāt, and in 1520 A. D. he also led a contingent of 7,000 horse to help Mahārānā Sāngā in driving away Nizamulmulk (Mubarizulmulk), and seated Rāo Rāyamal on the gaddī of Īdar once more.

In 1527 A. D. he sent a force of 4,000 warriors to assist Mahārānā Sāngā in meeting Emperor Babar in the battle. (App. B. 20, pp. 185).

In 1529 A. D. Shēkhā, the uncle of Rāo Gāngā, invaded Jōdhpur with the help of Daulatkhān, the ruler of Nāgaur, but in the battle fought near Sēvakī, Shēkhā was killed and Daulatkhan was forced to leave the field.

There after he resumed Sōjat from his elder brother Bīram, who at the time was creating unrest against him in the country and gave him the village of Bālā for his maintenance.

He died in 1532 by accidentally falling through a window where he was sitting to enjoy the cool breeze.

(19) Rao Maldeo

Rāo Māldēv, his eldest son, succeeded him. At the time of his accession to the throne, only the districts of Jōdhpur and Sōjat were under his sway, but soon afterwards he subdued the Sīndhals of Bhādrājun and Rāipur.

When Sultān Bahādur Shāh of Gujrāt invaded Mēwār in 1532 A. D., he sent his Rāṭhor contingent to render help to Mahārānā Vikramāditya.

In 1534 A.D. when Daulatkhān of Nāgaur attacked Bīramdēv, the grandson of Rāo Jōdhā, in order to annex Mērtā, then Rāo Māldēv seized Nāgaur and drove the Khān away towards Ajmer.

In the following year Bīramdēv defeated Shamsher-ul-mulk, the representative of the Sultān of Gujrat and captured Ajmer. When this news reached Rāo Māldēv, he asked Bīramdēv to hand it (Ajmer) over to him, as he (Bīramdev) would not be strong enough to hold it against the army of Gujrāt. But Biramdev refused to agree to it, consequently Rāo Māldēv took over Mērtā and Bīram had to retire to Ajmer.

As Rao Māldēv favoured Sahasā, the grandson of Barsingh, by the bestowal of the Jāgīr of Rīān on him, Bīram got jealous of him and once attacking Rīān killed him on the field. This enraged Rão Māldēv to such an extent that he at once despatched his generals Jaitā and Kūnpā against him, who soon captured Ajmer. Bīramdēv had to remain a fugitive for some days and was everywhere pursued by the warriors of Rão Māldēv and driven away, till at last he took refuge at the court of Shērshāh at Delhi.

Rão Māldēv conquered Siwānā and imprisoned Sikandarkhān of Jālore.

In 1539 A. D. when Emperor Humāyūn and Shershah were contesting the throne of Delhi, Rão Māldēv taking advantage of their pre-occupation extended his possession up to Bayānā. He routed the Sōlankīs, who ruled somewhere near Tōnk and Tōdā, posted his garrisons at Jaunpur (Mēwār) and annexed Sāmbhar, Kāslī, Fatehpur, Rēwāsā, Chhota Udaipur (in Jaipur State), Chātasū, Lawān, Malāranā, etc. He also subdued the Chauhāns of Sānchore, took possession of the portion of Gujrat up to the borders of Rādhanpur and Khābar and plundered Nābarā.

In 1540 A. D. he aided Mahārānā Udayasingh in rescuing the throne of Mēwār from the clutches of Banabīr, the illegitimate son of Prithvīrāj. He also took possession of Khairwā and a large part of Gōdwād.

In 1542 A. D. Rão Māldēv invaded Bīkānēr, put its ruler Rão Jaitsī to the sword and annexed it along with the district of Jhūnjhanū to his possessions.

Emperor Humāyūn, after his defeat by Shērshah in 1542 sought the help of Rão Māldēv, but due to some misunderstanding he left the place and went towards Umarkōṭ by way of Phalōdī. This afforded an opportunity to Bīramdēv and Bhīm, the second son of the late Rão Jaitsī of Bīkānēr, to poison the ears of Shērshāh against Rão Māldēv, and in 1543 A.D. Shērshāh marched with a huge army against the Rão. On receipt of this news, Rão Māldēv too proceeded towards Ajmer with an army of 80,000 strong to give battle to the invader. When Shērshāh was apprised of the strength of Rão Māldēv's force, his enthusiasm cooled down, and he wished to turn back. But Bīramdev persuaded him to wait and himself despatched some forged letters to the address of some of the leading nobles of Māldēv. He also managed to let these letters fall into the hands of the Rāo instead of those of the addressees. This strategem succeeded and Rāo Māldēv being ignorant of the trick got suspicious that his nobles were in league with the enemy and retreated towards Jōdhpur under cover of night. But his noble generals Jaitā and Kūnpā as well as some others refused to retire beyond Girarī (in Jaitaran District) and with a force of only 12,000 horse turned back to attack Shērshāh in the night. Unfortunately they lost their way in the darkness, and only half of their number was able to reach Sumēl to face the enemy at day break.

Under these circumstances, it was not prudent enough for them to attack an army of 80,000 men, but the brave Rāṭhōṛs did not care for the odds against them and atonce charged on the Pathān army. They fought with such valour and recklessness that Shērshāh was about to quit the field with his army. But as the fortune did not favour the Rāṭhōṛs from the very beginning, Jalālkhān, a noble of Shērshāh, reached there with a fresh army at that critical moment and his joining the army at that time changed the fate of the day. The brave Rāthōrs, already reduced to a small number, fell fighting to a man after laying low a yet greater number of the opponents.

Shērshāh did not believe this news of victory at first when it was conveyed to him, but when he came to know of the facts as they stood, he uttered "Thank God that the victory is mine, otherwise I would have lost the Empire of Hindustan for a handful of Bājrā" (a kind of corn).

When Rāo Māldēv became aware of the true facts, he repented very much for his unjust suspicion, but as the time for action had passed away, he was obliged to go away towards Siwānā for the time being.

After this battle Shērshāh, the victorious Paṭhān king atonce marched towards Jōdhpur and captured it in 1544 A. D. He returned Mertā to Rāo Bīramdēv and Bīkānēr to Rāo Kalyānmal, the elder son of the late Rāo Jaitsī.

Shērshāh was burnt to death by an explosion at Kālanjar in 1545 A. D.

After his (Shērshāh's) retreat Rāo Māldēv collected sufficient men and material from the districts of Mārwār and in 1546 A. D. first captured Bhāngēsar (in Pali district) and then Jodhpur. In course of time he took possession of Phalōdī Ajmer, Pokaran, Bāhadmēr, Kōtarā, Mērtā, Jālore and Badnore also.

He chastised the Bhātis of Jaisalmēr and twice put the armies of Mahārānā Udayasingh to rout.

In 1562 A. D. when the Emperor Akbar was on his way to Ajmer and was stationed at Sāmbhar, Jaimal, the son of Bīram, approached him and complained against Rāo Māldēv and sought his help. The shrewd Emperor who was looking for an opportunity to avenge his father's insult, took advantage of this family dissension and ordered Mirzā Sharfuddīn to render assistance to Jaimal. The fort of Mērtā was eventually taken after great efforts. This was the place where Rāthor Dēvīdās, at the head of his 400 Rāthōr horsemen, played havoc among the Imperial forces. Some time later Akbar annexed the district of Parbatsar also.

Rāo Māldēv, whose territory once extended up to Hinḍaun, Bayānā, Fatehpur, Sīkrī, and Mēwār, and whose assistance was sought even by Emperor Humāyun against Shērshāh, breathed his last in 1562 A. D. Had not the foolish followers of Emperor Humāyun hurt the religious sentiments of the Rājpūts by slaughtering a cow and had not the internal dispute between Rāo Māldēv and Bīramdēv taken place, the Rāo would have moulded the Mārwār State into quite a different shape worthy of his name.

He according to the wish expressed by him was succeeded by his sixth son Rāo Chandrasēn, who was a brave, independant and spirited ruler.

(20) Rao Chandrasen

Though Akbar tried his utmost to make him accept his allegience, yet all his efforts proved of no avail. (For his detailed history please refer App. B 20, pp. 65-80).

His glorious life came to an end in 1581 A. D. at Sāran a village near Sōjat.

He was succeeded by his two younger sons, who both were killed in 1581 A. D.[1]

(21) Rao Rayasingh

When the news of the tragic end of both his brothers and the call of the Rāthōṛ nobles reached Rāo Rāyasingh (the eldest son of Rāo Chandrasēn), who had joined the Imperial service and was then serving at Kabul, he after obtaining the permission of the Emperor reached Sōjat and ascended the Gaddī in 1581 A. D. He was killed at Datānī (in Sirohi State) in 1583 A. D. where he had gone, under Imperial orders, to help Devaṛā Jagmāl against Devarā Surtān.

(22) Raja Udayasingh.

Rājā Udayasingh was the fifth son of Rāo Māldēv who owing to certain domestic circumstances had joined the service of the Emperor Akbar. He had occasion to crush the risings at Samāvalī, Khīchīvārā, Ōrchhā, and Bundēlkhand at the Imperial command. Pleased with his brave deeds, Akbar rewarded him in 1583 A. D. with the throne of Mārwāṛ and the hereditary title of "Rājā"

At the time in 1570 A. D. when Akbar was encamped at Nāgaur and the ruler of Bīkānēr etc. had accepted his allegiance, Rāo Chandrasēn totally refused it. This led the Emperor to favour Udayasingh, who was afterwards known at the Imperial Court as "Mōtā Rājā"

In 1583, he (Rājā Udayāsingh) helped Mirzā Khān (Abdul Rahīm Khān-e-Khānān) in routing Muzaffar at Rājpīpalā. The year following this event Akbar also granted him the district of Sōjat.

---

1. Rao Chandrasen was succeeded by his two younger sons (21)Rāo Āskaran and Rao Ugrasēn. They divided between themselves the district of Sōjat, which was all that remained in the possession of their father at the time of his death. In 1581 A. D when they were passing their leisure hours by playing an indoor game, a dispute arose about the result of the game and both were killed on the same spot.

He also was of help to the Imperial nobles in subduing Daulatkhān at Khambhāt.

He subdued the Sīndhals of Sīndhalvāti (in Jālore district) and avenged the death of Rāo Rāyasingh by deposing Dēvarā Surtān and installing Dēvarā Kallā on the throne of Sirōhi.

In 1587 A. D. he invaded Siwānā in conjunction with the Imperial Army and after the death of Rāo Kallā (the grandson of Rāo Māldēv) the fort was taken.

In 1592 A. D. when Akbar went to Kāshmīr, he deputed Rājā Udayasingh to look after the affairs of Lāhore.

The following year he took possession of Jasōl and also rendered help to prince Dāniyāl in conducting war in the Deccan.

He died at Lahore in 1595 A. D. and was the first ruler of Marwar who, owing to the circumstances given below, accepted the allegiance of the Emperor Akbar :—

1. That at that time the rulers of the Rājpūt States in Rājpūtānā considered the Imperial Mansabs as an honour.

2. That even in the presence of Udayasingh the throne of Jōdhpur was given to his younger brother.

3. That besides this, later on, Mārwār was annexed by the Emperor Akbar on account of the treatment meted out to Humāyun (his father) in the past.

In similar circumstances Jagmal, the brother of Mahārānā Pratāpsingh of Mēwār, was also obliged to accept the allegiance of Akbar, but as he died soon after, in 1583 A.D., he could not succeed to the throne of Mēwār.

Rājā Udayasingh held a Mansab of fifteen hundred horse.

He was succeeded by his sixth son, Savāi Rājā Shūrsingh at Lahore. In 1596 A. D. when Prince Murād was transferred as governor of the province to the Deccan, Savāi Rajā Shūrsingh was appointed in his place to look after the affairs of Gujrāt. But when he reached Sirōhī,

(23) Savai Raja Shursingh.

on his way to Gujrāt, he again exacted a huge sum from Dēvaṛā Surtān as a compensation for the loss incurred at the death of his cousin Rāo Rāyasingh.

The following year he put to flight Bahādur, the son of Muzaffar, who had ventured to plunder Gujrāt.

Some three years later, in 1600 A. D., he was ordered to proceed to the Deccan to assist Prince Dāniyāl in suppressing the revolt of Saādatkhān and his minister Rāju of Ahmadnagar. He twice suppressed their risings in 1600 and 1601 A. D. and also that of Khudāvandkhān Habshī in 1601 A. D. at Pathari as well as at Pālam.

Rājā Shūrsingh, with his contingent, led the vanguard of the Imperial army on its march against Ambar Champū, the commander of the army of Nizām-ul-Mulk, which was further strengthened when Habshi Farhād also joined it. But when the opposing forces met each other in the field so dashing was the charge, led by Rājā Shursingh himself, that Ambar Champū had to leave the field. This event occurred in 1602 A. D. and was highly spoken of even by Prince Dāniyāl. When this news reached the Emperor, he himself rewarded him for this act of gallantry with the title of 'Savāi Rājā' and the bestowal of a Jāgir.

After the accession to the throne of Emperor Jahangir in 1605 A.D. Savāi Rājā again rendered aid to the Imperial armies in suppressing the rebellion in Gujrāt.

In 1608, he was ordered to proceed to the Deccan with Khān-e-Khānān to maintain law and order in the said province, but when he reached Pāḍīv (in Sirohi State), on his return from the Deccan in 1613 A.D., he was received by Rājsingh, the then Rāo of Sirōhī with great honour and a treaty was concluded between them, which ended the dispute between the two States created by the death of Rāo Rāyasingh.

Savāi Rājā Shursingh helped Prince Khurram in subduing Mahārānā Amarsingh of Mēwār in 1614 A. D. He also defeated Rāthōr Bīram, but on his submission bestowed upon him the title of Rāval and the Jāgīr of Mahēvā.

The following year when Emperor Jahangir and the Savāi Rājā were camping at Ajmer in 1615 A.D., his brother Rājā Kishan Singh, the founder of the present Kishangarh State, attacked his camp in the night and murdered his minister Bhāṭī Govinddās to avenge the death of his nephew, but was himself killed by the Savāi Rājā's guards.

Some time afterwards the Savāi Rājā got himself weighed in gold and silver at Sūrsāgar (a suburb of Jodhpur) and the weight in gold and silver was disposed off in charity. He then returned to the Deccan along with the other Imperial nobles to crush the risings of the enemies there.

In 1617 A. D. when the Emperor Jahāngīr realised that Prince Khurram was unable to control the affairs of Jālore, he entrusted them to Shūrsingh. Thereupon Rājkumār Gajsingh laid a siege to the fort and after reducing the Bihārī Pathāns captured it.

He took a leading part in most of the battles fought out by the Imperial armies in the Deccan and a great many of them were mainly won due to his prompt and bold action for which he was promoted to the Mansab of 5,000 Zāt and 3,300 Sawārs.

He died in the Deccan at Mahkar in 1619 A. D.

It was during his reign that the old system of administration was replaced by a new one on Imperial lines.

According to the chronicles he received five Districts in Gujrāt, one in Malwa, and one in the Deccan in addition to his own territory of Mārwār.

(24) Raja Gajsingh

He was succeeded at Burhānpur by his eldest son Rājā Gajsingh. According to Col. Tod, at this time his horses were freed from receiving the Imperial Brand.

When he was at Mahkar, Ambar Champū, the minister of

Ahmadnagar, again raised the banner of revolt and surrounded the Imperial forces, but after three months hard fighting, he was forced to flee before the valour of Rājā Gajsingh.

In 1621 A.D. after severe fighting he again subdued Malik Ambar, for which he received the title of 'Dalthambhan' and his Mansab was raised to 4,000 Zāt and 3,000 Sawārs. As he snatched the banner of Malik Ambar Champū in this battle, so in order to commemorate this event, he added a red stripe to his own flag.

In 1623 A. D. he was deputed with Prince Parvēz to drive away Prince Khurram from Mālwā, and later received the districts of Phalōdī and Mērtā in Jāgīr with a further rise in his Mansab by 1,000 Zāt and 1,000 Sawārs.

The following year Prince Khurram again endeavoured to capture the throne of Delhi. But in the battle fought on the banks of the river Tōns near Benāres, Rājā Gajsingh turned his victory into defeat and killed Sīsōdiyā Bhīm, the commander of his forces. For this unique service the number of his Sawārs was again raised by 1,000.

After this event, he performed the ceremony of getting himself weighed with silver at Prayāg (Allahabad) and later returned to the Deccan. He drove away Prince Khurram for the third time, when he made a surprise attack on Burhānpur.

In 1625 A. D. when Mahābatkhān was transferred to Bengal, according to the wishes of Nūr Jahān, he wanted to take away with him almost all the Imperial nobles stationed in the Deccan. Rājā Gajsingh frustrated the vile plans of the said Khān and thus saved the Deccan from falling into the enemy's hands.

When the Emperor Jahāngīr died in 1627 A. D., Prince Khurram succeeded his father with the title of Shāhjahān at Āgrā. He received Rājā Gajsingh with great honour in appreciation of the brave deeds performed by him in the past and forgiving him for his hostilities against himself, conferred on him a robe of honour and recognised his previous Mansab of 5,000 Zāt and 5,000 horse.

Some time afterwards on receiving the commands of the new Emperor, he invaded the fortress of Sīsōdari (near Fateh-pur-Sikarī) and brought the rebels to their senses.

When the Emperor Shāhjahān despatched three armies in 1630 A. D. towards Bālāghāt to punish Nizām-ul-Mulk and Khān-e-Jahān Lodī, one of them was placed under the command of the Rājā, which he led with great success.

From Bālāghāt he returned to the Emperor, who rewarded him with a sword of honour, and then again sent him to the Deccan where his Rāthōr warriors played a conspicuous part.

The following year he was again sent to Bālāghāt along with Yāminuddaulāh (Āsāfkhān) to punish Mōhammad Ādil-khān and was appointed the general of the vanguard.

From this place he returned to Jōdhpur, but in 1633 A.D. he again went to Āgrā, and the Emperor honoured him again with a robe of honour etc., and deputed him to the Deccan to keep a watch on the affairs there. In 1636 A. D. he returned from the Deccan with the Emperor and came down to Jōdhpur, where he resided for about one year and a half.

After that, taking along with him Mahārāja-Kumār Jasvantsingh, he again went to Āgrā in 1637, where the Emperor again honoured him by the bestowal of a robe of honour.

He died at Agra in 1638 A. D. and was cremated on the banks of the river Jumna.

Rājā Gajsingh was a brave Rāthōr warrior and according to the chronicles, he took part in about fifty-two battles in all. He was honoured by the Emperor a number of times, and was himself a generous ruler.

25 Maharaja Jasvant Singh 1.

He had two sons—Amarsingh and Jasvantsingh. Maharaja Jasvantsingh succeeded to the throne of Jodhpur at the age of only eleven years, according to the wishes of Rājā Gajsingh

1. This chapter was read at the XI All India Oriental Conference held at Hyderabad Deccan) in December 1941 A. D.

and received the Mansab of 4,000 Zāt and 4,000 Sawārs from the Emperor, while Amarsingh was given the title of Rāo and the district of Nāgaur in Jāgīr (App. B. 4, pp. 81-86).

In 1639 A. D. Mahārājā Jasvantsingh's Mansab was further raised by the Emperor to 5,000 Zāt and 5,000 Sawārs and the district of Jaitāran was also given in Jagir to him.

He mostly remained in service with the Emperor and received honours on several occasions.

In 1641 A. D. one thousand Sawārs of his Mansab were raised to the rank of Du-Aspa[1] and Seh-Aspa[2].

In 1642 he was sent with Prince Dārāshikōh to defend Kandhār against Shāh Shafi, the king of Iran, but as this king while on his way to Kandhār died at Kāshān, he along with the Prince returned from Ghaznī.

Three years later in 1645 A. D. he was deputed to Agra to help in keeping peace and good government and the following year two thousand Sawārs of his Mansab were raised to Du-Aspa and Seh-Aspa rank and he visited Kābul with the Emperor.

In 1647 A. D. first two thousand five hundred and then three thousand Sāwārs of his Mansab were made Du-Aspa and Seh-Aspa, but in 1648 all the five thousand sawārs under his mansab received the said rank.

In 1649 A. D. he accompanied Prince Aurangzēb to Kandhār, who was sent there to punish Kazalbāshes of Iran, but on receipt of fresh orders from the Emperor both of them halted at Kābul till the Emperor himself reached there.

On his return from Afghānistān, he helped Rāval Sabalsingh against Rāval Rāmchandra in usurping the throne of Jaisalmēr, and in return got the districts of Phalodi and Pōkaran from him.

---

1. He who received the pay of 2 horses.

2. He who received the pay of 3 horses.

His Mansab was further raised to 6,000 Zāt and 5,000 Sawārs of the Du-Aspa and Seh-Aspa rank in 1653 A. D. and he was sent with Prince Dārāshikōh to conquer Kandhār, but this time the Imperial army could not succeed.

In 1655 A. D. his Mansab was again raised to 6,000 Zāt and 6,000 Sawārs (out of which 5,000 were Du-Aspā and Seh-Aspā) and the title of Mahārājā was conferred on him. Soon after receiving this honour he was also favoured with the district of Jālore.

In 1657 A. D. when Emperor Shāhjahān fell ill and his younger sons Aurangzēb and Murād marched from the Deccan and Gujrat respectively to seek their chances for the throne, Dārāshikōh, the eldest of the sons of Shahjahan, deputed Mahārājā Jasvantsingh I with the consent of the Emperor to check the advance of the aforesaid rebel princes, and besides bestowing on him various precious things appointed him governor of Mālwā. In addition to these honours his Mansab was raised to 7,000 Zāt and 7,000 Sawārs of which 5,000 were Du-Aspā and Seh-Aspā. In the battle, which was fought at Dharmat also known as Chornarāna (some fourteen miles to the South-South-West of Ujjain), against the combined forces of both the rebel princes, he displayed extra-ordinary valour, but unfortunately Qāsimkhān, the commander of the Imperial Army with him, in league with the other Muslim nobles, secretly joined with the rebel princes and treacherously deserted him at the nick of time. Therefore, inspite of the heroic and courageous efforts to gain the day, the tables were turned against him and after receiving serious wounds in the fight he was forced by his devoted nobles and kinsmen to leave the field against his will. The officers in Aurangzēb's forces wanted to pursue the Maharaja, but Aurangzēb, who had already seen the dreadful effect of the Rāṭhōr blades, warned them to desist from committing such a folly, which might have changed victory into an utter defeat.

We learn from "Tawārīkh-e-Muhammad Shāhi" that Aurangzeb often used to say "As God willed that the religion of Muhammad should survive in Hindustan that is why Jasvantsingh retired from the field that day."

According to Bernier Mahārājā Jasvantsingh lost about 7,400 out of his 8,000 warriors and returned to Jodhpur (App. B. 5, pp. 87-93).

After deposing his father and throwing him into prison Aurangzēb captured the throne of Hindustān and in order to deprive Prince Dārā of the help of the powerful Rāthōr ruler of Mārwār, opened negotiations with the Mahārājā (Jasvantsingh) through Mahārājā Jayasingh of Āmbēr. Hence when the Maharājā met him in the Punjāb, the new Emperor received him with honour, and at the same time awarded him a robe and sword of honour together with many-other precious gifts. After a few days, when they both reached the Sutlej, the Emperor again rewarded him with pearls etc., and bestowing on him a big Jāgīr sent him to look after the affairs at Delhi.

At the end of the same year, when Aurangzēb marched against Prince Shujā, the Mahārājā was in command of the right flank. Prince Shujā in the meantime had appealed to the Mahārājā to help him at this critical moment to clear the way for the release of the old and invalid Emperor. Mahārājā Jasvant, whose Rājpūt heart was touched at the mention of the miserable plight of the old Emperor, agreed to his entreaties and in reply informed Shujā that he would attack the army under Prince Muhammad (Aurangzēb's son) in the rear before day break and so he too should simultaneously attack it on the front at that hour. Accordingly the Mahārājā on his part attacked Prince Muhammad's army on the rear at the pre-arranged time and in the confusion, which followed, he looted the treasures of the army chest as well as its equipment. But Shujā on his part failed to attack at the right moment and delayed his action. The Mahārājā after carrying out his portion of the agreement left the army and waited at some distance until daybreak and then returned to Mārwār. This delay on the part of Shujā sealed his fate and he was obliged to run away leaving the field in his enemy's hands. All this took place in the beginning of 1659 A. D.

According to Bernier, when the Mahārājā, on his way to Mārwār, arrived near Agra, Shāistākhān, the maternal uncle of Aurangzēb, who was in-charge of the city, got so much overawed that he would have committed suicide by taking poison, had not the ladies of the harem snatched the cup from his hands and thus saved his life.

Aurangzēb, soon afterwards, despatched Amīnkhān, the Mīrbakhshī, with a force of 9,000 horse to invade Jōdhpur, and at the same time commanded Rāo Rāyasingh, the son of Rāo Amarsingh to accompany him after bestowing on him the title of 'Rājā' as well as the throne of Mārwār.

As soon as this news reached the Mahārājā, he too prepared himself and marched on to meet the invaders. In the meantime Prince Dārāshikoh requested the Mahārājā for help, which he gladly undertook to render. The Emperor was alarmed by this development and he again tried to win over the Mahārājā to his side through Rājā Jayasingh of Āmbēr, and gave orders to recall the forces dispatched against him. Rājā Jayasingh's earnest and insistent requests obliged him to refuse the promised help to Dārā under the excuse that unless some other person of note came forward to assist him, he could be of little use single-handed.

Soon afterwards Aurangzēb favoured him with the governorship of Gujrāt, and a robe of honour and at the same time confirmed his Mansab of 7,000 Zāt and 7,000 horse (including 500 Du-Aspā and Seh-Aspā). Further, after a few months, he bestowed on him a second time the title of 'Mahārājā' and also honoured more than once Mahārāja-Kumār Prithvīsingh his heir apparent.

About 1661 A. D. the Mahārājā after appointing his own deputy in Gujrāt, marched towards the Deccan to help Amīr-ul-Umarā Shāistākhān against the well known Mahārattā leader Shivājī. Though there soon arose dissensions between Shāistākhān and the Mahārājā, yet the latter captured a number of fortresses which were in the possession of the Maharaṭṭā leader.

In 1663 A. D. when Shivājī made a surprise attack on Shāistākhān at night time, the Emperor recalled Shaistākhān and appointed Prince Muazzam in his place. At the same time he bestowed on the Mahārājā a robe of honour etc.

Mahārājā Jasvantsingh showed great valour in the capture of the Kuṇḍā fort. But the Emperor wanted to crush down Shivājī as early as possible, which the Mahārājā did not like as he was fully aware that as soon as the Emperor was free from the menace of Shivājī, he would devote all his attention to give vent to his communal feelings. Therefore, in 1664 A. D. Aurangzēb deputed Rājā Jayasingh of Āmbēr in his place, and recalled him to Delhi.

Two years later in 1666 A. D. he was sent along with Prince Muazzam to Kābul, with a force of 20,000 strong, to check the advance of King Abbās II of Īrān, who was intending to invade India. But by the time they reached in the vicinity of Lāhore, King Abbās II died, and so after resting there for some time, they turned back to Delhi.

In 1667 A. D. the Emperor appointed Prince Muazzam as governor of the Deccan, and showing due honour to the Mahārājā deputed him to assist the Prince in his task. After fully surveying the situation there, the Mahārājā persuaded Shivājī to send his son Shambhājī to Prince Muazzam and conclude a treaty with him. But the Emperor did not approve of this and so he recalled him from the Deccan, and later in 1671 A. D. sent him to Jamrūd, after awarding on him a robe of honour and a horse worth about 600 gold mohurs. In course of time, the Mahārājā suppressed the rebellious Pathāns, and cleared the road leading from India to Kābul through the Khyber Pass.

Some three years later, in 1674 A. D., the Paṭhāns attacked Shujāatakhān near the river Gandāb, and killed him in the fray, but the Mahārājā soon inflicted an examplary punishment on them for their misbehaviour. When this news reached Aurangzēb, he himself marched towards Hasanabdāl and reaching Rāwalpindī awarded the Mahārājā with a robe of honour worth Rs. 7,000 along with other precious articles.

Mahārājā Jasvantsingh had two sons; the elder one of whom died in 1667 A. D. and the younger one breathed his last in 1676 A. D. The Mahārājā took this shock to heart so much that due to grief he himself left this mortal world in 1678 A. D. at Jamrūd in his fifty second year.

According to 'Tawarikh-e-Muhammad Shāhi', when the news of the demise of the Mahārājā reached the Emperor he said "Today the door of opposition to the Muhammedan religion has got broken." But when the Empress heard of this news she exclaimed "Today is the day of grief that this selected pillar of the Empire has fallen down."

Mahārājā Jasvantsingh I of Mārwar was a ruler of independent nature, and owing to the pro-muslim policy pursued by the Emperor, he always tried to pinch him whenever an opportunity occurred. The Emperor himself was always afraid of him, and as long as the Mahārājā was alive, he dared not impose a punitive tax like 'Jaziā' on the Hindus. Though Aurangzēb desired very much to take revenge on him, yet he dare not openly do so and therefore he always tried to keep him pleased by awarding honours and precious gifts, and at the same time always kept him far away from his own country.

26 Maharaja Ajit Singh.

Mahārājā Ajitsingh was the posthumous son of Mahārājā Jasvantsingh I.

He finally took possession of his patrimony in 1708 A. D., at the age of about 29 years, after a prolonged struggle with the Moghuls During this long period Mārwār was occupied and ruled by the agents of the Emperor Aurangzēb and his successor Bahādurshāh. But the Rājpūt nobles of this land fought for the liberty of their country for about three months without even having any ruler in this world as their head. Then for about eight years more they struggled on with the conviction that their beloved ruler was kept concealed somewhere in a place of safety, and then for about 21 years more under the command of their ruler.

When Mahārājā Jasvantsingh I died, the Rajput nobles, who were with the late Mahārājā at Jamrūd, returned to Delhi, enroute to Mārwār, with his two widowed queens and his two posthumous sons who were both born at Lāhore. In the meantime the Emperor, to avenge the insults suffered by him from time to time at the hands of Mahārājā Jasvantsingh, annexed his country soon after his death, and planned to take possession of both the infant princes too. But all his efforts were frustrated by the undaunted and devoted Rāthōrs and they managed to send away their infant Mahārājā Ajitsingh to Mārwār secretly and kept him concealed in a village in Sirōhī State while his younger brother died at Delhi. Thus freeing their infant ruler from the clutches of the tyrant monarch the Rājpūt warriors also fought their way back to their beloved country. Here, under the wise direction of their sagacious and intrepid leader Durgādās Rāṭhōṛ, they commenced harrasing the imperial posts all over the country by guerilla warfare. The Emperor, in order to divide the Rājpūts in opposition, tried to instal Rāo Indrasingh, the grandson of Rāo Amarsingh, as ruler of Mārwār, but all his efforts ended in a fiasco. Thus finding all his plans falling flat to the ground, the Emperor, accompanied by his youngest son Mohammad Akbar, came down to Ajmer in person and from this place he himself directed the operations of the army to crush the rebellious Rāthōrs.

In 1681 A. D. Rāthōr Durgādās won over Prince Mohammad Akbar to his side and persuading him to tread the path shown by his own father, proclaimed him Emperor of Hindustān at Nādole. When the news of this event reached the ears of the Emperor, he was stunned for a while, but on recovering his senses, he wrote a letter to prince Akbar and attempted to deceive him wherein he utterly failed (App. B. 6, pp. 94-101). But being a shrewd monarch, he again tried to entrap the Rāthōṛs in his snare by indirectly impressing upon them that Prince Akbar was only acting upto this intrigue under the instructions of his father. Fate however favoured him this time and his methods were successful to some degree.

The Rājpūt nobles tried to ascertain the facts from Prince Akbar himself in his camp, but it being night time they could not get access, and when they came to know that his (Akbar's) general Tahavvarkhān had also gone back to the Imperial camp, their suspicions were fully confirmed. They therefore deserted Prince Akbar in a body.

Next morning when the Prince realised his delicate position, he at once went to the Rāthōrs for refuge and removed all their ill-founded suspicions. The Rāṭhōrs repented much for their false step which had lost them an opportunity. At this Durgādās, leaving the affairs of Mārwār in the hands of Chāmpāvat Sōnag, started with the unfortunate prince Mohammad Akbar towards the Deccan to divert the attention of the Emperor and in June, they arrived at the court of Shambhāji. This action taken by Durgādās produced the desired effect, and the Emperor too, leaving the chastisement of Mārwār in the hands of Prince Azīm went to the Deccan in person. This afforded the Rāṭhoṛs a breathing space, and after collecting their men and money they began to threaten the invaders with redoubled vigour, all over the country at each and every place. Thus these well directed combined or individual efforts of the Rāthors continued in harrassing the Imperial officers, as well as the army of occupation until the death of Emperor Aurangzēb in Deccan in 1707 A. D. and after frustrating the efforts of his successor Emperor Bahādurshāh, Mahārājā Ajitsingh was able to take possession of the fort of Jōdhpur in 1708 A. D. finally.

As stated above, Mahārājā Ajitsingh was kept in concealment in the mountains near Sirōhī from 1679 to 1687 A. D.. In the year 1687 he was brought out of his place where he resided and was proclaimed the ruler of Mārwār. When he became major, he personally took more and more active part in routing his enemies. Rāthōr Durgādās also returned from the Deccan in 1687 A. D. and played a most prominent part in this prolonged struggle.

After capturing Jōdhpur in 1708 A. D. Mahārāja Ajitsingh also aided Rājā Jayasingh in recovering Āmbēr, which had also been occupied then by the Imperial forces. At the same time the combined armies of Mārwār and Āmbēr also took possession of Sāmbhar, and this spoil was shared by both the rulers among themselves.

Mahārājā Ajitsingh then invaded Nagaur to avenge the hostile attitude shown by Rāo Indrasingh, but when he reached Mūṇḍwā, the latter's mother approached him and apologized for all that had happened uptill that time. Thus Mahārājā Ajitsingh had to yield to her entreaties and forgiving Rāo Indrasingh returned to Jōdhpur.

Bahādurshāh, after his success in killing his own rebellious brother Kāmbakhsh in the Deccan, came towards Ajmēr to dispossess Mahārājā Ajit of Jōdhpur, who also prepared himself and marched out to measure arms with him. But in the meantime the Sikhs had revolted in the Punjab, so the Emperor was obliged to conclude a treaty with the Mahārājā in 1710 A. D. and recognised his right over Jōdhpur. After this the Mahārājā proceeded to a pilgrimage.

In 1712 A. D. Mahārājā Ajitsingh invaded Kishangarh and thence he went to Sāṁbhar where he met Rājā Jaysingh of Āmbēr as well as some other rulers of Rajpūtānā.

Moizuddīn Jahāndārshāh, the then Emperor, did not think it prudent to start a fresh quarrel with the Mahārājā as at that time Farrukhsiyar was threatening the throne of Delhi.

Soon after it when Farrukhsiyar ascended the throne, Rāo Indrasingh and Rājā Rājsingh (of Kishangarh) succeeded in poisoning the ears of the new Emperor against Mahārājā Ajitsingh. He therefore despatched Amir-ul-Umrā Husainalikhān with a strong force to invade Jōdhpur. As soon as the news of this invasion reached the Mahārājā, he appointed a trustworthy noble to look after the routine work of the administration and himself went towards the Western part of the country to collect men and money (App. B. 7, pp. 102-108), but in 1714 A. D. a treaty was concluded near Mērtā, and the Amir-ul-Umrā returned with Mahārāj-Kumār Abhayasingh to Delhi accordingly. The Mahārāj-Kumār was well received by the Emperor and was appointed Faujdār of Sōrath.

The following year, the Emperor appointed the Mahārājā Governor of Gujrāt and bestowed on him a Mansab of 5,000 Sawārs, but he returned from Gujrāt in 1717 A. D and later took Nāgaur in his possession and had it recognised from the Emperor in his Jāgīr.

In 1718 A. D. on a dispute, which arose between the two Sayyad brothers and the Emperor, Farrukhsiyar called the Mahārājā to his aid.

But the man through whom he negotiated was a secret friend of the Sayyad brothers and he exposed to the Mahārājā the fikle-mindedness of the Emperor and turned his sympathies from him (the Emperor). Anyhow when the Mahārājā reached Delhi, the Emperor sent one of his nobles to receive him. But as he was now well aware of his fickle nature, he gained audience of the Emperor in the company of his minister Qutub-ul-Mulk. This action of the Mahārājā displeased the Emperor and he, as advised by the Rājā of Āmbēr etc., endeavoured to get him murdered secretly, but in this he was not successful. Thereafter he again tried to win Mahārājā Ajitsingh on his side and bestowed upon him the State of Bīkānēr, the Governorship of Gujrāt and the title of 'Rāj Rājēshvar'. Though both sides attempted to arrive at a compromise, yet owing to the unstability of the Emperor's mind, the Mahārājā as well as the Sayyad brothers lost their faith in him. Therefore, in February 1719 A. D. Rafiud-darjāt was seated on the throne of the Moghul Empire, and Farrukhsiyar was first cast away in prison and some time later murdered there (App. B. 9, pp. 113-118).

Rafiuddarjāt, the new Emperor, abolished the 'Jaziā' as well as the tax levied on the sacred places of the Hindus (App. B. 8, pp. 109-112) in order to gain the good will of the Mahārājā.

Sometime afterwards the Mahārājā wished to leave Delhi for Gujrāt, but as there was a rebellion at Āgrā, he could not proceed.

About three months afterwards, Rafiuddarjāt fell seriously ill and his elder brother Rafiuddaulāh was placed on the throne (as desired by the sick brother), under the title of Shah Jahan II (Sānī). The party then marched towards Agra to supress the rebellion. Sayyad Abdullāh Khān intended to invade Āmbēr too, and punish Rājā Jayasingh, but Mahārājā Ajitsingh persuaded him to give up this idea.

In the month of September of the same year Rafiuddaulāh also died at Vidyāpur, but the news of his death was disclosed only after the installation of Raushan Akhtar on the Moghal throne, under the title of Nāsiruddīn Mōhammad Shāh. Soon after his accession the new Emperor honoured Maharājā Ajitsingh by the Governorship of Ajmēr and also raised his Mansab by 300 Sawārs and probably promoted the rank of his 2,500 Sawārs to Du-Aspā and Seh-Aspā. The province of Gujrāt minus Sōraṭh, which was given to Rājā Jayasingh, also remained in his possession.

When Sayyad Husainalikhān was murdered in 1720 (A. D.) the Mahārājā took possession of Ajmēr and severing all connections with the Emperor, ruled there as an independent king. He forbade cow-slaughter in the province under him and annexed Sāmbhar, Ḍīdwānā, Tōḍā, Jhāṛōd, and Amarsar.

When Mōhammad Shāh was apprised of these happenings, he tried to dispossess the Mahārājā of the province of Ajmer, but the four biggest nobles at his court, who were offered the Governorship of Ajmer, refused to accept the honour one after another. Anyhow, in 1721 a representative of Haidar Qulīkhān took charge of the Governorship of Gujrāt from the representative of the Mahārājā, while Sayyad Muzaffar Alīkhān marched towards Ajmer with an army of about 20,000 strong. The Emperor entertained the belief that as soon as Ajitsingh will hear of the march of the Imperial forces against him, he would surrender the province to the Emperor. But on the contrary when he knew that the Mahārājā was prepared to oppose him, he at once ordered Muzaffar Alīkhān, the newly appointed Governor of Ajmer, to halt at Manōharpur. He therefore waited there for about three months for further instructions from the Emperor, and during this period of inactivity his army chest was exhausted; and by the end of this time many of his soldiers deserted him and he was reduced to a pitiable plight. Though he was invited by the Rājā of Āmbēr to go to his territory, yet he felt so much aggrieved that he returned the Imperial order about the Governorship of Ajmer as well as the robe of honour, and turned an ascetic.

Thereupon the Emperor asked Sayyad Nusaratyārkhān to march against Ajitsingh. When this information reached the Mahārājā, he despatched his heir-apparent Abhayasingh with a sufficient force who, as desired by his sire, plundered the Imperial territories of Nārnole, Alwar, Tijārā, Shāhjahānpur, and reached Sarāya Aliwardīkhān, only 18 miles distant from Delhi itself.

Hearing of these inroads upon the Imperial territories, the Emperor asked his nobles to punish the Mahārājā for this audacity, but three of them expressed their inability in turn. At last after much persuasions Nusratyārkhān accepted this task. In the meantime Mahārājā Ajitsingh himself left Ajmer and returned to Jodhpur and thus the situation was saved.

In 1722 A. D. Mahārājā Ajitsingh sent his representative to the Emperor to protest against his order in taking away the province of Ajmer from him. Where upon the Emperor restored the said province to the Mahārājā and further gave a promise of returning the province of Gujrāt too after some days. Further to appease Mahārājā Ajitsingh, he again honoured him with a robe of honour, etc.

Some months afterwards the Mahārājā got two of the Imperial officers murdered for their using abusive language against him. This act again enraged the Emperor and he issued orders to a number of his nobles to invade Mārwār, and at the same time he again bestowed the province of Nāgaur on Rāo Indrasingh. When the combined forces of the Imperial nobles reached Ajmer, Ūdāwat Amarsingh, the commander of the Mahārājā's army, bravely gave them a battle. In the meantime Rājā Jayasingh succeeded in bringing about a treaty between the Emperor and the Mahārājā and persuaded Ajitsingh to hand over the fort of Ajmer to the Emperor and, as a further proof of good will, to send his heir-apparent to attend at the court of Mōhammad Shāh.

Accordingly, when the Mahārāj-Kumār reached Delhi, the Emperor received him with due respect worthy of him.

Though everything was thus settled, yet the Emperor lived in constant dread of the Mahārājā. He therefore won over Bhandārī Raghunāth to his side through the efforts of the Rājā of Āmbēr and after getting a forged letter signed by Mahārāj-Kumār Abhayasingh had Mahārājā Ajitsingh assasinated while asleep, by his younger son Bakhat Singh in the year 1724 A. D. (App. B. 10 & 11, p.p. 119-133).

Mahārājā Ajitsingh, who lost his father before he was born and his mother in his infancy, had to face an enemy like Emperor Aurangzēb. He was kept concealed in the mountains for about eight years and after which he had to roam all over his country for about 21 years. But by passing through all these vicissitudes of life; he turned out such a powerful ruler that he, in league with the two Sayyad brothers, dethroned Emperor Farrukhsiyar, and seated three new Emperors in succession on the Mughal throne of Delhi.

He also helped Mahārānā Jayasingh twice when his eldest son Amarsingh revolted against him in 1691 and 1695 A. D. (App. B. 20, pp. 186).

(27) Maharaja Abhaya-singh

Mahārājā Abhayasingh, the eldest son of Mahārājā Ajitsingh, succeeded his father at Delhi as he was there at the time of his father's death.

The Emperor personally paid him a visit to his residence and honoured him with a robe of honour, and also bestowed on him the province of Nāgaur in Jāgīr.

The following year (in 1725 A. D.) he went to Gujrāt along with Sarbuland Khān to suppress the trouble caused there by Hamīd Khān as well as the Dakkhanīs. After accomplishing this task he returned to Jōdhpur via Delhi, set right its affairs, and then invaded Nāgaur and granted it to his younger brother Bakhatsingh, and exalted him with the bestowal of the title of 'Rājādhirāj'.

The Mahārājā also gave shelter to Hādā Budh Singh, the ruler of Būndī and Rāwal Akhairāj, the ruler of Jaisalmer. In 1727 A. D. he again went to Delhi, and thence proceeded on a pilgrimage to Gadhamuktēshwar.

In 1728 A. D. his younger brothers, Anand Singh and Rāya Singh, took possession of Īdar, which was then included in the Mahārājā's Mansab, but he did not oppose their action keeping in view the maintenance of undisturbed peace in Mārwār (App. B. 12, pp. 134-135).

Emperor Mōhammadshāh got displeased with Sarbulandkhān, the Governor of Gujrāt, and appointed Mahārājā Abhaya Singh in his place in 1730 A. D. as a mark of favour. He bestowed on him (the Mahārājā) a robe of honour (as well as the province of Ajmer). Accordingly he took possession of Ajmer and then marched with his brother Rājādhirāj for Ahmedabad, by the way of Sirōhī and Pālanpur. But when he reached there he found Sarbulandkhān unwilling to hand over charge of the governorship and was prepared to oppose him After a fierce battle between Sarbulandkhān and the Mahārājā, which was fought on the banks of the river Sabarmati (App. 13 & 14, pp. 136-153), the old governor was obliged to hand over the province to the Mahārājā and to retire towards Agra.

The following year Pēshwā Bāji Rāo I invaded Gujrāt, but the Mahārājā managed him to side with the Emperor and sent him with the army against Tryambak Rāo Dābhārē, who was helped by the Nizām. The invaders were defeated. But Nizām-ul-Mulk poisoned the ears of Nawāb Khān Daurān, the minister of the Emperor, against the Peshwā and tried to get him punished. On coming to know of this intrigue the Mahārājā sent a letter of protest to the Nawāb, in which he conveyed to him in plain words that even if the Nizām, who was in league with the enemies and who yet possessed the confidence of the Nawāb, dares to come this side, he too would be chastised in the same way (App. B. 15 & 16, pp. 154-165).

In 1732 A D the Mahārājā managed to get Pīlāji, the founder of the Gaekawad dynasty, murdered, and annexed Barōdā. He also captured a number of forts, which were in the hands of these Mahrāttā intruders (App. B, 17 & 18, pp. 166—176).

Owing to these Maharāttā raids the revenue of the province had dwindled, and a horrible famine which ravaged in the land made the condition all the more pitiable, yet the Imperial court did not send the expected help in men and money, even on repeated demands.

Under such circumstances Umābāī Dābhārē, the widow of Khāndērāo Dābhārē, invaded Gujrāt the following year. A treaty was concluded with her, and was also approved by the Emperor. For this foresight the Emperor honoured the Mahārājā with a robe of honour, after which, the Mahārājā having appointed his own deputy to look after the Gujrāt affairs returned to Jōdhpur.

The same year a boundary dispute arose between Rājādhirāj Bakhat Singh and Rājā Sujān Singh of Bīkānēr. The Rājādhirāj invaded Bīkānēr, and the Mahārājā also went to his help, and they captured the city. In the end, a treaty was concluded with the Bīkānēr ruler by the terms of which the Bīkānēr ruler promised to pay Rupees twelve lacs as indemnity, out of which 8 lacs were paid in cash and for the remaining four lacs, he had to cede the villages of Kharbūjī and Sārūndā Besides this he also promised to serve the Mahārājā with the whole of his army whenever called for to do so (App. B. 19, pp. 177-182).

In 1734 A. D. he held a grand assembly at Hurdā, which was attended by the rulers of Jaipur, Udaipur, Kōtāh, Bīkānēr and Kishangarh and all of them signed a pact of mutual assistance. After this pact he accompanied Samsāmuddulāh to deal with Malhār Rāo Hōlkar, who threatened Ajmer and Sāmbhar, but by the mediation of Rājā Jayasingh a treaty was concluded between them. He then went to Delhi with the Nawāb in 1735 A. D.

Malhār Rāo getting displeased with the Mahārājā for his siding with the Emperor invaded, in his absence, some of the provinces of Mārwār in 1736 A. D., but was soon opposed and forced to withdraw his forces by his (Mahārājā's) nobles.

In 1737 A. D. the Muslim nobles poisoned the ears of the Emperor against the Mahārājā who, thereupon appointed Momin-Khān as Governor of Gujrāt in his place. But when the new Governor did not find himself strong enough to take possession of the province, he asked for the help of the Maharattā-general Rangojī, promising him a share in the income of the province in return for his services. When the Mahārājā came to know of this clique he got so much enraged that he left the Imperial court, even when the Emperor was holding it. All the courtiers present there were alarmed by his behaviour, and entreated him to return back to the court, where a fresh Farmān, under the signature of the Emperor, for his governorship of Gujrāt was issued. But as Mōmīnkhān had occupied Ahmedabad, even in disobedience of the orders conveyed in this Farmān, the Mahārājā left Delhi and returned to Jōdhpur.

Sometime afterwards he again invaded Bīkānēr, but when, in 1741 A. D. Rājā Jayasingh of Āmbēr marched against Jōdhpur, he was obliged to come back from there (Bīkānēr). Peace was soon patched up between both the rulers of Jōdhpur and Jaipur without any bloodshed and Rājā Jayasingh returned to his capital.

Later on Mahārājā Abhaya Singh, in order to take revenge upon Jayasingh, asked Rājādhirāj Bakhat Singh to take possession of Ajmer, which was then under Jaya Singh. As soon as this news reached Rājā Jayasingh, he marched against him with an army of 50,000 strong. At Gangvānā, near Ajmer, Rājādhirāj Bakhat Singh measured swords with him, with great bravery, with a force of 5,000 warriors only and according to Col. Tod, Rājā Jayasingh had to flee away towards Khaṇḍēlā. But Bakhat Singh also lost almost all of his warriors and thinking it imprudent to stay there in this condition, moved on to Riān, where Mahārājā Abhaya Singh was camping with his army. Soon after both the brothers again marched against Rājā Jayasingh, who being afraid of the Rāthōr might dared not give them a battle, and handing back the seven provinces, which fell into his hands in his invasion of Mārwār and returning all the material which Rājādhirāj left behind at Gangvānā concluded a treaty with them.

After the death of Rājā Jayasingh in 1743 A. D. Ajmer was again taken possession of by Mahārājā Abhayasingh. Rājā Īshwarīsingh tried to recapture it, but failed.

In 1747 the Mahārājā again invaded Bīkānēr, but peace was soon restored.

The following year Ahmadshāh Durrānī invaded the Punjab. The Emperor called the Mahārājā and the Rājādhirāj to his aid. But as Mahārājā Abhaya Singh was too busy with his own State affairs, Rājādhirāj Bakhat Singh alone went there and helped Prince Ahmadshāh in defeating the Afghāns at the battle of Sirhind and in re-taking Lahore.

In April of the same year Ahmadshāh ascended the throne after the death of his father. He bestowed on the Rājādhirāj the Governorship of Gujrāt, but as the Maharaṭṭās were at that period, over running the whole country, he did not think it prudent to go to Gujrāt and so returned to his own country.

The same year, at the request of Mahārānā Jagatsingh II, the Mahārājā helped Madhosingh with 2,000 horse against his elder brother Rājā Īshwarisingh of Jaipur.

Mahārājā Abhaya Singh died in 1749 A. D. Like his father and grandfather he too was a brave ruler.

He was succeeded by his only son Mahārājā Ramsingh.

(28) Maharaja Ramsingh.

Though he was a brave ruler yet, was not so sober minded. A dispute arose between him and his uncle Bakhat Singh. Some of his nobles also deserted him and joined hands with the Rajādhirāj. Thereupon Mahārājā Rāmsingh invaded Nāgaur, but on the Rājādhirāj agreeing to return Jālore, peace was not disturbed and the Mahārājā returned to Jōdhpur.

But sometime later the Rājādhirāj showed his unwillingness to part with Jālore and went to Delhi. There he intrigued with the Amir-ul-Umrā Salābatkhān (Zulfikar Jang) and instigated him to secure for himself the governorship of Ajmer and promised him full support against the Maharaṭṭās. In return for this help he demanded assistance from him (Amir-Ul-Umra) in occupying Jōdhpur.

As soon as this news reached the Mahārājā, he too sought help from his would-be father-in-law Rājā Īshwarī Singh of Jaipur and Malhār Rao Hōlkar. Rājā Gajsingh of Bīkānēr and Rājā Bahādur Singh of Rōōpnagar (Kishangarh) sided with the Rājādhirāj.

Some days afterwards when Zulfikār, after being appointed governor of Ajmer, reached Pīpār, a fierce battle ensued between his army and that of the Mahārājā. In a short time the

Muslim army was routed from the field, and in the intense heat of the day wandered hither and thither in quest of water to quench their thirst and also that of their horses. According to the author of "Sehrul Mutākharīn" when Zulfikar's vanquished and thirsty soldiers happened to come across with the Mahārājā's warriors, while out searching for water, then out of pity for their miserable condition the Mahārājā's soldiers supplied them with sufficient water to quench the thirst of both the men and their horses and after that asked them to leave the place instantly for their own camp.

This is a unique instance of the Rāṭhōr magnanimity of heart and its parallel can scarcely be found in the annals of other Rājpūt races[1].

Zulfikār was so much disheartened by this defeat that even the assurances of Rājādhirāj Bakhat Singh could not deter him from returning to Delhi by way of Ajmer. This event took place in 1749 A.D.

In 1751 A. D. when Mahārājā Rāmsingh was camping with his forces at Mērtā to meet the possible onslaught of the Rājādhirāj, he (Bakhat Singh) took the fort of Jodhpur by a surprise attack and thus deprived Mahārājā Rāmsingh of his possession for ever.

In 1752 A. D. Rāmsingh, with the active support of Sindhiā, was able to get hold of some portion of Marwar.

---

1. Munshi Ghulam Husain Khen, the author of Sehrul-Mutākharin, describes this event as follows —

It was so heard that about the mid-day when the guns became too hot for discharge and the battle somewhat cooled down, in those parts of Rājputānā and at that place particularly, where the battle was being fought, there was an acute scarcity of water, some of the followers of the Amirul-Umra, who were feeling thirsty and were wandering in quest of water reached the vicinity of the camp of Ramsingh Coming to know of their calamity, betrayed by their looks, the Rājput nobles commanded their servants to draw water and quench the thirst of their foes, including their horses, and bade them to depart instantly, remarking they were at war with them The story about the clash with Zulfikarjang and the supply of water by the Rājputs to their foes bear credence as Sayyad Ismailalikhān Bahādur, son of Abdulalikhān Bahādur, cousin of the author, was accompanying that army The author has recorded this happening after personally hearing the story from the Sayyad This virtue of the Rājputs is one of the rare qualities May the Almighty God bestow such rare qualities on all mankind (Vol. III., pp. 883—885)

Two years later (in 1754 A. D.) by the efforts of Jayā Āpā Sindhiā, a fresh treaty was concluded between Ramsingh and his cousin Bijaya Singh by the terms of which the former was given the districts of Siwana, Marōth, Mērtā, Sōjat, Parbatsar, Sāmbhar and Jālore.

He breathed his last in 1772 A. D.

(29) Maharaja Bakhat-Singh.

Maharaja Bakhatsingh, who wrested the throne of Mārwār from his nephew Mahārājā Ramsingh in 1751 A. D., was a brave and sagacious ruler. We have already narrated that he once utterly routed the Jaipur army 50,000 strong under the personal command of Rājā Jayasingh with only a force of 5,000 brave warriors under him.

Mahārājā Bakhatsingh also proposed to enter into a pact with Rājā Mādhōsingh of Jaipur in order to drive away the Maharattās from Malwa, but the latter had not the courage enough to agree to it.

He died at Sīndhōlī (in Jaipur) in 1752 A. D. while conducting negotiations regarding his aforesaid proposal.

(It is also said that he was poisoned under the instigation of the Rājā of Jaipur).

(30) Maharaja Bijaya Singh.

Maharaja Bijayasingh, his only son, succeeded him to the throne of Jōdhpur.

In 1754 A. D. in a sharp encounter with Jayā Āpā Sindhiā, who had come to help Mahārājā Ramsingh, he defeated him at Gangarda, but in another battle his artillery could not reach him in time and the Maharattās won the day. The Maharattās, elated with success, pursued the Mahārājā upto Nāgaur.

Seeing no other way to raise the seige Mahārājā Bijayasingh contrived to get Jayā Āpā murdered by treachery. Soon after this happening, the other Maharattā leaders, hearing of this news, invaded Nāgaur and Jodhpur to avenge the death of Jayā Āpā. But sometime later a treaty was drawn up, by which Ajmer was ceded to the Maharattās and a number of districts in Marwar were assigned to Mahārājā Ramsingh for his maintenance. These internal dissensions afforded opportunities to the Maharattā free-booters to invade this country from time to time, and also to the Jāgīrdārs (feudatories) to become unruly.

In 1760 A. D. four of the leading Jāgīrdārs were imprisoned.

In the years 1766 and 1772 A. D. the Mahārājā went twice to Nāthdwārā for pilgrimage. He also actively supported Mahārānā Arasī (Arisingh) against his grand nephew Ratnasingh at the end of 1770 A. D. and in return for his help, got the district of Gōdwār. (App. B. 20, pp. 186-188)

He chastised the Talpuras and annexed Umarkōt in 1782 A. D. He gave sanctuary to Mahārāj—Kumār Rājsingh of Bīkānēr and sent a force of his Rāthor warriors to the succour of Rājā Pratāpsingh of Jaipur against Mādhōjī Sindhiā. The force played havoc in the Maharattā army at Tungān in 1787 A. D. He also gained success in his invasion on Kishangarh.

Mādhōjī Sindhiā invaded Mārwār in 1790 A. D. to avenge the serious reverse of his army at Tungān. The battle of Tungān was fought to further the interests of Rājā Pratāpsingh, yet he refused to come to the aid of Jodhpur at the time of this crisis. On the other hand De Boigne, the French general of the Maharattā army, kept the Rāthōrs under deception by negotiating a false treaty with them. Thus the Maharattās gained victory this time and Mahārājā Bijayasingh was compelled to agree to pay in future the same tribute to the Maharattās, which was formerly given to the Mughul Emperors.

He died in 1793 A. D. after a reign of about 41 years.

With the permission of Shāh Ālam II, the then Emperor, he coined his own silver coins in 1780 A. D., which since came to be known as Bijaya Shahī, or Baī Sandā (for having twenty second regnal year of Shāh Ālam II imprinted on them).

We learn from an Imperial Sanad, dated 7th August 1775 A. D., that the village Rāisinā or the area of land over which the present New Delhi has been built was granted to him in his ancestral Jāgīr in perpetuity. (App. B. 21, pp. 189-195).

(31) Maharaja Bhimsingh

As two of his elder sons had left this world in his own life time, he was succeeded by his grandson Bhīmsingh (the son of his second son Bhōmsingh).

The struggle for the throne continued going on between him and his uncles and cousins throughout his life. The Maharattās also invaded Mārwār in 1794 A. D., but he bought them off.

(32) Maharaja Mansingh

He died in 1803 A D. after a reign of about ten years. As he left no male issue, he was succeeded by his cousin Mahārājā Mānsingh, the son of Gumānsingh.

In the same year a treaty was drawn up between the Mahārājā and the East India Company, but the Mahārājā did not approve of its terms, and wanted some modifications in them.

The following year, when the East India Company was waging war with Sindhiā, Mahārājā Mānsingh subdued Ajmer and also gave refuge to the family of Jaswant Rāo Hōlkar. At this action of the Mahārājā, the East India Company was forced to annul the treaty of 1803 A. D. In the meantime some of the dissatisfied nobles of Mārwār took up the cause of Dhōnkalsingh, an alleged posthumous son of the late Mahārājā Bhīmsingh, for the throne of Mārwār. A year later the relations between Mahārājā Mānsingh of Jodhpur and Mahārājā Jāgatsingh of Jaipur got strained to a breaking point on the question of the marriage of Krishnākumārī, the daughter of Mahārānā Bhīmsingh of Mēwar, who was previously betrothed to late Mahārājā Bhīmsingh of Jōdhpur.

Thākur Sawāīsingh of Pōkaran, taking his chance of this fued, instigated the Mahārājā of Jaipur to invade Jōdhpur. Mahārājā Suratsingh of Bikānēr and the ruler of Shāhpurā joined hands with the invader and most of the Jāgīrdars of Mārwār also rendered help to the Jaipur hordes. Although, in 1807 A D. the invaders gained some success for the time being in gaining possession of the city of Jōdhpur, yet soon afterwards, with the combined efforts of Singhī Indrarāj and some of the remaining loyal nobles, Amīr Khan, a freebooter siding with the Jaipur chief was bought over to help the cause of Mahārājā Mānsingh. Thus gaining ample strength and collecting sufficient men and money, the city of Jaipur was raided with this newly raised army. This news frustrated all the plans of the Mahārājā of Jaipur and he was obliged to retire post-haste to defend his own capital.

In 1808 Amīr Khan treacherously murdered the Thakurs of Pōkaran, Chandāwal, Pāli, Bagrī, etc., who were the most prominent rebel nobles of Marwar at Mūṇdwā.

After this event, the Jōdhpur forces also invaded Bīkānēr to take revenge on its Mahārājā, who took part in the invasion of Jōdhpur along with the Jaipur army, and forced him (Mahārājā Sūratsingh) to cede back the district of Phalōdi, which he had received for giving active support to the cause of Dhōnkalsingh. He was also compelled to write a bond for the payment of Rs. 3,60,001/- as indemnity (App. B. 22, pp. 196-198).

The following year Amīr Khan was sent against Jaipur to settle accounts with the Mahārājā for his previous invasion of Mārwār and he compelled Mahārājā Jagatsingh to return all the effects left behind by Mahārājā Mānsingh at the battle of Gīngōlī (in Parbatsar district), and to pay a large sum in cash to meet the expenses of his (Amīr Khan's) army.

In 1812 A. D. the Marwar forces invaded Sirōhī and plundered its capital.

The following year Mahārājā Jagatsingh of Jaipur called Singhī Indrarāj to his court in order to re-establish friendly relations with Mahārājā Mānsingh of Jōdhpur.

The same year Mahārājā Mānsingh captured Rao Udaibhān of Sirōhī, while he was camping at Pālī, and kept him in captivity for about three months. But when the Rao accepted the allegiance of the Mahārājā and also promised to pay Rs. 1,25,000 as indemnity, he was set free.

In 1815 A. D. Singhī Indrarāj, the minister and Āyas Devnath, the spiritual teacher (Guru) of the Mahārājā, were murdered at the instigation of the local faction by Amīr Khan's followers. The Mahārājā took this matter to heart so much that he shut himself up in seclusion and left taking any interest in politics or in the administration of the State The vile faction on their part set up in his place Mahārāj-kumār Chhatrasingh, his heir-apparent, against the wishes of the Mahārājā

In 1818 A. D. a new treaty was concluded between the East India Company and the Jōdhpur State.

Soon after this treaty Mahārāj-kumār Chhatrasingh died and the Mahārājā re-took the reigns of administration in his own hands. In 1800 A. D. he took a dreadful revenge on the intriguers for their misdeeds and disloyal activities against him.

In 1824 A. D. the East India Company, in order to suppress the unruly tribes there, took over 21 villages of Mērwāṛā from Jōdhpur under its direct control.

Three years later the Mahārājā gave sanctuary to Rājā Madhurājdeo Bhōnslē of Nāgpur, who came to Jōdhpur after his utter defeat by the East India Company. A year afterwards in 1828 A. D., he gave refuge to Rājā Kalyānsingh of Kishangarh.

In 1835 A. D. the Agent to the Governor General in Rajputana put 29 rebellious Jāgīrdārs of Mallānī under custody and put the administration of Mallānī district under the Political Agent.

The same year, the East India Company took seven more villages of Mērwārā under its direct control (which were returned in 1843 A. D.) and also renewed the agreement about the previous 21 villages. Further the Mahārājā agreed to pay Rs. 1,15,000 in cash instead of 1,500 Sawars according to the agreement in the previous treaty of 1818 A. D.

As the Mahārājā was a staunch devotee of the Nāth sect, so the Naths exercised an undue influence over the administration of the State. To eradicate this evil, the Agent to the Governor General in Rajputana and the Political Agent, with a contingent of ten thousand soldiers, came to Jōdhpur, and concluded a fresh treaty in 1839 A. D. By the terms of this treaty a Political agent was stationed at Jōdhpur to render advice and give help to the State whenever necessary, and the fort was temporarily put under his charge, but was returned back to the Mahārājā after a short period in 1840 A. D. The following year the A. G. G. as well as the Political Agent endeavoured to end the interference of the Nāths in the State administration, but their efforts proved of no avail. They therefore resumed the Jāgīrs of these Nāths, but even when this drastic action failed to produce any sobering effect they were constrained to deport two of the rebellious Nāths.

This action of the Agent to the Governor General hurt the religious susceptibilities of the Mahārājā to such an extent that he renounced the world, left all interest in the administration from that day and died at Maṇdōr after about four months in 1843 A. D.

Mahārājā Mānsingh was a scholar, brave and a wise ruler. But as he was too much under the influence of the Nāths and unforgiving for his rebellious nobles, so his reign was never free from internal troubles.

In 1822 A. D. Mahārājā Ranjītsingh of the Punjab, sought his advice about the political situation then prevailing in India. This bears ample testimony for his fame and statesmanship in which he was held by the other rulers. (App. B. 23, pp. 199-202).

With the assistance of the Agent to the Governor General and the Political Agent he also introduced some social reforms in the State in 1839 A. D. which were inscribed on marble slabs and installed at every district headquarters in 1843 A. D. (App. B. 24, pp. 203-204 .

As he left no male issue, so he was succeeded after his death by Mahārājā Takhatsingh of Ahmadnagar, in Īdar State, according to the will made by him.

(33) Maharaja Takhatsingh

In 1847 A. D. the East India Company in lieu of Umarkot agreed to pay Rs. 10,000 annually to the State. Three years later in 1850 A. D. the Mahārājā got himself weighed in silver.

The Mahārānā of Udaipur put forward his claim in 1853 A. D. for the restoration of the Godwar district back to Mēwār, but as this district was ceded to Mahārājā Bijayasingh of Jodhpur in 1770 A. D. in return for his help against the Mahārānā's grand nephew, the A. G G rejected this claim.

In the year 1855 A. D. he went on a pilgrimage to Hardwār, Muttra and Pushkar When the Indian Mutiny broke out in 1857 A. D. the Mahārājā unflinchingly rendered every sort of available military help to the Britishers and gave protection to some fugitives also.

From the year 1859 A. D. the name of Queen Victoria began to be struck on the coins of Jodhpur in place of the Mughal Emperor.

The right of adoption by the Mahārājās of Jodhpur was recognised by the Government of India in 1862 A. D. The same year the title of Rāo Rājā was conferred in general on all the male off-springs of Pardāyats (concubines of the rulers).

In 1865 the Mahārājā met the Governor General at Calcutta and the following year attended the Darbār held at Agra by Lord Lawrence, the then Governor General and was awarded the insignia of G. C. S. I.

In the same year the Mahārājā gave permission for giving land free for the building of the railway line passing through his territory and also abolished the transit duties on the goods carried on this railway.

In 1867 A. D. Queen Victoria conferred on him the hereditary honour of a salute of 17 guns.

The long standing dispute between the State and its Jāgīrdārs about their Jāgīrs was amicably settled in 1869 A. D. and the following year the Government of India took over the working of the Sāmbhar Salt area as well as the salt areas at Nāwā and Gudā.

In the same year as the Mahārājā did not approve of his seat arrangement made at the Darbār held at Ajmer by Lord Mayo, he left the place for Jodhpur without attending it. For this act his salute guns were reduced from seventeen to fifteen.

In 1872 A. D. the Mahārājā's second son Zōrāwarsingh took forced possession of the Nāgaur fort, but was soon compelled to vacate it.

In October of the same year, due to continued ill health, the Mahārājā entrusted the administration of the State to his heir-apparent Mahārāj-kumar Jaswantsingh and soon after left this world in 1873 A. D.

(34) Maharaja Jaswantsingh II.

He was succeeded by his eldest son Mahārājā Jaswantsingh II. During his reign the administration of the State was remodelled on modern lines and his younger brother Mahārāj Pratāpsingh took a leading part in it.

In 1874 A. D. Mahārājā Jaswantsingh went on a pilgrimage to Hardwār and Gayā and thence went further to Calcutta, where he met the Viceroy in 1875 A. D. The following year he was honoured at Calcutta with the insignia of G. C. S. I. by the then Prince of Wales

In the same year the school, which was opened at the capital for imparting English Education to the boys, was raised to the standard of a High School.

On the occasion of the Darbār held at Delhi in 1877 A. D., in honour of the assumption by Queen Victoria of the title of

Empress of India, his salute guns were raised from 17 to 19 and the following year this number was further raised to 21.

In 1879 A. D. the Government of India took on lease the salt areas at Dīdwānā, Pachpadra, Phalōdī and Bhawātarā.

In 1881 A. D. a census of the whole of Mārwār was taken for the first time, and about 17,50,000 souls were counted.

In those years the income of the State amounted to about Rs. 20,00,000, while the expenditure far exceeded it. The liability of the State neared about 40 to 50 lacs, but on the re-adjustment of the financial management in 1882 A. D. its former defects were removed and in a short time satisfactory results appeared.

The first State Railway line in Mārwār was opened between Pāli and Khārchī (Marwar Junction) in 1882 A. D., which was further extended up to Jōdhpur in 1885 A. D.

In 1884 A. D. the City Municipality was established at the capital to look after the civic affairs of the city, a State Council was also constituted to render advice on important matters and the land revenue settlement was taken in hand.

In 1885 A. D. the State Treasury came into being, arrangements for opening Post Offices were made, and an ice factory was started. Further the old agreement regarding the 21 villages of Mērwārā was renewed and a canal for supplying water from Bālsamand to the city tanks was constructed.

The following year the Jodhpur Press, which turned out mostly litho-work was reorganised.

The Mahārājā sent his younger brother Mahārāj Pratapsingh to attend the Golden Jubilee celebrations of Queen Victoria at London in 1887 A. D.

The following year the Historical Department was created to compile the history of the State.

In 1889 A. D. the cavalry unit known as Sardār Risālā was raised and in 1890 A. D. His Royal Highness Prince Albert Victor Edward of Wales visited Jodhpur.

The civil administration of the Mallānī District was handed back to the Jodhpur Darbar in 1891 A. D.

In 1893 A. D. an intermediate college named after the then Mahārājā, and known as the Jaswant College was opened at Jodhpur.

In 1895 this noble hearted, liberal minded, wise and generous Mahārājā breathed his last at the age of 58 years.

During his reign all sorts of facilities, such as judicial, medical, educational, and of communications were provided for the benefit of the public and the income of the State too, rose above 57 lacs.

The first hospital run on modern lines was also opened about 1886 A. D. at the capital during his reign.

(35) Maharaja Sardarsingh.

He was succeeded by his son and heir Mahārājā Sardarsingh, but as the latter was only 16 years of age at the time of his accession, his uncle Maharaj Pratāpsingh was appointed Regent during the period of his minority.

In 1896 A. D. the Jaswant Female Hospital and the Elgin Rajput School were opened and the local Jaswant College was raised to the status of a degree college.

Full ruling powers were invested to Mahārājā Sardārsingh in 1898 A. D. and the criminal justice of the Mallānī district (previously held back) was also vested in the State by the Political Agent.

The following year, owing to the failure of rains, Mārwār was ravaged by a severe famine. In order to relieve the sufferings caused by this calamity the State spent about 26½ lacs of rupees for the relief of the people and cattle.

Owing to the exchange difficulties felt by the State during these famine operations, the striking of silver coins in the State mint was discontinued and the Imperial coins in circulation in British India were introduced in their place.

In 1901 A. D. the Mahārājā paid a visit to Europe for reasons of health.

The following year Mahārāj Pratāpsingh was adopted to the Gaddi of Īdar in Gujrat. In the same year Mahārājā Sardarsingh joined the Imperial cadet corps at Meerut and afterwards from this place he went to Pachmaṛhi to recoup his health.

In 1906 A. D. the weight of the Jodhpur copper coin was reduced by nearly half. In the same year the Mahārājā retook the reigns of administration in his own hands while the State Council continued to function as before under the presidentship of the Resident. But in 1909 A. D. he (the Mahārājā) assumed full ruling powers again.

In the same year, at the time of the visit of Lord Kitchner to Jodhpur, a small industrial Museum was opened which is now known as 'Sardar Museum.'

In 1910 A. D. the insignia of G. C. S. I., was conferred on him by the Government and his personal salute was raised from 17 to 19 guns. But after about a year this noble and kind hearted Mahārājā died in 1911 A. D. at the age of 31 years only.

During his reign many reforms were carried out for the well being of his subjects.

(36) Maharaja Sumersingh

He was succeeded by his eldest son Mahārājā Sumērsingh, but as the latter was then only 13 years of age Mahārājā Pratāpsingh abdicated the throne of Idar in favour of his adopted son Mahārāj Daulatsingh and took over the charge of the Regency administration at Jodhpur once again.

In 1912 A. D. a chief court was inaugurated in Jodhpur. The following year the State donated 2 lacs of rupees for the Hardinge chair of Technology in the Benares Hindu University with Rs. 24,000/- as an annual recurring grant.

A new High School known as the 'Rajput High School' was opened at Chopāsnī in 1914 A. D. to impart education exclusively to the boys of the Rajpūts and some months later, when the World War broke out in Europe, Mahārājā Sumērsingh and the old veteran Mahārājā Regent Sir Pratāpsingh both proceeded to the front.

A Public Library called the Sumer Public Library came into being in 1915 A. D. and was housed in the building of the Museum.

Mahārājā Sumērsingh was invested with full ruling powers in 1916 A. D. and the following year the Electrical and Mechanical Department was established to electrify the city. In 1918 A. D., when the bubonic plague broke out in the city, the Mahārājā made excellent arrangements for the protection of the property of those subjects, who had left the city and were residing in the suburbs and for checking this scourge threw open all the State buildings around the capital to house the people of Jodhpur. Just after this calamity influenza broke out in the city in an epidemic form, when further relief measures were immediately undertaken on a large scale to cope with the situation.

Thereafter Māhārāja Sumērsingh met with a premature death in October 1918 A. D. at the age of 21 years only.

He was an intelligent ruler of self dependent nature. During his short reign, the State made an all round progress in all the branches of administration. The Jodhpur lancers fought against the Turks with extraordinary valour in the Jordan valley, Haifa in Palestine and Aleppo in Syria, etc.

Mahārājā Sumērsingh was also honoured by the Khedive of Egypt with the title of the Grand Cordon of the order of the Nile.

As he had no male issue, he was succeeded on October 14, 1918 A. D. by his younger brother Mahārājā Umaidsingh Bahadur. The latter was born on July 8, 1903 A. D. As he was only 16 years of age at the time of his succession to the throne a Regency Council was constituted to carry on the administration of the State and Mahārājā Pratāpsingh was appointed Regent for the third time.

(87) Maharaja Umaidsingh Bahadur.

In recognition of the meritorious services rendered by the Jodhpur State in the War his local salute guns were raised from 17 to 19 in 1921 A. D.

He attended the inauguration ceremony of the Chamber of Princes, and in the cold season of the same year His Royal Highness the Prince Edward of Wales graced Jodhpur by a royal visit.

Mahārājā Pratāpsingh, the old veteran Rāthōr, passed away in 1922 A. D. at the ripe age of 76.

On January 27, 1923 Mahārājā Umaidsingh Bahadur assumed full powers of administration of the State, but being a prince of constitutional and democratic nature, he rules the State through a Council of ministers.

The Mahārājā was blessed with an heir apparent named Mahārāj-Kumār Shri Hanwantsinghji on the 16th June 1923.

In order to facilitate speedy justice to the people District and Sessions Courts were established in 1924. The following year all the State employees were further allowed the benefit to contribute towards the State Provident Fund to be of help to them on their retirement from service.

In March 1925 he, accompanied by his family, took his polo team to England, where it scored many successes against world renowned teams.

In 1926 the Mahārājā accidentally encountered a rogue elephant in the jungles of the Nilgiri hills, where he showed rare presence of mind.

The same year, on his return from Ooty, he created the Archæological Department to preserve the ancient monuments in the State.

A year after, in order to facilitate the money transactions for the State as well as to give impetus to trade, a branch of the Imperial Bank of India was opened at Jodhpur. The same year the Mahārājā bestowed a Jāgīr of the 'Rēkh' of about 55 thousand on Mahārāj Shri Ajitsinghji his younge brother. He also sanctioned a grant of Rs. 3 lacs for the Hindu University for the Irwin Chair of Agriculture.

In 1928 the Mahārājā earmarked an amount of two lacs of rupees more to maintain 4 scholarships for higher studies in veterinary and agriculture science.

In 1929 A. D. he laid the foundation stone of the new Chhitar (Hill) Palace as well as of the Windham Hospital, the last named institution being one of the best equipped in the whole of India.

In 1931 A. D. the census of Mārwār was taken and the population of Mārwār totalled 21,25 982 souls. A Flying Club was also started at Jodhpur the same year.

In May 1933 the designation of the Jodhpur State was changed to that of the Jodhpur Government, and the members of the Council came to be designated as Ministers.

The Mahārājā paid a visit to East Africa for big game hunting and the following year he again went to complete his programme of wild sports there.

In 1935 the Silver Jubilee of His Gracious Majesty King George V was celebrated in Jodhpur, and a large sum of money was contributed to the His Majesty's Silver Jubilee Fund. Similarly a handsome amount was also subscribed towards the Quetta Earth-quake Relief Fund opened at Delhi.

In 1936 A. D. Lord Willingdon, the then Viceroy, performed the opening ceremony of the Willingdon Gardens as well as the new building of the Sardar Museum and Sumer Public Library situated there in the centre.

The same year on June 23, the Mahārājā was honoured with the title of G. C. S. I. by the British Government.

In 1937 he proceeded to England to take part in the coronation ceremony of King George VI.

In 1938 the Government of India retroceded to the Jodhpur State the 21 villages (along with 3 new ones) of the Merwāṛā district, the administration of which was taken under its direct control in 1824 A. D. and also freed the State from the obligation of the payment of a sum of Rs. 1,15,000, which was annually paid to the Government of India for maintaining the Erinpura corps. The same year, in order to remove the scarcity of water in the capital, the Mahārājā got constructed a canal with pumping stations at necessary intervals, now known as Sardār Samand Water Supply channel, and built a huge reservoir for the water storage, at a total cost of Rs. 25,50,000. In order to remove the impurities of the water supplied to the city, an up-to-date filter plant was also fitted at a little distance below the reservoir.

In the same year the Umaid Female Hospital was opened at a cost of Rs. 11,19,000 and in 1939 the Mahārājā was generous enough to donate a fabulous sum of Rs. 70,00,000 in order to combat the scourge of famine in Marwar.

In August 1941 A. D. His Highness, with his younger brother Mahārāj Shri Ajitsinghji, paid a visit to the Near East War Front to inspect the Jodhpur troops.

In the same year a Representative Advisory Assembly was constituted in place of the Central Advisory Board previously established in 1939 A. D.

Up to the end of 1942 A. D. Jodhpur Darbar contributed sum of about 30 lacs of rupees towards the World War as well as twelve fighters and one heavy bomber.

His Highness has also placed four of his personal aeroplanes and one glider at the disposal of the Government of India.

Further, he was one of the foremost princes to place at the disposal of the Government of India all the resources of the State as well as his personal services in the present World War to crush the Axis Powers.

The latest census of the State showed a figure of 25,55,904 souls.

In his benevolent reign Marwar has taken giant strides in improvements in all directions and the annual gross income of the State has reached near two and a quarter crores of rupees.

Air Commodore, His Highness Rāj-Rājēshvar Saramad Rājahāi Hind Mahārājādhirāj Mahārājā Shrī Sir Umaid Singh Bahadur G. C. S. I., G. C. I. E., K. C. V. O., A. D. C., LL.D., is beloved by his subjects and is a kind hearted ruler with democratic outlook. He is an air minded prince, a spirited Polo player and a keen sportsman of wide fame.

He has five Mahārāj-kumārs namely Mahārāj-kumār Shrī Hanwantsinghji, Himmatsinghji, Harisinghji, Devisinghji, and Dilipsinghji.

The Mahārānī of Jodhpur, who was married in 1921 A. D., is a dutiful and very devoted Rānī of the Mahārājā and is ever alert to help the needy and the poor.

May the Almighty bestow His choicest blessings on the Mahārājā, may he and his family have health, long life and prosperity and may his people enjoy his benevolent reign for long.

APPENDIX A.

1. Rājpūts

[Read at XIX Congresso Internazionale Degli Orientalisti, held at (Regia Università) Roma in September 1935 A D and published in its proceedings and transactions, (pp. 409—422 as well as in 'Indian Culture,' Calcutta, Vol. III, No 2 (Oct 1936 A D) pp 289—302]

We know from the Hindu 'Shāstras' that in the beginning, the Āryans had no caste system among them, but it was introduced later to facilitate the social and the industrial developments of the society. By its introduction particular kind of work was entrusted to the particular group of people, specially suited for the purpose, and this was the basis of the caste system in India.[1]

Like other 'Shāstras', the 'Bhāgavata'[2] and 'Mahābhārata'[3] also support this theory.

It is likely that the people of the old school may see in this statement a suggestion of the modern ideas but this is not so.

In support of this, we quote here from a book named 'Samarāngana Sūtradhāra'[4] compiled by Rājā Bhōja, the famous Paramāra ruler of Malwa. He ruled from about 1010 to 1053 A. D. (1066 to 1110 V. S.) and besides being a patron

---

1 ब्राह्मणोऽस्य मुखमासीद्बाहू राजन्यः कृतः ऊरू तदस्य यद्वैश्यः पद्भ्यां शूद्रो अजायत ।

Rigvēda—Purushasūkta.

2 एक एव पुरा वेदः प्रणवः सर्ववाङ्मयः ।
देवो नारायणो नान्य एकोऽग्निर्वर्ण एव च ॥

3 एकवर्णमिदं पूर्वं विश्वमासीद् युधिष्ठिर ।
कर्मक्रियाविभेदेन चातुर्वर्ण्यं प्रतिष्ठितम् ॥

4 Adhyāya 7, Shlōka 1-17.

of learning is considered to have been himself a scholar of repute:—

'Brahmā, for maintaining peace and order on the earth made Prithu the first ruler of the people and he too for the sake of administrative convenience and efficiency divided them in four "Varnas" or castes.'

'People who were God-fearing, pious, scholarly and able were designated as "Brāhmanas"; those who were courageous, energetic, strong and able to protect others were named as "Kshatriyas"; persons who were wise, desirous of wealth, reliable, smart and kindhearted were styled as "Vaishyas" and men lacking in a sense of respect, religion, truth and purity were called "Shūdras".'

The purpose of quoting these lines here is simply to show that these divisions of Varṇas or castes, in the beginning, were based on the quality, work and the nature of the individuals[1] and they had no connection with birth.

In our opinion this system might have served at that time, to avert the clash of interests and the hard competition which threaten our society this day.

Further for the sake of individual development, the period of our life was also divided into four parts called four 'Āshramas'.

Leaving this question of 'Varṇas' and 'Āshramas' in general, we take up now the question relating to 'Kshatriyas' in particular.

According to the 'Vedic' and 'Paurāṇic' literature, the Kshatriyas were divided into two dynasties, one of which was named Solar or 'Sūryavamsha' and the other Lunar or 'Chandravamsha'. On the basis of the close study of the Āryan languages of India, scholars are of opinion that the two different stocks of the Āryans migrated to India in two different periods and to differentiate them from each other, they were called the Solar and the Lunar stocks.[2] But later a third division known as Fire dynasty or 'Agnivamsha' also sprang forth among them.

---

1 चातुर्वर्ण्यं मया सृष्टं गुणकर्मविभागशः ।

Bhagavadgītā, Adhyāya 4, Shlōka 13.

2 The Inscription dated V. S. 1166 (1109 A. D.) of Gōvindachandra contains —

प्रध्वस्ते सूर्यसोमोद्भवविदितमहाक्षत्रवंशद्वयेऽस्मिन् ।

....

....

The first mention of this dynasty or division is found in 'Navasāhasānka Charita' of Padmagupta composed in the later half of the 11th century A.D. It states that Vashishṭha, a sage, to get back his cow from Vishvāmitra, his rival, created a warrior from his fire altar at mount Abu, and as this warrior killed his enemies and brought back his cow, the sage named him as Paramāra or the destroyer of the enemy.

On the basis of the above story, we presume that, to get rid of his enemies, a descendant of Vashishtha, purified (by a sort of penance) a clan of Kshatriyas whose forefathers had embraced Buddhism. But Halāyudha, a contemporary of Padmagupta, in his 'Pingala Sūtravritti' mentions Rājā Munja of the Paramāra dynasty as belonging to the 'Brahma-Kshatra-Kula'[1] or a combined Brāhmana and Kshatriya dynasty.

The book named 'Prithvīrāja Rāsō' also contains a reference to this Fire dynasty. The author of 'Rāsō' taking Paramāra, Chālukya (Sōlankī), Padihāra (Pratihāra) and Chauhāna as having originated from the fire altar of Vashishtha calls their descendants as Agnivamshīs. This is the main reason for which the Indian [2] and foreign scholars consider these four clans as non-Kshatriyas and descendants of a foreign and non-Aryan dynasty called Khazar or Gurjara. They also presume that these non-Kshatriya dynasties after undergoing a sort of penance were reckoned as Kshatriyas by the Brāhmanas.

But firstly the accounts of Prithvīrāja, his relatives and his contemporaries as given in the 'Rāsō' do not correspond to historical facts. Secondly according to the 'Rāsō' Mahārāval Samarasimha of Mewar was killed in 1192 A.D. (1249 V.S.) while fighting on the side of Prithvīrāja. In fact Samarasimha ascended the throne of Mewar after 1267 A.D. (1324 V.S.) and breathed his last in 1302 (1359 V.S.).

This shows that even at that time there were only the following two famous divisions among Kshatriyas —

(1) Solar and (2) Lunar

1 Owing to the use of this word some scholars presume that originally they were Brāhmanas of Vashishṭha's stock or Gōtra and afterwards were converted as Kshatriyas At present the Paramāras call themselves as descendants of Vikramāditya, the famous (but fictitious) ruler of Malwa.

2 Indian Antiquary, Vol XL. pp 7—36.

Thirdly the 'Rāsō'[1] mentions in the form of a prophecy, the victory of the king of Mewar over Delhi after 1620 A. D. (1677 V. S.). Under such circumstances, the accounts of 'Rāsō' cannot be accepted as authentic.

As a matter of fact these divisions of Kshatriyas are merely the imaginative creations of the poets intended to show the superiority and antiquity of the dynasty. For had it not been so in each and every record (inscriptions and copper grants) of the well-known Kshatriya rulers these divisions would have been surely mentioned. But it is not so. Moreover wherever the mention of these divisions is found they are confusing in the extreme. If at one place a certain clan of Kshatriyas is mentioned as 'Sūryavamshīs' at another the same branch is said to have belonged to the Chandra or the Agni Vamshīs.

We have already given, some such proofs about the Paramāra clan, here some similar proofs fòr the other clans will be given presently.

In the inscription, of V. S. 1133 (1076 A. D.) of Vikramāditya VI, the Chālukyas (Sōlankīs) are recorded as Chandravamshīs. But in 'Bilhana's Vikramānkadēvacharita' and in the inscription of Haihaya (Kalachuri) Yuvarājadēva II, found from Bilhari, they are said to have sprung from the handful of water of Brahma and Drōna respectively.

In the inscription of Pratihāra king Bhōja,[2] found at Gwalior, the Prātihara (Padihāras) are referred to as Sūrya Vamshīs, while in the inscription[3] of Pratihāra Bāuka, dated V. S. 894 (837 A. D.), they are mentioned as descendants of Brāhmana Harishchandra and his Kshatriyā wife Bhadrā.

In the inscription of Chauhāna Lumbhā (dated V. S. 1377=1320 A. D.), found at mount Abu, Chauhānas are said to have belonged to the Chandra-Vamsha. But in the inscription of Vīsaldeva IV they are mentioned as 'Sūrya-Vamshīs'.

---

1 सोरेसे सत्योत्तरे विक्रम साक वदीत ।
दिल्लीधर मेवातपति लैहि खग्गबल जीत ॥

Samaya II, Chhanda 44, p. 265.

2 He ruled from about 843 to 893 A. D. (900 to 950 V. S)

3 In the beginning of the same inscription a hint has also been made that the Pratihāras were descended from Lakshmana, who was a door-keeper to his elder brother Rāmachandra.

Taking into consideration all these facts, it is not advisable for scholars whether local or foreign to rely upon 'Prithvīrāja Rāsō' and to presume that these four dynasties are being the descendants of the foreign and non-Āryan Gurjara (Khazar) stock.

Now we quote, in brief the points on the basis of which the Rājpūts are considered as non-Āryans:—

(1) That in the 'Harivamsha'[1] and in the 'Vishnu Purāna'[2]; the Haihayas (Kalachuris) are classed with Shakas, Yavanas, Pāradas and Kāmbōjas; hence it is probable that the former also belonged to the foreign non-Āryan stock [3]

(2) That Bāna in his 'Harshacharita' mentions simultaneously the victories of Prabhākaravardhana of Thānēshvara over Gurjaras and Huns, hence, it seems that the Gurjaras were also foreigners and came to India along with Huns.

(3) That in the inscription of Pratihāra Mathanadēva, dated V.S. 1016 (960 A.D.) found at Rājōr (Alwar State) Mathanadēva is stated to have belonged to the Gurjara-Pratihāra clan. Further in the records of the Rāshtrakūta princes of the south, the Pratihāras of Kannauj are designated as Gurjarēshvaras while in the writings of the Arabs they are called as Juzrs. All these facts go to show that the Pratihāras were the offshoots of the Gurjaras.

(4) That the Gurjaras themselves belonged to a foreign stock known as Khazars, who in the sixth century A.D. inhabited the borderland of Europe and Asia. Some scholars are of opinion that they came to India in the time of Kanishka, while other think that they migrated to India along with the Huns. The province conquered by these Gurjaras came to be known as Gurjar or Gujrat.[4]

(5) That some of the Sassanian typed coins, found in the North-Western India, contain the legends in both the Nāgarī and Pahlvī characters. In the Nāgarī is written:—'Shri

1 (Bengal) Vs 764—776

2 Amsha IV, Chapt 3, V 16ff.

3 Indian Antiquary, Vol XL, p. 19.

4 Mr C V Vaidya presumes that as due to the connection of 'Mahārāshtrī' language one province of India was called Mahārāshtra in the like manner due to the connection of Gujrātī language another province of it came to be known as Gujrat The language known as Mahārāshtrī was used in India even at the time of Vararuchi, who flourished in the fourth century B.C.

Vahmana Vāsudēva' while in the Pahlvī—'Tukān Zāulastān Sapardlakshān.'[1] Some scholars taking the word Vahmana for Chāhamān consider this Vāsudēva of the coin as the first known ruler of the Chāhamāna dynasty. Further they take 'Sapād Lakshān' inscribed on the coins to mean the Himalayan hilly tract known as Siwālaks and also think that the Chāhamānas were Khazars or the Gurjaras who migrated to India along with the Huns and settled in the aforesaid hilly tract. As these coins of Vāsudēva resemble those of Khusru II (Parviz), struck in the 37th year of his reign, it is assumed that the time of the former comes to about 627 A.D. (684 V.S.).

Let us examine these arguments in the light of the facts available from other sources:—

(1) That in the old records of Haihayas (Kalachuris) they are mentioned as Chandravamshīs or belonging to the Lunar dynasty and in the 'Purānas' they are stated to be pure Kshartriyas, hence they being only mentioned in 'Harivamsha Purāṇa' along with Yavanas, Pāradas and Kāmbōjas cannot be taken to be foreigners.

Moreover, Manu,[2] the famous law-giver of India has counted even these Yavanas, Pāradas and Kāmbōjas among the Kshatriyas:—

शनकैस्तु क्रियाल्लोपादिमाः क्षत्रियजातय. ।
वृषलत्वं गता लोके ब्राह्मणाऽदर्शनेन च ॥ ४३ ॥
पौण्ड्रकाश्चौड्रद्रविडाः काम्बोजा यवनाः शकाः ।
पारदाः पह्लवाश्चीनाः किराता दरदाः खशाः ॥ ४४ ॥

That the Kshatriya clans known as Paundrakas, Chauḍras, Dravidas, Kāmbōjas, Shakas, Pāradas, Pahlvas, Chīnas, Kirātas, Darадas, and Khashas due to their gradual ignorance of the religious rites and their disassociation with the Brāhmanas came to be known as 'Vrishalas' (Shūdras).

(2) That in fact Bāna by putting 'Gurjara-prajāgarah' along with 'Hūna-harina-Kēsarī' and 'Sindhurāja- Jvarō'[3] mentions only the inhabitants of the Gurjara country, hence it is not advisable to drag there the Gurjaras or the Khazars of the foreign origin. Further the migration of the Khazars in India has not yet been proved by the historians.

---

1 In an another type of this king's coins the Pahlvī legend runs as below — Saf varsu Taf (Shri Vāsudēva) Vahmana X Multan Malka.

2. Manusmriti, Adhāya 10

3 Harshacharita, Uchchhvāsa 2, p. 243.

(3) That the adjective (Gurjara) used in the Rājōr inscription is not meant to denote the Pratihāras as belonging to the Gurjara clan but simply as the inhabitants or the rulers of the province. At that time a large part of Rajputana was called Gurjaratrā [1] or Gujrat and its capital was Bhinmal.[2] It is also probable that the mention of the residential province, in the records of the Pratihāras of Bhinmal, was meant to distinguish them from the Pratihāras who went to Kannauj.

The Pratihāras after defeating the Chāvadās [3] established their kingdom at Bhinmal. They then extended their sway up to Bharoch as is evident from the copper grant, dated V.S. 813 (756 A.D.) of Bhartrivaddha, a feudatory of Nāgabhata I (Nāgāvalōka). Further at the close of the 8th century A.D. they conquered Kannauj and made it their new capital. Under these circumstances, we see no reason to wonder if, in the records of Rāshtrakūtas and those of the Arab travellers, they are designated as Gurjarēshvaras or Juzr respectively.

(4) That firstly the migration of the Khazars to India is not proved by the known history; secondly in the copper grant[4] of Gurjara king Jayabhata III of Bharoch, dated Kalachuri Samvat 456 (762 V.S.=705 A.D.) the Gujaras are said to have been descended from Mahārāja Karna; and thirdly Hiuen-Tsang, the well-known Chinese pilgrim, who came to India in the first half of the seventh century A.D. had stated that the rulers of Bhinmal, the capital of Gurjara country, and that of Valabhī, were Kshatriyas.

The Badagūjaras are also Kshatriyas as they make their matrimonial alliances only with other pure Kshatriyas.[5]

---

1 Copper grant of Pratihāra Bhōjadēva, dated V S 900 (Epigraphia Indica, Vol V, p 211).

2 Hiuen Tsang's travels

3 Some people are of opinion that the Chāvaḍās too were Gurjaras But the copper grant dated Kalachuri Samvat 490 (796 V S.=739 A D) of Chālukya (Sōlankī) Pulakēshirāja of Lāṭa states —

"सौराष्ट्र-चावोटक-मौर्य-गुर्जरादिराज्ये"

This shows that at that time the Gurjaras and Chāvaḍās (Chāpōtkaṭas) were considered as belonging to the two different clans

Bombay Gazetteer, Vol. I, part I, p 109

4 Indian Antiquary, Vol XIII, p 77.

5 Though in the olden times 'Anulōma vivāhas' (Marriage of higher 'Varna' males with the lower Varna females) were prevalent among Brāhmaṇas, Kshatriyas and Vaishyas, yet later this was disallowed To support this we quote here from the writings of Megasthenese who visited India in the 3rd century B.C.

'No one is allowed to marry out of his own caste or to exchange one profession or trade for no ther.'

Ancient India (Megasthenese & Arrian), Mc. Crindle, pp.85-86.

(5) That the opinions of the scholars differ much on this point. General Cunningham takes this 'Vāsudēva' of the aforesaid coins to be a Huna. While Mr. Rapson considers him a Sassanian. Similarly some historians presume that the 'second word of the Nāgarī legend of the coins is 'Chāhamāna' while others read it as 'Vahmana'.

Moreover the time of Chāhamāna Vāsudēva as given by Rājashēkhara Sūri in the genealogy, attached to his 'Prabandhakōsha'[1] is V.S. 608 (551 A.D.), but the period fixed for the aforesaid coins by scholars is V.S. 684 (627 A. D.)

We learn from the history that Gūvaka I was the seventh descendant of Vāsudēva. The inscription, dated V.S. 1013, found at Harshanāth, states that Gūvaka due to his chivalrous nature acquired the title of a 'Knight' at the court of Nāgāva lōka. In the inscription of Chauhāna Bhartrivriddha, dated V.S. 813 (756 A.D.), he (Bhartrivriddha) is said to have been a feudatory of Nāgāvalōka. This shows that Bhartrivriddha and Nāgāvalōka were contemporaries and lived about V.S. 813. Now if we deduct 25 years for each ruling prince (i.e. 200 years for 8 kings). the time of the beginning of the reign of Vāsudeva comes near to the period fixed in 'Prabandhakōsha.'

Further the kingdom of the Chauhānas was first established not in Sind or Multan but at Ahichchhatrapura, wherefrom they proceeded to Shākambhari (Sāmbhar). General Cunningham, on the basis of the description of Ahichchhatrapura found in the travels of the aforesaid Chinese pilgrim, locates this town near Ramnagar about 20 miles west of Bareilly.[2] According to 'Mahābhārata' this Ahichchhatrapura was the capital of north Pānchāla country.

Moreover the scholars, instead of accepting the word 'Sapādalakshān' on the coins is to mean a Himālayan tract

---

Hiuen Tsang, the Chinese pilgrim who came to India in the first half of the 7th century A.D. writes —

'The members of a caste marry within the caste, the great and the obscure keeping apart . . .'

Yuan Chwang (by Thomas Watters), Vol. I, p. 168

Further the children born of the occasional 'Anulōma vivābas' were considered as belonging to the mother's 'Varna' (caste). For instance— the children of Rāthōd Mūban who were born of his Kshatriya wife were called as Mūhanōt Kshatriyas, while those born of the Vaishya wife were considered as Mūhanōt Vaishyas

1. This Kōsha (Dictionary) was compiled in 1405 V.S. (1349 A.D).

2 In the eastern part of Rohilkhand.

Yuan Chawang (by Thomas Watters), Vol 1, p. 332 and Ancient Geography of India, p. 369

containing 125 thousand peaks or ranges, think that it has here been used for a tract containing 125 thousand villages.[1] The country ruled by Chauhānas, which included the provinces of Sāmbhar, Nāgaur and Ajmēr, etc. is called 'Savālakh' even to this day. Therefore no one can believe that the Chauhānas belonged to the Gurjara race or they migrated towards Rajputana from the Himālaya.

The same is the position of the Rāshtrakūtas, Guhils, etc. belonging to the other Kshatriya clans.

Mr. V. A Smith, on his theory of the sudden appearance of the Rājpūts in the 8th or the 9th century A.D. has advanced the theory that they are foreigners and belong to the non-Āryan races.[2] But how far he is justified can be ascertained from the following facts:—

(*a*) That in the 5th century A.D one of the Rājpūt clans known as Rāshtrakūtas were ruling in the Deccan, and at the end of the same century they were overthrown by another Rājpūt clan called Sōlankīs (Chālukyas).

(*b*) That the copper grant of Sōlankī Trilōchanapāla, dated Shaka Samvat 972 (1107 V.S.=1051 A.D.) states that before their migration to the Deccan, the Rāshtrakūtas had their sway over Kannauj[3] and the words Rathika, Ristika, etc. found in the edicts of Ashōka prove that the Rāshtrakūtas existed even about 250 B.C.

(*c*) That Guhila (Guhadatta) the founder of the Guhil clan of Mewar was ruling in the later half of the sixth century A.D. ; and Bāpā Rāval, one of his descendants was the master of Mewar in the first half of the eighth century. A.D.

---

1 'Skandapurāna' (which is supposed to be composed in the 9th century A.D.) states that there were 1 25,000 villages under Sāmbhar, Mēwār, Karnāṭak, etc.

2. Mr V. A Smith considers that the Chandēls, the Rāthōrs and the Gābarwāls are the descendants of aboriginal tribes like Gōnds, Bhars and Kharwars But in fact it is not so For Rāṭhōrs and Gābarwāls, please see our 'History of Rāshṭrakūtas' and 'Bhārata-kē-Prāchīna Rājavamsha,' Vol III

The Inscriptions of Chandels state them as 'Chandra-vamshis

3 कान्यकुब्जे महाराज ! राष्ट्रकूटस्य कन्यकाम् ।

लब्ध्वा सुखाय तस्या त्व चौलुक्याप्नुहि सततिम् ॥ ६ ॥

Indian Antiquary, Vol. XII, p. 201

Further is it not strange that simply because the present Kshatriya rulers call themselves Rājpūts,[1] Mr. V. A. Smith and others hold them as the offshoots of non-Āryans? But Rājpūt is a corrupt form of 'Rājaputra'. And as the descendants of the younger sons of the present Rājpūt rulers, after a certain number of generations are called 'Thākurs' and as the younger sons of the chiefs of Oudh or their descendants use along with their names the title of 'Kunvar', in the like manner it is probable that the younger branches of these Kshatriya rulers, to distinguish themselves from the ordinary Kshatriyas, might have adopted this title of 'Rajaputra'. Further in course of time partly due to the increase in the number of such 'Rājaputras' by the rise and fall of the several ruling families and partly due to the changes in their domestic conditions, this group of Kshatriyas might have come to be known as Rājpūts, while the ordinary Kshatriyas by adopting different occupations submerged into the different clans.[2]

Col. Tod in his History of Rājasthān[3] states that in the Mughal army there were one hundred thousands Rāthōr warriors and we presume that a large number of them was of the descendants of Rāō Sīhā, the founder of the Marwar ruling family This also supports our theory of the increase in the number of 'Rājaputras'.

Pānini, the famous grammarian, who flourished in the sixth century B.C. has given a rule in his Sanskrit grammer named 'Ashtādhyāyī':[4]

"गोत्रोक्षोष्ट्रोरभ्रराजराजन्यराजपुत्रवत्समनुष्याजाद् वुञ्।"

In it he has advised the use of an affix called 'वुञ्' where the multitude of such 'Rājaputras' is meant.

1. The author of the 'Shabdakalpadruma' has quoted the following half couplet from the 'Pārāshara Smriti' —

"वैश्यादम्बष्ठकन्यायां राजपुत्रः प्रजायते।"

But it is not traceable in the printed copy of the said 'Smriti' Hence it is possible that some one acquainted with modern Rāvanā Rājpūts might have inserted this in the book

2. The subclans found in the different sub-castes of the people of Rajputana also support it

3. Annals and Antiquities of Rajasthan (edited by Crooke), p 105-106.

4. Adhyāya 4, Pāda 2, Sūtra 39.

Ashvaghōsha, the famous poet of the second century of Vikrama era has used this word (Rājaputra) in his poems called 'Saundarānanda Mahākāvya'[1]:—

"केचिदिक्ष्वाकवो जग्मू राजपुत्राः विवत्सवः ।"

The poet Kālidāsa had made use of this word in his drama called 'Mālavikāgnimitra'.[2]

"मया राजपुत्रशतपरिवृतं वसुमित्रं गोप्तारमादिश्य.. ।"

Bāna Bhatta, who wrote his 'Harshacharita'[3] about 620 A.D. (677 V.S.) has also used the word Rājaputra.

In 'Mahābhārata',[4] the famous Hindu epic, we find repeated use of this word for Kshatriyas.—

एते रुक्मरथा नाम राजपुत्राः महारथाः ।
रथेष्वस्त्रेषु निपुणा नागेषु च विशांपते ! ॥ २० ॥
भैक्षचर्या ततः प्राहुस्तस्य सद्धर्मचारिणः ।
तथा वैश्यस्य राजेन्द्र ! राजपुत्रस्य चैव हि ॥ १४ ॥

Ibna Khurdādbā, who in 912 A.D (H.S. 300=V.S. 969) wrote his book named 'Kitābul Masālik-Ul-Mamālik',[5] states:—

There are in all seven clans in India:—1. Sabfria, 2. Brahma, 3. Kataria, 4. Sudaria, 5. Baisura, 6. Sandalia, and 7. Lahuda.

(1) Sabfria.—This is the highest clan from which the rulers are selected.

(2) Kataria.—People of this clan can drink only three cups of wine. Their daughters can be married to Brāhmanas. But the Brāhmanas cannot marry their daughters to these Katarias.

These descriptions show that even at that time there were two divisions among the Kshatriyas. One was called Sabfria—'Sukshatriya' or Rājaputra, because the rulers were selected from this division and the other was Kataria—ordinary 'Kshatriya'. The matrimonial alliances of the Brāhmanas with the daughters of these Katarias undoubtedly prove that these Katarias too were of pure Kshatriya blood.

It is also probable that in the times of the Mohemmadan rulers these Rājaputras, having been considered as holding a higher status than those ordinary pure Kshatriyas, might have been called Rājpūts.

1. Sarga 1, Shlōka 18
2. Anka 5, p. 103
3 (पुष्पभूतिस्तु) अपरेद्युः उत्थाय कतिपयैरेव राजपुत्रैः परिवृतो भैरवाचार्यं द्रष्टुं प्रतस्थे ।" (Uchchhvāsa III, p. 241.)
4. Drōna Parva, Adhyāya 112, Shānti Parva, Adhyāya 64.
5. Elliot's History of India, Vol. I, pp. 16-17.

At the time of the census of 1901 A. D., Mr. H. Risley the famous ethnologist after examining the straight and thin noses, the long skulls, and the tall bodies of the Rājpūts, had certified that they undoubtedly belonged to the Āryan race.

Now we will consider this problem from another view point:—

According to the aforesaid scholars even if we take it for granted that the Rājpūts were the descendants of Shakas, Kushans and Huns who coming from the north, invaded India, the theory of their Āryan descent is not weakened in any way. On the strength of the data found in 'Rāmāyana', 'Mahābhārata', 'Smritis', 'Purānas' and records, as collected by the modern research scholars, it is clear that there was a time when the descendants of the Āryans of India in their northern conquest acquired the land of Shakas, the Northern Tibet and the lands of Kushans and Huns in the Central Asia.

In this manner several Āryan rulers belonging to the solar and the lunar dynasties had founded fresh colonies or kingdoms outside India. The mention of the kingdoms of the sons of Bharata at Gāndhāra and that of Prachētā to the north of India as well as the conquest of Pātāla (America) by Arjuna are sufficient proofs to support this.

In the old records also we find a mention of the victory of our rulers over 'Trivishtapa' which according to the modern historians was the name of Tibet.

In the records, written in the 'Kharōshthī' alphabets and unearthed by Dr. Stien in Chinese Turkishtān, the use of Prākrit language and the appearance of the Āryan titles like Mahānubhāva, Mahārāja, Bhattāraka, Vamshamani show that the place was once colonized by the Āryans.[1]

We give below some specimens of the language used and the titles found in the said records:—

प्रियदेवमनुशस्स प्रियदर्शनस्स प्रियभ्रतु ।
महनुभव महरय जिटुघवंशमणा देवपुत्रस मसे ।

In the like manner the images of the Hindu gods and the Sanskrit inscriptions found in the islands of Java, Sumatra, Borneo, etc. prove that at a time they were also under the influence of the Āryans. The traces of 'Maya' culture

1 On the basis of these facts the modern scholars call this land by name of Serindia

discovered at America may also be regarded as the remains of the past Āryan influence.

The Chinese called the tract lying between India and China by the name of 'Shen-tu'[1] (i. e. a part of Sindhu),[2] because it was once under the sway of the Āryans of India.

Under these circumstances, there should be no hesitation in accepting the Shakas, the Kushans, and the Huns, as the descendants of the Āryans, who migrated to their respective countries. Though as stated above, Manu has called the Paundrakas, Chaudras, Dravidas, Kāmbōjas, Yavanas Shakas, Pāradas, Pahlavas, Chīnas, Kirātas, Daradas and Khashas as 'Vrishalas' or irreligious, simply because they migrated to the countries outside India where no Brāhmanas were available to perform the religious ceremonies, yet he himself has accepted their Kshatriya origin. Further we cannot give much weight to the word 'Vrishala' used by Manu as we see that the Brāhmanas, due to the jealousy, had declared even the Indian provinces of Magadha and Kalinga as well as the people living there as unholy, simply because the majority of the inhabitants there followed Bhuddhism or Jainism. For all these reasons, it is not advisable to consider the Rājpūts as descendants of Shakas, Kushans or Huns inspite of the proofs adduced to the contrary which go to show that even the Shakas, Kushans and Huns were the descendants of the Āryans, who migrated to the north of India.

We give below some more facts in support of this theory:—

Coins struck by the Shaka kings contain the marks of Sun, Moon and Ganges The language used in their coins and inscriptions is Prākrit.[3] Their names mostly resemble the Indian names, as can be judged from the following:—Rudrasimha, Svāmī Satyasimha, Svāmī Rudrasēna, etc.

---

1. In the time of 'Han Wu Ti' (apparently about 123 B. C.) 'shen-tu' was not far from the western border of the Chinese empire

Yuan Chwang (by Thomas Watters) Vol I, pp. 133-134.

This name (Shen-tu) was given to this country about 4 or 5 hundred years after Ashōka. The Romans called this further India as trans Gangetic India

2. We learn from the travels of Yuan Chwang that about 630 A D a Kshatriya king ruled at Kapis (Kāfiristān).

Yuan Chwang (by Thomas Watters), Vol. I, pp. 122—123.

3. अप्रतिहतचक्रस रजबुलस ।

On the Kushan coins the images of 'Shiva' and his bull or of the King offering sacrifice to the Fire Altar are found. The language written on them resembles Prākrita.[1] Their titles are also similar to those of the Indian kings as quoted below:—

Mahārāja, Rājātirāja (or Rājādhirāja) Īshvara, Mahēshvara and Dēvaputra. The name of one of the Kushan kings was 'Vāsudēva' which is purely an Indian or Āryan name.

Coins of Huns have the marks of trident and bull. The language inscribed on them is Sanskrit,[2] and the titles borne by those kings are similar to those of the epithets of the Indian kings given below:—

Vrishadhvaja and Mahārāja.

The name of one Hun king was Mihirkula, who was a staunch Shaivite.

Mention of the Huns among the 36 clans of the Kshatriyas is found in the 'Kumārapālacharita' which was composed in the 15th century of the Vikrama era and the author of 'Rājataranginī' also enumerates the Kshatriya clans as 36.

Col. Tod comparing the similarity of some of the customs among the Rājpūts and the Scythians opines that both of them belonged to the same non-Āryan race of Scythians or Shakas. But this supposition is quite unwarranted for we have already cited some facts to show that even the Shakas themselves were Āryans. And therefore it is not strange if some of the customs of the Rājpūts and the Scythians are similar.

Before concluding this paper we wish to crave the attention of those scholars to this subject who consider the present Rājpūt rulers as non-Āryans and express the hope that if they think their opinion to be well-founded they will be pleased to let us know how and when those old Kshatriya clans, who ruled in India for a considerable period, disappeared from the surface of the earth ?

(1) If they think that due to the acceptance of Buddhism or Jainism those Kshatriyas lost their caste distinction we are not prepared to believe this because the Lichchhavīs

---

1. महरजस रजदिरजस सर्वलोगईश्वरस महिश्वरस हिमकपिशस ।

२. विजितावनि रवनिपति श्रीतोरमाणदेव जयति ।

of Vaishālī and the Rāshtrakūta king Amōghavarsha I of the Deccan who followed Buddhism and Jainism respectively, retained their 'Varna' or caste distinction unmolested.

(2) If they are of opinion that foreign invaders totally destroyed the Kshatriyas, this is also far away from the truth, because after the death of the Hun king Mihirkula in 542 A.D. (V. S. 599) India was free from any effective foreign invasion for about 475 years[1] (or up to the conquest of the Punjab by Mehmud of Ghazni), while the records[2] of the Lichchhavī Kshatriyas prove that they were ruling in India up to 754 A. D. (811 V. S.).

There are some people who quote the following sentence from the 'Pārāshara Smriti':—'कलावाद्यन्तयोः स्थितिः' and try to prove that according to this in 'Kaliyuga' or in the fourth and the last circle of the Hindus, there remain only two 'Varnas', the Brāhmanas and the Shūdras. But taking all the facts given above into consideration this theory too becomes unacceptable.

---

1 Though the Arab invaders took Sind in the eighth century A D, yet all the other provinces of India were free from their influence.

2 Indian Antiquary, Vol IX, pp 163 and 167.

2. The Early Rāshtrakūtas of the Deccan and the present Mysore State

[Read at the eighth All India Oriental Conference, held at Mysore in December 1935 A D, and published in Journal of Indian History, Vol XVI, Pt 3, (December 1937. A D) pp 253-258]

Before the re-establishment of the Rāshtrakūta kingdom in the Deccan, the north-eastern part of the present Mysore State was under the Pallavas of Kānchī, and, as a branch of these Pallavas was called 'Nōlamba,' the modern Chitaldroog district of the Mysore State came to be known as Nōlambavādī.

The north-western part or the present Shimoga district of the state was ruled by the Kadambas, whose capital was Bānavāsī.

The rest of the territory of the present Mysore State was governed by the Gangas, and was known as Gangavādī. The surname previously used by the rulers of this dynasty was "Kōngunivarma", but after the victory of Shrīpurusha over the Pallavas, in the latter half of the eighth century A.D., he (Shrīpurusha) and subsequent rulers bore the title of "Pēramānadi" which had been used by the Pallavas.

About A.D. 550 the Chālukya chief Pulakēsin I established his capital at Vātāpi (modern Bādamī) and in course of time subdued the Pallavas of Kānchī. His son Kirtivarman I extending his sway conquered the Kadambas.

About A.D. 615 this Chālukya dynasty was divided into the western and the eastern Chālukyas, and about A.D. 750 the Rāshtrakūta chief Dantivarman (Dantidurga II), after defeating the western Chālukya king Kīrtivarman II re-established the lost Rāshtrakūta kingdom in the Deccan. The eastern—Chālukyas, whose capital was Vēngī remained constantly hostile to it.

The Samangarh plate[1] of Shaka Samvat 675 (A.D. 753) states:

> यो वल्लभं सपदि दण्डबलेन जित्वा
> राजाधिराजपरमेश्वरतामुपैति [१७]
> काञ्चीशकेरलनराधिपचोलपाण्ड्य-
> श्रीहर्षवज्रटविभेदविधानदक्षम् ॥
> कर्णाटकं बलमनन्तमजय्यमन्यै-
> र्भृत्यैः कियद्भिरपि यः सहसा जिगाय [१८]

i.e. he [Rāshtrakūta Dantivarman (Dantidurg II)] after defeating Vallabha (Chālukya Kīrtivarman II), subdued the Pallavas of Kānchi and some other rulers of the Deccan. The inscription[2] of Dashāvatāra temple of Ellora also testifies to his victory over the Pallavas of Kānchī.

The Navasari grant[3] of Shaka Samvat 836 (A.D. 914) contains: —

काञ्चीपदे पदमकारि करेण भूयः

i.e. Dantidurga II, (on his return from the conquest of the Central Provinces) again marched to Kānchī (as the Pallava king had made a futile attempt to regain his lost freedom).

Thus a large part of the north-western and the north-eastern districts of the modern Mysore State came under the influence of the Rāshtrakūtas.

गङ्गान्नामुपरि विजयस्कन्धावारे मण्णनगरे. ....

of the Talegaon plate[4] of Shaka Samvat 690 (A D. 768) which was issued from Manne, a town in Gangāvādī (Mysore), undoubtedly proves that, at that time, the Rāshtrakūta king Krishṇarāja I, who was successfully leading an expedition against the Ganga king, (probably Shrīpurusha) was encamped there (at Manne).

The Radhanpur grant[5] of Shaka Samvat 730 (A.D. 808) states:—

> येनेह बद्धमवलोक्य चिराय गङ्गं ।
> दूरं स्वनिग्रहभियेव कलिः प्रयातः [६]
> * * * * *
> मातङ्गान्मदवारिनिर्भरमुचः प्राप्यानतात्पल्लवात्

1. Indian Antiquary, Vol XI, p. 111.
2. Archaeological Survey of India, Vol V, p 87
3. Epigraphia Indica, Vol IX, p. 21.
4. Epigraphia Indica, Vol. XIII, p. 275
5. Epigraphia Indica, Vol. VI, p. 242.

i.e., the Rāshtrakūta king Dhruvarāja imprisoned the Ganga king (probably Shivamāra) and obtained some elephants from the Pallava king of Kānchī.

After this Dhruvarāja appointed his son Stambha as the governor of Gangavādī.

We learn from the Pattadakal Plate[1] of Shaka Samvat 726 (A.D. 804) that the Rāshtrakūta king Gōvindarāja III defeated Dantiga (Pallava Dantivarman) of Kānchī.

The Radhanpur grant[2] mentioned above further states:—

एकीभूय समुद्यतान् वसुमतीसंहारमाधित्सया (?)
विच्छायान् सहसाप्यबद्ध नृपतीनेकोऽपि यो द्वादश
ख्यातानप्यधिकप्रतापविसरैः संवर्तकोर्कानिव [१३]
.. ..
येनात्यन्तदयालुनाथ निगडक्लेशादपास्थायताल्
स्वं देशं गमितोपि दर्पविसराद्यः प्रातिकूल्ये स्थितः ।
यावन्न भ्रुकुटी ललाटफलके यस्योन्नते लक्ष्यते
विक्षेपेण विजित्य तावदचिराद्बद्धः स गंगः पुनः [१७]
. . . .
तत्रस्थः स्वकरस्थितामपि पुनर्निश्शेषमाकृष्टवान्
विक्षेपैरपि चित्रमानतरिपुर्यः पल्लवानां श्रियम् [१८]

i.e., the Rāshtrakūta king Gōvindarāja III quelled the revolt of his brother Stambha (Shauchakhambha[3]—the Governor of Gangavādī) and his eleven supporters, and also released the Ganga king imprisoned by his father Dhruvarāja. But when he too 'joined the rebels, Gōvindarāja reimprisoned him (annexing the Gangavādī province to the Rāshtrakūṭa kingdom). Gōvindarāja also defeated the Pallavas.

Records[4] found in Chittaldroog district of Mysore State show that Chiruponnēra of Nōlambavādī also accepted the suzerainty of Gōvindarāja III.

It is evident from the Kadab plate[5] of Shaka Samvat 735 (A.D. 813) that Chākirāja, feudatory of Rāshtrakūta Gōvindarāja III, was the governor of Gangavādī.

1. Indian Antiquary, Vol. XI, p. 125.
2 Epigraphia Indica, Vol VI, p. 242.
3 भ्राताभूत्तस्य शक्तित्रयनमितभुवः शौचखम्भाभिधानो
(the Nelmangal plate of Shaka Samvat 724, (A.D. 802) Epigraphia Carnatica, No 61, p 51)
This Shauchakhambha was pardoned by his brother and was reinstated in the governorship of Gangavādī
4. Epigraphia Carnatica, Vol XI, Nos 33-34.
5. Epigraphia Indica, Vol. IV, p. 340.

We know from the Baroda grant[1] of Shaka Samvat 757 (A.D. 835) that Rāshtrakūta Karkarāja of Gujrat, suppressing the revolt, installed Rāshtrakūṭa king Amōghavarsha I on his ancestral throne of Mānyakhēta. But owing to this revolt some provinces like Gangavādī, etc. regained their independence.

The Konnur grant of Shaka Samvat 782 (A.D. 860) contains[2];

प्रचण्डमण्डलातङ्को बङ्केशः सेल्लकेतनः । [१९]
. . . .
मन्त्रसादेन संलब्धवनवासीपुरस्सरान्
ग्रामान् त्रिंशत्सहस्राणि भुनक्त्यविरतोदयः [२१]
महाप्रतापादुच्छेदमुदयच्छन् मदिच्छया
मूलादुच्छेत्तुमुत्तुङ्गां गङ्गवाडीवनाटवीम् [२२]

i.e., Bankēya, a feudatory of the Rāshtrakūta king Amōghavarsha I, and the governor of Bānavāsī, defeated the Ganga king (perhaps Prithvīpati II).

The Sanjan plate[3] of Shaka Samvat 793 (A.D. 871) states:—

त्रस्यत्केरलपाण्ड्यचोलिकनृपैः संपल्लवं पल्लवम्
. . . .
निष्कृतिविकृतगाङ्गाश्शृङ्खलाबद्धनिष्ठाः

i.e., Amōghavarsha I imprisoned the Ganga king and the Pallavas were also afraid of him.

We learn from the records of the Rāshtrakūtas that Krishnarāja II the son of Amōghavarsha I had also fought against the Gangas and the Nōlambas.

The Deoli grant[4] of Shaka Samvat 862 (A.D. 940) contains:—

श्रीवल्लभेन निहतौ भुवि दन्तिगवप्पुकौ दुष्टौ ॥ २२ ॥
रच्छ्र्यामल्लविषद्रुममुदस्य निहितेन योऽकृत सनाथाम्
भूतार्यपुण्यतरुणः वाटीमिव गङ्गपाटीरे ॥ २३ ॥
परिमलितानिष्टगपल्लवविपत्तिरासीन्न विस्मयस्थानम् ।

i.e., the Rāshtrakūta king Krishnarāja III killed Dantiga and Vappuka, and deposing Rāchamalla installed (his own brother-in-law, Satyavākya Kōngunivarma Pēramānaḍi) Bhūtuga II (of the western Ganga dynasty) on the throne of Gangavādī. He also defeated the Pallava chief Antiga.

1. Indian Antiquary, Vol XIV, p. 199
2. Epigraphia Indica, Vol. VI, p 25.
3. Epigraphia Indica, Vol. XVIII, p. 243-251.
4. Indian Antiquary, Vol. V, p. 192.

Scholars presume that Dantiga and Vappuka belonged to the Nōlamba family and were the feudatories of the western-Ganga king Rāchamalla.

We learn from the Atkur inscription[1] of Shaka Samvat 872 (A.D. 950) that Krishnarāja III, being pleased with Bhūtuga II, for killing the Chōla prince Rājāditya, bestowed upon him the districts of Bāṇavāsī, etc. (the north-western part of the Mysore State).

The Gundur inscription[2] of Shaka Samvat 896 (A.D. 974) shows that at that time the districts of Bānavāsī, etc., were ruled by Nōlambāntaka Mārasimha II, who was the son of Bhūtuga II.

Some more names of the feudatories of the Rāshtrakūtas like Kalavittarasa and Shankaraganda can be quoted here who governed the Bānavāsī district.

This Rāshtrakūta kingdom of the Deccan lasted for about 225 years, and was put an end to by the Chālukya king Tailapa II, who defeated the Rāshtrakūta king Karkarāja II at about 973 A.D. But the inscription[3] of Shaka Samvat 904 (A.D. 982) found at Shravana-Belgola (Hassan District) shows that even at that time Rāshtrakūta Indrarāja IV, grandson of Rāshtrakūta king Krishnarāja III, held sway over a part of the Rāshṭrakūta kingdom. This last known ruler of the Deccan Rāshtrakūta family died in Shravana Belgola in Shaka Samvat 904 (A.D. 982).

This recital of evidence undoubtedly proves that the larger part of the present Mysore State remained, for about 225 years, under the direct or indirect influence of the early Rāshṭrakūtas[4] of the Deccan.

1. Epigraphia Indica, Vol. II, p. 171
2. Indian Antiquary, Vol XII, p. 271.
3. Inscriptions at Shravana Belgola, No. 57.
4. Though the Rāshṭrakūṭas were "Sūryavamshī Kshatrīyas," yet at that time owing to misrepresentation of the old records and the influence of the Vaishnavism they were considered "Chandravamshī Yādavas."

3. The early Rashtrakutas of the Deccan and the Nizam's Dominions

(Read at the Tenth All India Oriental Conference held at Tirupati in March 1940 A.D.)

Miraj plates[1] of the Western Chālukya Mahārājādhirāja Jayasiṁha II state.

यो राष्ट्रकूटकुलमिन्द्र इति प्रसिद्ध
कृष्णाह्वयस्य सुतमष्टशतेभसैन्यम् ।
निर्जित्य दग्धनृपपञ्चशतो बभार
भूयश्चलुक्यकुलवल्लभराजलक्ष्मीम् ॥

i. e. Sōlankī Jayasimha I by defeating Rāshtrakūta Indra the son of Krishna and owner of eight hundred elephants re-established the lost Vallabha (Chālukya) kingdom in the Deccan.

This shows that up to the end of the fifth century A.D., Rāshtrakūtas were ruling at Lātūr in the Gulabarga District of the Hyderabad Deccan, but were overthrown about 507 A.D. (564 V.S.) by Sōlankī king Jayasimha I, who established his capital at Vātāpī (Bādāmī) in Bijapur District.

The Miraj plates further state:—

तद्भवो विक्रमादित्यः कीर्त्तिवर्मा तदात्मजः ।
येन चालुक्यराज्यश्रीरन्तरायिण्यभूद्भुवि ॥

i.e., in the time of Kīrtivarman II son of Vikramāditya (who was 9th in descent from Jayasimha I) the Sōlankī kingdom again disappeared.

This event might have taken place between 747 and 753 A.D. (805 and 810 V.S.).

In the genealogy of Rāshtrakūta kings found in the inscription[2] of the Dashāvatāra temple at Ellora, situated in the Aurangabad District, the first name which appears is of Dantivarman I, perhaps a descendant of Indra referred to above, who might have flourished before 593 A.D. (650 V.S.).

---

1 Indian Antiquary, Vol VIII, p 12.

2 Archaeological survey report of Western India, Vol. V, p 87.

We learn from the inscription[1], dated Shaka Samvat 556 (634 A.D.=691 V.S.) of Chālukya Pulkēshin II that—

लब्ध्वा कालं भुवमुपगते जेतुमाप्यायिकाख्ये
गोविन्दे च द्विरदनिकरैरुत्तरां भैमरथ्याः ।
यस्यानीकैर्युधि भयरसज्ञत्वमेकः प्रयात-
स्तत्रावाप्तं फलमुपकृतस्यापरेणापि भूयः ॥

i.e., at the time of Pulakēshin II Rāshtrakūṭa Gōvindarāja I (the grand-son of Dantivarman I) with the aid of his allies attempted to regain the lost ancestral kingdom. But as he could not succeed he concluded peace.

Between 748 and 753 A.D. (804 and 810 V.S.) Dantivarman (Dantidurga) II, the great grandson of Gōvinda I, defeated (the western Chālukya King) Sōlankī Kīrtivarman II, took possession of Vātāpī (Bādāmī) the northern part of his kingdom and re-established the Rāshṭrakūṭa rule in the Deccan.

A copper grant[2] of Shaka Samvat 675 (753 A.D.=810 V.S.) found at Samangad (Kolhapur) also supports this. It states:—

महीमहानदीरेवारोधोभित्तिविदारणम् ।
.... , ... ॥

यो वल्लभं सपदि दण्डबलेन जित्वा
राजाधिराजपरमेश्वरतामुपैति ।
काञ्चीशकेरलनराधिपचोलपाण्ड्य-
श्रीहर्षवज्रटविभेदविधानदक्षम् ॥
कर्णाटकं बलमनन्तमजय्यरथ्यै-
र्भृत्यैः कियद्भिरपि यः सहसा जिगाय ॥

i.e., the elephants of Dantivarman II reached up to the rivers Mahī, Mahānadī and Narbadā (This shows that he invaded Gujrat, Malwa and Orrisa successfully). Further after defeating Vallabha (the western Chālukya king Kīrtivarman II) he assumed the title of Rājādhirāja and Paramēshvara and taking with himself a small cavalry defeated the powerful Karnatik army, which had won victories over the kings of Kānchī (Conjeveram), Kērala (Malabar coast, including modern Travancore and Cochin States), Chōla (Coromandal coast) and Pāndya (further south west of the Coromandal coast) as well as over king Harsha of Kanauj and Vajraṭa.

1. Epigraphia Indica, Vol. VI, p. 5-6
2. Indian Antiquary, Vol. XI, p. 111.

The Karnatik army referred to was the army of the Chālukyas.

He also defeated the rulers of Kanchi (Pallava rulers of Nōlambavādī or Chitaldroog district of Mysore State), Shrīshaila (in the Karnul district of Madras), Kalinga (the country near the sea coast between the rivers Mahānadī and Gōdāvarī), Kōshala (southern Kōshala-Gondwānā including the eastern portion of the Central Provinces), Malwa (Central India), Lāṭa (southern and central Gujrat), Tanka and Sandha Bhūpa (or Sindh).

A copper grant[1] of Shaka Samvat 679 (757 A.D.=814 V.S.) of Mahārājā Dhirāja Karkarāja II of Gujrat shows that Dantivarman II made this Karkarāja, who was his relative, the ruler of Lāṭa (southern and central Gujrat).

Paithan (Aurangabad District) grant[2] of Gōvindarāja III, dated Shaka Samvat 716 (794 A.D.=851 V.S.) states that he (Dantivarman II) extended his sway all over India from Rāmēshwaram in the south to the Himālayas in the north and from the western coast to the Eastern coast.

From the above facts it is evident that Dantivarman (Dantidurga) II was a powerful king of south India and his dominions extended from the northern borders of Gujrat and Malwa to Rāmēshwaram in the south.

The famous Kailāsa Bhavana (or Shiva temple) of Ellora caves in the Aurangabad division of the Nizam's dominions was built by Rāshtrakūta king Krishnarāja I, the uncle of Dantivarman II. This temple is carved out of the rock and is famous for its architecture. Here he also constructed a "Dēvakula" known after him as "Kannēshvara" where many scholars used to live.

It is evident from the Talegaon grant[3] of Shaka Samvat 690 (768 A.D.=825 V.S.) that he (Krishnarāja I) invaded the country ruled by Ganga king (or the south-eastern and south-western part of Mysore State).

It is stated in the Alas plates[4] of Shaka Samvat 692 (770 A.D.=827 V.S.) of Gōvindarāja II, that when he (Gōvinda rāja) was encamped near the confluence of the rivers Krishṇā,

---

1. Journal of Bengal Asiatic Society, Vol. XVI, p 106
2. Epigraphia Indica, Vol. III, p. 105
3. Epigraphia Indica, Vol XIII, p. 275
4. Epigraphia Indica, Vol. VI, p. 209.

Vēṇā and Mūsī, the king of Vēngi[1] (the eastern Chālukya king) acknowledged his supremacy. A large part of this Vēngi-Mandal comprises the south-eastern districts of Nizam's dominions.

We learn from the copper grant[2] of Begumra that Dhruvarāja, the younger brother of Gōvindarāja II had seized a canopy from the king of Northern Kōshala (Ayōdhyā).

He also defeated the Pallava king of Kānchī (Conjeveram or Nōlambavādī), imprisoned Ganga king of Chērā (Coimbatore or Gangavādī) and attacking Paḍihār ruler Vatsarāja drove him towards Bhīnmāl (Marwar).

The copper grants[3] of Shaka Samvat 730 (808 A.D.=865 V.S.) of Gōvindarāja III (the son of Dhruvarāja) show that he released and reimprisoned the king of Chēra (Coimbatore or Gangavādī), attacked Gujrat and conquered Malwa. After subjugating Mārāsharva on his invasion of Vindhyāchala he camped at Shrī Bhavana (Malkhed) till the end of the rains. On the advent of winter he advanced towards the river Tungabhadrā (which is the southern boundary of the Nizam's dominions) and defeated the Pallava king Dantivarman of Kānchī (Conjeveram or Nōlambavādī). Later in obedience to his command the king of Vēngī, probably Vijayāditya II of the Eastern Chālukya dynasty, attended his court and acknowledged his supremacy.

As his expedition up to the Tungabhadrā is mentioned in the grant[4] of Shaka Samvat 726 (804 A.D.=861 V.S.) it is obvious that some of the events took place before this year.

We learn from his copper plate[5] of Shaka Samvat 735 (813 A.D.=870 V.S.) of Torkhede (Khandesh District) that he having conquered Lāta-the central and southern part of Gujrat-made it over to his younger brother Indrarāja who founded the second branch of the Rāshtrakūta kings of Gujrat.

From the above facts, it is quite clear that he was a powerful king of the south, ruling over the tract lying between the rivers Narbadā and Tungabhadrā, and his

1. The district lies between the rivers Krishnā and Gōdāwarī
2 Journal of Bombay Asiatic Society, Vol XVIII, p 261.
3 Indian Antiquary, Vol XI, p. 157 and Epigraphia Indica, Vol VI, p. 242
4 Indian Antiquary, Vol. XI, p 126.
5 Epigraphia Indica, Vol. III, p. 54.

commands were obeyed by the kings of Vindhya or Malwa in the north to Kānchī (Conjeveram or Nōlambavādī) in the south.

Nilgund inscription[1] of Shaka Samvat 788 (866 A.D.=923 V.S.) points out his victories over Kērala (Malabar coast), Mālava, Gauda (perhaps Northern Bengal), Gurjara and Chitrakūta (Chittor).

We learn from the Radhanpur grant[2] of Shaka Samvat 730 (808 A.D.=865 V.S.) that he got built the city wall round the town or fortress by the eastern Chālukya king of Vēngi. Kanharicave- inscription[3] of Shaka Samvat 799 (877 A.D.=934 V.S.) shows that king Amōghavarsha I, son of Gōvinda III, being pleased with his feudatory Kapardi II of the Shilāhāra clan made over to him the kingdom of Konkan[4].

It is known from the Konnur grant[5] of Shaka Samvat 782 (860 A.D.=917 V.S.) that at that time Bankēya the feudatory of Amōghavarsha I was the Governor of Bāṇavāsī (Shimog District of Mysore) and at the desire of this king he invaded Gangavādī successfully.

The Shaka Samvat 793 (871 A.D.=928 V.S.) grant of Sanjan states that mobilisation of Amōghavarsha's army struck terror in the hearts of the kings of Kērala (Malabar coast), Chōla (Coromandal coast), Pāndya (further south-west of Coromandal coast), Kalinga (the country between the Mahānadī and the Gōdāvarī on the border of the sea), Magadha (Bihar) and the Pallavas of Kānchī (Conjeveram.)

We learn from the Sirur grant[6] of Shaka Samvat 788 (866 A.D.=923 V.S.) that the rulers of Anga (the country about Bhagalpur including Monghyr), Banga (Bengal) Mālava (Central India) and Vēngi (the tract lying between the Krishnā and the Gōdāvarī or south-eastern part of Hyderabad-Deccan) acknowledged his superiority. There may be some exaggeration in this statement.

1. Epigraphia Indica, Vol. VI, p. 102.
2. Epigraphia Indica, Vol. VI, p. 242.
3. Indian Antiquary, Vol. XIII, p. 135
4. Its capital was Tana It denotes the whole strip of land between the Western Ghats and the Arabian sea.
5. Epigraphia Indica, Vol. VI, p 25
6. Epigraphia Indica, Vol. VII, p. 203.

He shifted his capital perhaps from Nasik or Laṭalūr to Mānyakhēta (Malkhed) 90 miles to the south east of Sholapur in the Nizam's dominions.

We learn from the Rāshtrakūṭa grants that Krishnarāja II, the son of Amōghavarsha I, also conquered Āndhra (the country between the rivers Gōdāvarī and Krishnā including the districts of Krishṇā), Banga, Kalinga, Magadha, Gurjar and Gauda and annexed the province of Lāṭa.

He also fought against the Gangas, the Nōlambas and the eastern Chālukyas.

We learn from the Begumra copper grant[1] of Shaka Samvat 836 (915 A.D.=972 V.S.) that Indrarāja III, the grandson of Krishnarāja II, moved from Mānyakhēta to Kurundaka for his coronation. This Kurundaka was situated at the junction of the rivers Krishnā and Panchagangā. It also states that Indra III devastated Mēru perhaps Mahōdaya or Kanauj.

Karhad plates[2] of Shaka Sāmvat 880 (958 A.D.=1015 V.S.) indicate that Krishnarāja III, the nephew of Indrarāja III, while subduing the south, laid waste the province of Chōla (Coromandal coast, perhaps the capital of which at that time was Tanjore), conquered the territory of Pāndya (further south-west of Coromandal coast) and Chēra (Coimbatore), subjugated the king of Ceylon and erected a monumental tower at Rāmēshvaram to commemorate these victories. The invasion of Chōla country (Coromandal coast) probably took place in 947 A.D. (1004 V.S.). He also defeated Haihaya (Kalachuri) king Sahasrārjuna. "Yashastilaka Champū", a poem completed in Shaka Samvat 881 (959 A.D.=1016 V.S.), by Sōmadēva also praises his victories over Chēra, Chōla Pāndya and Simhala.

Further he awarded the district of Bānavāsī to Bhūtuga II (his own brother-in-law) whom he first installed in place of western Ganga king Rāchamalla I at Gangavādī. He also defeated king Anniga of Pallava dynasty and killed king Dantiga of Kānchī.

---

1. Epigraphia Indica, Vol. IX, p. 29
2 Epigraphia Indica, Vol IV, p. 281.

He was also a powerful ruler and his territory extended beyond the Ganges in the north.

Udayapur (Gwalior) inscription[1] of Parmāra Udayāditya points out that at the time of Khōttigadēva the younger brother of Krishnarāja III, Shrī Harsha (Sīyaka II) of Malwa invaded his capital.

'Pāiyalachchhī Nāmamālā' of Dhanapāla states that in 972 A.D. (1029 V.S.) the king of Malwa plundered the city of Mānyakhēta (Malkhed).

After this event the great power of the Rāshtrakūtas of the Deccan began to decline, and at the time of Karkarāja II, the nephew of Khōttiga, Sōlankī Tailapa II, attacked their kingdom and re-established the Chālukya kingdom at Kalyānī after 973 A.D. (1030 V.S.).

The Kharepatan copper grant[2] states.

कक्कलस्तस्य भ्रातृव्यो भुवो भर्त्ता जनप्रियः ।
आसीत् प्रचण्डधामेव प्रतापजितशात्रवः ॥
समरे तं विनिर्जित्य तैलपोऽभून्महीपतिः ।

i.e., the powerful king Karkarāja II was the nephew of Khōṭṭigadēva and after defeating him, Tailapa usurped his kingdom.

Vikramānkadēvacharita[3] of Bilhaṇa also supports the above statement. It states:—

विश्वम्भराकण्टकराष्ट्रकूटसमूलनिर्मूलनकोविदस्य ।
सुखेन यस्यान्तिकमाजगाम चालुक्यचन्द्रस्य नरेन्द्रलक्ष्मीः ॥

i.e., the state passed on the Chālukya king Tailapa (II), the destroyer of the Rāshtrakūta kings, who were a menace to the world.

Here the adjective used for the Rāshtrakūta kings shows that they were very powerful kings and all other rulers were afraid of their invasion. This fact is also supported by the writings of the contemporary Arab writers, like Sulaimān, Abūzaīdul Hasan, Ibn-Khurdādbā, Almasūdī, Al Istakharī and Ibn Haukal, who considered these Rāshtrakūta rulers of Malkhed eminent and most powerful kings as their supremacy

1. Journal of Bengal Asiatic Society, Vol. IX, p. 549
2. Epigraphia Indica, Vol. III, p 297.
3. Sarga I, stanza 69.

was acknowledged by all the other rulers of India who came in touch with them.

After this we find mention of only one more Rāshṭrakūta king named Indrarāja IV, a grand son of Rāshṭrakūṭa king Krishṇarāja III, who died in 982[1] A.D. (1039 V.S.)

This summary of the History of the Rāshṭrakūṭas of Malkhed shows that the kingdom established by Rāshṭrakūta king Dantivarman (Dantidurga) II by defeating Sōlankī (Chālukya) king Kīrtivarman II, between 748 and 753 A.D. (804 and 810 V.S.) lasted for about 225 years and nearly the whole of the Deccan including the present dominions of His Exalted Highness the Nizam as well as Trivendrum and Cochin etc., went under direct or indirect sway of the rulers of this dynasty.

In conclusion, I may add that a small village named Jaswantpura comprising of 1459 Bighas of land in the Aurangabad district of the Nizam's dominions is still held by the Rāthōr rulers of Jodhpur. It was founded by Mahārājā Jaswantsingh I of Jodhpur in about 1667 A.D. when he was sent by the Emperor Aurangzeb to subdue the well known Mahraṭṭā ruler Shivāji.

---

1. Epigraphia Indica, Vol. IV, p. 182.

4. False statements about king Jayachandra and Rao Siha.

(Read at the Fifth All India Oriental Conference, held at Lahore, in November 1928 and published in Indian Antiquary, Vol LIX, (January 1930 A D) pp. 6—9 as well as in the History of Rashtrakutas, pp 134-143.)

Jayachandra, king of Kanauj has often been accused of having caused the downfall of the last Hindu kingdom in Northern India. His grandson Rāo Sīhā also has been accused of having usurped Pālī, by treacherously murdering the Pallīvāl Brāhmans of that place. No reasons are, however, offered for these suppositions, but the only argument resorted to by these critics is that these stories are handed down from generation to generation or that they are so mentioned in the Prithvīrāj Rāsō and in Tod's *Annals and Antiquities of Rajasthan.*

In fact, none has yet taken the trouble of investigating the truth or otherwise of the problem. For the consideration of scholars I lay down my views on the subject here. The brief story of the Prithvīrāj Rāsō may be told as follows.

Once Kamdhaj Rāya, with the assistance of king Vijayapāl Rāthōr, of Kanauj invaded Delhi. At this, Tunvar Anangpāl, king of Delhi, requested king Sōmēshvara Chauhān of Ajmer for help. Sōmēshvara thereupon marched with all his forces and joined Anangpāl. A battle was fought in which the latter won a victory, and the hostile forces retreated. As a mark of gratitude for this timely succour, Anangpāl married his younger daughter Kamalāvatī to Sōmēshvara and simultaneously his another daughter[1] to Vijayapāl of Kanauj.

In V.S. 1115 Kamalāvatī gave birth to Prithvīrāja. Once Nāhad Rāo, king of Mandor, had paid a visit to king Anangpāl of Delhi, and beholding the handsome features of prince Prithvīrāja there, he declared his intention to marry his

1. Jayachandra was born to this lady

daughter to him. But later he abandoned the idea. On this Prithvīrāja invaded Maṇḍor in about V.S. 1129, and having defeated Nāhad Rāo, took his daughter in marriage. Later, in V.S. 1138, Anangpāl, disregarding the right of his elder daughter's son Jayachandra, made over the kingdom of Delhi to Pṛithvīrāja. Subsequently Pṛithvīrāja having abducted the daughter of the Yādava king, Bhān of Deogiri, who was engaged to Vīrachandra, nephew of Jayachandra, the armies of Prithvīrāja and Jayachandra had to meet on the battlefield. Sometime after this, Anangpāl also invaded Delhi to recapture it from Prithvīrāja, on the complaints of his former subjects being now oppressed by Prithvīrāja's coercive policy, but he did not succeed.

In V.S. 1144, when Jayachandra proposed to perform a Rājasūya-yajna and the *Svayamvara* of his daughter Samyōgitā, Prithvīrāja, considering it inadvisable to confront him, thought out another plan to render both the above ceremonies abortive. He at first repaired to Khokhandpur where he killed Jayachandra's brother, Bāluk Rāya, and afterwards eloped with Samyōgitā. Jayachandra was therefore obliged to wage war against Prithvīrāja. The latter managed somehow to escape, but as many as 64 of his generals were killed and his power was almost annihilated. According to the Rāsō, Pṛithvīrāja was 36 years of age when this event took place. So the date of the event must be Vikrama-Samvat 1151.

The bravery of the young general Dhīrasēn Puṇḍīr in the struggle with Jayachandra attracted Prithvīrāja's attention, and the king favoured him most. At this his veteran generals Chāmund Rāya and others became jealous and carried on intrigues with Shihābu'd-dīn. But Prithvīrāja, being too much engrossed with Samyōgitā, did not pay any heed to these affairs. His government, therefore, gradually showed signs of disintegration. This gave an opportunity to Shihābu'd-dīn to invade Delhi. Pṛithvīrāja was obliged to come out with his army to meet him. On this occasion Rāval Samarsī of Mewar, his brother-in-law, had also joined Prithvīrāja in the battle. But due to disorganisation of the army Shihābu'd-dīn eventually won a victory, and Prithvīrāja was captured and taken to Ghazni. Shortly after this, it is related, Shihābu'd-dīn met his death at the hands of Pṛithvīrāja at Ghazni, who immediately after killed himself.[1] Shortly after, Rainsī, son

1 According to the Rāsō Pṛithvīrāja had died at an age of 43, so the date of this event comes to V.S. 1158.

of Prithvīrāja, attacked the Mohemmadans of Lahore, to avenge his father's death, and drove them out. Thereupon Qutbu'd-dīn marched against Rainsī and killing him in the battle that followed, advanced further upon Kanauj. Hearing of this Jayachandra also arranged his army to encounter him. But in the battle that ensued Jayachandra was killed and the Mohemmadans were victorious.

The above story cannot stand any historical test. The Kamdhaj Rāya mentioned in it is a fictitious name, in as much as we know of no individual of that name in history. Similarly the name of Jayachandra's father was not Vijayapāl, but Vijayachandra, who lived not in the beginning of the twelfth century of the Vikrama era, but in the first half of the thirteenth century, as is evident from his copper plate grants[1] and inscriptions of V.S. 1224 and 1225. Again although the period of Anangpāl has not yet been precisely ascertained, yet this much is certain that Sōmēshvara's third ancestor Vigraharāja (or Vīsaladēva IV) had acquired possession of Delhi, which is borne out by the inscription[2] of V.S. 1220 (1163 A.D.) on the pillar of Firōz Shah at Delhi. Under these circumstances we do not understand how Sōmēshvara could have gone to Delhi to help Anangpāl. Moreover, in the *Prithvirajavijaya-Mahakavya*, which was written in Prithvīrāja's time, the name of Prithvīrāja's mother is mentioned not as Kamalāvatī, but as Karpūradēvī[3], who is stated to be the daughter not of Tunvar Anangpāl, but of a king of the Haihaya dynasty (of Tripurī). In the *Hammira-Mahakavya* also, the name of Prithvīrāja's mother is mentioned as Karpūradēvī. The author of the *Raso* has mentioned the date of the birth of his hero Prithvīrāja[4] as V. S. 1115, but in fact Prithvīrāja should have been born in V. S. 1217 (1160 A.D.) or somewhat later, as at the death of his father in about V.S. 1236 (1179 A.D.) he was a minor and his mother took charge of the administration.

Let us now consider the tale of Prithvīrāja having married a daughter of Nāhad Rāo, king of Mandor. This, too, is an absurdity, because from an inscription of V.S. 894 of king Bāuka, who was tenth in descent from this Nāhad Rāo,

1. Kielhorn's *Supplement to Northern List* (*Ep Ind*, vol VIII, Appendix I), p 13.
2. Epigraphia Indica, vol XIX, p 218   3 *JRAS*, 1913, p 275 f
4 The names of Prithvīrāja's ancestors mentioned in the *Raso* appear also to a large extent incorrect.

we conclude that the latter must have lived about V.S. 714, i.e., nearly 500 years before Pṛithvīrāja. Sometime between V.S. 1189 and V.S. 1200 the Padihār dynasty of Maṇḍor had ceased to exist, having been overthrown by Chauhān Rāyapāla, whose son Sahajapāla ruled at Maṇḍor about V. S. 1202, as appears from his inscription found at Maṇḍor.[1] Besides this, the name of the prime ancestor of the Paḍihār dynasty of Kanauj was also Nāgabhata (or Nāhaḍ). From the copper grant[2] dated V.S. 813 of the Chauhān king, Bhartṛivaddha II, found at Hansot, it appears that this Nāhad lived in the beginning of the ninth century of the Vikram era. Further, the first Padihār conqueror of Kanauj, too, was Nāgabhata (Nāhad II,) who was fifth in descent from the aforesaid Nāhad. He had died in V.S. 890, as appears from the *Prabhavaka-charitra*. No fourth Nāhad besides these has been heard of in the history of India.

We have already mentioned above V.S. 1217 as the approximate birth year of Prithvīrāja. In such a case it would certainly be impossible to assume that Anangpāl made over the kingdom of Delhi to Prithvīrāja in V.S. 1138.

Further, the story of Prithvīrāja having abducted the daughter of the Yādava king, Bhān of Deogiri, and of the consequent battle between Prithvīrāja and Jayachandra, also seems to be spurious. The founder of the city of Deogiri was not Bhāṇ, but Bhillam, who had founded the city about V.S. 1244 (1187 A.D.). Neither does this event find place in the history of Bhillam nor does the name Bhāṇ occur in the pedigree of the dynasty. Similarly, Vīrachandra, the name of a nephew of king Jayachandra, occurs only in the Rāsō and nowhere else.

We have mentioned above that an ancestor, third from Prithvīrāja's father, had acquired possession of Delhi. Thus the talk of Tunvar Anangpāl's effort to regain his kingdom from Prithvīrāja on complaint from his subjects about the latter's high-handedness is an untenable proposition.

There now remains the affair of the *Rajasuya* and *Svayamvara* ceremonies performed by king Jayachandra. Had Jayachandra performed such a grand ceremony as the

---

1 The Mandor inscription referred to here is not dated. *Archæl. Surv. Ind, An. Rep.* 1909-10, pp. 102-3.

2 *Ep. Ind.*, vol. XII, p 197

Rājasūya, some mention of it would have been found in the inscriptions of that monarch, or in the *Rambhamanjarı-Natıka* by Nayachandra-sūri, of which Jayachandra himself is the hero. Fourteen copper plates and two stone inscriptions[1] of Jayachandra have been found, the last of which is dated V.S. 1245[2] (1189 A.D.). Although there are thus as many as sixteen epigraphic records belonging to him, not one of them contains any reference to his having celebrated a *Rajasuya*.

The story of Prithvīrāja's elopement with Samyōgitā seems to be a creation of the fertile brain of the author of the *Raso*. Neither the *Prıthvırajavıjaya-Mahakavya* written in Prithvīrāja's time, nor the *Hammıra Mahakavya* compiled in the last half of the fourteenth century of the Vikrma era,[3] makes any mention of any such event. To rely on the story under these circumstances is to tread on uncertain ground. The dates[4] of the events given in the *Raso* are alike incorrect.

The story of Mahārāval Samarsimha of Mewar being a brother-in-law of Prithvīrāja and being killed in the battle with Shihābu'd-dīn, while helping his brother-in-law Prithvīrāja, is also an idle tale. This battle had in fact been fought in V.S. 1249, whereas Mahārāval Samarsī died in V.S. 1359. Under these circumstances, the above statement of the *Raso* cannot be admitted as either true or possible.

After this, there is the mention of Prithvīrāja's son Rainsī, but in fact the name of Pṛithvīrāja's son was Gōvindarāja.[5] He being a child, his uncle Harirāja had usurped his dominion of 'Ajmer, whereupon Qutbu'd-dīn, having defeated Harirāja, had protected Gōvindarāja.

---

1 *Bharat-ke-Prachın Rajvamsha*, part III, p. 108-110

2 Annual report of the Arch Survey of India (1921-22), pp 120-121.

3. Further there is no trace of Sōmavamshī Mukundadēvā of Kaṭak in the History of that period, whose daughter is mentioned as the mother of Samyōgitā in the *Raso*

4 Mr Mohan Lal Vishnu Lal Pandya had however assumed the dates of the *Raso* to be based on the 'Anand Vikrama Samvat', which he takes for granted on the basis of the words विक्रमसाक अनन्द According to this the Vikrama Samvats are arrived by adding 91 to the Samvats stated in the *Raso*. Thus by adding 91 to the Samvat 1158, the date of Prithvīrāja's death arrived at according to the *Raso*, we come to 1249 This date alone can be proved to be correct by this method But the other dates and the periods assigned to Nāhad Rāo, etc , still remain quite unreliable

5. *Bharat-ke-Prachın Rajvamsa*, part I, page 263,

In the end there is the mention of an invasion by Qutbu'd-dīn against Jayachandra, but, according to the Persian histories of India, this invasion is said to have been made not after Shihabu'd-dīn's death, but in his lifetime, and that he himself had taken part in it. He was killed at the hands of the Gakkhars or Khakkars in V.S. 1262 (1206 A.D.). Besides, in the Persian chronicles there is no mention of Jayachandra's collusion with Shihabu'd-dīn.

When all these circumstances are taken into consideration, the historical value of the *Prithviraja-raso* becomes vitiated. Besides, even if we accept for a moment the whole story of the *Raso* as correct, yet nowhere in that work is there any mention either of Jayachandra having invited Shihabu'd-dīn to attack Prithvīrāja or of his having any other sort of connection whatsoever with the Mohemmadan ruler. On the other hand, at various places in the *Raso* we read of Prithvīrāja's aggressive attacks, his elopement with the princess, his neglect of state affairs through his devotion to Samyōgitā, his proud and overbearing behaviour towards his brave and wise general Chāmund Rāya, whom he had sent to prison without any fault on his part and his high-handedness which gave rise to the complaints of the subjects of a state left as a legacy to him by his maternal grandfather. Along with this we also learn from the *Raso* that his unwise steps obliged his own generals to conspire with his enemy Sultān Shihabu'd-dīn. In the light of these circumstances readers will be able to judge for themselves how far it is just to dub king Jayachandra with the title of *Vibhishana* and thus malign him as a traitor.

Let us now examine the attack made on Rāo Sīhā, grandson of Mahārājā Jayachandra[1]. Colonel James Tod writes:—

"Here in the land of Kher amidst the sandhills of Luni (the salt river of the desert) from which the Gohils were expelled, Sihaji planted the standard of the Rathors.

"At this period a community of Brahmans held the city and extensive lands about Pali, from which they were termed Pallivals, and being greatly harassed by the incursions of the mountaineers, the Mers and the Minas, they called in the aid of Sihaji's band, which readily undertook and executed the

1. Annals and antiquities of Rajasthan, vol. I, pp. 942—43.

task of rescuing the Brahmans from their depredations. Aware that they would be renewed, they offered Sihaji lands to settle amongst them, which he readily accepted.

"Afterwards he found an opportunity to obtain land by putting to death the heads of this community and adding the district to his conquests."

From this narrative it is evident that before rendering aid to these Pallīvāl Brāhmans Rāo Sīhā had acquired possession of Mehwa and Kherdhar. It does not seem reasonable that an adventurer, hankering after land, should have renounced possession of these two large districts, merely to content himself with a few acres of land granted to him by his proteges, the Pallīvāls. Further, he had not at that time enough men with him to look after his possessions of Kher and Mehwa as well as for keeping under subjection the Mērs and Mīnās of the hilly tracts, who often overran Pālī. Besides, from the narratives of the old chronicles of Marwar we learn that the Pallīvāls of Pālī were a class of rich traders. It is nowhere recorded that they were masters of the town of Pālī; nor do we find any mention that Rāo Sīhā had murdered them. In the temple of Sōmnāth at Pālī there is a stone inscription[1] of V.S. 1209 of Sōlankī Kumārapāla, which shows that at that time the latter held sway over Pālī. It also appears from this inscription that one Bāhadadēva, a feudatory of Kumārapāla, ruled over Pālī at this time on behalf of Kumārapāla. There had also been one Ālhanadēva, a Chauhān feudatory and favourite of king Kumārapāla. An inscription dated V. S. 1209 of Kirādū shows that this Ālhanadēva had acquired possession of the districts of Kirāḍū, Rādadharā and Shiva by the favour of king Kumārapāla[2].

On the death of Kumārapāla about V.S. 1230, his nephew Ajayapāla succeeded to the throne. From this time the power of the Sōlankīs began to decline. Presumably the Mīnās and Mērs might have taken advantage of this weakness and plundered Pālī, which was then one of the richest cities in the vicinity. In the inscription dated V.S. 1319 at Sūndhā of Chouhān Chāchigadēva it is stated that Udayasimha, father

---

1. Indian Culture, Calcutta, vol. II. No. 1 pp. 136—138.
2. Epigraphica Indica, vol. XI. p. 70

of Chāchigadēva, and great-grand son of the aforesaid Ālhaṇadēva, was master of the districts of Nāḍōl, Jālōr, Maṇḍōr, Bāhadmēr, Ratnapur, Sānchōr, Surāchand, Rāḍadhaḍā, Khēḍ, Rāmsīn, and Bhīnmāl. Udayasimha is also described in this inscription as invincible to the kings of Gujarat[1]. We have found four inscriptions of this king ranging from V. S. 1262 to V.S. 1306 at Bhīnmāl. We conclude therefore that at sometime in this period, this Chauhān feudatory might have thrown off the yoke of the Sōlankī kings of Gujarat. At the same time, when we consider the geographical position of the above mentioned districts, we are led to believe that the city of Pālī, too, must have passed into the possession of the Chauhāns from the Sōlankīs. So that at the time of Rāo Sīhā's arrival in Marwaṛ, such an important city as Pālī must have either been in possession of the Sōlankīs or the Chauhāns. What circumstances, then, could have obliged Rāo Sīhā to butcher his helpless and trading supplicants of the Brāhmans a caste so sacred to a Rajput for the possession of Palī?

Besides this, when finding themselves too weak to ward off the marauding incursions of the hill tribes, these Brāhmaṇs had themselves applied to Rāo Sīhā for help, and having gained experience of his prowess, and having appointed him to be their protector, how could they have ever dared to incur his wrath by an act of effrontery?

Thus automatically Sīhā became master of the city, and so his interest lay in fostering its trade by conferring favours upon its merchants, the Pallīvāl Brāhmans, and not in laying waste the country by killing these traders, as is supposed by the learned scholar, Colonel Tod.

---

1. Ep. Ind., vol. IX, p. 78, v. 46.

5. The Gahadvals of Kanauj.

[*From about V. S. 1125 to 1280 (1068 to 1223 A. D.)*]

[Published in the Journal of the Royal Asiatic Society of Great Britain and Ireland, London (January 1932, pp. 1-21) and also included in the History of the Rāshṭrakūṭas (pp 113-133)]

---

6. The Rashtrakutas and the Gahadvals.

[Read at the Fifth All India Oriental Conference held at Lahore in November 1928 A. D. and published in the Journal Royal Asiatic Society of Great Britain and Ireland, London (January 1930 A D pp. 111-121.)]

There is much difference of opinion among historians as to the Rāshtrakūtas and the Gāhadvāls being indentical.

Dr. Burnell, observing the Rāshtrakūtas mentioned as *Ratta-vamshis* in some of their inscriptions,[1] was led to infer that they are members of the Reddi tribe. He believed that it is the Telugu word *Reddi* which has been distorted into *Ratta.* In Telugu this epithet is applied to the aboriginal agriculturists of that province.

Mr. V.A. Smith held that the Gāhadvāls and Rāshṭrakūtas of Upper India, at least, seem to have come from the same stock.[2]

For some time they held sway over Kanauj, as appears from the copper grant dated Shaka-S. 972 (V.S.1107=A.D.1051) of king Trilōchanapāla of Lāṭa (Gujrat), which contains:—

कान्यकुब्जे महाराजराष्ट्रकूटस्य कन्यकाम् ।
लब्ध्वा सुखाय तस्यां त्वं चौलुक्याप्नुहि सन्ततिम् ।

(*Indian Antiquary,* vol. xii, p. 201.)

1. Researchers of history are well aware that in the inscription of the Rāshṭrakūṭa king Amōghavarsha I, as also in that of Indra III found at Navasārī, the word "Raṭṭa" only stands instead of "Rāshṭrakūṭa" to denote the race of these kings, which shows that "Raṭṭa" is another form of the word 'Rāshṭrakūṭa."

2. "The Northern Rāṭhōrs are off-shoots of the Gāhaḍvāls." V. A. Smith, *Early History of India,* (4th Ed.), p. 429.

i.e. "O, Chaulukya! seek the hand of the daughter of the Rāshtrakūta king of Kanauj, and produce offspring."

In an article in the *Indian Antiquary*, vol. iii, p. 41, Mr. J.W. Watson, Political Superintendent, Palanpur, writes that on Thursday[1] the Mārgashīrsha Sudi 5 of V. S. 936, the Rāthōr Shrīpati, king of Kanauj, on the occasion of his accession to the throne, made a charitable grant of sixteen villages in North Gujrat to the Chibadiyā Brāhmans. One of those villages, named Ētā, is still held by the descendants of those Brāhmaṇs. He also adds that the Mohemmadan historians of Gujrat have acknowledged the king of Kanauj to be master of Gujrat.

In the above grant this Shrīpati is designated *Kanaujeshvara*, either perhaps as being a member of a Kanauj royal family of Rāshtrakūtas, or because the Rāshtrakūta king Dhruvarāja II of the southern branch may, after defeating king Bhōjadēva Padihār of Kanauj, have granted an appanage to Shrīpati's father, who belonged to a section of Northern Rāshtrakūtas, and on his death this Shrīpati may have made this charitable grant.

In the *Bombay Gazetteer* also the village of Ētā is stated to have been granted by the Rāshtrakūta king of Kanauj Dr. Fleet also holds that the Rāshtrakūtas had migrated to the South from the North.

But on this point it may, however, be asked how the Rāshtrakūtas of the Deccan, who are described as Chandra-vaṁshīs in their inscriptions, can be considered descendants of the Sūrya-vamsha. My reply to this is that in the first place the distinction of Chandra, Sūrya, and Agni Vamsha, is only a Paurānic idea, because in different places the same clan is designated as of different lineage.[2] Moreover, if at all the

1 In fact, Sunday falls on this date

2 In some inscriptions of the Sōlankīs (Chaulukyas), in the *Dvyashraya Kavya* of Hēmachandra, and in the *Vastupala-Charita* written by Jina Harsha Ganin, the Chaulukya race is said to have sprung from the Lunar stock But in the *Vikramankadeva Charita*, written by Bilhana, the origin of the race is held to be from Brahmā, which view is also supported by the inscription of the Sōlankī king Kumārapāladēva

In the Mount Abu inscription dated V S 1377 of the Chauhān Lumbha the Chauhān clan is stated to belong to the Lunar Stock, in the inscription of the time of Vīsaladēva IV, in the *Hammira-Mahakavya*, and in the *Prithvi-raja-vijaya* this clan is said to be of the Solar stock, while in the *Prithviraj Raso* it is mentioned as having sprung from Agni, the Fire God

Similar is the case of the other clans

matter deserves notice, it will be seen that in fact nowhere before S. 782 are the Rāshṭrakūṭas stated to be Chandra-vamshīs. Further, among the 1,800 silver coins of the Rāshtrakūta king Krishṇarāja I, found at Dhamōrī (Amrāoti), we find the phrase:—

" परममाहेश्वरमहादित्यपादानुध्यातश्रीकृष्णराज(:) "

Here the word 'महादित्य' alludes to the king's being of the Sūrya vamsha, because in the documents hitherto discovered *Mahadıtya* appears neither as a title nor as a name of his father. Thus it doubtless refers to his prime ancestor, the sun.

Besides this the copper grant dated Shaka-S. 730 (V.S. 865=A.D. 808) of the Rāshtrakūta king Gōvindarāja III, contains the verse:—

यस्मिन्सर्वगुणाश्रये क्षितिपतौ श्रीराष्ट्रकूटान्वयो
जाते यादववंशवन्मधुरिपावासीदलङ्घ्यः परैः ।

i.e. "just as the Yādava clan became invincible owing to the birth of Shrī Krishna, in like manner the Rāshtrakūta clan also became invincible by the birth of this able king."

This shows that until this date the Rāshṭrakūṭa clan must have been considered distinct from the Yādava[1] clan; but later on the scribe of the copper grant of king Amōghavarsha I dated Shaka-S. 782 (V.S. 917=A.D. 860), probably misinterpreting the simile in the aforesaid plate of king Gōvindarāja, may have taken this king for a Yadu-vamshī. The later writers of the subsequent seven grants, as also Halāyudha, seems to have copied this mistake.

In the *Rashtroda-vamsha-Mahakavya*, written in Shaka S. 1518 (V.S. 1653=A.D. 1596), it is stated that a Chandra-vamshī prince had been adopted by the Sūrya-vamshī king of Kanauj[2] and that the former was the first prince to be designated Rāshṭrōda.

---

1. This fact is borne out by the inscription of the Yādava king Bhīma, dated V. S. 1442, found at Prabhāsa Paṭṭana, which contains the words —

वशो(शौ) प्रसिद्धो(द्धौ) हि यथा रवीन्दो(न्द्वो): ।
राष्ट्रोडवंशस्तु तथा तृतीय· ।

2. पुरा कदाचित्रतये समेतान्देवाननुज्ञाप्य गृहाय सद्यः ।
कात्यायनीमर्द्धशशाङ्कमौलिः कैलासशैले रमयाम्बभूव ॥ १२ ॥
अन्योन्यभूषापणबन्धरम्यं तत्रान्तरे द्यूतमदीव्यतां तौ ॥ १४ ॥
कात्यायनीपाणिसरोजकोशविलोलिताक्षच्युपितादयेन्दोः ।
गर्भान्वितैकादशवार्षिकोऽभूदभूतपूर्वप्रतिमः कुमारः ॥ २० ॥
तस्मै वरं साम्बशिवो दयालुः श्रीकान्यकुब्जेश्वरतामरासीत् ॥ २१ ॥

Besides this, it is also possible that in course of time owing to the influence of Vaishnavism, the Rāshtrakūtas may have been considered Yadu-vamshīs. I quote, for instance the case of the Gōhil house of Bhaunagar (Kāthiāwār). When, in the thirteenth century of the Vikrama era, they had been ruling in Mārwār, they were considered Sūrya-vamshīs, whereas now, owing to their present abode being in the vicinity of Dwārakā, they allege themselves to be Chandra-vamshīs, as is evinced by the following stanza:—

चन्द्रवंशि सरदार गोत्र गौतम वखाणुं
शाखा माधविसार मके प्रवरत्रय जाणुं
अग्निदेव उद्धार देव चामुण्डा देवी
पाण्डवकुल परमाण आद्य गोहिल चल एवी
विक्रमवध करनार नृप शालिवाहन चकवे थयो
ते पछी तेज ओलादनो सोरठ मा सेजक भयो ॥

A further proof of Vaishnavism influencing the lineage is that in the seal of a copper grant, of the sixth century of the Vikrama era, of the Rāshtrakūta king Abhimanyu, there is an image of the goddess Ambikā seated on a lion, while in their subsequent copper grants Garuda has been substituted.

Here it may also be asked why, if the Rāshtrakūtas in reality were not Chandra-vamshīs, did they themselves allow the repetition of a mistake committed by a scribe. In reply I beg to say that the royal family of Udaipur is popularly styled Sūrya-vamshī, but the learned Mahārānā Kumbhakarna himself, concurring with the opinion of previous scholars, stated in his *Rasika-priya* (a commentary on the *Gitagovinda*) that the founder of the dynasty was a Brāhman:—

"श्रीवैजवापेन सगोत्रवर्यः श्रीवप्पनामा द्विजपुङ्गवोऽभूत् ।"

Next I shall take up the question of the Rāshtrakūtas and the Gāhadvāls being one and the same.

अत्रान्तरे काचन लातनाख्या समेत्य देवी गिरिजाहराभ्याम् ।
त्रिलीनभूमिपतिकान्यकुब्जराज्याधिपत्याय शिशु ययाचे ॥ २४ ॥

. . . . . .

नारायणो नाम नृपः सुतार्थी यज्ञेश्वर ध्यायति सर्ववश्यः ।
सा रुद्रदत्तेन सहामुनास्मिन्नवातरत्काञ्चनमेखलेन ॥ २८ ॥
अलक्ष्यदेहा तमवोचदेषा राजन्नसावस्तु तवैकसूनुः ।
अनेन राज्यं च कुल तवोढं राष्ट्रौ(ष्ट्रो)ढनामा तदिह प्रतीतः ॥२६ ॥
(प्रथमः सर्गः)

An inscription of king Lakhanapāla[1] has been found at Badāyūn. It is of the thirteenth century A. D. It contains the lines:—

प्रख्याताखिलराष्ट्रकूटकुलजक्ष्मापालदोःपालिता
पाञ्चालाभिधदेशभूषणकरी वोदामयूतापुरी
.. ..

तत्रादितोभवदनन्तगुणो नरेन्द्र-
श्चन्द्रः स्वखड्गभयभीषितवैरिवृन्दः ।

i.e. "Protected by the famous Rāshṭrakūṭa kings, the city of Badāyūn is an ornament of the province of Kanauj (Pāṇchāla). Having conquered his foes by his prowess, Chandra became the first king of that place."

Similarly, we have found a copper grant of the Gāhaḍvāl Chandradēva of V.S.1148 which contains the lines:—

विध्वस्तोद्धतधीरयोधतिमिरः श्रीचन्द्रदेवो नृपः ।
येनोदारतरप्रतापशमिताशेषप्रजोपद्रवं
श्रीमद्गाधिपुराधिराज्यमसमं दोर्विक्रमेणार्जितम् ।

i.e. "Chandradēva, son of Yashōvigraha, became a powerful monarch. Having vanquished his enemies with the force of his arms, he took the kingdom of Kanauj." The lineage of Chandradēva is not mentioned in this copper grant. But his descendants were afterwards known as Gāhadvāls.

Comparing both these inscriptions and taking into consideration the contemporaneousness of the two Chandradēvas mentioned therein, we conclude that both refer to one and the same. Chandradēva, having first taken Badāyūn, later took possession of Kanauj also. After him his eldest son Madanapāla ascended the throne of Kanauj, while the younger son Vigrahapāla received Badāyūn as a *jagír*. The Badāyūn family stuck to the original racial name, but the descendants of Madanapāla, being sovereigns of Gādhipura (another name of Kanauj), assumed the title of Gāhaḍvāl, just as some Rāshṭrakūtas, residents of village Renka of the United Provinces, came to be known after it as Renkvāls. In the

1. This Lakhanapāla was seventh in descent from Chandra. By assigning twenty years to each generation we arrive at about the same period which is assigned to the Gāhaḍvāl Chandra of Kanauj.

In the United Provinces this Lakhana is generally supposed to be a nephew of king Jayachandra, and I think that the author of the *Raso* has also somewhere in his work mentioned him as such.

'Apabhramsha' *Gahad* can easily be a corruption of *Gadhipura*.

It may also be noted that, when Rāo Sīhā, having severed all connections with Kanauj, migrated to Mārwār, he at once abandoned his surname Gāhadvāl and acknowledged himself as simple Rāshtrakūta.

We conclude that, when the power of the Padihārs became weak owing to the invasion of the Rāshtrakūta king Indrarāja III of the Deccan, their feudatories began to assume independence. Consequently in about V. S. 1111 some member of the Rāshtrakūta family, having carved out an independent state of Badāyūn, soon after took possession of Kanauj. Afterwards, when Jayachandra was killed and when, shortly after, Shams-ud-dīn began to drive out the Rāshtrakūtas from that region, Jayachandra's grandson Sīha migrated to Mārwār *via* Mahuvi.

Certain ruins at Mahuvi (Dist. Farrukhabad) are still called Sīhā-rāo-kā-khēdā.

Again, from a copper grant of Rāo Dhūhar, grandson of Rāo Sīhā, we gather that in his reign a Brahman had brought down the idol of their tutelary deity from Kanauj. Similarly, in the inscription of V. S. 1686 of Rāthōr Jagmal, the latter's ancestor Dhūhar is mentioned as Sūrya-vamshī Kanaujīyā Rāthōr.

Taking all these facts into consideration, we are led to believe that in reality the Rāshtrakūtas and the Gāhaḍvāls were of the same lineage. Besides this, in the *Rajatarangini* (written in the twelfth century of the Vikrama era) there is a mention of thirty-six clans of Kshatriyas, and in the *Kumarapala-charitra* (written in V. S. 1422), where thirty-six clans are enumerated, the Rāshtrakūta clan is designated "Rat", while no specific mention is made of Gāhadvāls.

Again, finding a mention of the name of Gōpāla and his successor Madanapāla in a Bauddha inscription of V. S. 1176 (A. D. 1118) from Set Māheth, and Gopāla being entitled therein as *"Gadhipuradhipa"*. or ruler of Kanauj, Mr. N. B. Sanyāl thinks that these two, Gopāla and Madana, were the ancestors of the aforesaid Rāshṭrakūṭa king Lakhanapāla of

Badāyūn; that Gopāla had acquired possession of Kanauj in the last quarter of the eleventh century of the Christian Era, sometime between the overthrow of the Pratihāra dynasty of Kanauj in A. D. 1020 (V. S. 1077) and the acquisition of that kingdom by Gāhaḍvāl Chandra in almost the last part of the eleventh century of the Christian Era, and that Gāhaḍvāl Chandra had seized the kingdom of Kanauj from Gōpāla, which accounts for the title of "*Gadhipuradhipa*" being affixed in the inscription of Set Māheṭh to the name of Gopāla alone, and not to that of his son Madana.

Further, Mr. Sanyāl quotes a stanza from the copper grant dated Shaka-S. 972 (A. D. 1050=V. S. 1107) of Trilōchanapāla found at Sūrat, in which there is a mention of the Rāshtrakūtas having ruled over Kanauj. Mr. Sanyāl supports this view on the basis of the Set Māheth inscription.

In regard to the above opinion the following points deserve consideration:—

There have been found a copper grant of Trilōchanapāla dated A. D. 1027 (V. S. 1084), and also an inscription of Yashahpāla, dated A. D. 1036 (V. S. 1093), from which we conclude that the Pratihāras held sway over Kanauj for some time even after this period. Moreover, a stanza in the copper grant[1] of the Gāhadvāl Chandra, dated V. S. 1148 (A. D. 1091), found at Chandrāvatī, runs as follows:—

तीर्थानि काशिकुशिकोत्तरकोसलेन्द्र-
स्थानीयकानि परिपालयताभिगम्य ।
हेमात्मतुल्यमनिशं ददता द्विजेभ्यो
येनाङ्किता वसुमती शतशस्तुलाभिः ॥

From this we understand the Chandra had conquered Kanauj long before the date of this inscription. The propositions that Chandra had conquered Kanauj in the last part of the eleventh century of the Christian Era and that the Rāshtrakūṭa Gōpāla of the Badāyūn inscription ruled over Kanauj in the last quarter of the eleventh century do not appeal to reason.

Again in the Badāyūn inscription it is thus stated about Madanapāla, successor of Gōpāla—

"यत्पौरुषात्प्रबलतः सुरसिन्धुतीरहम्मीरसंगमकथा न कदाचिदासीत्" (I ४)

i. e. "under the powerful influence of Madanapāla there was

1. *Epigraphia Indica*, Vol. ix, p 304.

no talk even of the Mohemmadans ever attempting an approach to the bank of the Ganges."

As to this Mr. Sanyāl himself thinks that Madanapāla may have fought with the Mohemmadans as a feudatory general in the army of the Gāhadvāl Gōvindachandra.

If it were so, it would be more open to question how the scribe, who delights in recording even the ordinary act of his patron's forefather Madana in having kept the Mohemmadans from the banks of the Ganges, forgot to take notice of such a great deed as the conquest of Kanauj by Madana's predecessor, Gōpāla ?

Mr. Sanyāl holds V. S. 1257 (A. D. 1200) as the probable date of the Rāshtrakūta Lakhana's Badāyūn inscription. This Lakhana was seventh in descent from Chandradēva. According to the prevalent practice of assigning a period of twenty years to each ruler, if we count back 140 years from the date V. S. 1257, we arrive at V. S. 1117 (A. D. 1060), as the time of Chandradēva of Badāyūn.

We have found a copper grant of V. S. 1148 (A. D. 1091) of Chandra of Kanauj, referring to his many past conquests and ceremonies; also we know that this Chandra retired from the throne in V. S. 1154 (A. D. 1097), having made over the kingdom to his son Madana, and died only three years after. From these facts we conclude that this Chandra was rather old at the time of issuing this copper grant (V. S. 1148); and this is further borne out by the fact that even his son Madana having attained old age, retired in V. S. 1161 (A. D. 1104), i. e., only four years after Chandra's death, and died in about V. S. 1167 (A. D. 1110).

Hence, to suppose that Chandra of Badāyūn is identical with him of Kanauj would not be improbable. The same Chandra, having acquired Badāyūn, may soon after have conquered Kanauj, as has been stated before.

In the circumstances, if we presume Gopāla of the Set Maheṭh inscription to be identical with the one mentioned in the Badāyūn inscription, it may be said that the scribe of the former inscription may have affixed the title *"Gadhipuradhipa"* to Gopāla in consideration of the Badāyūn family being closely related to the Kanauj family.

In the foregoing we have referred to the copper grant dated Shaka-S. 972 (V. S 1107=A. D. 1050) of Trilōchanapāla. This inscription has reference to some past, and not to any contemporary, Rāshtrakūtas of Kanauj. It therefore finds no support in the Set Māheth inscription.

Further, is it not strange that, owing to a fancied resemblance between the names of Yashōvigraha and Vigrahapāla and Mahīchandra and Mahīpāla, Dr. Hoernle came to the conclusion that the Gāhadvāls belonged to the Pāla Dynasty ? In the first place, the names of all the kings of the Pāla dynasty ended in the termination Pāla; secondly, Mahīpāla of the Pāla dynasty was a powerful king, while the Gāhadvāl Mahīchandra was not even an independent chief. Thirdly, in all the inscriptions of the Pāla kings, excepting one of Mahīpāla, the dates are given in their regnal years, whereas in all the inscriptions of the Gāhadvāl kings the Vikrama Samvat is used. Lastly, kings Dharmapāla and Rājyapāla of the Pāla Dynasty married the daughters of kings Parabala and Tunga respectively of the Rāshtrakūta dynasty, while, as shown above, the Rāshtrakūtas and Gāhadvāls were identical.

Some people hold the Rāshtrakūtas and the Gāhadvāls to be of distinct origins on the ground of their different *Gotras*. But Vijnānēshvara has clearly said—

राजन्यविशां....पुरोहितगोत्रप्रवरौ वेदितव्यौ

i. e. "the *Gotras* and *Pravaras* of kings accord with those of their priests."

Accordingly, having shifted their residence from one province to another, they may probably have been required to change their Purōhitas, and so their *Gotras* may also have changed.

The quotation given below from Ashvaghōsha's *Saundarananda-Mahakavya* will also be sufficient to show that the difference in *Gotras* does not necessarily indicate difference of the clans:—

गुरोर्गोत्रादतः कौत्सास्ते भवन्ति स्म गौतमाः ॥ २२ ॥
(सर्ग १)

i. e. "owing to the change of the priest they adopted Gautama's *Gotra* instead of their previous Kautsa *Gotra*".

Thus, on giving a careful consideration to the subject, the doubts raised against the collateralness of the Rāshtrakūtas and the Gāhadvāls will be seen to be groundless.

7. History of the Rashtrakutas and Prof. Majumdar.[1]

[Published in the Journal of Indian History, Madras, (April 1937 A.D), Vol. XVI, Part I. pp. 19-23]

A CRITICISM of my history of Rāshtrakūtas, by Professor R. C. Majūmdār of the Dacca University, was published in the 'Modern Review' of May 1934. There the Professor begins as under:—

"The title of the book is somewhat misleading as it is not a systematic history of the Rāshṭrakūṭas as it professes to be."

But can Dr. Majumdār mention the name of a more systematic history of Rāshtrakūtas published before the one in question ?

1. Then the Professor refers the Hāthī Gumphā and sātavāhana inscriptions. But I don't think they will go against the theory that at the time of "Mahābhārata" Rāshṭrakūtas lived in the Punjab and thence they migrated to the south. In the time of Ashōka they were at the north-western part of India, Saurāshṭra and Kalinga, and from these places they advanced towards the Deccan.

This is the only reason that we find mention of the dynasty in the edicts of Ashōka found in those provinces as well as in the Khārvēla inscription, of B. C. 165, of Hāthīgumphā and in the records of Sātavāhanas on the southern bank of the Gōdāvarī.

Sir George A. Grierson in his letter of 13-6-33 writes that "There are no less than five dialects in India called "Rāṭhī", and perhaps the most important is that spoken in the eastern Punjab. It is described in Volume IX, part I, pp. 610 and 696 of the 'Linguistic survey'. I there gave the local explanation of the word "Rāṭhī" as meaning ruthless but it is quite possibly really connected with "Rāshṭras"."

1. Vice Chancellor Dacca University.

2. The Professor hesitates to accept[1] the Rāshtrakūta sway over Kanauj prior to Chandradēva. But had it not been so how would it have been mentioned in the inscription of Sōlankī Trilōchanapāla of 1068 A.D., as Chandradēva took possession of Kanauj after that date.

3. The article of Pandit Ramkarna mentioned by Dr. Majumdār contains only 2 pages devoted to the hypothesis that the Gāhadvāls were a branch of Rāshtrakūtas while my book named 'Bhārata-kē-Prāchīna Rājavamsha', Vol. III, published in 1925 A.D., contains more proofs in support of the theory.

4. As regards the association of Gādhipura with the name of Gāhadvāl, I may point out that as a branch of Rāshtrakūtas has been called Renkwāl for their association with a village named Renkā and a branch of Chauhans owing to their being the masters of "Suvarnagiri", are known as Sōnagarā, in the like manner if a branch of Rāshtrakūtas came to be known as Gāhadvāl, owing to their association with 'Gādhipur', there seems no reason to disbelieve it.

5. As regards the classification of the Rāshtrakūtas as "Sūryavamshīs", I have given a number of proofs and have illustrated the mistakes committed by old writers.

Further the Professor writes that "while only six lines have been devoted to the art of Rāshtrakūtas, almost as many pages have been devoted to the determination of their gōtra and Vamsha". But he should note that the author considered it more important to deal fully with their Vamsha than art.

Going further the learned Professor writes—'The penultimate chapter of the first part entitled—"The Glory of the early Rāshtrakūtas" betrays the real motive of the author which is not so much to write a sober history of the Rāshtrakūtas as to make the present Rāthōds of Jodhpur shine in the reflected glory of the ancient Rāshtrakūtas.'

I think the expression of such views is only due to prejudice, or to ignorance of the facts and to remove this I give below the summary of the chapter devoted to the "Glory of the

1. In this connection, he may also see 'Indian Antiquary', Vol. III, p 41, and Bombay Gazetteer Vol V, p. 329.

latter Rāshtrakūṭas" in the second volume of the history, at present, in press:—

The Ghōsuṇḍī inscription[1] of Mahārāṇā Rāyamal, of Mewar, dated V.S. 1561 (1504 A.D.), contains:—

श्रीयोधक्षितिपतिरुग्रखड्गधारानिर्घातप्रहतपठानपारशीकः ।
पूर्वानतार्प्सीद्गयया विमुक्तया काश्यां सुवर्णैर्विपुलैर्विपश्चितः ॥

i.e. Rāo Jōdhā killed the Pathāns and Persians by his sword.

He satisfied his ancestors by freeing the holy city of Gayā from the tax, and pleased the scholars by giving a huge quantity of gold in charity at Kāshī (Benares).

Muhammad Kāsim in his "Tārīkh-i-Farishtā", which he wrote in V.S. 1671, states[2]:—

Shērshāh, at the end of the battle fought with Rāo Māldēva's army, abruptly uttered—"Praise be to God by whose grace, anyhow, I have achieved the victory, otherwise I would have lost the kingdom of Hindustān for a handful of Bājrā."

Abulfazal in his 'Akbarnāmā'[3] mentions Rāo Māldēva as the greatest ruler among the Rāos and Rājās of the time.

The author of "Tuzuk-i-Jahāngīrī[4]" refers to Rāo Māldēva holding larger territory and bigger army than Mahārānā Sāngā (Sangrāmsingh I of Mewar). The numerical strength of Māldēva's army is given as 80,000.

A poet of Rājasthān describes Mahārānā Pratāp and Rāo Chandrasēn, son and successor of Rāo Māldēva, as under:—

अणदगिया तुरी ऊजला असमर, चाकर रहण न डिगियौ चीत ।
सारे हिन्दुस्थान तणै सिर, पातल ने चन्द्रसेण प्रवीत ॥

i.e. Mahārāṇā Pratāp and Rāo Chandrasēn were only two persons who neither accepted the suzerainıty of the Mughal emperor nor allowed their horses to be branded with Akbar's mark.

Besides this Mahārānā Pratāp himself followed the path trodden by Rāo Chandrasēn some ten years back.

1. Journal Bengal Asiatic Society, Vol 56, part I, No. 2.
2. Vol. I, chapter 2, p 228.
3. Vol. II, p. 160.
4. Preface, p 7.

"Ālamgīr Nāmā"[1] mentions Mahārājā Jaswantsingh I as being the greatest of all in power and prestige and a pillar of the Mughal empire

The author of 'Maāsir-ul-Umrā'[2] writes that this Mahārājā Jaswantsingh I, due to his largest army and biggest paraphernalia, was the greatest of all the rulers of Hindustān.

He demolished mosques and built temples[3] in their places even in the time of emperor Aurangzēb and the emperor dared not lay 'Jaziā' as long as the Mahārājā survived, but was able to impose it only after his death.[4]

Mahārājā Ajitsingh, the son of Mahārājā Jaswant I, joined hands with 'Sayyad' brothers and massacring emperor Farrukhsiyar placed in succession three emperors on the throne of Delhi.

The chivalry of Rāthōd Durgādās is well known to almost every Indian.

As regards the magnanimity of the Rāthōrs the author of 'Sehr-ul-Mutākharīn'[5] states:—

"After fighting for some time when the army of Amīr-ul-Umrā (Zulfi-kār-Jang) was confounded owing to lack of water the opponent Rāthōr army of Mahārājā Rāmsingh of Marwar quenched the thirst of his men and horses by supplying water freely and then bidding them go unmolested."

As regards Mahārājā Bakhatsingh Col. Tod writes[6]:—

"....and but for that one damning crime[7], he would have been handed down to posterity as one of the noblest princes Rājwārā ever knew."

1. P. 82.
2. Vol. III, p. 608.
3. Sarkar's History of Aurangzeb, Vol. III pp 368-369
4. V. A. Smith's Oxford History of India, p. 488.
5. Vol. III, p. 885.
6. Annals and Antiquities of Rajasthan (Ed. by Crooke), Vol. II, p. 1057.
7. Committed under special circumstances (see Indian Antiquary, Vol. LVIII, pp. 47-51.)

The Colonel further states[1]:—

"The Moghal emperors were indebted for half their conquest to the 'Lākh Tarwār Rāthōrān', the 1,00,000 swords of the Rāthōrs."

Further in the recent Great War, besides the help given by other Rāthōr rulers, Mahārājā Sumērsingh of Jodhpur, aged only 16 years, and his grand uncle Mahārājā Pratāpsingh, aged 69, laid an example before the princely order by voluntarily joining the armies in the field.

The chivalry shown by the Jodhpur lancers in the eastern front, during the Great War, can be judged by the speech[2] of Lord Chelmsford, the Viceroy and the Governor-General of India, delivered at Jodhpur, wherein he said:—

"By their exploits at Haifa and in the Jorden valley they recalled the deeds of their ancestors who fought at Tongā, Mērtā and Pātan. The reputation which they have gained is well worthy of the glorious annals of Marwar."

Now I only quote two more events of individual Rāthōr chivalry from Akbarnāmā. Abulfazal writes:—

(1) "That when the army of Akbar invaded Mērtā, in the time of Rāo Māldēva, Rāthōr Dēvīdās came out of the fort with his four hundred followers, and fought in such a way against the vast army of Mughals that the people who witnessed the event forgot the well-known warrior Rustam[3]".

(2) "That when Akbar invaded Chittor Rānā Udaisingh was obliged to seek shelter in the mountains leaving the responsibility of guarding the fort, against the enemy, upon the shoulders of Rāthōr Jaimal. And as long as this Rāṭhōr warrior survived Akbar did not get a chance to capture the fort.

1. Annals and Antiquities of Rajasthan (Ed. by Crooke), Vol. I, pp. 105-106.
2. Delivered on 20th November, 1920.
3. Akbarnāmā, Vol. II, pp. 162.

It only slipped into the hands of the Mughal emperor[1] after Jaimal's death."

These few facts, I think, will convince the scholars that the Rāthōrs are famous for their chivalry and magnanimity and for this they are called—'रण-बंका राठोड़'

As regards the glorious military exploits of Dhruvarāja and Gōvindarāja III, if the Professor will go through carefully the history of these two rulers given in the book his doubts will soon be removed.

In conclusion, scholars will judge for themselves, by the words of Dr. Majumdār used in his criticism of the book, how far he was prejudiced against the writer, the book and the dynasty with which it deals.

1 Akbarnāmā Vol II pp 320-321

APPENDIX B.

1. Pali inscription of the time of Chalukya (Solanki) Kumarpala, dated V.S. 1209

[Published in Indian Culture, Calcutta, Vol II, No 1, (1936 A D.) pp. 136-138.]

This inscription has been inscribed on a pillar, in the 'Sabhāmandapa' of the temple of Sōmnāth at Pali, a town, situated 40 miles south-east of Jodhpur. It was first noticed by Dr. D. R Bhandarkar in the Proceedings of the Royal Asiatic Society, WC. 1907-08, p. 45. It is dated the 4th day of the dark half of second Jyēshtha, V. S. 1209. The year being a Shrāvanādi it corresponds to 13th May, 1153 A. D. It consists of twenty lines and covers a space of 1′ 7″×1′ 6″. The characters belong to the northern type of alphabets, and as regards orthography it is needless to write anything as its middle part from lines fifth to twentieth has peeled off. Though this state of the inscription has deprived people of the knowledge about the object of the inscription, yet the matter which has escaped the hands of time has preserved very valuable information for the history of the Rāthōr rulers of Mārwār.

The first seven lines of the inscription state that in Vikram Samvat 1209 (1153 A. D.) the town of Pali was under the kingdom of (Sōlankī-Chālukya) Kumārapāla[1] of Anahillapātan (Gujrat), who subdued the king of Shākambharī (Sāmbhar), and his feudatory Bāhadadēva was in charge of the place (Pali). Most probably he might have been a Chauhān Rājpūt related to Chauhān Ālhanadēva of Kirādū as an inscription[2] of the same year (V. S. 1209=1152 A. D.) found at Kirādū states

1. He ruled from V S 1199 to 1230 (1142 to 1173 A.D.)
2. Epigraphia Indica, Vol XI, P. 45

that Chauhān Ālhanadēva was a favourite of Kumārapāla and had acquired the possessions of Kirāḍū, Rādadhaḍā, and Shiva due to his favour. From the death of king Kumārapāla, about V. S. 1230 (1173 A. D.),[1] the power of the Chālukyas began to decline. The inscription dated V. S. 1319 (1262 A. D.) of Chauhān Chāchigdēva states that his (Chāchigadēva's) father Udayasimha, who was a great-grandson of the aforesaid Ālhanadēva, held an independent sway over Nādōl, Jālōr, Maṇdōr, Bāhadmēr, Ratanapur, Sānchōr, Surāchand, Rādadhadā, Khēd, Rāmsīn and Bhīnmāḷ. We have got four inscriptions of this Udayasimha ranging from V. S. 1262 to V. S. 1306.

All this prove that in the beginning of the thirteenth century of Vikrama era, Pali was under the rule of the Chālukyas and then it passed away to the Chauhāns as is evident from the situation of the towns mentioned in the Sūndhā inscription of V. S. 1319. It never remained under Pallīwāl Brāhmans and therefore Rāo Sīhā, the founder of the Rāṭhōr dynasties of Jodhpur, Bikānēr, Kishangarh, Īdar, Ratlām, Sītāmau, Sailāna, Jhābuā, etc. had no occasion to murder the Brāhmans of Pali treacherously to usurp the town as is stated by Lt.-Col Tod in his Annals and Antiquities of Rājasthān (Vol. II, pp. 942-943). There he has written:—

"At this period a community of Brahmans held the city and extensive lands about Pali, from which they were termed Paliwal; and being greatly harassed by the incursions of the mountaineers, the Mers and Minas, they called in the aid of Sihaji's band, which readily undertook and executed the task of rescuing the Brahmans from their depredations. Aware that they would be renewed, they offered Sihaji lands to settle amongst them, which were readily accepted; and here he had a son by the Solankani, to whom he gave the name of Asvatthama. With her, it is recorded, the suggestion originated to make himself lord of Pali; and it affords another example of the disregard of the early Rajputs for the sacred order, that on the Holi, or Saturnalia, he found an opportunity to "obtain land", putting to death the heads of this community, and adding the district to his conquests. Sihaji outlived his treachery only twelve months, leaving his acquisitions as a nucleus for further additions to his children."

1. Epigraphia Indica, Vol. IX, P. 78

But his unauthentic statement cannot stand before the Pali inscription reproduced below:—

१-ॐ सं० १२०६ द्वि० ज्येष्ठ वदि ४ अद्येह पल्लिकायां श्रीमदणहिल-
२-पाटकाधिष्ठितसमस्तराजावलीविराजितपरमभट्टारकमहारा-
३-जाधिराजपरमेश्वरउमापतिवरलब्धप्रौढप्रतापनिजभुजविक्रम-
रणांग-
४-णविनिर्जितशाकंभरीभूपाल श्रीमत्कुमारपालदेवकल्याणविजयरा-
५-ज्ये तत्पादपद्मोपजीवि ········ श्रीकरणादौ सम-
६-स्त पोरारपारपथ अद्येह श्रीमत्पल्लिकाधि-
७-ष्ठित समस्त श्री विराजमान श्रीवाहडदेव प्रति-
८-पत्तौ नेत्रपाला
९-नीजा समदंत जावेरद्द
१०-धर्म्म तस्यका
११- विंश
१२- नकरणी-
१३- हराजेक
१४- करापितो
१५- श्रीनदूल
१६- भावि
१७- यत् नाति तन्व
१८-ते दत्तहर
१९-यितः रक।
२०-से सूत्र० केल्हणेन

2. False challenge against the seniority of the Jodhpur House

Published in the special number of the Journal of Indian History, Madras.
Vol. XX, pt. 1 (April 1941) pp 22—27.

Rao Jōdhājī, the founder of Jodhpur had 20 sons.—

Nīmbājī the eldest of them was wounded while fighting with Sīndhal Jaisā in 1521 V. S. (1464 A. D.) and died after five months in Jōdhājī's lifetime.

Jōgājī, the second son, according to old chronicles, being a lazy fellow, was discarded by his father and the nobles of Marwar. He was deprived of the throne of Marwar and was obliged to rest content with some villages in the Bilārā District. We learn from an inscription found at the village Khāriā that he died in 1570 V. S. (1513 A. D.)

Sātaljī, the third son, who was born in 1492 V. S. (1435 A. D.), succeeded his father after his death, in 1546 V. S. (1489 A. D.), and died in 1549 V. S. (1492 A. D.).

Sūjājī, the fourth son, who according to the chronicles, was born in 1496 V. S. (1439 A. D.), ascended the throne of Marwar, after the demise of his elder brother Sātaljī.

Bīkājī, the fifth son, accompanied by his uncle Kāndhaljī and helped by Jāt Nikōdar and Sānkhalā Nāpā etc., went towards Jānglū and subduing Jāts, Sānkhlās and Bhātīs, founded Bīkānēr in or about 1542 V. S. (1485 A. D.).

In the chronicles of Marwar his birth-year is given as 1497 V. S. (1440 A. D.), while in those of Bīkānēr as 1495 V. S. (1438 A. D.).

The History of Bīkānēr written by Munshī Sōhan Lāl, the Additional Member of the Regency Council, Bīkānēr, and published in 1947 V. S. (1890 A. D.) states:—

> "Bīkājī the sixth and Bīdājī the twelfth son of Jōdhājī were born of the same mother. The former, who was born in 1495 V. S. (1439 A. D.), went towards the north of Marwar, in 1522 V. S (1465 A. D.) and there with the help of Nāpā Sānkhlā etc., established his new State.
>
> In 1546 V. S. (1489 A. D.) his uncle Kāndhaljī was killed at Hisār, while commanding the Bīkānēr forces and therefore Bīkājī with the help of his own father Jōdhājī avenged his death and killed Sārang Khān. While back at Drōnpur Jōdhājī asked his son Bīkājī not to demand any share from Jodhpur and present the town of Lādnū to him. Bīkājī agreed to it but at the same time requested his father that if indeed he considered him a worthy son he should also grant him the insignias of the Royalty brought from Kannauj. As the request was granted, but those articles were not handed over, Bīkājī after the death of Jōdhājī and his successor Sātāljī attacked Jodhpur and obliged his brother Sūjājī, the then ruler, to deliver those articles to him" (see pp.89-104).

This clearly shows that Bīkājī was the fifth or the sixth son of Jōdhājī and he went towards Jānglū and there, with the help of his uncle Kāndhaljī, Jāt Nikōdar, Shānkhlā Nāpā, etc., took advantage of the internal dissensions of the petty land-holders and subduing Jāts, Sānkhlās, and Bhātīs established his new estate. In time when he grew stronger and his father asked him to give up the share of Marwar and present the town of Lādnū to him, he, in turn, requested him (Jōdhājī) to accept his estate as an independent State and for this sort of recognition also grant him all the insignias, required for an independent ruler. This request, it seems, was made to avoid any future claim of sovereignty of the Jodhpur branch over Bīkānēr as was the case with the estates of other brothers of Bīkājī, namely, Dūdājī, Karamsījī, Rāyapāljī, etc.

Further the Jodhpur Branch of the Rāthōr rulers enjoys undisputed seniority among all the present Rāthōr States in India and is recognized as the premier branch of the Rāthōr rulers by all the other States as well as by the Government.

In November 1912 when His Excellency the Viceroy visited Bīkānēr, Mahārājā Ganga Singhjī, the present ruler of the State, himself in his State banquet speech, said.--

"In this connection may I be permitted as one who is closely associated by family ties and as senior in age of the rulers of the Rathore States in Rajputana, to say how indebted we are for the arrangements which Your Excellency was pleased to make for the administration of the Jodhpur State during the minority of His Highness the Maharaja."

(Report on the administration and Pioneer, 2nd December 1912).

This also proves that up till 1912 A.D. His Highness Bīkānēr considered himself senior only in the age, but not in lineage or rank.

But Dr. Gauri Shankar Hira Chand Ojha has made a departure from this well established fact in his "Rājpūtanē-kā-Itihās", Vol. IV, without any sound basis and for the reasons best known to himself. Let us now, with due respect, examine his proofs and arguments. He writes:—

"बीका सातल से बड़ा न रहा हो अथवा उसने पिता को वचन दिया था इस कारण से सातल के गद्दी पर बैठने पर उसने कोई हस्ताक्षेप न किया, परन्तु जब सूजा ने सातल की मृत्यु पर जोधपुर की गद्दी अपने हाथ में करली तब तो बीका ने ससैन्य उस पर चढ़ाई करदी। इस चढ़ाई का उल्लेख जोधपुर तथा बीकानेर की ख्यातों में मिलता है।"

....

"उक्त ख्यातों आदि के अनुसार यह स्पष्ट हो जाता है कि बीका, कमसे कम सूजा से अवश्य बड़ा था, जिनसे तख्त, चमर, भुंजाई की देग आदि पूजनीय वस्तुएं उसे प्राप्त हुई"

(जिल्द चौथी, खण्ड प्रथम, पृ० २५७-५८)

" i.e. Bīkā might not have been elder than Sātal, or owing to the promise given by him to his father he did not interfere when Sātal ascended the throne. But when on his demise Sūjā usurped the throne of Jodhpur, Bīkā invaded it as is evident from the chronicles of Jodhpur and Bīkānēr."

According to those chronicles it becomes clear that atleast Bīkā was really elder than Sūjā hence he got the throne, the fly-flaps (an insignia of royalty), the big frying pot, etc., the things of adoration.

We are unable to understand that when Dr Ojha himself accepts the seniority of Sātaljī and when Sūjājī was his (Sātaljī's) successor, what led him to challenge the seniority of the Jodhpur House.

According to Jodhpur chronicles and horoscopes it is quite clear that Sūjājī was older than Bīkājī by one year. But if we suppose him younger than Bīkājī, by one year, does Dr. Ojha mean that if a member of a senior house adopts a younger brother or his son, the senior house loses its seniority?

So far as history is concerned Jodhpur was the seat of the Government of Jōdhājī the father of Bīkājī, and was succeeded by Sātaljī, the elder brother of Bīkājī, and if he (Sātaljī) adopted one of the younger brothers of Bīkājī (though it has not yet been proved) Bīkānēr cannot claim its seniority over Jodhpur.

Moreovor Dr. Ojha himself writes:—

"इन जन्म पत्रियों में परस्पर विभिन्नता होने के कारण कौनसी विश्वसनीय है यह कहना कठिन है।"

....

"ख्यातों आदि में प्राय. कुंवरों के नाम राणियों के नामों के साथ दिये रहते है, अतएव उनके आधार पर पुत्रों के छोटे-बड़े होने का निर्णय करना कठिन प्रतीत होता है।"

(राजपूताने का इतिहास, जिल्द ४, खण्ड १, पृ० २५७ और २५८)

"i.e. there being differences in these horoscopes, it is very difficult to decide which of these is correct".

....

"In the chronicles the names of the princes are given with the names of their mothers, hence the decision of their seniority, on the basis of this, becomes difficult".

These are again the clear admissions that there is no basis for this challenge.

Let us now examine the verses quoted from a poem named "Karmachandravamshōtkīrtan" composed by Jayasōma, in 1650 V.S. (1593 A.D.) while residing at Lahore:—

"नींबा सूजा सातल नाम सुतत्रययुता महाराज्ञी ।
जसमादेवी नाम्नी राज्ञो जीवस्य सर्वस्वम् ॥ ११० ॥
नींबाख्ये संजाते दैवनियोगात्सुते कथाशेषे ।
जातिस्वभावदोषाज्जातामर्षा सपत्नीषु ॥ १११ ॥
विक्रमनामसपत्नीसुतेऽसति स्वात्मजे कथां रम्यां ।
भावीति विभाव्यात्मनि विजने राजानमाचष्टे ॥ ११२ ॥
ततो निजात्मजं जाया मायया मोहितोऽधिपः ।
विक्रमं जांगले मोक्तुं समाहूयेदमुक्तवान् ॥ ११३ ॥
पित्र्यं राज्यं सुतो भुंक्ते किं चित्रं तत्र नन्दन ! ।
नव्यं राज्यं य आदत्ते स धत्ते सुतधुर्यताम् ॥ ११४ ॥
तेन देशोऽस्ति दुःसाधो जांगलो जगतीतले ।
त्वं साहसीति कृत्येऽस्मिन्नियुक्तोऽसि मयाधुना ॥ ११५ ॥

"वि० सं० १६५० में लाहोर में रहते समय जयसोम द्वारा रचे हुए 'कर्मचन्द्रवंशोत्कीर्तन' काव्य में लिखा है:—"दूसरी महाराणी जसमादेवी के तीन लड़के नींबा, सूजा और सातल नाम के थे और वह राजा का जीवन सर्वस्व थी। जब दैवयोग से नींबा नाम के पुत्र की कथा ही बाकी रह गई (अर्थात् वह मर गया) तब जसमादेवी ने जिसे स्त्री स्वभाव से अपनी सौतों के प्रति द्वेष उत्पन्न हुआ यह होनहार ही है, ऐसा सोचकर एकांत में विक्रम नाम के अपनी सौत के पुत्र की अनुपस्थिति में राजा को अपने पुत्र के विषय की कुछ रोचक कथा कही। तब राजा ने पत्नी के कपट से मोहित होकर अपने बेटे विक्रम (बीका) को जांगल देश में निकाल देने की इच्छा से अपने पास बुलाकर कहा–हे पुत्र ! बाप के राज्य को बेटा भोगे इसमें कोई अचरज की बात नहीं, परन्तु जो नया राज्य प्राप्त करे वही बेटों में मुख्य गिना जाता है। पृथ्वी पर कठिनता से वश में आनेवाला जांगल नामक देश है, तू साहसी है इसलिए तुझे मैंने इस काम मे (अर्थात् उसे वश करने में) नियुक्त किया है।"

(जिल्द ४, खण्ड १, पृ० २५५-२५६)

"i. e., Another queen Jasmādēvī had three sons-Nīmbā, Sūjā and Sātāl by name, and she was the light of the king's soul. When as destined, nothing but the story of Nīmbā was left (i.e. he died), then Jasmādēvī, who according to her sex weakness, became jealous of the other queens thinking this to be an act of fate, one day in the absence of Vikram, son of the other queen, narrated some interesting stories about her (own) son, when the King was alone. The king enamoured by the viles of the queen called his son Vikram (Bīkā) and with the intention of driving him away in Jāngal district, said "O son! there is nothing new if a son enjoys the state of his father, but he, who acquires new state, is considered worthy of all. On the surface of this earth, the district of Jāngal is difficult to be conquered: you are brave and therefore I appoint you to carry out this task". (Vol. IV, part I, pp. 255-256.)

Our objections regarding it are as under:—

(1) That the poem is composed by a poet who himself belonged to Bīkānēr and was also connected through Karmachandra with its ruler.

(2) That the order in which the names of the three sons of the queen Jasmādēvī are given in the verse 110, betrays the ignorance of the author, as Sātal is admitted on all hands to have been elder to Sūjā, and therefore had he written the first part of the verse as नींवा सातल सूजा there would have been no difficulty in the meter.

(3) That the verse 112 is itself grammatically incorrect or confusing.

(4) That the translation of the verse 112 given on p. 255 of Dr. Ojha's history shows the ignorance of the translator

(5) That the author of the poem himself in the face of the well established facts about the seniority of Jodhpur house and Sātaljī, the successor of Jōdhājī, could not dare use a single word to repudiate the fact directly, but simply tried to flatter his patron, the ruler of Bīkānēr indirectly.

(6) The seniority of Sātaljī to Bīkājī is already admitted by the chronicles of Jodhpur and Bīkānēr as well as by Dr. Ojha himself and therefore against that well established fact the hypothesis of this poem falls to the ground in the eyes of the scholars.

Further Jodhpur was founded by Rāo Jōdhājī, the father of Bīkājī, and when Bīkājī was trying to establish Bīkānēr, the former (Jodhpur) was a well established and larger parental State, which helped Bīkājī to conquer the tract of Jāngal and prepare the ground for a new state.

Moreover even against all the well established facts given above, if we accept Dr. Ojha's supposition that Bīkājī was the eldest son of Rāo Jōdhājī, it makes no difference whatsoever as we find that Rāo Chūndājī, Rāo Māldēvjī, Rājā Udayasinghji, Rājā Gajsinghjī, etc., the rulers of the same ruling family, selected for one reason or the other their younger sons to succeed them, but the estates of the eldest sons could not deprive the Jodhpur line of its seniority.

We think we have fully discussed the facts, and if in Dr. Ojha's Vth volume there will be some fresh proofs to establish his theory, we will again try to discuss their merits.

3 Rao Chandrasen, a forgotten Hero of Rajputana.

Read at the Sixth All India Oriental Conference held at Patna in December 1930 A. D. and published in its proceedings and transactions pp 153 168

Its major portion was also published in Indian Antiquary, vol LXII, (1933 A. D) pp 29-34.

The name of the magnanimous hero, Mahārānā Pratāp of Mewar, and the memory of his noble deeds thrill the heart of every true Indian—young or old—with emotion even to this day. But the name of Rāo Chandrasēn, the first hero of Rājasthān, who, in protecting his independence against the covetousness of the great Moghal Emperor Akbar, sacrificed his ancestral throne and took all the calamities upon himself; and whose trodden path was followed by Mahārānā Pratāp after a period of about 10 years, looks quite new to history. Aye, the very name of such a great hero is lost in his own domains by circumstances.

Short summary of the life of Pratap.

Mahārānā Pratāp was born on the 3rd day of the bright half of Jyēshtha Vikram Samvat 1597 (9th May, 1540 A. D.) and ascended the throne of Mewar in V. S. 1628 (1572 A. D), when many districts of his country had passed under the sway of the Moghals and his own brothers had rebelled against him. In spite of all these calamities he opened life-long hostilities with Emperor Akbar, to deliver his ancestral capital Chittor from him and missed no opportunity of breaking down from his impregnable mountain fastness upon the imperial odds. The Islamites, too, left no stone unturned to compel him to subjugation. On one occasion the imperial army being defeated either took to their heels or dispersed; while on another the Mahārānā had to seek shelter in the impregnable mountains.

This state of affairs lasted up to A. D. 1586 (V. S. 1643), when Akbar's attention was diverted to the affairs of Punjab. And the Mahārānā getting some rest regained some of his lost districts, but he could not acquire the possession of Chittor in his life-time and took away this sorrow to the grave.

Such is the brief summary of the noble deeds of Mahārānā Pratāp, and for such inflexible honour, bravery and patriotism, he, in spite of the lapse of over three and a quarter of a century,[1] is honoured in the hearts of all the lovers of freedom.

But now scholars will judge for themselves how the nature of our hero, whose life we are going to narrate here, compares with that of the Mahārānā.

Life of Rao Chandrasen

Rāo Chandrasēn, the hero of this biographical sketch, was born on the 8th day of the dark half of Shrāvaṇa, V.S. 1598 (16th July, 1541 A.D.). He was the sixth[2] son of Rāo Māldēv,[3] the well-known and powerful ruler of Marwar, who, by the force of his arms, had acquired supremacy among all the contemporary rulers of Rājpūtānā, with whom shelter was sought by Humāyūn,[4] the Emperor of India in his days of adversity and by whose overwhelming might the pride of Shēr Shāh,[5] the Pathān Emperor of India, had been crushed. Towards the close of the reign of this eminent Rāo a large part of his dominion had gone out of his possession due to family discord.

---

1 Mahārānā Pratāp died on the 11th day of the bright half of Māgh, V. S. 1653 (19th January, 1597 A. D.)

2 When only a child of three, i. e. in V. S. 1600 (1543 A. D) he was granted the big fiefship of Sīwānā and Bīsalpur, where he used to live when of age. A day after his father's death he hastened to Jodhpur to try his luck in taking the reins of government in his hands according to the wish of his father. When a king, he granted that fief of Sīwānā to his elder brother Rāo Rāymal (the 2nd son of the deceased Rāo).

3 In the preface to the *Tuzuk-i-Jahangiri* it is stated 'Rāo Māldēv was a very great and powerful Rājā whose army consisted of 80,000 cavalry Although Rānā Sāngā, who had fought with Bābar, possessed equal wealth and ammunition yet in respect of dominions and arms, Rāo Māldēv surpassed him. Whenever Rāo Māldēv fought with Rānā Sāngā the former was victorious.'

4 In the *Tabaqat-i-Akbari* it is stated· 'The Emperor Humāyūn, obliged by circumstances, started towards Māldēv who was, at that time, among the big Rājās of Hindustān and to whom no other Rājā was equal in respect of power and army.' (Page 205)

5 Shēr Shāh on his victory was obliged to utter these words —'Thank God, at any cost victory has been attained, otherwise I would have lost the Empire of Hindustān for a handful of millets' (*Tarikh Farishta*, part I, page 228 and *Muntakhibullubab*, part I, page 101).

On the demise of Rāo Māldēv, Rāo Chandrasēn, in accordance with the wishes of his father, was installed upon the throne of Marwar on the first day of the dark half of Mārgashīrsha, V. S. 1619 (11th November, 1562 A. D.), shortly after which some of his nobles, being displeased with him on an insignificant incident[1], began to intrigue with his three elder brothers[2]. They persuaded them to raise trouble in different quarters. His eldest brother Rām rebelled in Sōjat, the second Rāymal towards Dundāḍā, while the third Udayasingh having made a surprising attack took the two villages Bāoḍī and Gāngānī. At this Rāo Chandrasēn immediately marched against Udayasingh who, relinquishing the possession of his newly acquired villages, retreated towards Phalōdī. At Lōhāwaṭ however, he was overtaken and wounded by the Rāo in a battle which resulted in a victory for the latter. After some time Rāo Chandrasēn again prepared to invade Phalōdī at the time when the power of the Moghal Emperor Akbar was fast rising. But some considerate nobles intervened and made peace between the two brothers, as they (nobles) apprehended danger to the Rāthōr power through family dissensions at such a time.

In 1620 V. S. (1563 A. D.) the Rāo led an army against his eldest brother Rām. At first Rām came out and opposed the army of the Rāo at Nàdōl[3]. But seeing no chance of victory he went to Husain Qulī Bēgh, the imperial Hākim at Nāgaur, stated his prior claim by primogeniture to the throne of Mārwār; and asked for help. Husain Qulī seeing a chance of benefitting himself by this internal discord readily accepted the proposal and suddenly laid a siege to Jōdhpur. The Rāo fought for some days, but being obliged by the shortage of provision had to make peace[4], and agreed to restore Sojat to

1 An offender, having deserted the court of Rāo, took shelter with one of the nobles named Jaitmāl (son of Jaisā). When he was arrested and brought back, the said noble requested the Rāo to punish him in any way other than death. Incensed at this uncalled for interference the Rāo ordered the unfortunate wretch to be instantly put to death. Jaitmāl and his colleagues did not like it.

2 At this time the three elder brothers of the Rāo were in their respective Jāgīrs. The eldest Rām was at Sōjat, the second Rāymal at Siwānā and the third Udayasingh at Phalōdī.

3 Another version is that it was Rāo Rām, who, with the assistance of Mahārānā Udaysingh had at first marched out in order to obtain the throne of Mārwār.

4 It is stated in *Tarikh-i-Palanpur* (part I, page 77) 'That Mirzā Sharfuddīn rebelled against Akbar and invaded Mērtā after the demise of Rāo Māldēv, and that Rāo Chandrasēn saved Mērtā by concluding a peace with him in 1615 V. S (1559 A. D.).' These facts are doubtful, for Merta had been made over to Jaimal by Sharfuddīn during the life-time of Rāo Māldēv. After this when Sharfuddīn rebelled Akbar took Mērtā from Jaimal and made it over to Jagmāl. Sharfuddīn rebelled in 1620 V S. (1563 A. D =971 A. H.) while Rāo Māldēv died in 1619 V. S.

Rām and to pay indemnities of war to Husain Qulī Bēgh. As a consequence of this the possessions of the Rāo were limited to the districts of Jōdhpur, Jaitāran and Pōkaran only. But after the return of the Mohemmadan army the terms of the treaty were not fulfilled to the satisfaction of Rām. He, therefore, approached the Emperor in 1621 V. S (1564 A.D.) for help. As this was a good chance for the Emperor (Akbar) to avenge his father's[1] wrongs, he accepted the request of Rām and sent an army under Muzaffar Khān.

Simultaneously he ordered Husain Qulī Bēgh to dispossess the Rāo of Jōdhpur and settle Rām at Sōjat. Husain Qulī, accordingly, laid siege to Jōdhpur, but the Rāo bravely defended the fort. When the imperial army failed to take the fort by open attack it attempted to enter it by an inlet[2] towards the Rānīsāgar tank, but in vain.

As the siege continued for many months the provision failed, the leading sardars therefore prevailed upon the Rāo to escape from the fort. He reluctantly, went to Bhādrājan[3] with his family while his Sardārs, who remained behind, fought in open battle and died glorious deaths. The imperial army then got the possession of the fort.

The following is an extract from *Akbarnama*[4]:—

'After the accession of Chandrasēn to the throne Husain Qulī Bēgh and the imperial army besieged Jōdhpur. Hearing this, Rām, the eldest son of Rāo Māldēv, came and joined them. The officers of the army sent him to the Court where he was received by the Emperor with due honour. The latter sent him to Husain Qulī Bēgh with a fresh army under Muinuddīn Khān and others. The imperial army soon took the fort.'

The Rāo collecting men and money began to harass the Mohemmadans now and then.

---

1 When Humāyūn had sought the assistance of Rāo Māldēv against Shērshāh his followers had slaughtered a cow in Mārwār. Displeased with this the Rāo (Māldēv) had desisted from helping him and Humāyūn had to turn back disappointed.

2 This inlet was meant for carrying water to the fort from the tank.

3 This event is stated in the chronicles to have occurred on the 12th day of the dark half of Mārgashīrsha, V. S. 1622 (19th November, 1565 A. D.).

4 *Akbarnama*, Vol. II, page 197.

In 1627 V. S. (1570 A. D.=978 A. H.) when the Emperor after visiting Ajmēr reached Nāgaur, many princes of Rājpūtānā attended his court[1] there. The Rāo, too, went there to read his mind, and was received by the Emperor with due honour. His intimate desire was that if the Rāo were to own his allegiance even in name he might restore Jōdhpur to him. But the unbending nature of the Rāo defied all courtly allurements and he returned to Bhādrājan rejecting the offers of the Emperor.

Soon after this the imperial army laid siege to Bhādrājan while the Rāo defended it for some time. As the provision here, too, failed he went to Sīwānā.

In 1629 V.S. (1572 A.D.) he made a recruiting tour and on his way when encamped at Kānujā (district Jaitāran) Ratan, son of Khīnvā, the chieftain of Āsarlāī, disregarded the summons of his court. The Rāo, therefore, marched on Āsarlāī and laid it waste.

Next year (1630 V.S.=1573 A.D.) the inhabitants of the town of Bhināya (district Ajmēr) approached him for protection against the depredations of Mādaliā, the Bhīl chieftain. Accepting their appeal the Rāo attacked the residence of the Bhīl. As many other Bhīls of the neighbourhood happened to be at his residence to join some ceremony, they all took up arms to repulse the attack. But as soon as Mādaliā was killed they all fled[2] away leaving the place and the district in the possession of the Raō.

---

1 Udaysingh, the third son of Rāo Māldēv, and Rāo Kalyānmal and his son Rāyasingh of Bīkānēr, etc., had had an interview with Emperor at this place The Emperor deputed Udaysingh to suppress the Gūjar rising in Samāolī and kept prince Rāyasingh in the court, to whom afterwards the administration of Jōdhpur was also entrusted. Prince Rām was also appointed in Jodhpur to participate in guarding the highway to Gujrāt.

It is stated in Tabaqāt-i Akbarī that Akbar reached Nāgaur on the 16th Jamādiul Akhir, 977 A.H (3rd day of the dark half of Paush, 1626 V S =26th November, 1569 A.D) and sojourned there for 50 days (page 289) But in the 'Akbarnāmā" this event is said to have occurred in 978 A.H. (1570 A.D.). (Vol II, pages 357-58).

2 From that day the following proverb is prevalent in Marwar—
'मादलियो मारियो नै गोठ बीखरी,' i e as soon as Mādaliā (the Bhīl chief) was killed the guests to the feast dispersed.

Bhināya is in the possession of the decsendants of Rāo Chandrasēn up to this day

It is stated in the chiefs and leading families of Rajputana, 'Chandrasēn, the grandson of Rāo Māldēv of Marwar, (1581) came to Ajmēr and, having by stratagem intoxicated Mādaliā, the chief of a band of Bhīls who ravaged the country near Bhināi, slew him and dispersed his followers. For this service Bhināi and seven other parganas were bestowed on him in Jāgīr by the Emperor Akbar,' (1916, pages 96—98).

The same year (i.e. 1630 V.S.=981 A.H.) Akbar despatched a strong army to take Siwānā.[1] Besides, the Mohemmadan commanders Shāh Qulī etc., Hindu princes and chiefs like Rāysingh of Bīkanēr, Kēshavadās of Merta, Jagat Rāya etc., were also deputed to accompany it. As the Emperor was very anxious that somehow the Rāo might own allegiance, he had, therefore, instructed his commanders to try to subdue him by promises of imperial favour. At first the army went towards Sōjat where it defeated prince Kallā,[2] a nephew of the Rāo, whence they set out for Siwānā taking his (Rāo's) relatives Kēshavadās, Mahēshdās and Prithvīrāj with them. When this large army came near Siwānā,[3] plundering the surrounding country, and defeating those, who opposed them, the retainers of the Rāo suggested him to take refuge in the neighbouring hills and to wait there for an opportunity.

Chandrasēn, accordingly, went into the hills leaving the defence of the fort to his Commander-in-chief, Rāṭhōr Pattā, but he let slip no opportunity of breaking down upon the besieging army and pressed it hard by destroying its flanks and rear at times. The garrison, too, gave a good account of its deeds. Though the besieging army was immense and formidable, yet neither the Rāo nor his retainers were discomfited and missed no opportunity of attacking the opponents. In 1631 V.S. (982 A.H.) disappointed at the state of affairs Rāo Rāyasingh, who then administered the affairs of Mārwār on behalf of the Emperor, left Siwānā for Ajmēr and informed the Emperor, that the army deputed by him at Siwānā was not adequate to capture the fort and reinforcement was necessary.[4] The Emperor, therefore, sent Tayyab Khān, Sayyad Tōqbāī, Subhān Qulī Khān Turk, Khurram, Azmatkhān, Shivdās, etc. with a large army to help the imperial forces at Siwānā. The strength of the imperial army being thus

1 *Akbarnama*, Vol III, pages 80—81.

2 Prince Kallā, at first, bravely opposed the imperial army, but was eventually obliged by his far outnumbering assailants to leave the fortress of Sojat and to take refuge in the fortress of Sināri. The imperial army finding it difficult to take this latter place set fire to it which obliged Kallā to retreat to Kōrnā. But when he was pursued by the army to this place too, he had to conclude peace and though by some pretence he exempted himself from accompanying the army he had to send his relatives with it

3 The allies of Rāo Chandrasēn Rāval Mēghrāj, Sukhrāj, Sūjā and Dēvīdās had bravely fought with batches of the imperial army that had been out to plunder in the neighbourhood. (*Akbarnama*, Vol III, page 81).

4 *Akbarnama*, Vol. III, pages 110-111.

redoubled, the Rāo at the request of his Sardārs escaped via Rāmpurā to the impregnable hills, the Emperor was much resented to hear the escape of the Rāo and reproached his commanders.

Next in 1632 V.S. (993 A.H.) Jalāl Khān was deputed[1] to suppress the Rāo and Sayyad Ahmad, Sayyad Hāshim, Shimālkhān and other nobles were also ordered to accompany him.

As the previously sent army suffered continued failure it became disheartened; and as they had no good provision of fodder and had to wander fruitlessly in the hilly tracts the horses, too, became weak and unserviceable.[2] The Emperor, therefore, instructed these newly appointed nobles to relieve it. Accordingly the nobles went to their respective Jāgīrs to make preparations.

When Jalāl Khān reached Mērtā Rāmsingh, Sultānsingh,[3] Alī Qulī, etc. nobles of the Siwānā army, sent him words, that, though they were trying their best to suppress the Rāo, yet they had not been able to win him, for being himself a brave warrior, surrounded by retainers, brave alike, and finding an impregnable shelter in the mountains, he was invincible. But if Jalāl Khān would instantly help them with his army they would achieve some success. So Jalāl Khān immediately marched on Siwānā. Hearing this the Rāo arranged an ambush to surprise and rout Jalāl Khān in the way, but somehow the latter got scent of his movement, he, therefore, advanced forward and attacked the Rāo. This surprising attack upset all his (Rāo's) projects, yet for some time, he continued the conflict with the imperial army from his mountain fastness.[4] Afterwards anticipating destruction of his handful brave soldiers in thus falling upon an immense army he again had to take refuge in the mountains

As the imperial army had had a bitter experience of entering into the mountains in pursuit of such a dangerous enemy as the Rāo this time they retired to the fortress of Rāmgadh, and from there they tried their best to find out his

1 *Akbarnama*, Vol III, page 158 2 *ibid*, Vol III, page 167.

3 These were younger brothers of Rāo Rāyasingh of Bikānēr

4 *Akbarnama*, Vol. III, pages 158—159.

whereabouts, but all their efforts proved fruitless. In the meanwhile they learnt through a person, who called himself Dēvīdās,[1] that the Rāo was with his nephew, prince Kallā. At this they went with him to Kallā who positively denied their information. The army had to return in despair and Shimālkhān was much displeased with Dēvīdās. Therefore inviting the latter to his camp under some pretence he tried to take him prisoner, but at the right moment Dēvīdās effected a brave escape to the disappointment and shame of Shimālkhān. Further, thinking his stay, in the imperial camp, unsafe, Dēvīdās went away to Kallā and as he was determined to avenge himself on Shimālkhān, he together with Rāo Chandrasēn fell upon the imperial army. But, as they were in a hurry, they mistook Jalāl Khān for Shimālkhān. However, the former was killed. They then proceeded to attack the latter (Shimālkhān) but, by that time, Jaimal[2] at the head of a fresh imperial army happened to come there and the Rāo and Dēvīdās thought it wise to retire to their residence.

This last attack had much reduced the strength of the imperial army, which afforded a chance to prince Kallā (son of Rām) once again to try his lot. He collected men and money, garrisoned the fortress of Dēvkōr[3] and prepared for battle with the imperial army.

To overcome the new difficulty the imperial army was obliged to give up the siege of Siwānā and began to prepare for an attack upon Dēvkōr. The Emperor seeing his prestige thus endangered, sent more men under Shāhbāzkhān to put down the anarchy in these parts. This new general, on reaching Dēvkōr, saw that the imperial army besieging the fortress, was engaged in fruitless attempts. He, therefore, advanced ahead and attacked the fort. This reinforcement greatly added to the strength of the imperial army and the

---

1 The strange story related by this man at Rāmgaḍh was that he was the same Dēvīdās who was supposed to have been killed in the battle with Sharfuddīn at Mērtā. That when he had been left on the field in a senseless state, an ascetic picked him up, took him to his hermitage and healed his wounds. That he remained with the ascetic for some time and had come there with his permission to try his fortune by serving under the imperial banners. He was believed by some of the imperial commanders, while others disbelieved him (*Akbarnama*, Vol. III, page 159).

2 In *Akbarnama* this man is named Jaimal, while in some other histories the name of Mēritiā Jagmāl' occurs instead (*ibid*, Vol III, page 159).

3 (*Ibid*, Vol. III, page 167). The site of this fortress remains yet unexplored.

handful and fatigued retainers of Prince Kallā could not stand its charges for long. The fortress was captured and Shāhbāz-khān left some portion of the army in the fortress under the Sayyads of Bārāh, while he himself proceeded to Siwānā. On his way there were some Rāthōr warriors, stationed in the fortress of Dunārā,[1] to whom the commander of the imperial army (Shāhbāzkhān) proposed subjugation and imperial service But these brave Rāthōrs preferred death to loss of independence and engaged the great Moghal army in a furious battle till each of them had fallen on the field. The Moghal army then took possession of the fortress (of Dunārā), proceeded further, laid siege to Siwānā; and relieved and sent back the old army, as instructed by the Emperor. The new general, after some days' strenuous efforts, perceived that it was very difficult to take the fort by fighting in the open field with the brave Rāthōrs. He, therefore, began to press the garrison by employing stratagems; and cut off all supplies to the inmates of the fort. Seeing further defence impossible the commander of the garrison proposed to evacuate it on condition of being allowed to retire peacefully. Shāhbāz welcomed the proposal as he foresaw only loss in pressing them any further. After great and prolonged difficulties the fort of Siwānā came in the possession of Akbar in 1633 V. S (984 A.H.) and the surviving Rāthōr defenders retired to the mountains of Pīplūn where the Rāo resided. But still they did attack the Moghal army whenever possible.

The same year in the month of Kārtik (October, 1576 A.D.) Rāval Hans Rāj of Jaisalmēr, seeing the Rāo engaged with the imperial army invaded Pōkaran, which was defended by Panchōlī Ānand Rām, the fort officer of the Rāo, for about 4 months. But in the end both the armies, seeing no advantage, concluded a treaty by which the Rāval was to advance a loan of one lakh of Phadiās (Rs. 12,300) to the Rāo and the Rāo was to hand over the district of Pōkaran to the Rāval on the condition to return it on the repayment of the said loan. Consequently the fighting was stopped and the draft treaty was submitted to the Rāo for his approval. Rāo Chandrasēn, being engaged in war with the Moghals, was in need of money, he therefore welcomed the treaty.

1 At present there is no fortress in Dunārā.

When the imperial army pursued the Rāo even in his mountain fastness of Pīplūn, he, after fighting for a time, was obliged to retire towards Sirohī[1]; Dūngarpur[2] and Bānswārā.

After some time, when Sojat also fell in the hands of the Moghals on the death of Kallā in the battle field, Kūmpāvat Sādūl, son of Mahēshdās, Jaitāvat Āskaran, son of Dēvīdās, and other Sardārs of Marwar went to the Rāo and requested him to return and protect his native land. Accepting this, he set out for Marwar via Mewar and routing the imperial post at Sarwād took possession of the district in 1636 V. S. (1579 A.D.). Later he overran the adjacent districts of Ajmer also. At this Emperor[3] sent an army against him under his nobles like Pāyandā Mōhammad Khān, etc. The Rāo, after fighting for some time with this odd, thought it inadvisable to remain in the open field and retired to the nearest mountain in 1637 V. S. (1580 A. D.=988 A. H.).

Shortly after this the Rāo again collected men and money, invaded Sojat and took possession of it on the 11th day of the dark half of Shrāvaṇa, 1637 V S. (7th July, 1580 A.D.). He then established his residence in the hill fortress of Sāran close by, but he could not enjoy it for long as he died on the 7th day of the bright half of Māgha, 1637 V.S. (11th January, 1581 A.D) at Sachiyāya. Thus ended the thorny but brilliant career of this unyielding hero of Marwar.[4] On the spot where he was cremated there stands a marble tablet[5] to this day.

1 Rāo Chandrasēn is said to have stayed here for about a year and a half.

2 It is said that though Rāo Chandrasēn, owing to the dissension between the Rāval and his son, had acquired the possession of the Dūngarpur fort, but was obliged to vacate it on arrival of the imperial army.

3 In 988 A H (1637 V. S =1580 A D.) it was reported that Rāo Chandrasēn (son of Māldēv) in spite of his (formerly) attending the imperial court had rebelled. But as he was afraid of the imperial army, was waiting for an opportunity in his hiding place And now finding a chance had begun to plunder the district of Ajmer (*Akbarnama*, III, page 318)

But Rāo Chandrasēn had only once met Akbar at Nāgaur in 1627 V. S (1570 A D.). His subsequent interview with Akbar is neither stated in any of the Persian Chronicles, nor in the Khyāts. The statement therefore, merely alluded to his meeting with the Emperor (Akbar) in 1627 V. S

4 It is stated in the chronicles of Marwar that when Rāo Chandrasēn had taken possession of Sōjat a large number of Rāthōr Sardārs from far and near had flocked under his banner But Rāṭhor Bairsal and Kunpāvat Udaisingh paid no heed to him out of pride Rāo Chandrasēn, therefore marched upon Dūdōr the jāgīr of Bairsal On the way as Āskaran, son of Rāthōr Dēvīdās promised to negotiate with Bairsal and to bring him in the service of the Rāo the latter gave up the idea of invasion. But when Āskaran saw Bairsal for the purpose, the latter feigning terror, requested the former to assure him of the favour of the Rāo by bringing him (the Rāo) to his house for dinner. It was done accordingly But soon after his return from there the Rāo suddenly expired, hence treachery on the part of Bairsal is generally suspected

5 In this tablet there is an image of Rāo Chandrasēn on horse back along with five ladies standing in front of him to show that five of his wives became Satis This fact is also borne out by the inscription below the image which runs as follows.—

"श्रीगणेशाय नमः। सवत् १६३७ शाके १५[०]२ माघमासे सु(शु)क्लपक्षे सतिव (सप्तमी) दिने राय श्रीचद्रसेणजी देवीकुला सती पंच हुई"।

Rāo Chandrasēn was a ruler of very inflexible and independent disposition. He took upon himself the calamities of a wandering life in mountains after being deprived of his paternal state of Marwar. He continued to fight for 16 long years with the armies of Emperor like Akbar, and never thought of ending his miseries by yielding to the supremacy of the great Moghal. Even from *Akbarnama* it is evident that it was an ardent desire of the Emperor to bring the Rāo in his allegiance like other rulers of Rājpūtānā, he, therefore, used to give special instructions to all his nobles sent against him to try their best to subjugate the Rāo by temptations of imperial favours. But this desire of the Emperor had never been fulfilled. Rāo Chandrasēn[1] had three sons, Ugrasēn, Rāyasingh, and Āskaran

Comparison

At that time Mahārānā and the Rāo were the only two thorns pricking at the heart of Akbar. A contemporary poet has very well expressed this fact in the following couplet :—

अणादगिया तुरी ऊजला असमर, चाकर रहण न डिगियौ चीत ।
सारै हिंदुस्थान तणै सिर, पातल नै चंद्रसेण प्रवीन ॥

i. e. at that time there were only two renowned rulers throughout India, viz. Rānā Pratāp and Rāo Chandrasēn, whose horses could not be enslaved by the imperial brand, who could never be tempted by imperial services and whose arms ever remained drawn against the imperial armies.

In the following we shall note some similar events that happened in the reign of the Rāo and the Rānā :—

1. Though the rulers of Mārwār and Mēwār had from the past been at daggers drawn with the Mohamedan Emperors yet the Rāo defying the offer of service had positively declared war with Akbar in 1621 V. S. (1564 A. D.). And a discord between the Rānā and Kunvar Mānsingh arose in 1630 V. S. (1573 A.D.) as a consequence of which Akbar began his invasions of Mēwār.

---

1 Rāo Chandrasēn made a charitable grant of village Araṭhnadi to a Brāhman named Sānga.

2. Though Rāṇā Pratāp was the eldest son of Rāṇā Udaisingh yet the latter had nominated his younger brother, Jagmāl, as heir to the throne of Chittor. And when Rāṇā Pratāp ascended the throne against the right of his brother, there ensued discord between these two. With the advice of the Subēdār of Ajmer Jagmāl went to Akbar via Jahāzpur and the Emperor granted that district to him in Jāgīr. After a time Sagar, another brother of the Mahārāṇā, also deserted him and went to Akbar.

On the other hand, the Rāo was nominated heir-apparent by his father in spite of his three elder brothers. His eldest brother Rām being displeased with him, went to Akbar as advised by Husain Qulī Khān and received Sojat in Jāgīr (as stated in the Khyāts). In 1627 V. S. (1570 A.D.) his second brother Udaisingh, too, went to the opposite side.

3. At the time of the accession of Pratāp to the throne, Chittor, Māṇḍalgarh, etc. (districts of Mēwār) were under the possession of the Moghals; similarly at the time of the accession of the Rāo to the throne, Ajmer, Mērta, etc. (districts of Mārwār) were also under the possession of the Moghals.

4. Prior to the accession of Pratāp most of the great generals of Mēwār had fallen in battles, fought with Bābar and other Mohemmadan kings; in the like manner, prior to the accession of Chandrasēn the great generals of Mārwār had been killed in the battle with Shērshāh.

5. The Rāṇā opposed the great Moghal armies to protect his and his country's independence, taking shelter in the mountain range between Gōgūnda and Khamnōr; similarly the Rāo fought with the great Moghal armies from his sheltering place in the mountains of Siwāṇā.

6. Obliged by the continued attacks of the Moghal armies, the Rāṇā had to wander away towards Bānswārā[1] and in Chhapan-kā-Pahār (in Mēwār), similarly the Rāo had to go to Dūngarpur and Bānswārā, while Chhapan-kā-Pahār near Siwāṇā was his main place of shelter for a long time.

---

1 *Akbarnama*, Vol. III page 238.

7. Mahārānā Pratāp could not take Chittor, though he regained the possession of some of his lost districts; similarly the Rāo could not regain the possession of Jodhpur, though Sojat was taken by him in his last days.

8. Abul Fazal says (*Akbarnama*, Vol. II, pages 357-58), 'In 978 A. H., i. e. in the 15th regnal year, when Akbar came to Nāgaur, Chandrasēn, son of Māldēv, presented himself and received many imperial favours.'

But from the chronology of events it appears, that, though Akbar had a wish to bestow favours on Chandrasēn, the latter rejected his proposal of allegiance. This fact is proved by the following version of the same history.[1]

'Early in the 19th regnal year (981 A.H.) when the Emperor came to Ajmer, he heard that Chandrasēn, son of Rājā Māldēv, had rebelled; that he had repaired the fortress of Siwana, one of the strongest forts in Ajmer "Sūbā" and had made it his abode. Hearing this the Emperor was moved to pity for the subjects of the district and deputed Shāh Qulī, Rāo Rayasingh, Shimālkhān, Kēshavdās (son of Jaimal) and Jagat Rāi (son of Dhan Chand) with a powerful army to punish him. He also instructed the generals that, should the Rāo repent for his actions, he may be assured of imperial favours.

After the former narrative of A.H. 978, the foregoing one of 981 A.H. is the first containing mention of the Rāo in the *Akbarnama* Under the circumstances, as stated by Abul Fazal, if the Rāo had acquired imperial favour at Nāgaur, what then had been the cause of rebellion by him? Moreover, there appears no mention of the Emperor's favour to the Rāo in the History.'

The author of the *Akbarnama* further adds[2]:—

'In the 25th regnal year (i.e. in 988 A.H.) Chandrasēn in spite of his attending the imperial "Darbār", again rebelled as has been mentioned hitherto.'

---

1 *Akbarnama*, Vol III, pp. 80-81

2 *Akbarnama*, Vol. III, p 318.

But in the history there appears no mention of the meeting of the Rāo with the Emperor excepting the one at Nāgaur. This version, therefore, alludes to the same meeting.

Following are the similar statements for Mahārānā Pratāp in *Akbarnama*[1]:--

'According to the imperial orders Mānsingh with other nobles went to Udaipur. The Rānā came to receive them and respectfully wore the "Khilat". He took Mānsingh to his palace as a guest and begged pardon for his mischief. The nobles did not agree. The Rānā making promises saw Mānsingh off and adopted mildness.'

'In the 18th regnal year (981 A.H.) Rājā Bhagvantdās. Shāh Qulī Khān, and Lashkar Khān together with a large army were ordered to go into the Rānā's land via Īdar to suppress all the landlords of those parts, chastising those who dared to oppose.[2]'

'Within one month Bhagvantdās with his army came to the court and brought the son of Rānā Partāp with him'; the details are as below:—

When the imperial army reached Gōgūndā, the place where the Rānā lived, the Rānā came and saw Rājā Bhagvantdās. He repented for the faults done in the past, and prayed to be recommended to the Emperor. At the same time he took Mānsingh to his palace, entertained him and sent his son with him. He further said that, unfortunately, he was hitherto awe-struck, but that now through him, he was entertaining the Emperor and sending his son to the court. After a time when his mind would be pacified he would present himself in the court personally.[3]

A perusal of the various histories of Rājpūtānā shows that the above statements are only the products of the author's fertile brain. He (the author) at least, has branded both the unyielding heroes with the imperial slavery. But this is far from truth.

---

1 Akbarnama, Vol. III, p. 40. 2 *ibid.*, Vol. III, p. 64. 3 *ibid.*, Vol. III, pp. 66-67.

9. There is a further statement concerning Rānā Pratāp in *Akbarnama*.[1]:—

'The Emperor ordered Kutubuddīn Khān, Rājā Bhagvantdās, and Kunvar Mānsingh to go with a small imperial army to hunt out the Rānā in the mountains But when the Rānā was not found they went to Gōgūndā.'

'As Rājā Bhagvantdās and Kutubuddīn Khān returned without obtaining the permission of the Emperor; he was much displeased and refused them audience which was allowed when they begged his pardon and expressed repentance for their mistake[2].

Similar statement in *Akbarnama* regarding Rāo Chandrasēn[3]:—

'In 982 A.H. when the Emperor came to Ajmer, Rāo Rayasingh coming singly from Siwana prayed that Chandrasēn, son of Māldēv, had raised much disturbance in the boundaries of Jodhpur; that the imperial army at Siwana was not adequate to suppress him, and that he can be suppressed if a strong reinforcement be despatched. The Emperor very kindly accepted his request and deputed Tayyab Khān, Sayyad Bēgh Tōkbāī, Turk Subhanqulī, Khurram, Azmat Khān, and Shivdās with some brave warriors for this purpose. Chandrasēn retreated in the mountain via Rāmpurā. The imperial army went in pursuit of him, many surrendered and many were killed. Chandrasēn could not resist Taking his retreat for his defeat the imperial army, through foolishness, returned. When the Emperor heard this he was much incensed and lost confidence in those nobles.'

Both the above narratives of Abul Fazal narrate similar events

Again, in the *Muntakhibut-tavarikh*,[4] it is stated:—

'But they did not go after the Rānā and he escaped alive; the Emperor took it ill'

---

1 *Akbarnama*, Vol. III, p 191

2 *Akbarnama*, Vol III, page 195

3 *Akbarnama*, Vol III, pages 110-111

4 *Muntakhibut-tavarikh*, Vol. II, page 235

This event is much more similar to that of Rāo Chandrasēn.

A Special Event

The following story of Rānā Pratāp is current in Rājpūtānā.

On one occasion the Mahārānā greatly distressed by the miseries of his children, thought of acknowledging the supremacy of the Emperor. But Prithviraj, brother of Rayasingh (of Bikaner), being informed by Akbar, addressed the Mahārānā in the following lines:—

पटकूँ मूँछाँ पाण, के पटकूँ निज तन करद ;
दीजे लिख दीवाण, इण दो महली बात इक ।

i. e. should I feel proud on your account or kill myself, kindly let me know the alternative I should adopt.

The Mahārānā being encouraged by it sent this couplet in reply:—

खुशी हूँत पीथल कमध, पटको मूँछाँ पाण;
पछटण है जेतै पतौ, कलमाँ सिर केवाँण ।

i. e. right gladly you should feel proud, as long as the lance of Pratāp shines over the head of the Moghals.

But no similar tail about Rāo Chandrasēn has been heard.

The Probable Causes of the obscurity of the Rao.

Why the name and history of such a memorable hero are forgotten? The chief cause of it seems to be that, unlike Mahārānā Pratāp, the throne of Mārwār was lost to the descendants of our hero—Rāo Chandrasēn. Some time after his death his elder brother, Udaisingh (alias Mōtā Rājā) got the possession of the throne in 1640 V.S. (1583 A.D.). This new sovereign was not on good terms with our hero. The poets and historians of the time, therefore, thought the recital and narration of his heroic deeds to be fruitless and a cause of displeasing the contemporary rulers.

We hope true Indians and specially the Rāthōr Rājpūts will cherish the memory of the magnanimous Rāo in their hearts like that of Mahārānā Prātap.

4. Rao Amarsingh the well known hero of Rajputana.

(This paper was written for the Fifth Session of the History Congress to be held at Hyderabad (Deccan), in December, 1941.)

Rāo Amarsingh, the elder son of Mahārājā Gajsingh of Marwar, was born on the 17th April 1613 A.D.[1] and was by nature an independent, reckless and unyielding prince. This was the main reason why his father selected his younger son Mahārājkumār Jaswant Singh I to succeed him on the throne of Marwar. As soon as Amarsingh came to know of this decision, he, losing hope of his ancestral throne, took a band of selected Rāthōrs and went to serve at the Mughal Court. Emperor Shāh Jahān impressed with his gallantry soon got pleased and awarding him an elephant made him his courtier.[2]

After this, Amarsingh took part in several expeditions with the Imperial armies and was bestowed on by the Emperor a mansab of 2000 Zāt and 1300 horse[3] on the 14th December 1629 A. D.

Later on the 10th December 1634 A. D. the Emperor pleased with his bravery raised his Mansab to 2500 Zāt and 1500 horse and again awarded him an elephant, a horse and a flag.[4]

Next year he accompanied Sayyad Khān Jahān to punish Bundēlā Junjhār Singh.[5] In this expedition, when the fort of Dhāmunī was captured by the Imperial army, Amar Singh

---

1 In some chronicles the birth date is given as 12th December

2 Bādashah Nāmā, Vol I, chapter 1, p. 227

3 do do Vol I, do 1, p. 291

4 do do Vol I, do 2, p 65.

We learn from the chronicles that on the invitation of Mahārājā Gajsingh, he (Amarsingh) reached Lahore on the 9th day of the dark half of Pausha, V. S. 1691 (4th December 1634 A. D.) and was presented before the Emperor, who bestowed on him a Mansab of 2500 Zāt and 1500 horse and Jāgīr of five Parganās But Col. Tod has written the Vikram year of this event as 1690 (1634 A D.).

Annals & Antiquities of Rājasthān (Edited by Crooke), Vol 2, p. 976.

5 Bādashah Nāmā, Vol I, chapter I, p. 96.

decided to wait with his soldiers outside the fort till dawn. But in the meantime, the magazine in the fort caught fire by the sparks from the torches of the free booters, and blew up a portion of the rampart which killed three hundred men of the Imperial army encamped on the other side of it. Though the casuality list contained a greater number of Amarsingh's own warriors,[1] yet he managed to help the wounded and kept order in such a splendid manner that no confusion reigned in the army.

This presence of mind of Amar Singh again pleased the Emperor and on the 19th January 1635 A. D., he raised his Mansab to 3000 Zāt and 1500 horse.[2]

After this, when Sāhū Bhōnslē, taking out a descendant of Nizāmul Mulk's family from the prison in the Gwalior fort raised the banner of revolt, Emperor Shāh Jahān himself marched up to Daulatābād and from that place despatched three armies to punish the Bhōnslē. In one of these armies which was sent under the command of Khān Daurān, Amar Singh with his brave Rājpūts, was placed in the vanguard.[3] After supressing this rebellion successfully, when Amarsingh returned to the Imperial Court in 1637 A. D. the Emperor awarded him a robe of honour, a silver caparisoned horse and a Mansab of 3000 Zāt and 2000 horse.[4]

The following year when Shujā was sent to Kandhār with the Imperial army, the Emperor again awarded Amarsingh a robe of honour, a silver caparisoned horse and a trumpet and bade him farewell to accompany Shujā.[5] On the 6th May 1638 A.D. when Amarsingh was at Kābul with Shujā, his father Mahārājā Gajsingh died at Agra. In fulfilment of the Mahārājā's wishes, Emperor Shāh Jahān bestowing the title of Rājā on Amarsingh's younger brother Jaswant Singh I made him the ruler of Marwar, and awarding the title of Rāo to Amarsingh gave him Nāgaur as Jāgīr. Further the Emperor raised his (Amarsingh's) mansab to 3000 Zāt and 3000 horse.[6]

---

1 Bādshāh Nāmā, Vol. I, chapter 2, p. 110.
2 do do Vol. I, do 2, p. 124.
3 do do Vol. I, do 2, pp 136-138.
4 do do Vol. I, do 2, pp 246-248.
5 do do Vol. II, p. 37.
6 do do Vol. II, p 97.

In 1639 A. D. the Emperor was again pleased with his bravery and first gave him a horse and afterwards an elephant[1].

In the month of March 1641 A. D. the Emperor again ordered Rāo Amarsingh to accompany Shāh-Zādā Murād towards Kābul and awarded him a robe of honour, a silver caparisoned horse and an elephant.[2] But after five months, when Jagatsingh, son of Rājā Bāsū, rebelled, the Emperor ordered Shāh Zādā Murād and Rāo Amarsingh to leave Kābul and go to Paithan via Siālkōt to supress the rebellion.[3] After about seven months when Jagatsingh accepted the allegiance of the Emperor, the Shāhzādā and Amarsingh both returned to the Imperial Court[4].

In the meantime the king of Persia had mobilised his army to capture Kandhār. As soon as this news was received, the Emperor raised the Mansab of Rāo Amarsingh to 4000 Zāt and 3000 horse and awarded him a robe of honour and gold caparisoned horse,[5] and ordered him to accompany Dārā Shikōh to check the advance of the Persian army. But as the king of Persia died, he returned with Khān Daurān Nasrat Jang in October 1642 A. D.[6]

Sometime after this event Rāo Amarsingh fell ill and could not attend the Imperial Court. But when after recovery he attended the court Salābat Khān the Shāhī Bakhshī being jealous[7] of the Rāo uttered some harsh words,[8] which the Rāo

1 Bādshah Nāmā, Vol. II, p 145
2 do do Vol. II, p. 228.
3 do do Vol. II, p 240.
4 do do Vol. II, p. 285
5 do do Vol II, pp. 293-294.
(This Mansab has also been mentioned in Bādshāh Nāmā, Vol. II, p 721).
6 Bādshāh Nāmā, Vol, II, p. 310.

7 It is already stated that the Rāo received Nagaur from the Emperor in Jāgīr and as the boundaries of Nagaur and Bikaner were adjoining a boundary dispute arose on a trifling matter between the servants of Rāo Amarsingh and of Karansingh, the ruler of Bikaner But as Rāo's servants were unarmed at the time, Karansingh's men, who were well armed killed many of them When this news reached Rāo Amarsingh at Agra he sent words to his servants to avenge the death of their brethren In the meantime Rājā Karansingh, who was in the Deccan, also wrote a letter to Salābat Khān the Shāhī Bakhshī and persuaded him to help the cause of Bikaner. The Bakhshī therefore issued orders to appoint a Shāhī Amīn to inquire into the dispute and forbade both the parties to take any further action into the matter. This was the main cause of anmity between the Shāhī Bakhshī and the Rāo (Bādshāh Nāmā, Vol. II, P 382)

8 It is stated in the chronicles that Salābat Khān addressed the Rāo as 'Ganvār' (rude) as is also evident from the following couplet.—

उवा मुखते गग्गो कह्यो, इवा कर लई कटार ।
वार कहण पायो नहीं, जमदढ होगइ पार ॥

took as an insult to himself. This was enough to enrage the brave Rāthōr, who, setting aside the etiquette of the Imperial Court as well as ignoring the presence of the Emperor, thrust his dagger and pierced the heart of Salābat Khān, thus killing him at the spot.

We learn from the chronicles that at that time Amarsingh lost himself so much in anger that he advanced towards the Emperor and attacked him also with his sword, but it struck the throne instead, and the Emperor, escaping death, took to his heels and entered the ladies apartments.[1]

Seeing this, Khalīl-ulla-Khān and Arjun Gaud[2], two of the attending nobles, attacked the Rāo, but when they could not face the enraged brave Rāthōr successfully some six or seven other Mansabdārs and mace bearers also joined them. Though Rāo Amarsingh faced them bravely yet, being encircled by

---

(i. e.) as soon as Salābat Khān uttered the letter 'गं' the Rāo took out the dagger and before the Khān could utter the word 'वार' (rude) the dagger of the Rāo went through the heart of the 'Bakhshī.'

'Bādshāh Nāmā' describes the valour of Rāo Amarsingh in the following words —

"A young man like Amarsingh who surpassed all the other Rājpūts of the well known families in nobility and valour and for whom the Emperor thought that he accompanied with other Rājpūt nobles, will die in a great battle fighting against the enemy and will achieve good fame". (Vol. II, P. 281).

Col. Tod writes —"Amra was conspicuous for his gallantry, and in all his father's wars in the south was ever foremost in the battle."

(Annals & Antiquities of Rājasthān (Edited by Crooke), Vol. II, P 975)

1 Col. Tod writes —"He absented himself for a fortnight from court, hunting the boar or the tiger, his only recreation. The emperor (Shāh Jāhān) reprimanded him for neglecting his duties and threatened him with a fine. Amra proudly replied that he had only gone to hunt, and as for a fine he observed putting his hand upon his sword, that was his sole wealth."

"The little contrition which this reply evinced determined the king to enforce the fine, and the paymaster-general, Salābat Khān, was sent to Amra's quarters to demand its payment. It was refused, and the observations made by the Sayyid not suiting the temper of Amra, he unceremoniously desired him to depart The emperor, thus insulted in the person of his officer, issued a mandate for Amra's instant appearance. He obeyed, and having reached the Amm-khas, or grand divan, beheld the king, "Whose eyes were red with anger' with Salabat in the act of addressing him. Inflamed with passion at the recollection of the injurious language he had just received, perhaps at the king's confirmation of his exclusion from Marwar, he unceremoniously passed the Omrahs of five and seven thousand, as if to address the king, when with a dagger concealed in his sleeve, he stabbed Salabat to the heart. Drawing his sword, he made a blow at the king, which descending on the pillar, shivered the weapon in pieces. The king abandoned his throne and fled to the interior apartments."

(Annals and Antiquities of Rājasthan (Edited by Crooke), Vol. II, pp. 975-977.)

2 Col. Tod has written him as the brother-in-law of Rāo Amarsingh.

(Annals and Antiquities of Rājasthān (Edited by Crooke), Vol. II, p 977.)

those nobles—like Abhimanyu a young hero of Mahābhārat was laid low.[1] This event took place on the 25th July 1644 A.D.[2]

Hearing the death of their master, fifteen brave Rājpūts of the Rāo, who were present in the fort at the time attacked the Emperor's servants and within a short time, after wounding two imperial officers and six mace bearers, were themselves killed.

When this news reached the camp of the Rāo and was known by the neighbours Chāmpāvat Ballū and Rāthōr Bihārī Singh[3] joined the retainers of Rāo Amarsingh and got ready to kill Arjun Gaud. But before they could put their idea into action they were surrounded by an Imperial detachment and shared the fate of their master after laying low a number of Imperial officers.[4]

Col. Tod writes.—

"The Bokhara gate by which they gained admission was built up, and hence-forward known only as "Amarsingh's gate", and in proof of the strong impression made by this event it remained closed through centuries, until opened in 1809 by Capt. Geo. Steell of the Bengal Engineers.[5] "

---

1 Bādshāh Nāmā Vol., II, pp. 380-381.

The Rāo was cremated on the bank of the Jumna at Agra Two of his Rānīs became 'Satīs' with him there, three got themselves burnt afterwards at Nagaur and one at Udaipur

The cenotaphs which were built to commemorate them or the Rāo's descendants are still standing at Nagaur.

In some chronicles it is stated that the corpse of Rāo Amarsingh was thrown in the Jumna

Col. Tod in his Annals and Antiquities of Rājasthān writes —". and his wife, the princess of Būndī, came in person and carried away the dead body of Amra, with which she committed herself to the flames " (Vol. II, p 978).

2 In 'Bādshāh Nāmā' the date of this event is given as H S 1054, Salkha, Jamādi-ul-Avval, Thursday (Vol. II, p. 380)

3 Previously both of them served Mahārājā Gajsingh (the father of the Rāo) and Rāo Amarsingh himself, but at present were in the Emperor's service

In the chronicles of Marwar we find the name of Kūmpāvat Bhāvasingh in place of Bihārīsingh.

Col Tod writes—" To avenge his death, his retainers, headed by Balu Champavat and Bhao Kumpawat, put on their saffron garments and a fresh carnage ensued within the Lal Kila—— The faithful band was cut to pieces "

(Annals & Antiquities of Rājasthān, (Edited by Crooke) Vol II, pp 977-978)

4 Bādshāh Nāmā, Vol II, pp 383-384

5 Annals & Antiquities of Rājasthān, (Edited by Crooke) Vol II, p 978

Col. Tod further states —

"Since these remarks were written, Captain Steell related to the author a singular anecdote connected with the above circumstance While the work of demolition was proceeding, Captain Steell was urgently warned by the natives of the danger he incurred in the operation, from a denunciation on the closing of the gate, that it should thenceforward be guarded by a huge serpent —when suddenly, the destruction of the gate being nearly completed, a large cobra-de-capello rushed between his legs, as if in fulfilment of the anathema Captain Steell fortunately escaped without injury "

(The south gate of the Agra Fort is known as that of Amar Singh).

(Annals & Antiquities of Rājasthān, (Edited by Crooke) Vol. II, pp 978-979)

Sometimes after the death of Rāo Amarsingh the Emperor bestowed a Mansab of 1000 Zāt and 700 horse on Rāyasingh, the elder son of the Rāo,[1] who gradually rose to rank in the Mughal Court.

In 1659 A.D. when Aurangzēb defeating Shujā near Khajwā made him flee from the field, the former, to avenge himself on Mahārājā Jaswant Singh I, raised the Mansab of Rāo Rāyasingh to 4000 Zāt and 4000 horse, honoured him with the title of 'Rājā' and gave him the State of Jodhpur.[2] But his plan was frustrated by the said Mahārājā.

In 1676 A. D. when Rāyasingh died the Emperor (Aurangzēb) bestowed a Mansab on his son Rāo Indrasingh.

When Mahārājā Jaswant Singh I died in 1678 A. D., the Emperor, to avenge himself on the deceased, granted Indrasingh the title of 'Rājā' and the administration of Jodhpur State.[3] But this time the loyal nobles of the late Mahārājā did not allow him to succeed.

Indrasingh rose to a Mansab of 5000 Zāt and 2000 horse. In 1716 A. D. Mahārājā Ajitsingh of Marwar deprived him of Nagaur but in 1723 A. D. Emperor Mōhammad Shāh, being displeased with the Mahārājā, re-granted the Jāgīr of Nagaur to Indrasingh. At last in October 1726 A. D. Mahārājā Abhaya Singh snatched the 'Paraganā' of Nagaur from Indrasingh and awarded it to his younger brother Rājādhirāj Bakhat Singh.

At the time of Indrasingh's death at Delhi in 1732 A. D. he held provinces of Sirsā, Bhatnēr, Pooniā and Baihanīvāl[4] as a mark of Imperial favour.

1 Bādshāh Nāmā, Vol. II, p. 403.
2 Alamgīr Nāmā, p 288.
3 Maāsir-i-Ālamgīrī, pp. 175-176.
4 These facts are corroborated by a letter, dated the 4th October 1732 A. D., of the minister of Rājādhirāj Bakhat Singh addressed to the agent of Mahārājā Abhaisingh of Marwar at the Imperial Court.

5. False charges against Maharaja Jaswantsingh I of Jodhpur and one of his queens.

(Read at the fourth History Congress held at Lahore in December 1940.)

On hearing about the illness of Emperor Shāh Jahān when princes Aurangzēb and Murād marched towards Agra in 1658 A.D., prince Dārāshikōh, with the consent of the ailing Emperor, deputed Mahārājā Jaswant Singh I, the ruler of Jodhpur to check their advance. But unfortunately, almost all the imperial nobles intrigued with prince Aurangzēb, and therefore the Mahārājā could not get any information regarding the movements of the opponents, until the armies of both the princes (i.e Aurangzēb and Murād) joined near Dēpālpur and finally moved towards Ujjain.

Later on, in a pitched battle between the Mahārājā and the two princes Qāsimkhān, the commander of the Imperial forces, and fifteen other Muslim nobles with their associates, pretending shortage of munitions stopped firing of their guns and slipped away from the field.

Under these circumstances the Mahārājā was obliged to face the enemies with only seven Hindu nobles. But in the course of the fray when the Mahārāja himself got wounded, and many of his warriors had fallen and further resistance became impossible, Rāṭhōr Ratansingh, the Rājā of Ratlām, took over the command to save the life of the Mahārājā, the leader of the Rāṭhōr clan, and with repeated and earnest requests made him retire in spite of his reluctance to do so.

We quote here some authorities in support of the above fact:—

1. Ishardās writes in his "Fatūhāt-i-Ālamgīrī":—
"Jaswant wanted to ride into the struggle and get slain, but Mahēshdās, Āskaran and other Pradhāns seized his bridle and brought him away" (see p. 21 b).

2. Mīr Muhammad Māsūm writes in his "Tārīkh-i-Shāh Shūjāī":—

"The Mahārājā was wounded and fell down from his horse. His devoted Rājpūts wanted to take him to a safe place. He forbade it, saying——. They did not listen to him, but removed the wounded man full of severe pains". (see p. 50 b)

3. Āqilkhān writes in his "Vāqayāt-i-Ālamgīrī":—
"The Rājā, in spite of his receiving two wounds, stood firmly and encouraged the Rājpūts as far as possible" (see p. 31).

4. Manucci writes in his "Storia Do Mogor":—

"The Rājā never ceased to fight most desperately until at length he saw himself left with only the smallest remnant of his force". (See Vol. I p. 259).

5. Francois Bernier writes in his "Travels in the Mughul Empire":—

"Jaswantsingh displayed extraordinary valour, disputing every inch of ground with skill and pertinacity. With regard to Qāsimkhān, although it cannot be denied that he deserved the celebrity he had hitherto enjoyed, yet upon the present occasion he approved himself neither a dexterous general nor a courageous soldier: he was even suspected of treachery, and of having concealed in the sand, during the night that preceded the battle, the greater part of his ammunition, a few volleys having left the army without powder or ball. However this may be, the action was well supported and the passage vigorously, opposed.——It was then that Qāsimkhān ingloriously fled from the field, leaving Jaswantsingh exposed to the most imminent peril. That undaunted Rājā was beset on all sides by an overwhelming force, and saved only by the affecting devotion of his Rājpūts, the greater part of whom died at his feet. Fewer than six hundred of these brave men, whose number at the commencement of the action amounted to nearly eight thousand, survived the carnage of that dreadful day. With this faithful remnant, the Rājā retired to his own territory." (See pp. 38—39).

6. Col. Tod writes in his "Annals and Antiquities of Rājasthān":--

"..... as soon as the battle joined, when the Moghul horse deserted and left him at the head of his thirty thousand Rajputs, deemed, however, by their leader and themselves sufficient against any odds." "Jaswant, spear in hand, mounted his steed Mahbub, and charged the Imperial brothers; ten thousand Muslims fell in the onset, which cost seventeen hundred Rathors,———. Aurang and Murad only escaped because their days were not yet numbered. Mahbub and his rider were covered with blood, 'Jasa' looked like a famished lion, and like one he relinquished his prey." The bard is fully confirmed in his relation of the day, both by the Moghul, historian and by Bernier," (See Vol. II, pp. 980—981,edited by Crooke).

7. Sir Jadunath Sarkar writes in his "History of Aurangzeb":—

Raisingh's flight had already uncovered Jaswant's right flank, the fall of Iftikhar Khan exposed his left. Meantime his van had almost entirely melted away; part of it had perished around Mukundsingh in his heroic charge; of the rest, the Chandravat Rajputs and Bundelas had fled, and the Musalmans under Qasimkhan, who had kept aloof from the fighting, prepared to run away as they saw Aurangzeb's host advancing on them. Only one course was left to a Rajput general under such circumstances, he must charge into the thickest press of the enemy and die amidst a heap of the slain. And this Jaswant wanted to do. He had fought valiantly for four hours and by firmly keeping his own ground he had so long saved the Imperial Centre, the pivot on which his whole army rested. In spite of two wounds, his voice and example had cheered the Rajputs. But now Aurangzeb from the front, Murad from the left, and Safshikankhan from the right, were converging on him like a tumultuous flood, to envelop his small remnant of clansmen. Such a combat could have only one issue: victory was impossible but a hero's death—no less dear to the Rajput heart—was within his reach. He wanted to drive his horse into the advancing enemy's ranks and get slain. But his generals Askaran and Maheshadas Gaur, and Goverdhan, and other ministers seized his bridle and dragged his horse out of the field. Mughal princes might cut each others throats, but why should the head of the Rathors and the hope of Marwar give up his life in their domestic quarrel? With a few Rathors, mostly wounded—the sole remnant of his gallant band the vanquished general took the road to Jodhpur." (See Vol. II, pp. 20-21).

Now in the presence of so many proofs, how a sane man can rely on the version of Khāfīkhān (Mōhammad Hāsham), who writes in his book called "Muntakhibullubāb":—

"Every minute the dark ranks of the infidel Rājpūts were dispersed by the prowess of the followers of Islām. Dismay and great fear fell upon the heart of Jaswant, their leader, and he, far from acting like one of the renowned class of Rājās, turned his back upon the battle, and was content to bring upon himself ever lasting infamy. Qāsimkhān and other imperial nobles were also obliged to follow him". (See Vol. II, p. 18).

The language used by Khāfīkhān is itself a proof of his malignity against the Hindu Mahārājā and therefore it is apparent that he simply tried to divert the charge of treachery and cowardice from one of his co-religionists to a Hindu ruler.

As regards the charge of pride or delay in action brought against Mahārājā Jaswant I by Col. Tod in his "Annals and Antiquities of Rājasthān" as under:—

"The battle which ensued......was lost by the temerity of Rathor commander-in-chief, who might have crushed the rebellious hopes of Aurangzeb, to whom he purposely gave time to effect a junction with his brother Murad, from the vainglorious desire to conquer two princes at once. Dearly did he pay for his presumption, for he had given time to the wily prince to sow intrigues in his camp, which were disclosed as soon as the battle joined." (See Vol. II, p. 980).

we quote here two passages from Bernier's travels which themselves will repudiate the above charge:—

(1) "But Shah Jahan privately suggested the same measures of caution and forbearance, which were practised in the case of Sultan Suja". (See p. 37)

(2) "It appears certain, indeed, that he (Aurangzeb) was at this time totally incapable of opposing any effectual resistance, and that Qasimkhan and the Raja might have obtained an easy victory. ... ..The two commanders, however, were compelled by their secret orders quietly to take a position on the banks of the river, and to content themselves with disputing the passage". (See p. 38).

Further Sir Jadunath Sarkar also writes in his "History of Aurangzeb":—

"Jaswant had been charged by Shah Jahan to send the two rebellious princes back to their own provinces with as little injury to them as possible, and to fight them only as a last recourse." (See Vol. II, p. 5)

These lines also support Bernier's version.

Later comes the charge of folly or obstinacy, whatever we may call it, against one of the queens of the Mahārājā. Francois Bernier writes:—

"I may here relate the disdainful reception experienced by the valiant Jaswantsingh from his wife, a daughter of the house of Rana. When it was announced that he was approaching with his gallant band of about five hundred Rajputs, the melancholy remnant of nearly eight thousand, at the head of whom he had fought with noble intrepidity, quitting the field from necessity, but not with dishonour, instead of sending to congratulate the gallant soldier on his escape, and console him in his misfortune, she dryly commanded that the gates of the castle should be closed against him. "The man is covered with infamy," she said, "and he shall not enter within these walls. I disown him for my husband, and these eyes can never again behold him. No son-in-law of Rana can possess soul so abject. He who is allied to his illustrious house must imitate the virtues of the great man: if he cannot vanquish he should die." The next moment the temper of her mind took another turn. 'Prepare the funeral pile', she exclaimed, "The fire shall consume my body. I am deceived, my husband is certainly dead; it cannot possibly be otherwise;" and then again, transported with rage, she broke into the bitterest reproaches. In this humour she continued eight or nine days, refusing the whole of that time to see her husband. The arrival of her mother was attended, however, with a beneficial effect: she, in some measure, appeased and comforted her daughter, by solemnly promising, in the Raja's name, that as soon as he should be somewhat recovered from his fatigue, he would collect a second army, attack Aurangzeb, and fully retrieve his reputation.

This anecdote may serve as a specimen of the spirit, which animates the women of this country. I might mention several instances of the same kind,........" (See pp. 40-41).

We find almost a similar story in Khāfīkhān's "Munta-khib ul-lubāb", but there the place of the Shīshōdanī Rānī, who according to Bernier, belonged to Rānā's family has been given to Hādī Rānī, said to be the daughter of Hādā Chhatrasāl (See Vol, II, pp. 44).

Col. Tod has also quoted this story from Bernier. But the well known historian of the Rānās of Udaipur and the author of 'Vīrvinōd,' relates this story with Hādī Rānī and not with the Shīshōdanī Rānī of Jaswant. (See Vol. II, pp. 824-825).

Moreover, though no such event is traced in the old chronicles of Būndī, yet Sūrajmal, the bard of Būndī, who being specially prejudiced against the Rāthōr rulers of Jodhpur, could not restrain himself from tarnishing the glory of a well known ruler of Jodhpur, and giving false credit to a Būndī princess, which was not at all her due. In his "Vamsha Bhāskar" he writes:—

"The day on which Jaswant, fleeing from the battle field arrived at Jodhpur had been allotted to his Hādī Rānī and therefore he entered her apartment. The Rānī, coming to know of the flight of her husband ordered the cooks to stop the rattle of the metal utensils, got removed all the weapons from her apartments, covered her ivory bangles with cloth, and put off all the jingling ornaments and thus she received her lord.

But when he asked the reason of her covering the ivory bangles she replied—"Perhaps the rattling of metal, the sight of weapons and ivory, and the jingle of ornaments may frighten you my lord and thus interrupt us in our meeting." The Rājā was much ashamed to hear these words". (See pp. 2698-99).

Manucci writes this story in his Storia Do Mogor as under: –

.... .."Things remained thus for some years, until Aurangzeb, who had then become king, offered himself as a mediator to restore friendship between them . . ... As a mark of respect to the king's requests, she reluctantly consented. Nevertheless, she never forebore from showing the rajah a wry face as a token of her disapproval, which she persisted in with much rancour. Once the Rajah wanted to eat a melon, and along with it the serving maid presented a knife. Thereupon Raniji suddenly fell upon the maid and seized her by the hair, beating and thumping her, saying: 'Knowest thou not the courage of this runaway, that when he sees a bit of iron of any sort he swoons?' 'This was her behaviour for the rest of her life." (Storia Do Mogor Vol. II, P. 261-262).

These baseless and conflicting stories show that Bernier or some one else, who heard about the brave deeds performed by the Rājpūt ladies all over Rājpūtānā and specially at Mewar, invented such a story and the later writers followed him blindly with some modifications.

It is quite clear that though the Imperial Muslim nobles, as well as some Hindu Mansabdārs left the battle field and a large number of the Mahārājā's own warriors were killed, he went on facing the princes bravely even after being wounded more than once, but was forcibly removed from the field by his kinsmen and ministers. Moreover the fight was a domestic quarrel among the princes and did not effect Marwar, as is stated by Sir Jadunath Sarkar and quoted above, hence there seems to be no reason for a sane Rājpūt wife to adopt such a foolish attitude towards her husband. The different versions found in different books also prove its fabrication. Dr. Ōjhā has also discredited this story in his Rājpūtāne-kā-Itihās, (Vol. IV, part I, p. 436).

6. Letters exchanged between Emperor Aurangzeb and his son Prince Mohammed Akbar.

(Read at the XX Congress International Des Orientalists held at Brussels in September 1938 as well as at Second Indian History Congress held at Allahabad in October 1938 and published in its proceedings, pp. 355-360)

After the death of Mahārājā Jaswant Singh I, at Jamrūd in 1678 A. D., the Emperor Aurangzēb annexed Marwar and the Rāthōr nobles were obliged to keep their newly born ruler, Mahārājā Ajitsingh, concealed in the mountains and raise the banner of revolt against the oppressor. When the pressure of these Rāṭhōrs grew untolerable the Emperor himself reached Ajmer and sent his son Prince Mōhammed Akbar to quell the rebellion. But soon Durgādās, Sōnag and other chiefs of Rāthōr nobility prepared Akbar to usurp the throne of Delhi, like his own father, and proclaim himself the Emperor of India on the 3rd January 1681 A. D.

It was a great shock to the Emperor, as at that time he was camping with a very small army and so he tried to deceive his son by sending him the following letter:—

Translation of the letter.

"Dearest son, light of the eyes and dearer than life being blessed with special favours should know—Almighty knows well that we loved him better than all his other brothers. Our benevolent self had always kept his health, wealth, prosperity and comfort at heart. But due to his unworthiness he has fallen into the trap of the deceitful Rājpūts and being driven away, like Adam from the lap of his mother and the side of his father, is now wandering in the forests and mountains of misery and is contemplating to execute malicious plans and conspiracies.

Learning the mournful news of his roaming about in wilderness and discomfort, we are greatly pained and have lost the charm of our own pleasures. Fie! it is a great pity that leaving aside the regal dignity, that simple and inexperienced boy neither took pity on his own self nor his wife and children and has given himself over to beastly and cruel Rājpūts and is rolling here and there like a ball fallen into the hands of rude people.

Father has a natural love for his sons. Though this son has committed great faults, yet we do not want that he be treated according to his deserts.

"If the son is a heap of ashes yet he is the collyrium of his parents' eyes[1]".

Done is done. But even now, if on showing him the right path, he repents for his misdeeds and returns in our service the pen of pardon will be struck through the records of his faults and those gifts and favours, which he could not have even dreamt before, will be bestowed on him.

Though for the bestowal of those favours his presence in person is not essential, yet his evil reputation is now widely known and every young and old has heard about his follies, it is necessary that once he should present himself in the court and efface this black spot from his forehead.

How Jaswant, the leader of these Rāthōrs, behaved with Dārāshikōh and how far he helped him is so well known that it requires no repetition. That son who has built castles in air on the promises of these Rāthōrs will reap nothing else but repentence.

He should bear all this well in mind and may wisdom and light guide him".

Prince Mohammed Akbar's reply to his father.

"Mōhammad Akbar, the youngest son, humbly informs his father, who is revered in both in this world and the next that the mandate, which was addressed to the youngest son for

1 The matter given in inverted commas in both the letters re-produced here is in couplets in the original letters.

the special purpose, was received in good time and on auspicious occasion. After humble submission its ink has been anointed in the eyes of wisdom as collyrium and by knowing its favourable purpose eyes of the heart were enlightened.

In reply to each and every instruction, inscribed by the paternal pen, a few words are written which are true and if judged impartially, will be found not far from justice.

You have written that you had loved him (the youngest son) more than all the other sons, but his own unworthiness ignored this great generosity and has thrown himself in the whirlpool of folly.

Emperor of spiritual and temporal world! may he be safe, as the duty of a son is to serve and please his father, likewise the duty of a father is to bring up, educate and guard the health and life of his son. Praise be to God, uptill now I have left no stone unturned in service and obedience, but how can I enumerate the favours of Your Majesty. As one from a thousand or as if a drop from the ocean it is brought to the notice that to help and side with the youngest son is the foremost duty of a revered father always and everywhere, but Your Majesty, leaving aside the love of all the other sons, have bestowed the title of "Shāh" upon the eldest son and declared him the heir-apparent. How this action can be justified ?

Every son has got equal right in his father's property. Which religion permits of preference of one over the others? There is another true and omniscient Emperor, in whose workshop of power and wisdom there is no place for false logic. To elevate or degrade rests upon His will, which is not devoid of prudence. But what to speak of Your Majesty's religious mindedness, justice and wisdom, which are an open book to all.

'Let us see whom the beloved Almighty loves and favours'.

Your Majesty is the originator and preceptor of this path. How can this path which has been chosen by Your Majesty be called wrong ?

'When my father sold the garden of paradise for 2 grains of wheat,[1] shall I not be called unworthy of him if I do not sell it for a grain of barley'.

'Worthy son is he who follows in the footsteps of his Sire'.

If one wants to prosper like his father he should learn to act like him.[2]

Your Majesty! man has always faced difficulties and dangers. Mighty monarchs like Taimūr[3] and Akbar[4] had gained their objectives after surmounting numerous difficulties.

'He who is not prepared to face difficulties will never gain any pleasure.'

It is proved by history that he who bears no hardship of darkness cannot qualify himself to taste nectar and he who faces no troubles cannot taste the fruits of pleasure, as there is no flower without thorn and no treasure without serpent.

'He who kisses the blade of sword embraces the goddess of the kingly fortune.'

When every hardship is followed by prosperity, by the grace of Almighty, there is every hope that in a few days the fulfilment of desires will be within sight and the state of perplexity and wandering may change into success and pleasure.

Your Majesty hints that to what extent Jaswant, the leader of the Rāthōrs, helped Dārāshikōh is well known and that the promises and words of the Rāthōr clan are not to be relied upon, may be quite correct. But Your Majesty has not

1 According to Mōhmedan belief God created Adam and kept him in paradise instructing him not to eat the fruit of knowledge (wheat). But Adam disobeyed His command. Being displeased God hurled him down in this mortal world.

The well known Persian poet Hāfiz of Shiraz has composed a poem expressing the idea—if I shall not do something more than what my father has done I shall be called an unworthy son. Prince Akbar has quoted this couplet in his letter here declaring "When my father has done such things, either I must do something more or give myself up to be called an unworthy son".

2. This is from Sheikh Sādī of Shīrāz the well known Persian poet

3. The word 'Sāhib Qirān' used for Taimūr here means—the Lord of happy conjunction of stars or a fortunate and invincible hero

4. The word 'Arsha Ashiyānī' used for Emperor Akbar here means nestling at the foot of the divine throne.

reached the depth of the facts, because Your Majesty has no brains. In fact, Dārāshikōh had a dislike for this clan and therefore he met just what he deserved.

Had he been friendly with these people from the very beginning he would not have been reduced to such an extremity.

Emperor Akbar—peace be on him, strengthening the ties of alliance with them, conquered the whole of India and on their strength made his empire firm. This is the very race with whose help Mahābatkhān obtained control over the Emperor Jahāngīr. The bravery of Rājpūts cannot be easily forgotten, as only three hundred of them performed great deeds of valour, like Rustum, befitting their tradition, even when Your Majesty, himself was adorning the crown and throne at the capital.[1] Jaswant was the same who had disgraced Your Majesty more than once even in your campaigns against enemies and Your Majesty seeing no way of avenging the insults deliberately overlooked the matter. That was the same Jaswant, whom Your Majesty kept away by various promises and pretexts from joining Dārāshikōh and that was the very cause of your victory, over your brother.

Praise be to their loyalty who sacrifice their heads for their prince and even do not hesitate to put their lives at stake.

O Emperor of India! many princes and nobles are in search of Seva[2] since the last 3 years, yet it is only first day for them. All this does not cause surprise because ministers are helpless, nobles untrustworthy, soldiers inefficient, clerks worthless, merchants paupers and the people down-trodden. The Deccan, a land like heaven, has become deserted and abandoned as a forest and a mountain. Burhānpur—the abode of pleasure, which is like a mole on the cheek of the earth, gives a spoiled and deserted appearance. Aurangābād which bears Your Majesty's name and hence is an important city among others, shivers like quick-silver by the massacres and plunders of the enemy's forces. The administrators enjoy at home and the

1. The three hundred Rājpūts carried away their infant prince Ajitsingh to Marwar against the wishes of the Emperor.

2. Well known Maharattā knight Shivājī, who died on 5th April 1680, but probably the writer here might have meant Sambhā his son and successor.

people are at the mercy of the enemy.[1] Where such atrocities prevail, there is no wonder if the inhabitants of the place find themselves unable to praise and bless their king. High persons of old nobility and respected people live in obscurity, while the work of administration and the strings of advisors are in the hands of low born and wicked persons. Cotton cleaners, weavers, soap-sellers and sweepers wield power.

Persons dressed in loose garments, to hide their treachery and deceit, hold the net of the satan in the shape of a rosary and preach religion. While Your Majesty considering them friends, advisors and ministers, like Gibrāel[2], Michāel[3] and Isrāfīl[4], have delegated your powers in their hands.

Those knaves, who sow wheat but sell barley, getting opportunity declare a feather of a pigeon as that of a red duck and a straw a mountain.

'In the reign of king Ālamgīr, the champion of the faith, soap-sellers have become law givers and religious heads'.

'Carders and weavers take pride in knowing the secrets of the Emperor's court'.

'Rogues wield such powers that scholars wait at their doors'.

'Fools exercise such great authority as was never dreamt of by the wise'.

'God forbid, in these unsettled times horses are kicked by asses'.

Your Majesty's orders are thrown to the winds. Justice and wisdom have disappeared. The officials of the kingdom have become merchants and traders. They buy positions with money and sell them to fulfil their base desires.

He who eats salt breaks the salt-cellar. The time is not far away when the foundation of the kingdom may collapse.

1. Mahaṛaṭṭā army.
2. Gibrāel—an angel of God.
3. Michāel—another angel.
4. Isrāfīl—The angel of death, who is to blow the last trumpet.

When such conditions exist and there seems no hope of change in Your Majesty's policy, the kingly duties force me to clear the country of Hindustān by removing rubbish and thorns spread in the shape of rogues and oppressors and to uproot lawlessness by promoting the wise and learned. By doing so, the creation of God, after being free from anxiety and oppression, engage themselves calmly in their own pursuits and the fame which is real and eternal may everlast in the world.

How good it would be, if Your Majesty develops the desire of leaving this work in the hands of your youngest son and yourself start on a holy pilgrimage of Meccā and Madīnā to gain eternal bliss and make the world ever grateful and thankful.

Your Majesty has lost a greater part of your life in coveting the worldly objects, which are more unreal than dreams and more unsteady than the shadows of the clouds. Now the time has come when you should do something for the next world in order to atone for the past sins, which were perpetrated in your prime of life, to satisfy the greed of worldly desires, by your outrageous conduct towards your revered father and noble brothers.

'These sixty years are wasted in sleep. Yet try to make a better use of the rest'.

Besides this the trouble taken by the paternal pen in thrusting some more advices, deserves admiration.

'What good have you done to your father which you expect from your son'.

'You tender advice to others, but better try to hear yourself first whatever you have to say to others.'

'When you cannot cure yourself keep away from advising others.'

I regard it a stroke of good fortune that you advise me to return to you. But the memory of treatment meted out to your father and brothers. since early days of your youth, creates a just fear and suspicion in the mind of one, who, has become target of anger without sufficient cause and that fear and suspicion is not groundless. But if your gracious Majesty take the trouble to come here this suspicion will be dispelled and peace and pleasure reign in their place.

'We are unable to reach that elevated door, but if kindly grace steps forward it will be more appropriate.'

On Your Majesty's arrival when the mind will be appeased hearty obedience to the kindly commands will be deemed a good fortune.

In this unknown State. . ...

'Kill or grant pardon, my head lies at your door; I am not to give commands, but am at your mercy!'

With greatest respects. May the sun of kingship ever shine'.

A good deal of information is gained from these letters about the conditions prevailing at that time and the causes of the rise and fall of the Mughal Empire.

7. A Letter of Maharaja Ajitsinghji relating to the Emergency Administration of Marwar.

Published in 'New Indian Antiquary,' Bombay Vol. I No. 7 (October 1938) pp. 444-449.

On the death of Maharaja Jaswantsingh I, in 1678 A. D. the emperor Aurangzēb annexed Marwar. But after 28 years of continual fight his son Mahārājā Ajitsingh re-captured Jodhpur, the capital of the State, as soon as the Emperor Aurangzēb died, in 1707 A. D., in the Deccan. After this his son and successor Bahādur Shāh also invaded Marwar and compelled Mahārājā Ajitsingh to leave the State administration in the hands of the Mughal officials and to accompany him against his brother Kāmbaksh. But as soon as Bahādur Shāh crossed the Narbadā, Mahārājā Ajit returned to his capital and driving away the Mughal garrison took the reins of the administration in his own hands.

In 1713 A. D. Emperor Farrukhsiyar, who ascended the throne of Delhi after Jahāndār Shāh, sent an army under Sayyad Husainalīkhān against Marwar. As soon as this news reached Jodhpur, Mahārājā Ajitsingh went towards Tilwārā in the western part of Marwar for war preparations and sent his trustworthy and loyal noble Chānpāvat Thākur Rāo Bhagvāndās to Jodhpur with a letter containing a number of detailed instructions to be carried on.

This letter will give an idea of the condition prevailing then and the manner in which the affairs of the State were managed at the time of emergency and will also throw light on the administrative qualities of Mahārājā Ajitsingh of Marwar.

(महाराजा अजितसिंघजीके स्वहस्तसे लिखी पत्रके ऊपरकी पंक्तियाँ.)

तथा अजराह नीवाजसरै देसरी खीजमत फरमाय बीदा कीया है नै नसीयत बीगतवार फैरिसत फुरमावै सो फेम राख काम कर्णो हुकम छै सही।

(मुहर का लेख)

श्री हजूर छत्रपती महाराजाधिराज महाराजा श्रीअजीतसिंहजी देव विजयते।

......पती भूप तामरस....पख....पर राजत रा......हरि अंबे शिव सूर विनायक, ए सुर पंच सदा फल दायक॥

(महाराज के हस्ताक्षरोंमें)

"हुकम छै"

फरमांण अलीसांन दलकत खास मोहर खास ईनायत पातसाही।

जील सुभानी॥

(पत्र)

सिद्ध श्री अनेक सकल सुभ ओपमा विराजमांनानां श्री हिंदूपत पातसाह छत्रपती महाराजाधिराज महाराजा श्रीअजीतसिंघजी महाराज कंवार श्रीअभैसिंघजी देव वचनात तथा निवाजसरै राह राव भगवांनदास जोगीदासोतनूं पायतखत गढ जोधपुरनुं सारी बात रा जाबतारै वासतै बीदा कीया सो श्रीहुकम समारक रै माफक जाबतो करसी।

वीगत—

१. जोधपुर हीज रैणौ

२. अजमेर मेडतै नागोर खबरदारी राखणी आदमी भावै इनवारी बांभण साह कायथ सो सावधान रहीजो आदमी बावा के कांना नीसर होय सो जावतो करणो।

३. श्रीजी न करै पीण कदाच कांई आयंबणै तो श्रीहजूरसुं अरज लिखणी ईणांरै भरोसे न रहणो ने कासीद तथा मातबर आदमी मेलणो नैं श्रीहजुर नैं अरज लिखणी सो महासिंघरी मारफत अरज पोहचै जाब ईणांसुं हीज ईनायत होसी।

४. अरजदासत सीरकार रा कासीद साथे आई करै नै सुणी हकीकत लीखणी नैं कांमरी अरज लीखणी नैं श्रीजी हजूरसू पीण फुरमाण मेलो हीज हमेसा ईनायत होसी।

५. कांमकांज में सावधांन रैहणो।

६. कांम मामलै पांच आदमियांसु जोडै राखणो आपैणांसुं तथा गोढवाड सीरोही नागोर वाला तेडीया आवै।

७. गढ ऊपर संचो राखणो नै तोपां सारै चढावणी।

---

१ बाहर जायें। २ मौका आ पडे। ३ जवाब। ४ इन्हीं को। ५ साथ। ६ मेल। ७ अपनोंसे। ८ बुलानेसे। ९ संचय।

८. गढ रो पेसो जावतो राखणो रहे आय पोहचां जीतरै कायम रहै ने गई खबर हुवां श्रीजी थांने नां आवां नो वेगा पीण तीन बीस पचीस तो खरा ।

९. कोंगल थांरी नांवरो ने मुतसदीरा सकों ने भेलो लीखणो ।

१०. गोयंददास ने दयालदास नें हुकम हुवो छै सो थानुं ईसारो सारो करता रैहसी नें रीणीवतें ईणा ऊपर अनरोंजी होसी तो हुकम ईणानुं नै थानुं ईनायत होसी सो हमांरी मारफत रो कहे जीण मांन करजो ।

११. अजमेर सुं हरकिणी वहानै जोधपुर आदमी आवे काजी तथा मुला वाकांनवेस तो मेडतावालां था जावतो राखणो ने श्रीहजूर सुं पीण हुकम ईनायत होसी आघो आवणै न देसी पीणी कदासें आवे तो दखल वीना हुकम मत देवो ने खांण ने पीण मत देवो ने कदाचीत कोई रीजीलो होय तो रातरा बीस तीस असवार मेलणां के पौला सो जाय रातरा खूंद ने मारने परा जाय नें पछै सुहैरे कूटी वाहेर चढावजो ने मुलें तो बीसलपुर जावतो रहै।

१२. कार्फलो गुढा में होय जाय पीण जोधपुरमें नावै हुकम छै कठाहीरो सैहर नजीक नावै ।

१३. पेहमदावाद रो ही जावतो राखणो ।

१४. उदैपुर पीण जावतो रहे खबर आई करै कुण गयो रैहो ।

१५. दोय आवे नो घांणोरा चर्का सुं जावतो रहे ।

१६. हकीकत सुणो सो वाकानवेस ने पोंहचाजो सो लीखसी ने थांने हीज लीखणी होय सो थे लीखजो ।

१७. दरो पदा होय ने श्रीजी हजूर ने चाले के दीली नुं चाले सो के लीयो न लीयो स्यायत लागथाजी जीणरो फैमरोंखणो ।

१८. हरकोर किणीरी न करणी ।

१९ पेसलुक सूं चाले तो भली वात छै ने नही तो कहजो घेते माफक ।

२०. श्रीजी हजूर सुं ओलंभो आवे तो चमकजो मती दफेलथंका कांम में रैहजो ने पेसो कोई जरुर जांणसां तो महासिंघ री मारफत ने श्रीजी दरबार री तरफ दोनुं एक हुकम आवै नो उण माफक जावतो राखजो ।

२१. दीजमें दलेलो राखजो ।

२२. सीवांसांढांरो जावतो राखणो चांगीरैंद कांकैड छै तैठे ।

२३. कठीन फोज मेलणी देवल सीधैज राठैधरै ।

संवत् १७७१ रा भाद्रवा सुद ५ मुं ॥ तलवाडे

---

१० कायाज । ११ तुम्हारे । १२ किसीतरह । १३ ऐतराज । १४ होगा । १५ भवरनवीस । १६ आनै । १७ होंगे । १८ पर । १९ कमी । २० कमीना=नालायक । २१ भेजने । २२ पैदल । २३ सुबहको । २४ अनुसंधानकारीदल । २५ गाम । २६ याजीदल । २७ रहा । २८ मरजो । २९ बायेराव । ३० तुम्हें । ३१ दिल्ली को जानेवाले या नगर में आनेवाले सामान पर चुंगी ली या नहीं इसका पूरा ध्यान रखना । ३२ कुताहिग्रा । ३३ जिन्दीदा । ३४ ठीकतौर । ३५ मौके पे । ३६ शिकायत । ३७ दिलासे के साथ । ३८ दिलासा=विश्वास । ३९ समाप्रान्तका । ४० चारों तरफ । ४१ सीमा । ४२ वहां । ४३ किधर । ४४ भेजनी । ४५ देवल-राजपूतों पर । ४६ सींधल-राजपूतों पर । ४७ राठोड़ों के गांव पर ।

(ऊपर के वेष्टन का मज़मून)

अजराह नीवाजसरै ईलकाब इनायत नीज परमभगत परायणानां सुँकीइषु सदा परधानानां स्वामधरमेषु। वजीर आजम ज़ुमदुतुलमुलक मदारलमहाम राव भगवानदासै।

४८ स्वकीयेषु।   ४९ स्वामिधर्म पालनेवाले।

50. Champā, one of the younger brothers of Rao Jōdhājī, the founder of Jodhpur, was a well known warrior His eighth in descent Rao Bhagwardas to whom this letter was addressed, served Mahārājā Ajitsinghjī during the occupation of Marwar by the Mohemmadans. His loyal services had been summarised by the Mahārājā himself in the following couplet.

भगवानो जोगातणौ, सक सांवत सिरताज।
कियो बिखो मरुधर मझै लियां भुंजां कुललाज॥

(i e) Bhagvāndās, son of Jōgidās, who is the leader of all the brave nobles, fought the enemies of Marwar and kept the honour of his clan un-tarnished.

His ninth descendant was Rao Bahadur Thākur Mangal Singhji, C I. E., a noble soul, who served the Jodhpur Darbār loyally and faithfully as a member of the State Council. His eldest son the present Thākur of Pōkaran is Rao Bahadur Thākur Chain Singh, M A., LL. B., (who lately retired from the membership of the Council) and who enjoys the hereditary privilege of occupying the first seat on the right side row of the nobles of Marwar Darbār

Translation

The top lines written in Maharaja Ajitsinghji's own hand-writing run as below:—

"We have sent you as a special favour to serve the country and command you to carry out carefully the detailed instructions issued by us."

Then there is a royal seal which contains:—

"Glory be to Shrī Huzūr Chhatrapati, Maharājādhirāj, Mahārājā Shri Ajitsinghjī Dēva.

Hari, Ambā, Shiva, Sun and Gaṇēsh—may these five deities always bestow favours."

Then there is a mark of approval in his own calligraphy and another three lines which go as under:—

"It is our Command.

"This royal mandate under our own signature and royal seal is issued under the shadow of God."

Translation of the letter.

"By order of the—blessed, adorned with many auspicious qualities, protector of Hindūs, emperor, sovereign ruler, king of kings, Mahārājā Shrī Ajitsinghji and his heir-apparent Abhaisinghjī Rāo Bhagvāndās, son of Jōgīdās, has been sent to Jodhpur, our capital, as a mark of special favour, to look after all the State affairs and act according to our auspicious command.

1. He should remain at Jodhpur.

2. He should watch over the affairs of Ajmer, Merta and Nagaur, and be observant of Brāhmans, Mahājans and Kāyasths even if they are reliable, and find out the purpose of the people who leave the place openly or secretly.

3. May God forbid, even then, if anything untoward happens he should write to us and should not depend on others, but send a messenger or trustworthy man with a written report, which will be submitted to us through Mahāsingh and its reply too will be communicated through him.

4. He should send his reports of current rumours and matters related to the administration with State messengers and the orders from us will always be communicated to him and Mahāsingh jointly.

5. He should always be cautious in his duties.

6. He should, for the safety of the State, keep friendly relations with others, so that when need be they may come to our help from our land and from Gōdwād, Sirōhī and Nāgaur.

7. He should stock all necessary things in the fort and mount guns on all strategic points.

8. He should manage the affairs of the fort in such a way that it may stand the siege of the enemy till the time of our arrival. God willing, we hope to reach early on receipt of information, yet it may take at least twenty or twenty-five days.

9. Letters from other officials as well as from you should be sent together.

10. Gōyanddās and Dayāldās have been instructed to keep you in touch from time to time and if there will be any objection to their action simultaneous orders will be issued to both of you through them, then you should carry out their fresh instructions.

11. If a Qāzī (Law giver), a Mullā (religious preacher) or a newswriter comes from Ajmer on any pretext he should be kept away from the people of Merta. We shall also issue necessary instructions on such occasions. But such a man should not be allowed to approach nearer and if he comes at all you should not allow him to take possession and refuse rations. Moreover, if any wicked person dares to approach, you should stealthily get him killed at night by sending twenty or thirty mounted or foot soldiers and then the next morning institute a false search and investigate the matter. Special care should be taken of Bisalpur.

12. Carvans may pass through Gudhā but not through Jodhpur. It is our command that it should not come nearer to any town.

13. You should also guard the affairs of Ahmadābād.

14. You should watch the affairs at Udaipur and inform us of the departure and arrival of the people there.

15. If necessary, keep friendly with the people of Ghānerāo.

16. Whatever you hear communicate it to the news-writer, so that he may write it to us and whatever you think more important you should write yourself.

17. Take care of customs duty and see whether it has been duly charged on goods imported in Marwar or exported to Delhi. No partiality need be allowed.

18. None should be shown undue favours.

19. If they carry on well, all is for the good, otherwise take them to task according to circumstances.

20. If we censure your work do not lose heart. Whenever we would like to make a necessary change in the policy, we shall send you same instructions through Mahāsingh as well as directly, at the same time, and then you should make changes in your management accordingly.

21. Be always confident at heart.

22. You should keep watch on border lands all round the country.

23. You should arrange to send detachments on Dēval and Sindhal Rājpūts and Rāḍdharā town."

Dated 5th day of the bright half of Bhādaun, Samvat 1771 (3rd September 1714 A. D.). Camp Talwārā."

Reading on the cover.

"On account of special favour the titles conferred on you are—our devoted, loyal, trusted, premier and faithful noble, Chief Minister, (Jumdutulmulk) centre of important affairs and (Madārulmahām) the best in the country Rāo Bhagvāndās."

8. A Letter of Maharana Sangramsingh II addressed to Maharaja Ajitsingh of Marwar.

(Published in (Dr. A. C) Woolner Commemoration Volume pp. 206-208)

Mahārājā Ajitsingh, the posthumous son of Mahārājā Jaswantsingh I of Marwar was born, at Lahore, on the 4th day of the dark half of Chaitra in Vikrama Samvat 1735 (19th February 1679 A. D.).

Mahārājā Jaswantsingh I, being an independent-minded ruler, was a hindrance to the bigotry of Aurangzēb and though the emperor could not openly show his displeasure towards him, and tried to keep him calm by frequently bestowing on him honours and responsibilities of the administration of the countries far away from his motherland, yet he cherished a secret desire of revenge in his heart.

This was the main cause why as soon as Mahārājā Jaswantsingh I breathed his last at Jamrūd, on the 10th day of the dark half of Pausha in V. S. 1735 (28th November 1678 A. D.) emperor Aurangzēb took possession of Marwar, revived 'Jazia' and ordered building of the mosques and demolition of Hindū temples.

Further on the birth of Mahārājā Ajitsingh when the loyal Sardārs of Marwar requested him to return the Rāthōr State of Marwar to the newly born ruler, he on the one hand tried to keep them in the dark by putting forward one or the other pretext and on the other hand began to hasten his occupation of Marwar for ever,

No sooner was the intention of the emperor realised than did these Sardārs of Marwar resolve to take away their infant ruler secretly from Delhi and free him from the clutches of the emperor. Any how they brought him to Marwar, his ancestral state, at the risk of their lives. But as the country was by now in full occupation of the Mughals, they were obliged to seek shelter in the mountains, hiding the infant prince at some unknown and impregnable place.

The infant Mahārājā remained there for about 8 years and for 20 years his loyal Sardārs fought with Mughals to drive them away from the country. The Mahārājā himself on maturity took the lead in this struggle. Though he took back Jodhpur, the capital of Marwar, on the 5th day of the dark half of Chaitra in V. S. 1763 (12th March 1707 A. D.), yet he was not completely out of danger for some years to come. However in a dozen years the conditions were reversed, for in Bhādon of V.S. 1775 (August 1718 A.D.) Farrukhsiyar, the then emperor of Delhi himself was obliged to seek the help of the Mahārājā. But owing to the fickle mindedness of the emperor, the Mahārājā soon lost his confidence in him and making an alliance with the Sayyad brothers put Rafi-ud--darjāt on the throne of Delhi.

This new emperor under the guidance of Mahārājā Ajitsingh soon stopped the 'Jaziā' and other taxes levied in places of Hindū pilgrimage.

We quote below a letter of Mahārānā Sangrāmsingh II of Mewar which will show that Mahārājā Ajitsingh who having once been victim of the anger of the emperor of Delhi was brought from there in disguise and concealed in the mountains, in the course of time became one of the three king--makers of the Mughal empire.

पत्र की नक़ल

(सीधी तरफ़)

१—स्वस्ति श्री दीली सुथाने महाराजा [धिराज महा]-
२—[रा] जजी श्री महाराज श्री अजीत [सिंहजी ....
३—(उ) देपुर था राणा संग्रामसिंघ लिखावत [मुजरे]
४—वाचजो जी अठारा समाचार भला है जी रावला

५—कागद समाचार सदा कहावजोजी राज ठाकु [र]
६—हो वडा हो देन मया राखो हो तीधी वीसेस [रखा]—
७—घजोजी थां राज रो घर है उठा अठारा [यक वा]—
८—त कर आणजोजो जुदायगी कणी वात [न]—
९—लेखवोजी .. . ..
१०—अप्र [च] राजरो कागद आयो तथा राज ली [खी फ–]
११—रुखसेर कोता अंदेसरे कहे म्हां है बुलाया था
१२—सो सैदा थी ने माथी ओरतरे वीचारी थी जणी—
१३—प्रे अमीरल उमराव दोलण थी बुलावे ने. . . .
१४—साह रफीअलदरजात तखत वैठाया ने

(उलटी तरफ़)

१५—हिदुस्थान रो जेजीयो छुडायो ने तीरथांरो अ—
१६—टकाव थो सो मीटायो जीख्या सो सगली हकी—
१७—कत थांच्यां थी घणी खुस्याली हुइ सो राज स—
१८—रीखो अठा पेहली कोई हिंदुवां माहे. .. .
१९—हुओ ना असुं हेगो ईश्वर ईसा मोटा..... ..
२०—ना घणी घणी ऊपजावे ईणी वातम.... .
२१—है वडो नफो हे सो ईश्र दीन तुरकां रा अ. ......
२२—था सोवे आपणा आसीरत हुआ.... .. [ह]
२३—कीकत लीखी सो ईवारुं हिंदुस [था] नरो वोज. .....
२४—लो उणाहीज थी हे ने.. ...पण
२५—कर ठेठ थी जांणे हे सो आपां हे........
२६—दरकार हे ने कोता अंदेस तुरक
२७—री वात आगे ही हलकी नीज़र आ [ई........वि]
२८—[ना] वीचारे काम न करेगा ने हलका [ला] गा ने अ [ठा]
२९—री वात सदा राजरा घररी हे ज्यूंही जांणे काम चा-
३०—करी फुरमावेगा राज करे आखा हिंदुस्था[न में]
३१—नचीताई है म्हे तो घणा नचीता हां [घणो कांई]
३२—लीखां संवत् १७७५ वर्षे वेसाख वदी ११

(सीधी तरफ़ आड़ी लकीर में महाराणा की स्वहस्तलिपि मे)

१—श्री [राज] राजेश्वर जी हजुर मुजरो मालम व्हे श्री [जी] रा प्रताप
२—थी....[मो] टी फते कीई जणी....खी लखी सो [अणीरी] वात सारा हींदुसथांने

(उलटी तरफ़ आड़ी लकीर मे महाराणा की स्वहस्तलिपि मे)

३—कलस चड्यो—ईसी मोटी वात राज थीज वणे सवज......री
४—वाते नचीता [हां]........ईतरे राज जोग है।

(PURPORT OF THE LETTER)

Mahārājā Ajitsinghji at Delhi should accept the compliments from Mahārānā Sangrāmsingh of Udaipur. We all are doing well and you should inform us about your own welfare. You are great. You would continue showing more and more intimacy. Consider this state your own and do not see any difference in any matter. Your letter received. You wrote that the short-sighted Farrukhsiyar called you and tried to harm you together with the Sayyads. On this you called Amīr-ul-umrā from the Deccan and by putting Rafi-ud-darjāt on the throne (of Delhi) got the Hindustān freed from 'Jaziā' and the restrictions imposed on the sacred places. I am very glad to learn all this. No one like you had taken birth among the Hindūs uptill now nor is any expected in future. May God give you more success. This is a great gain to us all. Until this day the Mohemmadans were more powerful but now they seek our support ...(1.23-25)......The short-sighted Mughal had even lost his prestige once before. He would not do any thing in future without careful consideration as he has lost his prestige. You should consider this place as your own house. Please let me know if I may be of any service to you. On account of you all India is safe and specially we ourselves. What more should we write?

Dated 11th day of the dark half of Vaishākha Samvat 1775.

(Horizontal line in Mahārānā's own hand-writing on obverse of the letter)

The king of kings should accept my compliments. You wrote that by the grace of God you have achieved a great victory. This has———

(Horizontal line in Mahārānā's own hand-writing on reverse).

made your fame well-known all over India. You are the only person who can accomplish this. We are safe in your presence. You are fit to do all this.

9. A letter of Maharaja Ajitsingh relating to the death of Emperor Farrukhsiyar.

[Read at the Ninth All India Oriental Conference held at Trivendram in December 1937 and published in its proceedings and transactions, pp 839-842.]

In 1713 A. D. Emperor Farrukhsiyar, who had seated himself on the throne of Delhi, sent Sayyad Husain Ali Khān at the head of an army against Jodhpur. When this news reached Jodhpur the Mahārājā went towards Tilwārā (Western part of Marwar) for the war-preparations and appointed his premier noble Chanpāvāt Bhagvāndās, with detailed instructions, to look after the administration of the country. But soon a treaty was concluded and Farrukhsiyar recognised Mahārājā Ajitsingh as the lawful ruler of Marwar.

In 1718 A. D, displeased with the growing power of the Sayyad brothers, Emperor Farrukhsiyar sent for Mahārājā Ajitsingh, but before he saw him some courtiers found an opportunity to poison his (Emperor's) ears against him, and the king, being thus displeased with the Mahārājā, wanted to get him murdered. The events which took place since the arrival of Mahārājā Ajitsingh at Delhi to the accession of Rafiuddarjāt and the causes which compelled the Mahārājā to join in the assassination of the Emperor can best be known from the translation of Mahārājā Ajitsingh's own letter, to his loyal official, Sobhavat Dayāldās, given below:—

(स्वयं महाराजा के हस्ताक्षरों मे लिखी पंक्तियां ।)

(हा) थ पकड नखत — — — —
हँस म्हे घरे वेगा पधार्गं छां
तु (खुस्याली) न्रे हुरगा छै सही

(मोहर का लेख ।)

(छत्र प) ति श्री राजराजेस्वर महाराजाधिराज
महाराजा श्री अजीतसिंह देव विजयते भानुतेज सरूपेण महीमण्येषु राजते
हरि अंबे शिव सूर विनायक पे सुर पंच सदा फलदायक

(महाराजा की सही ।)

हुकम है

(पत्र ।)

स्वांरूपां श्री अनेक सकल सुभ ओपमा विराजमानानां श्री राजराजेस्वर महाराजाधिराज महाराजा श्री अजीतसिंघजी महाराज कंवार श्री अभैसिंघजी देव वचनात सीकदार दयालदास दीसे सुप्रसाद बाँचजो ।

तथा अरजदास्तां तथा उवाकारी फरदां श्री हजुर नीजर गुदरी हकीकत सारी तपसीलवार मालुम हुई ।
तथा पैलां तो म्हांनु फरकसेर ओर मनसोबै माथै बुलाया था सु अठै आया जरै जैसिंघजी कोता अंदेस थका फरकसेर रै कांने लागा सु म्हांसु नीजर फेरदी नै आगे सैदा सुं पीण इण तकररी नीजर ओरतरै थी हीज जरे नबाब अवधलाखाजी नै म्है बीचार नै नवाब हसनअलीखांजी नु दखणं सु ताकीद कर बुलाया सु फा । वद १४ अठै आया जरै म्है नै दोनु नबावां सलाह ठहराई जो फरकसेर लायक पातसाही रै नहीं इणां रा फैल ने तरे नीपट अ बुन ? के ईण नु उठाय देवां नै ओर हर कोई बाहदरसाहारा पोतां मै थापां आ सलाह ठैहराय नै फा । सुद २ कीलो घेरीयो नै फा । सुद १० बुधवार फरकसेर नु पकड़ कैद कीयो नै साह रफीयलकदर रै बेटै रफीयलदरजात सुं केद मांही सु काढ़ नै तखत बैसाय पातसाह कीयो नै श्री श्रीजी रा प्रसाद्कर जेजीयो पीण म्है छुडायौ नै तीरथां रो पिण अटकाव थो सु ही दुर करायो पे बरै ही बातां आज तक हींदु कीणा सु न हुई सु श्रीजीरा प्रताप अनुग्रीहे सु म्हे कीवी के थे इणां बातांरी घंणी खुस्याली करजो ।

तथा बेसाख सुद १० फरकसेर रै गले तसमो खैचने मारियो । तथा जेठ वद ११ अदीतवार रै दीन पातसाहाजी सु म्है देसरी सीख कीवी सु पातसाजी इतरो दीयो तीणरी विगत— सीरपाव । घोडो पलांण जडाव रो । मोती कांन रा भारी कीमत रा पातसाहजी हाथा सु कांनां मै घालीया । सीरपेच जडाउ पातसाहाजी हाथा सुं बांधीयो । तरवार जडाऊ । हाथी । हथणी-आगै कीणी अमीर नु पातसाहां दीया नहीं साहजादां रा दसतुर माफक म्हांनु दीया । तुमनतोग बडो मरातब के साहजादां रै हुवै और कीणी अमीररै आज तक न हुवो सु म्हांनु दीयो ।

तथा पातसाहाजी बीदा करतां कहो पेक वार थे जरूर मीजने चालजो सु मतलब श्रोछै फेर रश्रायत करसी सु हकीकत पाछां सु लीखसां हमै वेगा देस पधारां छां थे घणी खुस्याली करजो।

तथा फरकसेर सु पेहेले दीन म्हे मीलीया तरे ऊणांहीज बीरीयां जेसिंघ मीया सु वात करने म्हासु चुक कीयो पछै दुजै फेरे घावडीया मांह राखने म्हांनु बुलाया था तीजै फेरे सीकार मे दगो विचारनै बुलाया था चोथे फेरे नावाडे बेसांण ने दगो वीचारीयो थो पछै वागमै सोर र? वीछायो थो ने बगतरपोस बरकंदाज राखनै म्हांनु बुलाया था फेर भांत भांत सु दगो वीचारीयो थो सु म्हांरै तो श्री हीगुलाजजी हमेसा साहाय छै नै जेसिघरै तथा मीयांरै मुढै धुड पडी सु जेसिंघ री तो कमाई ईसडी थी म्हे मारता नै श्रांबेर बगेरे देस मांह सु काढने श्रांबेर श्रोर कोई बेठांण ता पण ईस्वर सांमो देखनै जेसिघ नुं म्हे जीवा बचायो पेहेला तो श्रठेहीज मारता था पछै फरकसेर थको श्रठा सु नाठो सु पाछै फौजां बीदा कीवी तरै म्है वीचारीयो जेसिघ रै माजनै उप्र नीजर म्हांनु राखणी नंही म्है हीदुसथांन रा सीरदार छां ईणांनु जीवा बचांवणो ने ठीकाणो पण ईणां नु देणो तरै नबाबां सु सलाह करने फोजां मोकुफ राखी नै श्रांबेर बगेरे उतन मनसबो म्हे दीयो ने बीदर दीखणं मे छै, श्रांबेर सु कोस सो सात छै, तठै फोजदारी दैने बीदा कियो सु उठै जावसी म्है बीचारीयो हाथी री श्रसवारी करनै पछै छोटी श्रसवारी न वीचारीजै दीली रो पातसाह फरकसेर तिण नु म्हे उठाय केद कीयो नै दुजो खातर मे श्रायो सु केद मांह सु काढने म्हे पातसाहा कीयो तरै जैसिंघ री कीसी गीणंत छै श्रांबेर पेकवार तो श्रागे बेसांणीयो थो नै दुजीवार हीमारु तो जीवा बचायो नै श्रांबेर बगरे उतन मनसब म्हे दीयौ ने श्रौ। केसरीसिघ नु म्हे जेसिघजी री दीलासारे उवासदै मैलीयो छै सु जेठ सुद १ रो करार फुरमायो छै सु श्री हजुर मे श्ररज श्रावसी श्री हीगुलाजजी रा प्रसाद सु श्री दरबार रो बोल उपर हुश्रो चाहो थो सु सारा थोक कीया थे खुस्याली जांणजो हुकम छै।

सं॥ १७७५ रा जेठ बद ११ मु॥ जांहनाबाद

Translation.

Top lines written in Maharaja's own hand-writing.

Holding his hand (we seated him) on the throne. Now we are soon returning home. You should feel happy. Written under our command.

Contents of the Royal Seal.

By the grace of almighty goddess Hingulāj, glory be to sovereign ruler, King of Kings, Mahārājādhirāj, Mahārājā Shri Ajitsingh Dêva who shines like the sun on the earth.

Visnū, Ambā, Shiva, Sun and Vināyak—may these five deities always bestow favours.

Approval of the letter in Maharaja's own calligraphy.

It is our command.

Letter

By order of nobleself, graced with all the good qualities King of Kings, Sovereign ruler, Mahārājā Shrī Ajitsinghjī and his heir-apparent Shrī Abhaisinghjī, the City Magistrate Dayāldās should note their favours.

Your requests and the reports of the events were submitted to us and the detailed account became fully known.

In the beginning, Farrukhsiyar had sent for us with some other motive, but during the time of our reaching here (Delhi) short-sighted Jaisinghjī poisoned his ears and set him against us. Farruksiyar had already been hostile with the Sayyads and therefore we and Abdullākhān, after taking stock of the situation, sent for Husain Alī Khān to come post-haste from the Deccan. He reached here on the 14th of the dark half of Phāgun (7th February 1719 A. D.) and the two Sayyad brothers and we thought it advisable to depose Farrukhsiyar, and seat any of the grandsons of Bahādurshāh on the throne, as the former is quite unfit to be a king and his manners are mean and debased. Accordingly on the 2nd of the bright half of Phāgun (10th February 1719 A. D.) the fort was surrounded by troops and on Wednesday, the 10th of the bright half of Phāgun (18th February 1719 A.D.) Farrukhsiyar was imprisoned and in his place Rafiuddarjāt, the son of Rafiulkadar, after being released from prison, was placed on the throne and proclaimed king. Further by the grace of God we got the jaziā (the tax levied on the non-Muslims) abolished and restrictions on the holy places removed.

These twelve successes, which we have achieved by the grace of God, were never acquired by any Hindū uptill now and therefore you should feel it a cause of great satisfaction.

On the 10th of the bright half of Vaishākh (18th April 1719 A. D.) Farrukhsiyar was dispatched by fastening a cord round his neck and on Sunday, the 11th of the dark half of Jēth (3rd May 1719 A. D.), when we obtained the permission from the Emperor to return to our country, he honoured us with the following things.—Robe of honour, horse with studded saddle, priceless pearls, which the Emperor himself put in our ears, studded 'Sarpēch" (a head ornament), which was also tied by the Emperor by his own hands, a studded sword, a male elephant, a female elephant, not bestowed on any noble but the princes of royal blood only ere this, was awarded to us and "Tumantōgh" a great rank, which too was not conferred on any other noble ere this except on princes only, was conferred on us.

Besides this the Emperor asked us not to leave before seeing him once again and it is concluded that he will bestow more favours, which will be communicated to you later on. Now we are coming soon to our country and hence you should feel happy.

Further when we saw Farrukhsiyar for the first time he after consulting Jaisingh (of Āmbēr) and Miyān (Mīrjumalā) devised means to get us killed. A second time he sent for us keeping murderers concealed inside the chamber. For the third time he summoned us and wanted to kill us during the hunt. A fourth time he calling us at a lonely place wanted to finish us. Afterwards he, spreading gun-powder in the garden and appointing sharp shooters, clad in armour, sent for us. In short he contrived by various means to make short work of us. But as the Goddess Hingulāj always guards us the mouths of Jaisingh and Miyān were filled with dirt. Jaisingh deserved all this for his misdeeds. We would have killed him and depriving him of Āmbēr seated some one else there on the "Gaddi", but for the sake of God we saved his life.

At first we intended to finish him here, but he had already fled away in the life-time of Farrukhsiyar. So a detachment was sent in pursuit, but however on a second thought, we, being a great noble of Hindustān, deemed it proper to overlook malicious deeds of Jaisingh and to save his life and state. Accordingly after holding consultations with the Sayyad brothers we recalled the detachment and giving him Āmbēr and 'Mansab' sent him to Bidar to take command of the forces there. The place in the Deccan is fourteen hundred miles away from Āmbēr and he will soon leave for it. We thought that after mounting on an elephant the other conveyances are below our dignity and as we could dethrone and imprison Farrukhsiyar and after releasing the other one of our choice from prison put him on the throne, this Jaisingh does not deserve our attention. Once before we aided him to take possession of Āmbēr and this second time too we saved his life and gave him—Āmbēr— his native land, and 'Mansab.'

We have sent Purōhit Kēsarīsingh to assure Jaisingh and have taken words for the 1st of the bright half of Jēth (9th May 1719 A. D.) when report will be submitted to us.

By the grace of Goddess Hingulāj Darbār's words deserved supremacy and they have achieved the same. You should feel satisfaction. Written under our command.

11th day of the dark half of Jēth, Saṁvat 1775 (4th May 1719 A. D.)

Camp—Jahānābād (Delhi).

10. William Irvine and Maharaja Ajit Singh.

(Published in Indian Antiquary, Vol. LV III, (1929 A. D.) pp. 47 51.)

William Irvine was born on the 5th July 1840, at Aberdeen. He joined the Indian Civil Service in A. D. 1863, at the age of 23, and retired in 1888, at the age of 48. After this, in England, he commenced writing his history of the decline of the Mughal Empire entitled *Later Mughals*. This work is in two volumes, and covers the century from the death of Aurangzēb in 1707 to the capture of Delhi by the English in 1808. But the author died in 1911, leaving the work unfinished and, though the first draft was revised from time to time, only chapters II to VI, section 24, could be published in his life-time, and to these he gave his finishing touches. Chapter I (Bahādur Shāh), and chapter VII (from the fall of the Sayyid brothers in 1720, to the death of Rustam Alī Khān in February 1725), bear marks of his revision and corrections, though not in a complete or final form, as even in them he left many gaps to be filled up, and query marks for verification or correction. Beyond this his draft remained unrevised.

Thus the burden of completion of the book, after Irvine's death, devolved upon the well known Mughal historian Jadunāth Sarkār, who, having ably edited the book, got it published.

The above lines will give an idea of the work *Later Mughals*, which is thus the fruit of the combined effort of two learned scholars, namely Messrs. Irvine and Sarkār; more presumably so, is the subject of our enquiry, falling, as it does, under chapter VII of the book.

In the following paragraphs we reproduce section 29, chapter VII, vol. II, of the book, headed "Murder of Ajit Singh by his Son."

"We shall conclude this section with the death of Rajah Ajit Singh. Tod admits that the bards and chroniclers pass over the event with a mere mention, one of them going so far as to leave a blank page at the critical point of his story. But in another part of Tod's book, we have a detailed narrative of the crime.[1] In any case, that Ajit Singh met a violent death at the hand of his second son, Bakht Singh, is admitted by the Rajputs themselves, and even by their ardent champion Colonel Tod." (Tod, I, 698, II, 88).

"According to their story, Bakht Singh, after saying goodnight, concealed himself in a room adjoining the one in which his parents were sleeping. When all was still he entered their room, seized his father's sword, and plunged it into him. The wife was awakened by feeling her husband's blood on her breast. Bakht Singh escaped. Ajit Singh's body was cremated on the 7th June 1724, when eighty-four wives and concubines sacrificed themselves on his funeral pyre. A dispute about the succession at once arose between the sons on the spot. On the 25th July 1724, Abhai Singh, then between twenty-one and twenty-two years of age, obtained through the intervention of Samsam-ud-daulah the title of *Raja Rajeshwar*, with the rank of 7,000 *zat* (7,000 horse), and was allowed to depart for Jodhpur to take possession of his father's succession. (Tod, I. 699, K. K. 974, Khush-hal 1044 b.)

"The fact of Ajit Singh's murder by his son, Bakht Singh, is not denied by any one; but a divergence of opinion exists as to the incentives to the deed. Tod's informants told him that Bakht Singh acted at the instigation of his elder brother, Abhai Singh,[2] then at Dehli, and in the power of the Emperor. The murderer's reward was to be the appanage of Nagor and its five-hundred and sixty-five townships. To account for

1 Tod, I, 699. This passage shows Tod at his weakest as an historian. His fastening of Ajit Singh's murder upon the Sayyids is a gross chronological error. Hardly less absurd is his assertion that Ajit Singh ever refused "sanction to the nefarious schemes of the Sayyids." He was their friend and partisan up to the end.

2 Warid 130, assigns the same reason as Tod for the murder. Cf. *M. U.* III, 755.

Abhai Singh's unholy desire we are told that his ambition had been stirred by the Machiavellin Sayyids, eager to wreak vengeance upon Ajit Singh for his opposition to their dethronement of Farrukh-siyar. Now let us apply some of the simplest critical tests. Can the offered reward be looked on as sufficient to impel Bakht Singh to an act of parricide? He may not have been a very clever man, but he was hardly such a simpleton as to incur the infamy of such an act, (1) for the benefit, not of himself, but of a brother, and (2) for the grant of an appanage which, by universal Rajput practice, would have been his as a matter of course whenever his father died a natural death. But coming finally to external tests, what is there left of the story? We find that its very foundation vanishes. The assassination of Ajit Singh took place in June 1724; one Sayyid had been assassinated on the 8th October 1720, and the other, after being defeated in battle and made a prisoner on the 14th November 1720, died in prison on the 11th October 1722. Obviously they could not have been in 1724 the instigators of Abhai Singh. Further, it is impossible, after even the most elementary study of the period, to ignore the fact that Ajit Singh, instead of opposing, helped the Sayyids to the utmost in getting rid of Farrukh-siyar. Tod's story is thus a mere legend, which falls to pieces directly it is examined; nor, as he admits, does his usual resource, the rhyming chronicles of the bards, afford him here any countenance. And Tod himself (II, 113) confesses that "but for that one damning crime, Bakht Singh would have been handed down to posterity as one of the noblest Princes Rajwara ever knew." Conceding the truth of even a part only of this glowing eulogy, is it not more unlikely than ever that such a paladin could have become the miserable tool of an ambitious brother, with no greater incentive than the offer of an appanage already his by family custom? Is it not rather to be believed that the father did something which the son felt was an attack on his personal honour?

"Although coming from Muhammadan sources, there is another version (Kamwar) of the facts, which, destructive though it is of any respect for the character of the "great Ajit," is much more satisfactory than that put forward by the champion of the Rajputs. It is one that furnishes a sufficient motive for the dreadful deed, and thus satisfies better the conditions of the case. We are told that soon after Ajit Singh had made his peace and returned to Jodhpur, he fell in love with the wife of his middle son Bakht Singh and was guilty of an incestuous intercourse. Overcome with shame and touched in the tenderest point of his honour, Bakht Singh sought his opportunity of revenge. One night when Ajit Singh, drunk and stupefied, was lying fast asleep, his son stabbed him to death. As a contrast to Tod's dithyrambs, we may here give the Muhammadan view of the Rājah's character. He was exceedingly wanting in good faith, a breaker of his oath, one who had slain unfairly many of his relations and dependants. Among his evil deeds was the abandonment of Farrukh-siyar to his fate, in spite of his relationship through his daughter; nay he took an active part in that Emperor's dethronement. In the end he attained the reward for his misdeeds.

> "He who sows the seed of evil and hopes for good,
> Racks his brain uselessly and imagines a vain thing."

Thus Irvine concludes his twenty-ninth section. We have to think over two main points of this opinion. Firstly, was Bakht Singh entitled to the appanage of Nāgaur with its 565 townships[1] according to the custom of the family, as Irvine alleged? To me the supposition appears almost an impossibility, because Mahārāja Ajit Singh had twelve sons. Had each of the eleven younger princes been allowed as big an appanage as that of Nāgaur, the heir apparent, Abhai Singh, would not have been left space enough to set his foot upon, outside the gates of the Jodhpur fort even. Moreover the district of Nāgaur was not at that time in possession of Mahārājā Ajit Singh himself. Though Mahārājā Ajit Singh had occupied Nāgaur having expelled Indrasingh, grandson of Rāo Amarsingh, in V. S. 1773 (A. D. 1716) yet in V. S. 1780 (A. D. 1723) Jai Singh, Rājā of Jaipur, by order of the Emperor, came with the imperial army and put Indra Singh again in possession of Nāgaur. After this, on the accession of

1 Tod mentions 555 townships under Nāgaur, as is proverbially known, to this day, in Marwar.

Mahārājā Abhai Singh to the throne, the Jāgir of Nāgaur being restored to him in V. S. 1782 (A. D. 1725) he occupied it by force and in the month of Kārtik of the same year, it was granted to Rājādhirāja Bakht Singh independently. How far Mr. Irvine's writing is true, under these circumstances, may be questioned.

History tells us that being terror-stricken with the formidable trio that installed kings on the throne of Delhi according to their sweet will, Muhammad Shāh arranged, on the one hand, to get rid of the two Sayyid brothers, and on the other, with the connivance of the Rājā Jai Singh of Jaipur and Bhandārī Raghunāth of Jodhpur, he overawed Abai Singh. And through him he enticed Bakht Singh, his younger brother, with the title of Rājādhirāja, and the State of Nāgaur, and thus prevailed upon him to murder Ajit Singh, who was now the only surviving thorn, out of the trio, aching at the Emperor's heart Had it not been so how could the perpetrator of such a heinous crime as parricide, have got the title of Rājādhirāja and an independent State like Nāgaur?

The second point pertains to the histories written by the Mohemmadans.

Mr. Irvine mentions within brackets the name of Kamwar as his authority for "another version" of the facts, which shows that the aforesaid queer ground for the murder of Ajit Singh has been borrowed by him from *The Tazkirat-us-Salatin-i-Chaghtaiya* of Muhammad Hādī Kamwar Khān.

Though the said history is not at present with us, yet in the VIIIth volume of Elliot's *History of India*, at pages 17-18 there is a reference to that work. It shows that its first part commences with an account of the origin of the Mughals, and of Chingiz Khān and goes down to the death of Jahāngīr. The second part, which is said to be the more important, and useful, begins with the death of Jahāngīr and ends with the seventh year of Muhammad Shāh A.H. 1137 (A.D. 1724=V.S. 1781). The writer himself admits that he had written this history without any royal order, and without the assistance of any of the nobles of the time, under various hardships and difficulties.

From the writings of Kamwar Khān, borrowed by Mr. Irvine, it is quite evident that he was maliciously disposed towards Mahārājā Ajit Singh, for which other grounds are also not wanting, as would appear from the following:—

Firstly, this Muhammad Hādī (Kamwar Khān) had remained in Aurangzēb's service, when he must have well experienced the antagonism of Mahārājā Ajit Singh to Mohemmadanism. Formerly the helpers of the Mahārājā had, with a view to baffle the crooked policy of Aurangzēb, made the heir-apparent, Prince Akbar, to follow the example of his father.[1] Some years after the death of Aurangzēb, Mahārājā Ajit Singh himself, having joined with the Sayyid brothers, had got the Emperor Farrukh-siyar deposed, and murdered, and had subsequently placed Rafī-ud-darajāt and his brother Rafī-ud-daulāh (Shāh Jahān II) on the throne, like mere tools in their hands. On the death of these Muhammad Shāh himself acquired the throne through this trio, in recognition of which he had to confer on Ajit Singh, the Subedārī of Ajmer and Gujarāt. But eventually, fearing the influence of the trio, Muhammad Shāh managed, at first, to get the Sayyid brothers killed, and afterwards Mahārājā Ajit Singh. Under these circumstances there is no wonder if a Mohemmadan writer of the Emperor's Court, with a view to bring a powerful Hindu Mahārājā's name to ill repute, and to screen the faults of his co-religionist Emperor, should ascribe such a foul reason for Ajit's murder. Moreover had this story not been the brewing of Kamwar Khān's own brain, the other Mohemmadan contemporary writers of the court, as also the writers of other Native States[2] would never have missed the opportunity of dwelling upon the affair at some length.

Shāh Navāz Khān (Samsām-ud-daulāh) has written a history named *Ma'asiru'-l-umara*, which contains history of the nobles of Imperial Court from the time of Akbar to A. H. 1155 (A.D. 1742). It is clearly stated in this history that when the

1 After the death of Mahārājā Jaswant Singh the Emperor had seized Mārwār, from his infant successor, Mahārājā Ajit Singh, thereupon the Rāṭhōr Sardārs of Mārwār had revolted. To quell them, the Emperor had sent out his son Akbar. The Rāṭhōrs set him against his father promising to acknowledge him as their Emperor (*Bharat ke Prachin Rajvamsa*, vol. III, p 209)

2 The writers of the Rājpūt States of the medieval age observed it as a sort of principle to give publicity to any weakness which they happened to notice in the affairs of another Native State. Such instances in the history of the Native States are not infrequent.

eldest son of Ajit Singh came to the court he got his father killed by his younger brother, being misguided by nobles of the court who offered him some temptation. Muhammad Shafī Wārid has written a history entitled *Mirat-i-waridat* about which he says "from the year 1100 A.H. (A.D. 1689, V.S. 1746) to A.H. 1152 (A.D. 1739=V.S. 1796) the greater portion of what I have recorded I have myself seen, and that which I heard from trustworthy persons I took the utmost pain in sifting and inquiring into, and whatever statements I had the slightest doubt about I discarded. But from the commencement of the war of the late Sultān Muhammad Āzam Shāh up to the present time (*i.e.*, from A.D. 1717 to 1739), or for twenty-two years, I have seen everything with mine own eyes." Mr Irvine himself admits in the footnote No. 2 to page 115 of the 2nd volume of his book, that Wārid "assigns the same reason as Tod for the murder." Besides this, in the *Muntakhabu'-l-lubab* of Khāfī Khān, which contains a history from A.D. 1519, up to the fourteenth year of Muhammad Shāh's reign, no such reason is ascribed for the murder of Ajit Singh, which has been very briefly noticed by that writer.[1] And this appears to be quite proper also, because the writer in order to evade reference to his co-religionist Emperor's evil doing, might have thought it proper to observe complete silence about the affair.

We fail to understand how Mr. Irvine, in the face of such reliable and authentic versions by contemporary writers, had admitted as correct the private and unauthorized history written by Kāmwar Khān.

As for parricide, the offence was not unprecedented among royal families. Kīrat Singh, the younger son of Mīrzā Rājā Jai Singh, had poisoned the latter at the instigation of Aurangzēb, for which he was granted the *jagir* of Kāmā. Is this event not quite on all fours with the one under discussion? Rānā Kumbhā of Mēwār was murdered by his son Udai Singh. Rājā Savāi Jai Singh of Jaipur had killed his son Shēr Singh. Bāgh Singh of Khētrī killed his son who was adopted unto the Jagīrdār of Sultānā, and amalgamated that *jagir* in his own estate. In the house of Taīmūr such offences for the sake of

1 Khushāl Chand in his *Nadir uz-zamani* has also perhaps observed the same course. This book was written about A.D. 1740.

power and territory had become almost a rule of the family. Similarly King John of England had got the rightful claimant, Arthur, murdered, and Richard III had got his two nephews killed. Many more such instances can be found in the world's history. The propriety of ascribing a slanderous reason for an offence, which, as shown above, has not been uncommon among princes of the land, is questionable. Moreover the idea of Mahārājā Ajit Singh's character borrowed by Mr. Irvine from the Mohemmadan writers, holds no water when examined from an historical point of view. They denounce the Mahārājā as "wanting in good faith," "breaker of his oath," "who had slain unfairly many of his kinsmen and dependents," and "had abandoned Farrukhsiyar." Had Ajit Singh ever broken faith with the Sayyad brothers? Had he not saved Sawāī Jai Singh of Jaipur in spite of his ill actions, as he was a relative, from perishing in the fire of the wrath of the Sayyad Brothers?

No mention is traceable[1] in any history of Ajit Singh having killed any relative or dependent. On the other hand, Tod speaks of his loveable nature in the following words, "so much was Ajit beloved, that even men devoted themselves on his pyre.[2]"

No doubt the fact remains that Mahārājā Ajit Singh had revenged himself fully for the wrongs done to him during his minority by the Mohemmadans. It is therefore that a Mohemmadan writer, out of jealousy, has falsely imputed such a conduct to the Mahārājā, without thinking over the actual facts.

As for the dethronement of Farrukhsiyar, it is evident from the autograph letters of the Mahārājā, and also from history that on the one hand the Emperor, immediately on arrival of the Mahārājā at Delhi, suspected him of his having joined with the Sayyad brothers, and on the other, Savāī Jai Singh of Jaipur, in order to maintain his own position, had commenced poisoning the Emperor's ears against Ajit, in consequence of

1 There is only one instance in Ajit's history which may be cited against him. He had removed the famous Durgādās from the administration on his regaining his authority, and Durgādās had gone out of Mārwār. But we come across such facts also in history, which show that the misunderstanding between them was not unjustifiable

2 Tod's *Rajasthan* (1880), vol. 1, p 637

which the Emperor had thoughtlessly begun his intrigues, seeking the life of Ajit. Being pressed by such circumstances, he was obliged to side with the Sayyads. A letter bearing on the subject has already been published in the May number of 1925 of the Hindī monthly magazine *Madhuri*

The reader will judge for himself how far the faults imputed to Ajit Singh are justifiable in the light of the above facts.

In support of the foregoing we give an extract[1], throwing light on the subject, from Mr. Forbes' *Rasmala*, a history of Gujarāt:—

"When Ubhai Singh from fear of the Padishah, wrote to Wukhat Singh to put his father to death, the Padishah gave him the Edur Parguna as a present."

A letter of V.S. 1784 from Rājā Savāī Jai Singh of Āmbēr addressed to Mahārānā Sangrām of Mēwār published in the *Rasmala*[2] just after the above narrative, also goes a great way towards bearing out the above fact.

Before concluding this note, and at the same time expressing our sorrow for the death of Mr. Irvine, we would like to suggest to Dr. Jadunāth Sarkār to think over the matter and to let us have his free and unbiased opinion on the subject, and also if there be a chance for the issue of a fresh edition of the book, to rectify the mistake or to add correcting notes as may be necessary.

1 Rasmala, Vol. II, Chapter 10, p 125.
2. Ibid., p 127.

Maharaja Ajit Singh of Marwar.

[Published in the Journal of Indian History, Madras Vol XII, No. 1 (April 1933.) pp. 85-89.]

In the second volume (chapter 7, section 29, pp. 114-117) of the book named "Later Mughals" written by Mr. William Irvine and edited by Sir Jadunāth Sarkār, it is stated:—"As Ajitsingh fell in love with the wife of his middle son Bakhat-singh, the latter stabbed him to death." The only authority quoted for this version is "Tazkirātussalātīn-i-chagatāī" of Muhammad Hādī Kamvarkhān.

A criticism on the above, headed "William Irvine and Mahārājā Ajīt Singh" published by me in a Hindī Magazine named "Mādhuri" (March 1928) as well as in the "Indian Antiquary" (March 1929, Vol. LVIII) shows that the emperor Muhammad Shāh after murdering the two Sayyad brothers resolved to assassinate Mahārājā Ajit Singh. The reason for this is quite clear as this trio were the most influential figures of the day, and Muhammad Shāh himself being placed on the Mughal throne by this trio was really afraid of them. Therefore to get rid of the said Mahārājā the Emperor first procured the help of Bhandārī Rāya Raghunāth of Jodhpur through Savāī Rājā Jaya Singh (the ruler of Jaipur), and then inducing the heir-apparent Kunvar Abhaya Singh, by threats and temptations, obtained a letter from him, in the name of his younger brother Bakhat Singh to get his plan fulfilled. This was the only reason that Bakhat Singh was given the fiefship of a large district like Nāgaur[1] and an extraordinary title of "Rājādhirāj."

1. The Emperor first gave this district to Mahārājā Abhaya Singh in V.S. 1782 (A. D.1725).

The fact that Mahārājā Ajīt Singh was murdered at the instigation of the Emperor is clearly admitted by the contemporary Mohemmadan writers like Shāh Nawāz Khān (Samsāmuddaula) and Muhammad Shafī Vārid in their respective books named "Maāsirul-Umarā' and "Mīrāt-i-Vāridāt".

If one sees the prefaces written by Kamvar and Vārid in their respective histories he will find that the former faced great difficulties while collecting the material for his book owing to the lack of help coming from any quarter, but the latter compiled his book after thorough investigation. Further for the events in the latter's history from A. D. 1717 to 1739 (V.S. 1774 to 1796) the author admits himself as an eye witness, and, as the murder of Mahārājā Ajit Singh took place in A.D. 1724 (V S. 1781), the statement of Vārid is naturally more reliable than that of Kamvar.

Is it not strange that in spite of all this a scholar like Sir Jadunāth Sarkār, even after perusing all the facts laid before him long ago, cannot feel bold enough to decide the matter one way or the other, but has fallen for the last 2 years between the horns of a dilemma in re-examining the manuscripts of Kamvar's history? I therefore think it necessary to put some more facts, in support of my view, which I hope will enable the learned scholar to decide the matter at an early date.

In the old chronicles of Mārwār it is stated:—"As Mahārājā Ajit Singh was murdered at the instigation of the Emperor his younger sons Ānand Singh, Kishōr Singh and Rāya Singh, soon after his cremation, left Jodhpur and revolted against their elder brother Abhaya Singh to form an independent territory in Mārwār. They were also joined by some of the nobles of the State. But when after long attempts no success was achieved, Ānand Singh and Rāya Singh took possession of Īdar which was then in the Mansab of Mahārājā Abhaya Singh; and the Mahārājā on his part, considering the restoration of peace in Mārwār necessary, did not openly interfere in the matter." From that time Īdar has been ruled by the descendants of Ānand Singh.

The same chronicles also mention:—"According to the wishes of the Emperor Muhammad Shāh, Savāī Rājā Jaya Singh of Jaipur and Bhaṇḍārī Raghunāth of Jodhpur induced Rājkumār Abhaya Singh to get his father murdered by his younger brother Bakhat Singh. This was the only reason that, when after ascending the throne[1] of Mārwār, at Delhi, in V. S. 1781 (A. D. 1724), Mahārājā Abhaya Singh was prepared to start for Muttra to marry the daughter of Savāī Rājā Jaya Singh of Jaipur, the Sardārs (nobles) of Mārwār, to put an obstacle in his way, pressed him first to pay a visit to Jodhpur. But when no heed was paid to their request some of them left Delhi for their respective Jāgīrs, without his permission, while others joined his rebellious brothers Ānand Singh, Kishōr Singh and Rāya Singh."

The letter of Mahārājā Abhaya Singh, dated the 10th day of the bright half of Bhādon V. S. 1781 (18th August 1724), addressed to Abhaya Karan son of the well known Rāthōr hero Durgādās, also supports the above fact. It contains the following:—"Abhayakaraṇ the son of Durgādās may know the pleasure of Rāj Rājēshvar Mahārājādhirāj Abhaya Singh. Some persons have left our attendance without obtaining permission and perhaps they may misrepresent the matter to you. But you being loyal to your master, should not pay any heed to their call, and, seeing this letter, present yourself in our court after making due arrangements there. This is the command. Dated Bhādoṇ Sudī 10, V. S. 1781, Camp Jahānābād (Delhi)."

The chronicles of Mārwār further state:—"To revenge the death of their late Master, the Sardārs of Mārwār soon began to influence Mahārājā Abhaya Singh against Bhaṇḍārī Raghunāth. Though owing to the ministry of Raghunāth, all the important offices of the State at that time, were under the Bhaṇḍārīs yet the new Mahārājā was obliged to order their imprisonment and in compliance with this order some of

1. At the time of Abhaya Singh's coronation the Emperor bestowed on him the title of "Rāj Rājēshvar" ("Abhayodaya. chapter 6, stanza 11-12). This may also be a reward for his keeping silence about the conspiracy of the Emperor.

them, who resisted, were killed. But even this action of Abhaya Singh could not appease the Sardārs, so the Mahārājā was compelled to put in custody Rāya Raghunāth himself while at Muttra.

In Vikrama Samvat 1782 (A. D. 1725) when the Mahārājā seeing the agitation subsided released Bhandārī Raghunāth and his brother Khīnvasī, the Sardārs raised a fresh unanimous protest against this action and pressed him to reimprison them."

This shows that the Emperor Muhammad Shāh got Mahārājā Ajit Singh murdered with the help of Savāī Rājā Jaya Singh of Jaipur and Bhandārī Raghunāth of Jodhpur, and, for this heinous crime, the Sardārs of Mārwār became his (Raghunāth's) bitter enemies. This was the reason which agitated the Sardārs and made them retire to their respective Jāgīrs without the permission of the new Mahārājā and compelled him to imprison Rāya Raghunāth twice.

Further this was the only cause which afforded an opportunity for Ānand Singh, etc., the younger sons of Mahārājā Ajit Singh, to revolt against their eldest brother as well as to get the help of some of the Sardārs in establishing their independent rule at Īdar, one of the "Mansab" Jāgīrs of Abhaya Singh.

These are the internal affairs of Mārwār which prove the version. Now I shall try to quote from some of the original documents, collected by me, in this connection, to support the same theory.

There is a letter[1] dated the 4th day of the bright half of Kārtik, V.S. 1782 (29th October 1725 A.D.), written by Savāī Rājā Jaya Singh of Jaipur to Mahārājā Abhaya Singh of Jodhpur, in which the writer after pressing Mahārājā Abhaya Singh to proceed to Ahmadābād states:— "Your Highness wrote about the money for expenses and the Jāgīr for which a request has been submitted (to the Emperor) and his reply on receipt will be communicated to you later on."

1. This original letter was shown to Sir Jadunāth Sarkār at Patna.

Another letter, dated 2nd day of the bright half of Mangsir (Agahan), V.S. 1782 (11th November 1725 A.D.), of the same Savāī Rājā of Jaipur addressed to Mahārājā Abhaya Singh contains:—"And a letter of Rāya Raghunāth has been received by Purōhit Budhrām instructing him to obtain the orders from the emperor's court regarding the Jāgīr. He has shown this original letter to me. But as Sarbuland Khān and the Gurjabardārs have informed the emperor that the Mahārājā has not yet started (for Ahmadabad) the emperor has become displeased and does not answer to any request made for Jāgīr or money for expenditure. I, therefore, write Your Highness to start at once as soon as this letter is received and after reaching the second or fourth stage inform the Emperor of the fact through Gurjabardārs so that Your Highness' Jāgīr may be sanctioned. It is not advisable to make the Emperor annoyed."

Letter,[1] dated the 13th day of the bright half of Āshvin, V. S 1784, (17th September 1727 A. D.), of Rajādhirāj Bakhat Singh contains:—

"And Bhandārī Anūp Singh informed me about the Governorship of Ahmadābād which the Darbār wants to get. You should inform His Highness that that Governorship is not so valuable now-a-days as the southern people have gained power and the raids of the Kōlīs have increased in the province. When Navāb Sarbuland, who went with such a large army, could not control it, how would "Bābāji"[2] who will go only with his own army, do that. At present I see no gain in the Governorship. It will be disgraceful if after accepting the job control becomes impossible. Perhaps there may be some other motive in it which I cannot grasp. Further you have written that the arrangement of the Jāgīr has been done satisfactorily but it requires one lac of rupees, for preliminary expenses, which is lacking. You should, therefore inform His Highness that if there is a delay of ten days the crop will be lost and even after that without paying the money nothing could be done. So, if no other arrangement for the money is possible the

1. Only last half of this letter has been found.
2. Elder brother

districts be mortgaged with banker and necessary arrangements made. In no case should there be any delay in obtaining the orders for the grant of districts."

These references show that the Emperor Muhammad Shāh to get his desire fulfilled, might have promised,[1] in addition a hand-some Jāgīr to Abhaya Singh through Savāī Rājā Jaya Singh and Bhandārī Raghunāth but could not bestow it for certain reasons. This led the Mahārājā to delay his departure for Ahmadābād and to press Savāi Rājā Jaya Singh and Rāya Raghunāth to get the Emperor's promise fulfilled. This action still more displeased the Emperor. At last the Mahārājā had to obey the Imperial command but he soon arranged for the above Jāgīr, promising a lac of rupees to the officials.

This letter of Bakhat Singh also informs us that, at the time, there was a talk of the bestowal of the Governorship of Ahmadābād on Mahārājā Abhaya Singh.[2]

I hope Sir Jadunāth Sarkār, in addition to the facts laid before him in 1928 and 1929 will consider these fresh references, and I am confident, will be able to realise that Kamvar's statement is incorrect.

---

1 My idea was that the Governorship of Gujrāt was also promised at the time but the letter of Rājādhirāj Bakhat Singh mentioned above shows that, in fact, the point was raised in V. S. 1784 (1727 A. D.).

2. "Maāsirul Umarā" also supports it. (Vol. III Page 756).

12. Mr. Forbes and the house of Jodhpur.

[Published in Indian Antiquary, Vol. LVIII (March 1929) p. 60]

Alexander Kinloch Forbes was born in July 1821. He came out to India in 1843 under orders of the East India Company and lived in Gujrāt for a considerable period, during which he collected the history of that province and wrote the book named "*Rasmala*" in two volumes. On page 123 of the 2nd volume of his history he writes that "[on the death of Ajit] the Ranees prepared to become satees; they took with them Abhyesingh's younger brothers, Anandsingh, Raeesingh and Kishorsingh, *in order that their eyes might not be put out according to the Jodhpur custom.*"

We are at a loss to understand on what historical facts the writer has based this idea. History tells us that all the younger offshoots of the Jodhpur family have regularly been granted *Jagirs* from the State, in consequence of which about 2270 villages of Mārwāṛ are at present in possession of His Highness' brethren and Sardārs including those of the Mallānī District, while only about 770 villages are in fiscal possession of the State. Under these circumstances it is open to question how far the writer is justified in making such a remark.

As for the princes, Ānandsingh, Rāyasingh and Kishōrsingh, the history of the period shows that they had commenced their rebellious attempts even in the life time of their father Mahārājā Ajitsingh.

It is stated in the history of Mārwāṛ, that when the Emperor made a grant of Nāgaur, in the name of Indrasingh, in Vikram Samvat 1780, and the latter got possession of the place, Mahārājkumār Ānandsingh was deputed by the Mahārājā to take back Nāgaur; but arriving at Dīdwāna he himself raised up a fresh revolt, with a view to encroach on the country here and there and was pacified with much difficulty. Autograph letters and other correspondence, bearing on the subject, are to this day preserved by descendants of the State officials of the time.

In spite of all this, Ānandsingh and Rāyasingh received signal help from their brother Mahārājā Abhayasingh in acquiring the principality of Īdar. This fact is borne out by the *Report*[1] dated 21st September 1821, of Major Miles, political agent, Māhī Kānthā, which runs as follows :—

"In Samvat 1785 Anandsingh and Raisingh, two brothers of the Raja of Jodhpur, accompanied by a few horses from Vanoo and Palanpur and the Koolees of Gudwara, took possession of Edur without much difficulty. They are said to have had an order from Delhi, but the truth seems to be that they were invited by the state of the country and most likely assisted by the Marwar Prince, who at that period held the Subedari of Ahmedabad."[2]

Kishōrsingh had been granted a separate estate by his father in his lifetime. From a *Sanad* issued by Kishōrsingh in V. S. 1806 it appears that even after 25 years of the death of his father the estate continued to be in his possession and no interference was made in it by his eldest brother Mahārājā Abhayasingh. This *Sanad* is preserved up till now by the descendants of its grantee.

It is hoped that from the above facts the fictitiousness of the above mentioned statement in the "*Rasmala*" is proved beyond doubt.

---

1. *Rasmala*, Vol. II, P. 125, footnote No 1

2 In spite of this, the rebellious nature of these princes made them forget these obligations, and they still did not cease to annoy the Mahārājā

13. Another Letter of Maharaja Abhayasinghji of Marwar.

(Read at the fifteenth session of the Indian Historical Records Commission held at Poona in December 1938, and published in its proceedings, pp. 124-126)

(Introduction)

At the time when the campaign mentioned in this letter started, Emperor Mōhammad Shāh was ruling in Dehli, but the Maharattā intruders were gaining ground in Gujrāt and the power of Sarbuland Khān or 'Mubārizul Mulk,' the Imperial Governor of Gujrāt, was reduced to such an extent that not only he was obliged to pay a tribute called Chauth (fourth part of the revenue) to them, but also the districts of Barōdā, Dabhōī, Jambūsar, etc., yielding a revenue of about rupees 30 lacs, were annexed by them.

We learn from a letter of Mahārājā Abhayasinghji, dated 12th day of the bright half of Kārtik, Vikram Samvat 1787 (10th November 1730 A.D.), that out of the districts of Gujrāt, 28 were held by Pīlū and remittance of their income to the Imperial Governor depended only on the sweet will of the former. Pāvāgaḍh was under Chimnājī and Chāmpānēr under Kanṭhājī. Apart from all this, the Maharattās also levied several other taxes called Dēshmukhī, Pēshkashī, Darōbast, etc., in the province.

When such conditions were prevailing the Emperor Mōhammad Shāh sought the help of Mahārājā Abhayasinghji of Mārwār and appointed him the Imperial Governor of Gujrāt.

The letter of 12th day of the bright half of Kārtik, referred to above, states that at the time of the appointment of the

Mahārājā as Governor of Gujrāt, the Emperor gave him 15 lacs cash, 40 guns, 200 maunds of gunpowder and 100 maunds of lead.

After this appointment Mahārājā Abhayasinghji returned to Mārwār, raised an efficient army, mostly of Rāthōr Rājpūts, took his younger brother Rājā-Dhirāj Bakhatsinghjī along with him and marched towards Ahmedābād *via* Jālōre, Pālanpur and Siddhpur.

How the Mahārājā encountered the enemy and in what way Sarbuland (Mubārizul Mulk) was compelled to submit will be known from the following letter of the Mahārājā, dated 2nd day of the dark half of Kārtik, Vikrama Samvat 1787 (16th October 1730 A.D.).

(स्वयं महाराजा के हस्ताक्षरों में लिखी पंक्तियां ।)

। तथा श्रीजी रा प्रताप सु वडी फते हु-
। ई छै ईण वातरी घणी पुसाली
। कीजो ने श्रे समाचार सगला नवा-
। व नु केजो ने केजो मै तो पातसाई वं-
। दगी पोचायी ही ? उण में
। कमी नी राखी छै ने श्रवे करणा श्रकत-
। यार पातसारो ने नीवाव रो छै श्रोर ह-
। कीकत हुसी सो फुरमासां हुकम छै ॥

(मुहर में का लेख ।)

महामाया श्री हिंगुलाजप्रसादात् छत्रपति श्री राजराजेश्वर
महाराजाधिराज महाराजा श्री श्रभैःसिंह देवः विजयते भानु-
तेजस्वरूपेण महीमध्येषु राजते
हरि अंवा शिव सूर विनायक ये सुर पंच सदा फलदायक

(महाराजा की सही ।)

हुकम छै

(पत्र ।)

॥ः॥ स्वारुप श्री श्री राजराजैस (वर म-)
हाराजाधिराज महाराजा श्री श्रभैस—
धजी देव वंचनात भा॥ श्रमरसीध श्रो ।
वरधमांन दीसै सुपरसाद वांच जो।
तथा श्रागै हकीकत पे द्रपे लीखी थी सो जा-
णी होसी गाव श्रडालेच पधार मीया नै कु-

हाडीयो सो उगारे दीनांरी जबुंनी कर मगरुरी सुं
काई बात चित में न आई अर लोग भेलोकर ल-
ड़ाई सारु तयार हुवो तरें आसोज सुद ५ कुच फर-
माय सेहर सुं उगोंणी तरफ कोस १॥······?
गांव हांसोल रे घाट साबरमती उपर डेरा कीया
ने नदी उपर डेरा करण सुं मीयां देलत खायने कु-
चकर स्याही बाग नै मैमद अमीखां रे बाग डेरा
कर भीतड़ा ने नदीरा नालां रो अड़तलो लीयो
ने तोपखांनांरी मोरचा बंधीकर बेठो तरें उठै
मोरचा लागण री जायगां न दीठी सो आसोज
सुद ७ उठारा डेरां सुं कुचकर सेहर सु आथवण
भद्र रे कोट रे मुकाबले नदी उपर फतैपुरे डेरा
फुरमाय ने नदी उपरलां सारां पुरां मोरचा का-
यम कीया ने उण ही बेलां भद्र नै सेहर पनाहा
रा मोरचां सुं तोपां रहकलां री लड़ाई सरु हुई सो
मांहला कोट बारे अठी री मार सुं माथो बारे
काढ सकीया नहीं तरे मीयां मैंमद अमींखां रा
बाग सुं फेर पाछो कुचकर मांयलां री मदद सा-
रु खांनपुर रा अराकांनी आण पड़ीयो सो दीन
३ सुधी तो मोरचां री लड़ाई हुई सो मीयां रो क-
बीलो भद्र मै थो सु गोलां री मार सुं भाग नै रुस-
तमखां री हवेली मै जाय पेठो तरें मीया दीठो हीमें
भद्र छुटे ने सेहर भीले तरें आसोज सुद १० सन-
वार मीयां सारी फोज ले असवार हजार ८ नै पा-
ला हजार १० सुं सीरकार रा मोरचां उपर— — — —
सो मोरचां रो साथ सांवठो थो सु बेढ हुई तठै आदमी सो
पांच मीयां रा कांम आया नै सीरकार री तरफ रा पीण
आदमी पनरे बीस कांम आया कीतराक घायल हु-
वा तीण उपर हजुर में अरज मालुम हुई तरें म्है नै रा-
जाधीराज असवार हुवा सो चलाय नें मीयां उपर
गया सु मीयां मुंढा आगे तोपखांनो देने पुरां रो अ-
ड़तलो लीयो ने तोपां री मार जादे करी तरें सको उ-
मरांवां सुं सलाह वीचार अणी तीन कर घोड़ा
उठाय मीयां उपर न्हांखीया सो तोपखांनो पुठ पाछे
दीयो ने मीयां सुं मुकाबलो हुवो सो घडी ४ माहो-
माह सखरो लोह आगो ने पछे मीयां रा पग छुटीया
सो कोस १॥ सुधां भाग ने कासमपुरे जाय पेठो ने
भीतड़ां रो अड़तलो पकड़ीयो ईतरे पुठ दाबीयां
ही पोहता सो जाय पुरा ने घेर लीयो सो मेहजीद—
रो अड़तलो पकड़ीयां घडी २ फेर लड़ीयो साथ सा-
रो भागतां मारीयो गयो ने असवार असी रे आ-

सरे कने रहा तीके ही घायल तरें दीठो बचुं नही सो
फेर उठा सु भागो सो नदी पार होय आपरे डेरां जा-
य पेठो सेख अलेयार सेहर में सुं मदन थांणा पो-
हतो छो सो आवतो ही मारीयो गयो ईतरे दीन आथव
गयो तरें डेरां पधार दाखल हुवा मीयां रो लोग मारीयो
तीण रा घोड़ा लसकर मैं लुट आया तोप रेहकला लैने
आयो आयो थो सो दरबार मै आया बडा बडा ज-
मातदार वगैरे कर मीयां रा आदमी हजार तथा बा-
रेसो मारीया ने आदमी सौ सात आठ घायल ग-
या श्री ईश्वर रा चाहा सुं नै पातसाहजी रा ईकबाल सुं
वडी फतै हुई ने सारी बातां बोलबाला हुवो असवारी
रा खासा घोड़ा रे झटका ३ तीर दोय लागा तीर ३ बीलेतरे लागा कारगर न हुवा खेर
हुई सीरकार री
फोज में लोग काम तो माफक आयो पीण लोग जखमी ज्या-
दे हुवो श्रीजी रे तेज परताप सुं सको रे खेर हुई छै तुं सा-
री बातां खुस्याली करै नै सारी हकीकत नवाब सु जाहर
करे उठै नवाब नै पीण परवाहरा लीखीया पोहता होसी
राजाधीराज रे गोलो लागो सु ईस्वर रा परताप सुं पा-
छो जाय पडीयो नै तीर ३ हलका सा सीले फोड़ नै छीवी-
या ने ओर तो टोप सील मै घणा छीवीया पीण लागा
नही राजाधिराज रै पीण असवारी रा घोड़ा रे झटका ३
नै तीर छै पीण ईसवर रा परताप सुं खेर हुई थे लीखी-
यो थो ईण सु कजीयो कीयां नै सम्भावार कीयां पातसाह
रजामंद होसी नै चाहा माफक मतालब सरंजाम होसी
सो पातसाह रा हुकम माफक हरांमखोर नै सम्भावार की-
यो छै हीमै अखतीयार पातसाहजी रो छै तीण सीवाय डेरां
पधारीया पछै मीया रो वीसटालो गुसांई वीठलरायजी
री मारफत आयो तरै तो वात कबुल करी नही तीण उपर पात-
साही लोग सारां ने सीरकार रा मोटा मोटा उमरावां ने
मीयां रो वीसटालो आयो छै सो इण रो जवाब पाछां सुं
लीखां छां फेर दुजै दीन सारी तयारी कर असवार हुवा
था सो मीयां डेरां बारै न आयो दबकनै बेस रहो सो
मीया मे कांई हलावत रही न छै अे समाचार सारा न-
वाब सुं जाहर करजो नै सीरकार रो लोग कांम आयो
तीण रो चोपानीयो मेलीयो छै सो जाहर करजो नै पा-
तसाहजी नै सारी हकीकत तरजमो करनै मालुम क-
रजो नै नवाब नै कहजो कांम री बोलबाला करण मैं
कमी न राखी छै अठा आगै तो नवाब रो करायो कांम
होसी——

। सं॥ १७८७ रा काती बद २ मु॥ अेहमदाबादरे पुरे फतैपुरे

(Translation.)

Top lines in Maharaja's own handwriting.

That by the grace of God a great victory has been gained. For this you should feel happy and convey the information to the Nawāb (Shamsāmuddaulā) and tell him that we have left no stone unturned in serving the Emperor, but now is the turn of the Emperor and the Nawāb to appreciate our efforts.

If there is some fresh event it will be communicated. It is our command.

Seal.

By the grace of almighty goddess Hingulāj, glory be to sovereign ruler, king of kings, supreme prince, Mahārājā Shrī Abhayasingh Dēva, who shines like the sun on the earth.

Hari, Ambā, Shiva, Sun and Vināyak—may these five deities always bestow favours.

Approval in Maharaja's own calligraphy.

It is our command.

Letter.

By command of the illustrious, king of kings supreme prince, Mahārājā Abhayasinghjī Dēva, fortunate Bhandāri Amarsingh and Prohit Vardhamān should note his favours. Ere this every event has been communicated to you one after the other, which you might have noted. On reaching the village Adālēch, we sent word to the Miyān (Sarbuland Khān), but owing to his misfortune and pride he could not comprehend it and collecting a number of men prepared himself to give battle. Under these circumstances on the 5th day of the bright half of Āsōj (5th October 1730) we left the place and encamped on the bank of the Sābarmatī river, at the village Hānsōl, about 3 miles east of the city. Seeing us encamped on the bank of the river Miyān (Sarbuland) got frightened, left the place, took shelter of the walls and rivulets and posting his guns at the strategic points encamped at Shāhī garden and Mōhammad Amīn Khān's garden. Finding no satisfactory stronghold there we marched on the 7th day of the bright half of Āsōj (7th October) towards the west of the city and encamped on the river at Fatehpur in front of the Bhādar Fort, occupied all the strategic points on the hamlets near the river. Soon the artillery of the enemy commenced firing from the Bhādar Fort and the city walls, but owing to the volley of our guns the besieged enemy could not raise his head to find out our position. On seeing this the Arākānīs of Khānpur marched back from the garden of Mōhammad Amīn Khān to help the besieged garrison. For three days both sides continued fighting from their strongholds, but the Miyān's family, who were in the Bhādar Fort, were forced by the shells of our guns to leave the place and take shelter in the house of Rustam Khān. When the Miyān realised that the fall of Bhādar was imminent and the city was to pass in the hands of the opponents, he on the 10th day of the bright half of Āsōj (10th October) came out with all his army of 8 thousand horse and 10 thousand foot and attacked us. But there were enough men to answer him. In the battle which ensued 500 men of the Miyān were laid low while on our side 15 or 20 men lost their lives and a number wounded.

When we received this information, we and Rājādhīrāj (Bakhatsinghjī) led our army against the Miyān. On this the Miyān posted his guns to the fore-front and himself took shelter behind the hamlets. When the guns of the enemy began to cause havoc, we, after holding consultation with all our nobles, and dividing the cavalry in three divisions, attacked the enemy, and leaving behind the line of his artillery fought a hand to hand battle with the Miyān's men. This fierce battle lasted for about one and a half hour, in which the Miyān was forced to quit the field and fleeing away for 3 miles entered Kāsimpur and took shelter in the houses there. But we too followed him on his heels and besieged the town. There again he took shelter in a mosque and put up a defence for about 50 minutes. But as nearly all his army was annihilated while fleeing and only about 80 horses remained with him, who too were wounded, he considered himself unsafe and again took to flight from the place, crossed the river and re-entered his former camp.

Soon Shēkh Alayār Khān led a contingent from the city to render help, but was killed in this action. By that time it was evening and we returned to our camp. The horses of the Miyān's cavalry, whose riders were killed, were brought to our camp along with the artillery which he took with him to fight us. In all one thousand or twelve-hundred of his men, including persons of position, were killed and seven to eight hundred wounded. By the grace of God and good luck of the Emperor a great victory was achieved and everything set right.

Our own charger received three sword-thrusts and two arrow-wounds. Three arrows flew past touching him, but by good luck left no fatal effect. In our army though the number of killed was small, yet that of wounded was fairly large.

By the grace of God every one has been favoured with luck You should make rejoicings and acquaint the Nawāb with every happening. He might have also received our letters sent direct.

A shell hit Rājādhirāj but by the grace of God could do little harm. He also received three slight wounds from arrows which could penetrate his armour. Some more arrows hit his helmet and armour but could not penetrate them. His charger also received three sword-thrusts and six arrow-wounds, but by the grace of God he was saved.

You wrote that by fighting and punishing the Miyān the Emperor will be pleased and will grant our desired object. Therefore according to his commands we have punished the disloyal governor and now everything else depends on the Emperor.

After we reached our camp, we received terms of surrender from the Miyān through Gusāīn Biṭṭhal Rāyajī, but we paid no heed to them. Now he has sent these terms to all the Imperial Officers as well as to our big nobles, for which we will send a reply later on.

Next day, we again marched, after making necessary arrangements, but the Miyān dare not come out of his camp and remained there hidden. Courage has deserted him now.

Convey all this information to the Nawāb. A list of men killed on our side has also been despatched which you should bring to his notice. Submit all this information to the Emperor after translation and inform the Nawāb that in fulfilling the task we have left no stone unturned and now every thing else is left to him.

Dated 2nd day of the dark half of Kārtik, Vikram Samvat 1787 (16th October 1730 A.D.).

Camp Fatehpur,
Suburb of Ahmedabad.

14. A letter of Maharaja Abhayasinghji of Marwar relating to the Gujrat affairs.

(Written for the XVIII Session of the Indian Historical Records Commission to be held at Mysore in December 1941, A. D.)

(Introduction).

The letter, dated 10th November 1730 A. D. was written by Mahārājā Abhaya Singh, from Ahmedabad, to his ambassador at the Mughal court. It discloses the devastated condition of Gujrāt as well as the weak administration of the Mughal Court, and commands the ambassador to ask Nawāb Khān Daurān, the minister of the Emperor Muhammad Shāh, for the early despatch of men and money in order to bring the affairs of Gujrāt under control.

The letter which is preserved in the Sardar Museum, Jodhpur, measures 5′ ½″ x 9″.

(स्वयं महाराजा के हस्ताक्षरों से लिखी पंक्तियां)

— — — — — —

अबै परवानारा समाचार नवा–

। व नु जीउ रा जीउ केजे ने नबाव कयो थे···

। थांरी ने मांरी आवरु अेक छै सो अबे वचन रो···

। ला छै तीण सु आठा डेनांरी खरची ने तईना–
ध सीताब मेले ने खरची सताव मेले नहीं तो पछै अठे ओर नु
[सर] वीलदखां दाही तो होय ने रयो को ही जा
— — — — — — ने केजो हुकम [छै]

। तथा थे अरज लीखती गुजरात सताव पधारे जीउ कांम नीकले सो गुजरात पीण पधारिया छां ने काम पिण ईसडो कीयो छै आज तांई न हुवो ने अबे थांरी बं-

। दगी रो मुजरो छै आठ महीनां री खरची जागीरां ने तईनाथ अे काम सताव करां-
जथी थांरो मुजरो छै थांरे बाव नीवाजस छै तीण कर सदा खुस्याल रेजो ॥

(मुहर में का लेख)

महामाया श्री हिंगुलाज प्रसादात् छत्रपति श्री राजराजेश्वर
महाराजाधिराज महाराजा श्री अभैःसिंह देवः विजयते भानु-
तेजस्वरूपेण महीमध्येषु राजते। हरि अंबे शिव सूर विनायक
ये सुर पंच सदा फलदायक

(महाराज की सही)
हुकम छै
(पत्र)

॥:॥. स्वस्ति श्री राजराजेसुर माहाराजधिराज माहारा-
ज श्री अभैसिंघजी देव वचनात भं॥ अमरसिंघ प्रे॥-[व-]
रध मांन दीसे सुपरसाद बाचजौ ————————
॥ तथा। परवांनो आगे ईनायत हुवै छै जीण माफक सारो
कांम सरांजांम कराजौ ओर खरची दीसा आगै हुक्म ईनाय-
त हुवो छौ सु नवाब सुं रद बदल करनै कांम पैस पोचायो
हुसी फेर ताकीद रो खत मेलीयो छै सु देजौ नै खरची रो जतन
करजौ मुदार सारो खरची उपर छै नै अठै खरीप मै कुं बा-
की रहो नहीं नवाब सारो टको उघायौ जीण रजावंदी दी-
यो सु लीयो ने मारकुट ही लीयो परगनां ईजारदार छा तीही
ईणतरे लीयो सु खरीप री या हकीकत छै कोठो वगैरै छै [सुतो]
वोपार चले तरे पईसो आवै सु लोक आवादांन होसी [तरै]
आवसी ने नबाब जांणसीज खालसो जागीर सारो जबत
कीयो छै सु अठे पईसारी आयगा नहीं छै थे सारी हकीकत क-
हजौ ने फेर पातसाही दीवांन वगेरे छै तां कना वासलात रो का-
गद कराय मेलां छां नै अठे जमीत छै ने खरच छै सु नवाब सुं
पीण छीपीयो न छै दस वारे लाख रो दर माहो छै ने पातसा-
ही तरफ सुं तो सारा पनरे लाख आया ने चालीस रेहकला
दोय सै मंण दारु सो मंण सीसौ ने तईनाथी में अजमतुला-
खां नु मेलीयो सु खरची अठा सुं दीयां जावां छां उठारा सुरंजां [म]
री खरची री आ हकीकत थी ने कांम ईसडो भारी उठायौ जीण
जायगा सीरवीलंदखां सरीखो आदमी छो ने कीरोड रुपीया पा-
तसाहजी दीधा ने उतरा तईनात था सो ही मीयां सेहर मै बे-
ठो रहो ने गनीम मुलक आरीयो खराब कीयो पीण वारै न नी-
कलीयो ने नेमवाज आय नै चोथ दीवी सु गनीम री आसुर-
त छै चोथ हीज उपर मुकदमो नहीं वडोदो डबोही जांबुसर वगे-
रे तीस लाख री जायगा सु दरोवसत गनीम रे हैठै सुरत २८ प-
रगनां सुं पीलु रे नीचै कुं हाथ उपाडीयो कदे दै कदे न दे पावोग-
ढ चीमना रे नीचै छै चांपानेर रो कीलो कंठा नीचै छै जमीदारी
पकड ने बेठा छै चोथ देसमुखी पेसकस ने कीतरीक जायगा द-
रोबसत ईण तरै रो फेल छै उठा रो ड सरंजांम थो ने वीच में सी-

रवीलंदखां री आ हरांम जदगी थी ज पातसाह रो हुकम लोप आगी होय बेठां छौ कीणवासतै ज आज १५ बीस वरस हुवा जां जायगा सोबायत छै सु सारा जायगा पकड बेठा छै कोई गयो तीण ने दखल न दीयो टयाके रा छै जां मारदीया सु ओ रग पातसाईत रो बणरह्यो छै ईण पीण उणीज तरे जांणीयो ने फेर वाजे हरांमजादां री से पीण थी नै तोपखांनो सरंजांम जमीत वेसने गुजरात सरीखो कीलो ने पातसाही रो सलुक ओ सारी वातां उपर नीजर देने बेठो छै सु उठारै सलुक नै सरांजांम देखतां तो उ जांणतो हुं हीज थो पीण मै आ वात कबुल कीवी तीण उपर नीजर राखने सरंजांम तोपखांना रो दारु सीसा वगैरै रो सारी सीरकार सुं कीयो नै जमीत तो ईसवर रे परताप सुं छै हीज सु ईसडी करडी आंगेज नै अेक घर री जमीत सुं ईतरो कांम सरंजांम कीयो पातसाही लोगां मै एक करीमखां छौ सु असवार २०० सुं छौ बाकी ईतरी थाट सारो घर सुं सरंजाम कीयो दस पनरे लाख रुपीया करज गांणो गांठो कर लोक ने दीया नै मीयां ने सजावार कीयौ सु ईसडो कांम ईण पातसाही मै न हुवो सु कर दीखायो बाईस सोबां रो बंदोबसत कर दीयो सीरबीलंदखां सरीसो आदमी थो तीण नै खारज कर तोपखांनो ले काढीओ सु घणी आऔज करने नीकलीयो लोक भला भला तो सारा मारीया गया ईणरो उ तोर छौ ज चालीस लाख तलबरा देसी जरे सेहर देसुं ने गनीमां सुं बुलाया था ओर ही सो तरदुद कीयो थौ सु तरवार री झाट ईसडी दीठी सु सो भुल गयो नै आही ज कहै ज श्री माहाराज मैरी तकसीर माफ करै नै आगलै ईकलास उपर नीजर देनै मेरा द्'न जबुंन था तद मै अेता हंगांमा कीया हजुर के लोगां नै मेरे वांई जडाया सु मैने कीया था सु पाया अब मेरा जीव वगसै इण हाल सु नीकलीयो सु कांम तो आछौ हीज कीयो छै हमै ईगतार पातसाहजी रो छै सु ओतो कांम मै आंगेज कीयो छै तीण उपर सीरकार सुं खरची सरंजांम कर नै पेस पोचायो उठे खरची री तईनाथां री कीणी वात दीसा न लीखीयो कीण वासतै ज नवाब उ जांणसी ज आंरै जांणरी मरजी नही तरे म्हांसुं लीखै छै तीण वासतै न लीखीयो पीण नवाब ने आवान जोग नही सु ईसडा मुकदमा उपर जतन न करे आ तो मांहरे घर री जमीत थी नै फेर मरणा मारणा सुं आंगेज कीवी तरे कांम पेस पोहतो पीण ओर कोई होय तो ईण खरची सरंजांम सुं खराब होय नै पातसाही कांम खराब हो तो ने बीजा पीण सोबांरो बंदोबसत नै पातसाही री खराबी ईणज तरै हुई छै सु नवाब सारी दान वांना छै नै म्हे तो सारो कांम नवाब रै भरोसै कबुल कीयो छै पीण बीजौ ही वंदवसत पातसाही रो नवाब सु करणो छै तीणासुं खरची ने तईनाथां रो कांम सीताब कराय वीदा करावसी गनीम रो मुकदमो नवाब सुं छीपो न छै आठ महीनां री सरंजांम करणौ असवार

असाढ तांई रो जतन करणो ने थांनां मारीयां गनीम पेस
न आवे तीण सुं असखर दरमाहो पांच लाख रो राखणो ती-
ण सुं आठ महीनां रा चालीस लाख रो सरंजांम करणो ने
गुजरात मे रयी तो कुं न छै खरीप रो या हकीकत छै फेर सीर-
बीलदखां उतरो टकां हजुर सुं पागो मुलक लुटीयां खालसो
जागीर जबत कीयां ने हमारा नीकलीयौ तरै दोढ वरस रो
सीपाई री तलब रही ने भार बरदास्त न जुडै तरै दारु सीसो
वेच ने सरंजांम कीयो सीरकार मै दारु सीसो न थो सु हजा-
र बीस पचीस रो लीणे और ही लोकां लीयो सु सेहर री मुल-
क री आ सुरत छै जीको सेहर बारै ही न नीकलायो ने जमीत
पीण सारकार जीनरी नही फेर खरीप पीण लीधी तो ही ईण
हाल सु नीकलीयो सु गुजरात ईण हद ने पोहतो छै औ संमा-
चार सारा नवाब रे दील नसीन कीजो ने कहजो जै गनीम रो
बंदबसत करण री मरजी होय तो सारो जतन करसो
ने गनीम रै गुजरात री चोथ रो कंठा चीमन रै कजीयौ छै सु दो-
नुं ईण तरफ आसी नै मालुम हुयो छै उजैण है सेमदखां बी-
दा हुवो छै सु छतीस लाख खरची रा दीया ने सीरकार मै त-
ईनाथ हाडा दुरजनसाल भदोरीया वगैरै रो ठेहराव छै सु
उ मांगे छै सु नवाब सुं कहजो आं माहलो उठी नै बीदा न
करावै नै छनरसंघ वगैरै बीदा हुवा छै तांनै ताकीद सुं
चलाय देजो मुकदमो सारो गनीम रो ईण तरफ छै जमी-
दारी छै सु उठावणी छै आवात सारी दीलनसीन करजो
नै तनखा आगली सीरकार री गुजरात उपर थी सु गुज-
रात मै तो कुं न छै नै पनरे लाख लोकरा चढीया छै सु तला-
स कर तनखा रुपीयां री सांभर उपर करावजो नै हाल रो
आठ महीनां रो सराजांम कराजो नै सीरकार री बाकी री
जागीर राजाधिराज री जागीर सीरकार रो राजाधिराज
रो ईजाफो कीताब वगैरे आगे हुकम ईनायत हुवो छै तीण मा-
फक नवाब सुं ताकीद कर सीताब पेस पोहचवाजो नै ओर
रोसनदौलै आगै पातसाह कनै झुठी वात कही तीण उपर
थे नवाब री नीसां कीवी नै नवाब पातसाह री नीसां की-
वी पातसाह उण नै माकुल कीयां रा अरज लीखी सुं हमै तो
पातसाह रै सारी वात नीजर मै आई नै थाजै सीरकार रा
बदखावां रै मुंढे धूड पडी पीण आज पातसाही रो रंग
इसडो ही ज छै तथा फतेपुर झुमण झुंझणु वगैरै हमार जैसंघ
जी लेण रो तलास कीयां छै सु सीरकार री जागीर मै लेजो नै
न समै तो उणां नुं तईनाथ कराय लेजो उणां हेठै पडण न
पावै राजगढ मसुदो खरवो भीणाय वगैरे रो तो आगे हुक
म हुवो ईज छै सु सीताब छुडाव जो सुरत रा मुकदमां रे-
ई अरज लीखी छी सु मुसतफीखां नु ने मुतसदी नुं बीदा की-
या छै उणारी पीण अरज आई छै छोड देसी नही तो सजा था-

र हुसी नै उठा तालक खरच कै तीणरी खरची री अरज ली-
खी थी सु मुतसदीयां नुं फुरमायो कै सु सरंजांम कर देसी
हुकम कै——————————————————
संवत १७८७ रा काती सुद १२ मु॥ साहीवाग

(Translation).

The lines on the top and margin written in the Maharaja's own hand.

..........You should inform the Nawāb precisely what is written.

Nawāb had remarked that in our honour lies his honour. The time has now come to make good his words, and so arrange for men and money to be despatched immediately. Send money atonce, otherwise it will be difficult for us to remain here under conditions in which Sarbulandkhān lived.

Convey this to the Nawāb. It is our command. Further you wrote us that we should atonce leave for Gujrāt, so that our object may be gained. We have accordingly, arrived in Gujrāt, and succeeded in performing an unparalleled deed which has not been performed by any one else before. Now it is your turn to render service. Your services will only be appreciated on your making arrangements for the 8 months' expenditure (to be now incurred), Jāgīr and getting the deputation of military assistants. You have our royal pleasure, so you may live in peace.

Inscription of the Royal seal.

By the grace of almighty goddess Hingulāj, glory be to the sovereign, king of kings, paramount sovereign Mahārājā Shrī Abhayasingh Dēva, who shines like the sun on the earth.

Hari, Ambā, Soor (sun) and Vinayāka—may these five deities always bestow favours.

Approval of the letter by the Maharaja in his own calligraphy

It is our command.

Letter

By command of the illustrious, king of kings, paramount sovereign, Mahārājā Shrī Abhayasinghjī Deva, Bhandārī Amarsingh and Purōhit Vardhmān should note his favours. We had already favoured you with a letter and everything should be carried out according to it. We had written in the aforesaid letter for the arrangement of money which we hope might have been arranged after discussion with the Nawāb. A fresh reminder has again been despatched, which you should hand over (to the Nawāb), and press him for money. Everything depends upon it. Nothing is left out of the Kharīff crop. Nawāb (Sarbuland) has squeezed every pie of the income, whether it was given willingly or under pressure. The district 'Ijārdārs' (lease holders) have also likewise collected the rent. This is the real condition of the Kharīff crop. As regards the income from customs, it can only be realised when the trade flourishes and that can only be collected when people will re-inhabit their homes. The Nawāb might also be knowing that there is no source of income left under this head as the whole of Khālsā and Jāgīr lands have been resumed. You should make him conversant with everything.

Further, we are sending the account of receipts after its preparation by the Imperial revenue officers etc., and the Nawāb is fully aware of the forces kept here and the expenditure required. Ten or twelve lacs per month are required here for expenses, while the Emperor provided us in all 15 lacs of rupees, 40 guns, 200 maunds of gunpowder and 100 maunds of lead. As regards assistants, only Azmatullākhān was sent, whose expenses also fell on our own pocket. Such was the poor condition of the equipment and finances when we undertook this difficult task.

A person like Sarbulandkhan was the Governor of the place, who, inspite of receiving a crore of rupees as well as a large number of military assistants from the Emperor, sat idle in the city, while the enemy devastated the province, and he (Sarbuland) dare not come out (to face them), but being over-powered paid Chauth (fourth part of the revenue). This shows the strength of the enemy. They are not even satisfied by the levy of Chauth, but Barōdā, Dabhōi, Jambūsar etc., yielding a revenue of 30 lacs, have also passed under their control. Sūrat including 28 districts is under the sway of Pīlū and any remittance of their revenue depends on his sweet-will.

Pāvāgarh is held by Chimnā, and the fort of Chāmpānēr is under the possession of Kaṇthā. They pretend to be lords of the land and collect Chauth, Dēshmukhi, Pēshkashi and administer some of the places also. Such is their audacity.

This was the condition prevailing in the province when Sarbulandkhān, by proving himself untrue to his salt, disobeyed the orders of the Emperor, and severed all his connections with him. The reason was that for the last 15 or 20 years, the Subēdārs of various provinces have thrown off the yoke of allegiance and have not conceded the control of their province to any one whom the Emperor was pleased to send. The mighty have dominated the weak. This is the condition of the empire.

He (Sarbuland) also viewed it in the same light and was also backed by some miscreants. He thought himself safe relying on his huge artillery, munitions, number of soldiers, a fort like Gujrāt and the tottering condition of the Imperial court. Looking to the weakness and the chaos at the court, it might have turned out as he had imagined, but we, on our part, taking into consideration that we have under-taken the task, collected artillery, gunpowder, lead etc. from our own purse, and as by the grace of God, we already possessed the forces we fulfilled this difficult task with the help of our own men only. Among the Imperial officials, only Karīmkhān joined us with 200 horse, while the rest of the show was staged from our own purse. We paid off 10 to 15 lacs of rupees to the forces by mortgaging our own jewellery and brought the Miyān (Sarbuland) to book.

The task which could not be performed till now in the present regime has been accomplished (by us) and we gained control over the administration of 22 districts. A man like Sarbulandkhān was defeated and driven away, after being deprived of his artillery, and he quitted the place after many entreaties. All of his big officials were put to the sword, yet he was so proud and arrogant to hand over the city to us only on condition of the receipt of 40 lacs of rupees as his dues. He also invited the enemy (Maharattās) and used all other tactics, but so felt the blow of our sword, that he lost his wits and begged for pardon saying—"Mahārājā, considering the old ties of friendship existing between us, kindly forgive me for the follies committed by me. It was due to my bad luck that I created so much fuss. Some of the Imperial nobles instigated me to oppose you and I reaped what I sowed. Now I may please be spared my life". This was his plight when he left the place.

We on our part have rendered sterling service and now it is for the Emperor to appreciate it. As we had undertaken to fulfill the task, we completed it by arranging for men and money from our own purse. We never pressed him for money and military assistance etc. at that moment, thinking that the Nawāb might not take it as an excuse for our unwillingness to proceed to Gujrāt. This was the main reason why we did not write to him in this connection. But it is not fair on the part of the Nawāb that he should sit silent over such a matter. Relying on our own forces and putting our lives at stake we have successfully completed the task, but had anybody else undertaken this task, he would have been utterly ruined by lack of men and the money and the Imperial cause would have also suffered. The laxity in the control of other provinces as well as the weakness of the Empire is due to such negligence.

The Nawāb is wise enough in every respect, and we, relying upon his word, had undertaken this task. As the Nawāb has the burden of the control of other affairs of the Empire so it is incumbent on him to arrange for the despatch of men and money at his earliest. The Nawāb knows every-thing about the enemy. To arrange for the upkeep of the force for a period of 8 months i.e. up to Āshādh is essential, and the enemy if not fully crushed will again raise his head. This is the reason why we have to keep a force at an approximate cost of Rs. 5,00,000 per month and accordingly will require rupees 40 lacs for the coming period of eight months. In Gujrāt the winter crop has been damaged and the condition of the crop of the rainy season has already been narrated.

Further, Sarbulandkhān, who had received a huge amount from the Emperor and in addition plundered the province and resumed Khālsā and Jāgīr lands, when departed from this place, left 1½ years salary of his forces in arrears, and as he could not arrange for the transport he managed for it by selling gunpowder and lead. As we too were short of gunpowder and lead, we purchased these things worth rupees 20 to 25 thousands. Others also purchased the same from him. This is the plight of the city and the province. He who dare not even come out of the city, did not maintain a force as large as ours and collected all the dues of the rainy season crop quitted the place in such a paucity of funds. This shows the devastation of Gujrāt.

You should impress upon the Nawāb all these facts and make him aware that if he wants to check the activities of the enemy, he should arrange for all these requirements. A dispute about the Chauth between Kaṇṭhā and Chimnā is going on, hence they both will return here. It has come to be known that Muhammadkhān has left for Ujjain, and has been given rupees 36 lacs to meet his expenses. Besides this, as per his wish, he has been promised the services of Hādā Durjansāl Bhadōriyā etc. to assist him. The Nawāb may therefore be informed not to despatch any one of them (Bhadōriyā etc.) to that side and acquaint Chhatarsingh, etc. who have already left the place to reach here as early as possible. The enemy seems to advance towards this side, and the Zamīdārī system is to be abolished. Explain all these facts to the Nawāb. Our previous dues were to be recovered from the revenue of Gujrāt, but nothing is left here and we owe rupees 15 lacs to the creditors, so try to get the amount of our pay charged to the revenue of Sāmbhar and also manage for the fresh sum required for 8 months. Further remind the Nawāb to carry out early the orders already issued regarding the rest of our Jāgīr, Rājādhirāj's Jāgīr, extra Jāgīr for ourselves and Rājādhirāj, and the grant of title. Formerly, when Roshan-uddaullāh put up a false complaint (against us) to the Emperor, you satisfied the Nawāb, who in his turn convinced the Emperor and the Emperor wrote (us) about his faith in our loyalty. Now the Emperor has realised the true facts, and the mouth of some of our enemies have been filled with dust. But at present, the condition of the Imperial court is as it is.

Jaisinghjī is at present trying to get Fatepur, Jhūnjhanu, Jhārōd etc. in his Jāgīr, but you should endeavour to get them included in our Jāgīr. In case you fail to do so atleast get them leased to us, but in no case they should pass in his (Jaisingh's) hands. As orders regarding Rājagarh, Masudā, Kharwā, Bhināi etc. have already been issued, so get their compliance immediately. You sent us a request about the affairs of Sūrat, therefore we have despatched Musatkīkhān and the Mutsaddī, who have written to us that either the enemy will vacate the place or he will be punished. As they have also mentioned about the money for their expenses required there, so we have instructed the officials to arrange for it accordingly. It is our command.

Dated 1787 V. S. 12th day of the bright half of Kārtik (10th November 1730 A. D.)

Camp Shāhibāgh (Ahmedabad).

15. Maharaja Abhayasingh of Marwar and the Nizam.

(Read at the sixteenth session of the Indian Historical Records Commission held at Calcutta in December 1939 and published in its proceedings, pp. 211-214.)

The letter of Mahārājā Abhayasingh of Mārwār submitted here, throws some interesting light on the underhand tactics to which the Nizām resorted in order to create an ill-feeling between the Pēshwā and the Mughal Court as also on the diplomatic genius of Mahārājā Abhayasingh.

The Nizām and the Pēshwā were jealous of each other's power. The former was the foremost soldier of the time. But being defeated by the Pēshwā Bājī Rāo I, he intrigued with Trimbak Rāo Dābhāḍē, the Maharattā Commander-in-Chief, with a view to reducing the influence of his rival. About the beginning of 1731 A.D. Bājī Rāo I decided to invade Gujrāt. But as soon as he reached Ahmadābād in February Mahārājā Abhayasingh, the new Governor of the province, so put diplomatic pressure on him as to win him completely over to the side of the Emperor.

How the Mahārājā set the Pēshwā against other invaders of Gujrāt and how the Nizām tried to deprive the Pēshwā of the imperial favours—will be known from the contents of the following letter.

(स्वयं महाराजा के हस्ताक्षरों में लिखी पंक्तियां ।)

॥श्री॥ श्री परमेसुरजी साय छै

। तथा श्रीजी रा प्रताप सु फते हुई छै नीजांमल-

। मुलक री कुमख साये भी सो ही मारीगी ने सगलो

। हरस कीयो छै पीछ ईण वात री खातर तस-

। ले बाजेराव री न हुई ने नीजांम श्रठी श्रायो सो म्हारे

। ने नीजांम रीई हुसी सो मे तो लीखण मे कमी न की
। ने मांसु हुवो सो कीयो ने ईणां रा समाचारां सु तो ख-
। रावी ज हुसी सो ईसुर रे ही उहीज ईणांरो करखो छै सो
तो कुतों हुसी जसमा गलां ? नावाव नु केजो ने कांम काज
नीवा———–जाव लीजो हुकम छै

। तथा खरची खामखा मेलजो नीवाव नु केजो वीना खरची श्रेक
। भी दीन न चलसी ने श्रठे की पईसो न छै तीणसु खरची नीवां-
वनु कैने जरूर मेलाजो ईण वात रो ज्यादा कासु फुरमावां
खरची बीना काम वीगडसी ने मै तो रजपुत क्षां ईसुर करसी
जीकु हुसी पीण मुलक पातसाजी रा सु जासी श्रे समाचार
सगला केजो खोलने ने कांम करेने खरची दे तो रेजो नीतर
श्रेक साईत रेजो मती सीख मांगने उरा आजो हुकम छै ॥

(मुहर में का लेख ।)

महामाया श्री हिंगुलाजप्रसादात् छत्रपति श्रीराजराजेश्वर
महाराजाधिराज महाराजा श्री श्रभैःसिंह देवः विजयते भानु-
तेजस्वरूपेण महीमध्येषु राजते
हरि श्रंबा शिव सूर विनायक ये सुर पंच सदा फलदायक

(महाराजा की सही ।)

हुकम छै

(पत्र)

॥ः॥ सिधि श्री श्री राजराजेसुर महाराजधिराज महाराजा
श्री श्रभैसिहजी महाराज कंवार श्री रांमसिंघजी देववचना
त भा॥ श्रमरसिंघ प्रो। वरधमांन दीसै सुपरसाद वाचजौ
॥ तथा श्ररजदासत थांहरी श्राई हकीकत मालम हुई श्रागे नी
वाव नै खत दीया छै सु वेनै सारी रद बदल की होसी तीकमराव
उभाडा रे नै सीरकार री फोज ने वाजेराव रे लड़ाई हुई नै तीरमक
राव ने नीमांज री फोज रो सीरदार मुगल मोमनयारखां मुल पंवा-
र कांम आया पंवार उदो चिमनो पंडत नीजांम री तरफ सुं छो ने पीलु
रो बेटो पकडीया सीरकार री फते हुई तीणरा संमाचार तो नवाब ने
कहा होसी पीलू कंठो श्रणदराव वगैरे फोज नाठी पीलु नास नै ड-
भोई मै पेठो छै ने वडोदे पीलु रो भाई छै सु दोनु जायगा फोजां ला-
गी छै सु सीताव खाली होसी ने कंठो नास ने नीजांमलमुलक क-
ने गयो छै सु नीवाव ने कहनै पातसाह सु मालम करनै हुकम मे-
लावजौ उणने तंवी करै नै नीजांम ने हुकम पोहचै सु दरबार
री मरजी माफक रहे कंठा पीलु वगेरे नु जायगा न देवै नै फोज नी-
जांम री ही मारी गई छै सु ईण कजीया उपर मत मवादा ? ईण तर-

फने आवे नो कजीयो होसी सु सारी हकीकत नीवाव ने कहने पातसाह मुं मालम कराय ताकीद लीखावजो ने हमार वाजेराव पातसाही वद्गी पोहच नै कीवी छै सु सिरपाव फुरवांन हाथी ने राजा साहु ने फुरवांण सिरपाव ने हाथी ने चिमना ने सिरपाव मेलावजौ ने नवाव सु वात करने ईणरे मुनसव रो तजवीज कराजौ ने वडा-कांम वावत मतालव छै तांरी नीवाव सुं रद् वदल करजौ कांम करण री मरजी होय तो सारी वात दुरस करजौ कांमं पेस पोहचसी आगे श्री हजुर सु वाजेराव रा मुकदमै रे वासते लीखीयो तरे वात नीजर में वाजै आदमीयां रे कहै लीखीये सु नाई छी पातसाहजी ने नीवाव कहो वाजेराव उण तोर सु आयो छौ सु मालम होय छै तीकमराय री देसत सुं मीलीयो छै ईण सुं वडा कांम री गरज नसरे सु तीकमराय रो नीजांमलमुल्क री फोज रो तो नीजर मै आयो ने वीजो ही पातसाह री मरजी होसी तो निजर में आसीहीज पीण नवाव ने खोलने कहजौ ज मै तो नवाव रे भरोसे सारो कांम कीयो छौ ने नवाव वात ईण तरे नांख दीवी छै सु नवाव री मरजी कासु छै सीरवीलदखां रो मुकदमो छौ सु तो मै म्हांरो हर तरे पांच टका वर रा खायने पेस पोहचायो कीण वासते म्है कांस उठायो छौ जीण उपर निजर देने पेस पोचायो ने गनीम रे मुकदमै उपर नीवाव नै तईनाथां खरची दीसा ईतरो लीखीयो सु कुं जतन न हुवो सु विचार देखै कांम पातसाही के मांहरे वर रो सु नवाव इतरी तगाफली करे नै हमार गनीम रो तो हंगांम जादा हुवो दोनुं फोजां आई उठारो जतन हुतो नीजर में नायो तरै कांम वीगडै तो ईलजांम आवै कु न कहै उठासु जतन न हुवो तिण उपर तरोदुद कर ने वाजेराव ने पातसाही वंदो कीयो मिलायो तसेले दीलवरी हद तक करने कंठा पीलु वगैरै रो तंवी विचारी फोज सीरकार री मजवुत तोपखांनो वग्रे देने विदा कीया ने ईणतरे माहोमाह फाडने फीसाद दुर करण रो मनसोवो ठेहरायो सु जांणता था ईण वात सुं वोहोत राजी होसी उठासु नवाव लीखीयो बाजेराव नै तंवी करजौ ने यां ने नीकाल देजौ मदत मत देजौ सु नीजुंम रा लीखीये उपर आ कही सु मांनु नवाव भलावे जीण जायगा मे ओरां रो कहो लीखीयो पेस आंणै आवात मनासव छै ज गरजगोयां रो लीखीयो साच जांणे ने कांम री वात सुं गाफल हुवै वीच्यार देखो कंठा पीलु ने आठ वरस हुवा गुजरात री जंमीदारी कर वैठा ने तांरो उपर कीजे ने वाजेराव ने ईणतरे वंदगी मे आंणीयो तीण री वात चीत मे न वेसै सु अै वातां नवाव नै खोलने कहजौ ज मै तो सारो कांम नवाव रे भरोसै कीयो छै सु नवाव वान्तरो जतन न करे तरे मांनु सोवौ राखणो नही आज गुजरात रा सोवा में कांहुं छै सांमो देस सुं पांच टका मंगाय ने खाधा कोई जागीर रो राजाधिराज री जागीर रो कांम न हुवो हमार गनीम रो मुकदमो छौ तिण उपर ओ जतन कीयो सु ओ तो ईश्वर रे

परताप सुं कांम रास आयो पीण उठारे भरोसे तो सो खरा-
बी हुवी क्री नीजांम ने बाजेराव री तंबी दीसा लीखै मे बाजेराव ने फाड-
ने मनसोबा सु चाकर कर उणांरी तंबी सुं बीदा कीयो ने उठासु
ओ लीखीयो आयां उ पीला कंठा री मदत हुय ने आवे तरे पख की-
ण भांत छोडणी आवे सु मालुम हुवे क्रै म्हांने उणां नुं लडावण
री हीज मनसोबो छो सु नीजांम री कुदरत कासुं सु आवो आवे
ने आवतो तो समाचार हीज होतो ने फेर आंवण री वीचारसां
तो समाचार होसी पीण जीणां रे भरोसे कांम कीयो छो जीणां री
काहुं तारीफ कीजै जीण सुं हीमे थे पातसाहजी ने अरजी देजौ ने सा-
री हकीकत नवाब नै खोलने कहजौ जै नवाब री मरजी उठे
राखण री होय तो जीकु उठासु लीखै जीण माफक जतन करे नवाब
वीचारे गुजरात रो ईसडो मुकदमो छै सु सुपारस भागे जांरो
कांम नीकले सु दरबार रा मतालबां रा कांम रां जबाब साल
ही नही सु आ मरजी होय जतन न होय तो ईगतीयार नवा-
ब रो छै ओ सोवो छै नीवाब री खबर आवे तीण ने मेलै ईग-
तीयार नवाब रो छै ने फेर कहजौ मे अठे छां सु नवाब कांम का-
ज तो कोई करे नही तो म्हांनि अवस खराब करांने करे कांम कर-
णो होय तो करदे नही तो मोनुं वधानुं सीख देवे हजुर जावां
सारी खोलनै कहजौ ने ईण मुकदमा उप्र सारी रदबदल क-
र कांम ठीक करजौ ने कांम हुंणा न हुणा री जीकाई हकीकत हो-
य सु वीगतवार अरज लीखजौ हुकम छै
संवत १७८७ रा चेत सुद १४ मु॥ अहमदाबाद

(*Translation*)

Top and side lines in Maharaja's own hand-writing.

May Almighty always protect us.

That by the grace of God we have achieved victory. The helping force of the Nizām-ul-Mulk, which too was with the enemy, has also been destroyed and all have turned well. But Bājī Rāo has not been favoured with thanks and assurance for his help. If the Nizām himself comes here we are prepared to deal with him (in the right manner). We have written as much as was adequate and have done as much as was possible. But the news received from the Nawāb would undo everything and if such is the will of God something of this sort must happen. You should tell everything to the Nawāb and settle everything... ......

Also arrange to remit money soon. Tell the Nawāb that without money we cannot manage the affairs of the province even for a single day. Here there is no source of income, and therefore inform the Nawāb and arrange to send money without fail. What more can we write in this matter? Without money every effort will be futile. We belong to the Rājpūt race and therefore believe that whatever the Almighty desires will happen, but the Emperor will lose the province. Tell him (Nawāb) all these facts plainly, and in case he is prepared to comply with our request and gives us the required money, you should stay at the court. If not you should take his leave and come back without wasting a single moment there. It is our command.

Writings of the Royal seal.

By the grace of Almighty Goddess Hingulāj, glory be to sovereign ruler, king of kings, supreme prince, Mahārājā Shrī Abhayasingh Dēva, who shines like the sun on the earth.

Hari, Ambā, Shiva, Sun and Vināyaka—may these five deities always bestow favours.

Approval of the letter in Maharaja's own Calligraphy.

It is our command.

Letter.

By command of the illustrious, sovereign ruler, king of kings, Mahārājā Shrī Abhayasinghjī,[1] and his heir-apparent Shrī Rāmsinghjī, Bhanḍārī Amar Singh and Purōhit Vardhamān should note their favours.

We have received your letter and noted its contents. Before this we addressed letters to the Nawāb,[2] which you must have delivered to him and must also have therefore discussed the points with him.

There was a fight between the armies of Trimbak Rāo Dabhādē[3] and those of Bājī Rāo[4] and ours. Trimbak Rāo, Mughal Mōmīnyār Khān, the commander of the Nizām's[5] army,

1. Mahārājā Abhayasingh was the ruler of Mārwār and the imperial Governor of Gujrāt.

2. The Nawāb or Khān Daurān was the minister of Emperor Muhammad Shāh.

3. Trimbak Rāo Dabhāḍē was the son of Khānḍē Rāo Dabhāḍē and succeeded him as commander in-chief of Shāhū's army in 1730 A.D He later joined the Nizām against the Pēshwā Bājī Rāo I.

4. Bājī Rāo I was the son of Bālājī Rāo Vishwa Nāth Pēshwā, whom he succeeded in 1720 A.D. and died in 1740 A.D.

5 Nizām-ul-Mulk (Āsāf Jāh) Chinkulich Khān was the son of Ghāzī Uddīn Firōz Jang. He first served as the Governor of the Deccan, then of Mālwā and afterwards raised troops and conquered the Deccan by a clever use of intrigue and money. He was for some time, the prime minister of the Emperor Muhammad Shāh, but resigned the post and became a virtually independent ruler of the Deccan. He died in 1748 A.D.

and Mūlā Panwār were killed; Panwār Ūdā, Chimmnā[1], and Pandit of the side of the Nizām and Pīlū's[2] son were captured, and we were victorious. You would have imparted these news to the Nawāb.

Pīlū, Kānthā[3], Ānand Rāo and others have fled away with their armies. Pīlū fled to Dabhoī, and his (Pīlū's) brother is at Barōdā. We have despatched our armies to both these places, and hope to get them vacated soon. As Kānṭhā has fled to the Nizām-ul-Mulk, you should ask the Nawāb to inform the Emperor[4], and get his orders issued to the Nizām with a strict warning, that he should comply with the commands of the Darbār (Mahārājā) and should not give shelter to Kānthā, Pīlū and others.

The army of the Nizām too is destroyed, and if he comes again to this place to avenge himself there will be a battle with him. Therefore, you should ask the Nawāb to bring all these facts to the notice of the Emperor and get his orders soon despatched.

This time Bājī Rāo has rendered meritorious services to the Emperor. So a robe of honour, a "Farmān" and an elephant should be bestowed on him as well as on Rājā Shāhū[5], and a rob of honour on Chimnā[6]. Further, after explaining everything to the Nawāb also arrange for the bestowal of a "Mansab" on Bājī Rāo. We also remind you of the important problem of our own "Jāgīr" and hope you will again discuss it with the Nawāb. If he is inclined to comply with our request settle the matter with him in such a manner that our mission may be brought to a successful end.

---

1. Chimnājī Dāmōdar was for some time the prime minister of Shambūjī II of Kōlhāpur.

2. Pīlājī Gaikwāḍ was the founder of the present Gāikwāḍ dynasty of Barōdā and one of the two most prominent Maharaṭṭā officers in Gujrāt. He was killed by Mahārājā Abhayasingh of Mārwār in 1732 A.D and was succeeded by his son Dāmājī Gāikwād.

3. Kanṭhājī Kadam Bhāndē was the other most prominent Maharaṭṭā officer of Gujrāt.

4 Emperor Muhammad Shāh Nāsiruddin ruled from 1719 to 1748 A.D

5. Shāhū, the Rājā of Satārā was the grandson of Shivājī and he appointed Bājī Rāo I as his Pēshwā in 1720 A.D.

6 I think the reference here is to Chimnājī, the younger brother of Pēshwā Bājī Rāo I and not to Chimnājī, who belonged to the opposite camp.

Some time back we wrote about the case of Bājī Rāo, but owing to the verbal or written misrepresentations, the Nawāb could not grasp the reality, and has informed the Emperor that Bājī Rāo, only being afraid of Trimbak Rāo, has joined us in this way and therefore he could not help us in any bigger task. But the part played by the armies of the Nizām-ul-Mulk and Trimbak Rāo has come to the notice of the Emperor, and if he wishes, other facts will also be brought to his (Emperor's) knowledge.

You should inform the Nawāb clearly, that we have done all this fully relying on him. Yet he has neglected it in such a manner. Let us know what the Nawāb wants. Even the expedition against Sarbuland Khān[1] was carried out at our own expense. As we had undertaken the task, it became our duty to finish it. We have written so much to the Nawāb for sending us men and money with a view to enabling us to face the enemy. But nothing has been done uptill now. He should consider well whether this mission, the progress of which he (Nawāb) has been delaying is of the Emperor or our own. These days there was a large concentration of the forces of the enemy, and both the armies arrived here. When we failed to see any provision being made by the Nawāb, (to meet the situation) we apprehended that in case there was any adverse result, it was we who would be blamed for it, as no one would say that the Nawāb did not do any thing in the matter. In these circumstances we tried hard to bring over Bājī Rāo to the side of the Emperor, and giving him every assurance despatched him with our own forces equipped with strong artillery to punish Kanthā, Pīlū and others. We have thus, created a split among them and managed to crush the rising.

We thought that the Nawāb would appreciate our action but instead of that he has written us to punish Bājī Rāo, drive him away, and give him no help whatsoever. It appears that the Nawāb has written all this at the instigation of the Nizām. Is it fair that the Nawāb should act on the advice of others when the task has been entrusted to us? He believes in what these sycophants write, and neglects the real facts. Only consider that though Kanṭhā and Pīlū usurped the land of

1. He was the Governor of Gujrāt, but was defeated and driven out by Mahārājā Abhaya Singh, the newly appointed Governor of Gujrāt in 1730 A.D.

Gujrāt for the last eight years, he (Nawāb) favours them and gives no weight to winning Bājī Rāo over to the side of the Emperor. Tell all these facts to the Nawāb plainly and inform that we have done all this with full faith in him. But if he does not care, we are not prepared to keep this province. What advantage can one have in Gujrāt these days? On the contrary though we have to bear all the expenses from the revenue of Mārwār, yet he (Nawāb) has neither done anything for our own 'Jāgīr' nor for that of Rājādhirāj[1].

Recently the enemy threatened us again and therefore we managed the affairs in this way. By the grace of God, we were successful. But had we depended on the Nawāb, it would have been worse. He writes to the Nizām to punish Bājī Rāo, while we brought him (Bājī Rāo), whole-heartedly to our side and sent him to punish the Nizām. (Is it not strange that inspite of all this) the Nawāb has written to us in such a way? If Bājī Rāo is left alone, he would join Pīlū and Kanthā. In such circumstances how can we leave him alone? It appears that though the Nizām wants to create misunderstanding between us and the Nawāb yet he has no courage to advance. Had he come forward, he would have been punished, and further, if he thinks of advancing against us, he shall be punished. But what should we say of the Nawāb on whose support we counted for completing this task.

You should now submit the case to the Emperor and put all these facts in detail before the Nawāb. If the Nawāb wishes to keep us here, he should manage according to our letters. He should also note, that the present condition of Gujrāt makes it imperative that he should give effect to our recommendations. Nothing has yet been done even about the 'Jāgīr' of Darbār (ourself), and if he does not like or cannot manage it he may do whatever he thinks proper. Here is the province of Gujrāt and he may send any one he likes, as its Governor. Again tell him that inspite of our remaining busy here the Nawāb does not do anything in the matter and wants to ruin us for nothing. He should either do the work, if he so wishes, or give us leave for personally approaching the Emperor. Tell him everything plainly, discuss this case in all its aspects, settle the matter favourably and let us know everything about the favourable or unfavourable turn of the case. This is our command.

Dated the 14th day of the bright half of Chaitra (Vikram) Samvat 1787 (Shrāvanādi) (10th April 1731 A.D.). Camp Ahmedābād.

---

1. Rājādhirāj Bakhatsingh was the younger brother of the Mahārājā.

16. Maharaja Abhaya Singh of Jodhpur and the tactics of the Nizam.

(Read at the third Indian History Congress held at Calcutta in December 1939 and published in its proceedings pp. 1112—1115.)

When Mahārājā Abhayasingh, the newly appointed Governor, took charge of Gujrāt in 1730 A. D. the condition of the province was deteriorating. The Maharaṭṭā officers were ravaging the country without any opposition and the Imperial revenue also was left to the mercy of these marauders. Consequently the whole province was threatened with severe famine.

Under these circumstances, when Pēshwā Bājī Rāo I, arrived at Ahmedābād to plunder the province, the Mahārājā persuaded him to side with the Emperor and sent him against Trimabak Rāo—the Commander of the Rājā of Satārā. But the Nizām, who had joined Trimbak Rāo on account of his jealousy with the Pēshwā, tried his level best to misrepresent the whole affair at the Mughal court and divide the Pēshwā from the Emperor.

This second[1] letter of Mahārājā Abhayasingh, reproduced here, will show the real condition of the province at that time and the underhand tactics as adopted by the Nizām.

(स्वयं महाराजा के हस्ताक्षरों में लिखी पंक्तियां)

। .. .. (प)

। तसाही अमलदस्तु (र)..........

। हुराम छै ने जोका व खे............

। र करन ने पातसाही मुलक आया......हुंवता हुक (म)

। कीयो थो पीश नीबाब रे ने पातसारे खानरमा आई.......

---

1. This is the second letter which was written by the Mahārājā, in this connection, on the same day.

। आई तो अबे फल हुसी सो नीजर आसी अबे स''
। व नीवडसी मानु कीणी वात रो दोस न छै समाचार
। ती नीवाव ने केजो ने खरची सीताब मेलजो थांनरो
अत कसालो छै ने सुतदात ? सुखो सो खाधो ने अबे तो
वीना खरची सरम न रेसी तिणरो नवाब नु साफ केजो
ने की न करे तो थे सीख कर आवजो हुकम छै ॥

(मुहर में का लेख ।)

महामाया श्री हिंगुलाज प्रसादात् छत्रपति श्री राजराजेश्वर-
महाराजाधिराज महाराजा श्री अभैःसिंहदेवः विजयते भानु-
तेजस्वरूपेण महीमध्येषु राजते
हरि अंबा शिव सुर विनायक ये सुर पंच सदा फलदायक

(महाराजा की सही ।)

हुकम छै

(पत्र ।)

॥ः॥ सिधि श्री श्री राजराजेसुर माहाराजाधिराज माहा-
राज श्री अभैसिंघजी माहाराज कंवार श्री रामसिंघजी
देव वचनात भं॥ अमरसंघ प्रो॥ वरधमान दिसै सु प-
रसाद वाचजौ———————

॥ तथा फुरवांन आगै ईनायत हुवो छै सु उण माफक सारी
रद वदल नवाब सुं करनै सारी वातां रो हुकम माफक जा-
वतो करजौ तथा हमारु वाजैराव री अरजदासत आई
थी तीण मै अरज लीखी छी ज मै तो श्री माहाराज रा वचन
ने हुकम सुं तीमकराव वगैरै री लडाई मै पोहच नै पातसा-
ही वंदगी कीवी नै श्री माहाराज रो फुरमायो पातसाह सुं दुजो
न जांणीयो ने पोहच ने बंदगी कीवी ने हीमार नीजांमलमुलक
पातसाह रा हुकम नीजाम रा वंगस रा मारा वीजनस वा-
जेराव ने भेजदिया ने कहायो ज पातसाह रो ओ हुकम छै
ने तु माहोमाह लडने गनीमांरी वात हलकी पाडै छै सु आ
वात कीण रै भरोसै करै छै पातसाह रो तो तोनुं पकडण रो तं-
वी पोहचावण रो हुकम छै औ समाचारां सुं वाजेराव दो दलो
जादा हुवो ईणरे तरफ तरफ सुं खवर तो आगेहीज पोहती थी
पीण तसले दीलासा करने राखीयो ने हीमार विजनस खत
वांचण सुं आजुरदा जादा छै ने वीसवास जादा पडियो छै
सु मरजी जांणरी राखे छै ने नवाब ने तो आगे ही लीखीयो
थो फरवांण मेलावजौ सु न पोहतो तिणसुं हमे फरवांण व-
गेरे आगे लिखिया छै तां माफक सिताव मेलावजौ ने तस-
ले कर राखां छां पिण निजांम विसवास जादा घालीयो छै सु
दोरो रहसी नवाब निजांम रो ईतवार करै छै ने ईणरी आ
हकीकत छै हीमार कंठो गयो छै ने ईण तरफ आंवण री वी-

म्हारी तो मारियो जासी थे नवाब नैं खोल ने कहजौ पछै पात
स्याह नवाब ओर नरे न कहे तिण सुं सारी हकीकत खोलने
कहजौ ईण तरे बाजेराव ने कहाडण सुं पातसाह री
कितरी खराबी हुई छै पिण आजरी पातसाही मे चाकरी
री ईसडी हीज खबर छै सारी हकीकत कहजो हुकम छै
संवत १७८७ रा चेत सुद १४————मु॥ अहमदाबाद

Translation

Top and marginal lines in Maharaja's own hand-writing.

....but the Nawāb and the Emperor did not care for it. Now they will see the consequences, but they cannot blame us for the result. Communicate all this to the Nawāb and arrange for early remittance of money. Here is a great scarcity of grain. Whatever was available has already been consumed, hence we cannot pull on any longer without money. Inform the Nawāb of every thing clearly, and if he does not do any thing, get his permission and come back. It is our command.

Contents of the Royal Seal

By the grace of Almighty Goddess Hingulāj, glory be to sovereign ruler, king of kings, supreme prince, Mahārājā Shrī Abhayasingh Dēva, who shines like the sun on the earth.

Hari, Ambā, Shiva, Sun, and Vināyak—may these five deities always bestow favours.

Approval of the letter in Maharaja's own calligraphy.

It is our command.

Letter.

By command of the illustrious, sovereign ruler, king of kings, supreme prince, Mahārājā Shrī Abhayasinghjī[1] and his heir-apparent Shrī Rāmsinghjī, Bhanḍārī Amarsingh and Purōhit Vardhamān should note their favours.

Some time back we had sent you a letter and therefore you should discuss the points mentioned therein with the Nawāb[2] and settle everything accordingly.

Recently we have received a letter from Bājī Rāo[3] in which he has stated that relying on the words and commands of the

1 Mahārājā Abhayasingh was the ruler of Mārwār and new Governor of Gujrāt
2. The Nawāb or Khān Daurān was the minister of Muhammad Shāh at that time.
3. Bājī Rāo I became Peshwā in 1720 A. D. and died in 1740 A. D.

Mahārājā (us) he has served the Emperor[1] whole-heartedly, in the battle against Trimbak Rāo[2] and others. He made no difference in the commands of Mahārājā (us) and the Emperor, and has rendered good services But the Nizām-ul-Mulk[3] has recently sent him the original orders of the Emperor communicated to him (Nizām), to Bangash[4], and to us, and informed him that while such are the orders of the Emperor he is weakening the side of the invaders by fighting against his own men. On whose assurance is he doing all this? The Emperor has already ordered for his capture and punishment. This information has disheartened him (Bājī Rāo). Though he was already getting such news from different sources, yet we retained him by giving assurances. At present, after reading the original letters, he is perplexed, relies more on this news and intends to leave us. We had already written to the Nawāb to send a 'Farmān' (a letter communicating Emperor's favours), but the same has not yet been received. Therefore arrange immediately to dispatch the 'Farmān' etc., as was stated in our previous letter.

We are yet keeping him here by giving assurances. But as the Nizām is gaining (his) confidence, he would hardly remain here. Though the Nawāb relies on the Nizām to such an extent, yet he (Nizām) behaves like this. At present Kanthā[5] has gone (to the Nizām), but if he intends to come to this side, he will be killed You should explain every thing to the Nawāb, so that afterwards he and the Emperor may not blame us. To avoid all this, bring every thing to the notice of the Nawāb. By disclosing the imperial secrets to Bājī Rāo the Nizām has done a great harm to the Emperor, yet the present Imperial court keeps such sort of information about the services of its officers. Tell every thing. This is our command.

Dated 14th day of the bright half of Chaitra (Vikram) Samvat 1787 (Shrāvanādi) (10th April 1731 A. D.). Camp Ahmedābād.

---

1. Emperor Muhammad Shāh ruled from 1719 to 1748 A D

2. Trimbak Rāo Dabhādē was the commander-in-chief of Shāhuji's army and had joined the Nizām to reduce the power of Pēshwā Bājī Rāo I

3 Nizām-ul Mulk (Āsaf Jāh) Chinkulich Khān conquered the Deccan by intrigues and money and in time became a virtually independent ruler of it.

4 Muhammad Khān Bangash, the Afghān soldier of fortune founded Farrukhābād as his capital and gradually acquired the territory from the modern Aligarh to the south eastern boundary of the present Cawnpore district He died in 1743 A D

5 Kanthaji Kadam Bhāndē was one of the two most prominent Maharattā Officers in Gujrāt

17. A Letter of Maharaja Abhaya Singh of Marwar.

(Read at the fourteenth meeting of the Indian Historical Records Commission held at Lahore in December 1937 and published in its proceedings pp 63—65).

The document, which I have the humble privilege of submitting before the I. H. R. C., is a letter of Mahārājā Abhayasingh of Mārwār, addressed to his Vakīl at the Mughal Court and describes his military achievements in Gujrāt. Thus it illuminates a forgotten episode in the history, not only of an illustrious man, but also of the illustrious Rāṭhōr race, which he represented.

The circumstances, in the face of which these military successes had to be won, were exceptionally critical. Emperor Muhammad Shāh was on the throne of Delhi, but his empire was threatened with disruption on every side. In the south, the situation was almost unbearable. Nizām-ul-Mulk had allied himself with the Maharaṭṭās and his uncle had been harassing Sarbuland Khān, the Imperial Governor of Gujrāt. The Maharaṭṭās had, under the leadership of Pīlājī, the deputy of Khāndē Rāo Dābhādē, Commander of the Rājā of Satārā (and ancestor of the Gaekwar's), established their sway over Barōdā, Dabhōī, etc., and had converted the province into a sort of marauding ground for themselves. Even Sarbuland Khān had been obliged to admit the Maharattā claim to *Chauth* and *Sardesh Mukhi*. This was the situation which Abhayasingh was called upon to meet when he was appointed by the Emperor to the Government of Gujrāt. The previous Governor was unwilling to vacate his office, but soon finding himself unable to maintain his position was compelled to hand over his charge to the Rāṭhōr Chief. There remained now the task of ridding Gujrāt of the Maharaṭṭā marauders and of giving it peace. How he acquitted himself in this, will be found in the document itself, which, with its English translation, is given below.

(स्त्रयं महाराजा के हस्तात्तरों में लिखी पंक्तियां)

।ः॥ श्री परमेसुरजी साय छै

। तथा अरजदासत थारी आई ने फेर (सु)

सदीयारे नावे कागज आया था सो हा (ला)-
त तपसीलवार सगली मालम हुई ने नबा-
ब सु रद्‌वदल अवल की थारो मुजरो हु-
वे जागीर रा कांम मतालव सताब क [रे इ-]
ण मां तमांम थारो मुजरो छै ने मांरे सगला दीख-
णीयां सु कजीयो पडीयो छै सो अबै मै तो चा-
करी मा पाछ काई राखी नही ने अबै तो नीवाव
ईण तरे करसी तो मांसु सोबा रो जावतो हुसी
ने सोबो राखसां नीतर हरगज म्हारे सोबो राख-
णो कोई नई ने इण तरे करसी तो राखसां जतरे ई
एक वरस दोय वरस जीतरे गनीम रो कजीयो
रे तीतरे सोबा तमांम रो मोसुल मांनु फोज रा ख-
रच सु देने तईनाथ मैलै फेर कोई जागीरदार नांव लेण पावे न-
ई तो मांनु रेणी आसी ने जावतो रेसी नीतर हरगज म्हारे सोबो
राखणो कोई नई खातर आवे जीण नु दो नै मांरे जागीर रो कांम
कर देई तरे कीयो राखां । ने मालवा रो मचकुर लीखीयो सो मांरे
कोई मतलव नही ने दुजी कांनी रो पीण मतहुण दे ने गुजरात
री पुरी मदत करसी नै मांरी सांहुंसी तो पछै आंणीजसी सो
तपसीलवार समाचार धनुडा रा लीखीया सु जांणसी ।
ओर तो यादगारखां रो ने जती रो मचकुर लीखीयो थो सो दोनां नु
हाथ राखै ने जीण वात मा सीरकार रो फाईदो नै कांम हुवे सो की-
जै केणै कीणीरा पर नीजर मत दीजे । मै वडोदे पधारीया छां ने
सुवारे कुच छै सो नरबदाजी पधारसां कोला २४ तो गनीम कनी-
सु छुडाय लीया छै तठै सीरकार रा थांणा कायम कीया छै नै कोईक
रया छैं सो सताव छुडाय लेसां ने श्रीजीरा प्रताप सु अबार तो गनीम
नरवदा उरे न रेसी नै पछै तो उठारे जावता सारु छै श्रीजीरा
प्रताप सु गनीमरी कुदरत नई सो पचास कोसां ही नजीक
रे सकै अठेरी तरफ सु सगली वात खुस्याली राखै थारे वाव
नीवाजस छै ने अबै बंदगी री वेला छै—कीयां नीजर आसी
ने नीवाजस हुसी हुकम छै ओर हकीकत तफसीलवार धनुडा रा
लीखीया सु जाणसी हुकम छै ॥

(मुहर में का लेख)

महामाया श्री हिंगुलाज प्रसादात् छत्रपति श्री राजराजेश्वर
महाराजाधिराज महाराजा श्री अभैःसिंह देव विजयते
भानुतेजस्वरूपेण महीमध्येषु राजते
हरि अंबा शिव सूर विनायक ये सुर पंच सदा फलदायक

(महाराजा की सही ।)

हुकम छै

(पत्र ।)

॥ : ॥ सिधि श्री श्री राजराजेसुर महाराज-

धिराज माहाराजा श्री अभैसिंघजी माहा-
राज कंवार श्री रांमसिंघजी देव वचनात
भं॥ अमरसिंघ दिसे सु परसाद वाचजौ
॥ तथा । गनीम पीलु असवार हजार १५००० पा-
ला आदमी ५००० सुं मही उतर उली तरफ आयो
थो ने दरबार री फोज रा डेरा वारेजे हुवा तरे पी-
लारा आदमी रद बदल ने आया उणां रद ब-
दल करतां या कही ज वडोदो न छोडां ने सखत
नरम वातां कही सु वात रो तो रंग न थो पीण
उणां ने धीरज देण ने अठा सुं वातरे वासते ई-
दा लखधीर भं॥ अजबसिंघ पं॥ रांमानंद ने
मेला तां सुं साजस कीवी थे लीखो तरे फोज मेलां
सु उणां रो लीखो आयो उण सायत असवार २०००
जरीदा बीदा कीया सु पीलारे लसकर नजी-
क गया तरे लखधीर सीख करण गयो उठे पी-
ला ने मारलीयो ने पीला रो भाई पुरां लोहां
छै सु मरसी ने सीरदार आदमी ५ कने था तां-
ने मारलीया ने ईतरा मै फोज पीण जाय पोह-
ती सु लसकर लुट लीयो घोडा ८०० दरबार
मे पडाड आया केईक जीव ले नाठा था सु मही-
रा घाट उपर कोलीयां लुट लीया ने फोज रो कु-
च हुवो सु भादरवे डेरो हुवो सु ईण घाट गनी-
म उतरतो सु जांमन लीया पाखटी रा भोमी-
यां तेजांम रा जांमन लीया ने बंदवसत कर कु-
च फुरमायो सु वेसाख सुद ८ वडोदे डेरा हुवा ने
गनीम रो साथ गांव कडाली री गढी मे तथा जा-
यगां २ त. ४ साथ थो सु फोज बीदा हुई थी सु पेच
काढीया छै हीमै गनीम नर्मांद गांव कोरल नर-
बदा उप्र छै तठे ने डभोई रा कीला में मेला हुवा छै
सु जमीत जादा छै ने पाछा सुं उमां तीमकरावरी
मा ने उदा पंवार री खबर आंवण री छै सु कु मुजा-
को म्हीं ईणां नु समाचार करां छां ने वे आसी तो पी-
ण सजा पासी पीलु री फते रा संमाचार पोतां री
अरजदासन आई उठारा पातसाह री खुस ब-
खती रा नवाब री रजामंदी रा संमाचार लो-
खीया था ने मतालवां वगेरे कांम री रद बद-
ल रा ने पातसाह री नीजर रा ने थारी मुलाज-
मत रा समाचारां री अरज लीखी थी सु मालु-
म हुई सारो कांम खातर खा ठीक लगायें ने
यादगारखां नवाब रे पेस छै सु वात तो ईण सु

राखजौ ने जती सुं पीण जवाब सवाल कराया
करजौ ने ललांपतो राखजो दोनां सु सुलुक रा-
खजो कांम रो जांणां तीण सु वीसेख राखजो हुकम छे
संवत १७८८ रा वेसाख सुद १३ मु॥ वडोदे

Translation

Top lines in Maharaja's own hand-writing.

May God always be our Protector.

Your petition as well as the letters addressed to other officials were received and the detailed information known. You have done excellently well in negotiating with the Nawāb hence your services have been appreciated. Settle early about the grant of Jāgīr, in this your loyalty will be known.

All the southern people have become hostile to us and we have left no stone unturned to serve the Emperor. Now if the Nawāb will comply with our request we shall maintain order in the province (of Gujrāt) and hold it, otherwise we certainly do not want to keep it. If the Nawāb does as desired by us and allots the whole revenue of the province to maintain an army as long there is the fear of invasion, for a period of a year or two, deputes assistants and permits no landlord to raise his head,

Lines on the margin in continuation of the above.

then we will remain here and care for the safety of the province, otherwise we are determined to leave it. He may entrust it to any one else whomever he thinks fit. If he sanctions the grant of our 'Jāgīr', we will hold the province.

You previously made a mention about Mālwā, but we do not like it and you should not accept any proposal about some other place but try to get the 'Jāgīr' in Gujrāt. Then our true metal will be known. You will gather full information from the letter of Dhannūdā.

You mentioned about Yādgārkhān and the Jatī (Jain priest). Better keep both of them under your palm and do whatever is useful and serves best the purpose of the Darbār. Do not care for whatever others say. We have reached Barōdā and tomorrow will march towards the Narbadā. We have captured 24 fortresses from the enemy and posted our garrisons in every one of them. The rest in possession of the enemy will be speedily taken.

At present by the grace of God the enemy will not be able to remain on this side of the Narbadā, but later on it will depend upon the arrangements made against him. By the grace of God the enemy dare not stay within 50 miles of us. Rest assured from our side. We are pleased with you. Now is the time to render your service. When performed satisfactorily it will be acknowledged and appreciated. It is our command. The detailed information will be known from the letter of Dhannūdā. By command.

Contents of the Royal seal.

By the grace of Almighty Goddess Hingulāj, glory be to sovereign ruler, King of Kings, supreme prince, Mahārājā Shrī Abhayasingh Dēva, who shines like the sun on the earth.

Hari, Ambā, Shiva, Sun, and Vināyak – may these five deities always bestow favours.

Approval of the letter in Maharaja's own calligraphy.

It is our command.

Letter.

By command of the illustrious, sovereign ruler, King of Kings, Mahārājā Shrī Abhayasinghjī and his heir-apparent Shrī Rāmsinghjī, Bhanḍārī Amarsingh should note their favours.

When Pīlū, the plunderer, after crossing the river Māhī with 15,000 cavalry and 5,000 foot, advanced in this direction and Darbār's forces were encamped at Vārējā his (Pīlā's) men came to negotiate the terms. In the course of discussion they showed reluctance to hand over Barōdā and also used some harsh words. Though there was no hope of arriving at a settlement, yet to pacify them we sent Īndā Lakhdhīr, Bhanḍārī Ajabsingh and Panchōlī Rāmānand to negotiate and secretly instructed them that on receipt of their written request we will send a contingent. Accordingly, on receipt of their letter we despatched 2,000 selected cavalry. When this force neared the camp of Pīlā, Lakhdhīr went to him (Pīlā) under the pretext of obtaining his permission for leaving the camp, and there he killed him. His (Pīlā's) brother is seriously wounded and is sure to die soon. Further there were other five nobles with Pīlā, who too have been killed on the spot. At the same moment the cavalry also reached there and plundered the camp. 800 (riderless) horses were captured by our men and the others who fled to save their lives, were looted by Kōlīs on the bank of the Māhī. After this our army marched and camped at Bhādarvā. As the enemy wanted to cross the river at this place, we made the local petty landlords responsible for checking their advance. After making all these necessary arrangements we again marched and encamped at Barōdā on the 8th day of the bright half of Vaishākh (21 April 1732 A. D.). As the contingents of the enemy were encamped in the fortress of Kandālī village and 2 or 4 other places, we sent our detachment which drove them away from their shelters. Now all the troops of the enemy have assembled in village Kōral on the bank of the Narbadā and in the fortress of Dabhōī. He has with him a large army and there is also a rumour that Ūmā (the mother of Trimbak Rāo) and Ūdā Panwār are coming from the rear to his help, but there is no danger on that score. We are going to punish the enemy and if Ūma and Ūdā will come to his help they will also meet the same fate. Your report acknowledging the receipt of the information of Pīlū's defeat reached us and the informations which you conveyed regarding the pleasure of the Emperor, satisfaction of the Nawāb, negotiations about the Jāgīr, etc., presenting 'Nazar' to the Emperor and the services rendered by you on this occasion have been noted.

Do all the work satisfactorily, be friendly with Yādgarkhān, who is in favour of the Nawāb, and also negotiate through the Jain saint. Try to please both of them and keep them friendly.

Hold this cause of Jāgīr extremely important to all others.

It is our command.

Dated 13th day of the bright half of Vaishākh, Samvat 1788 (Chaitrādi 1789) (26th April 1732 A.D.). Camp Barōdā.

18. Capture of Baroda by Maharaja Abhayasingh of Marwar.

(Read at the Seventh All India Oriental Conference held at Baroda in December 1933 and published in Indian Culture, Calcutta Vol. I, No 2 pp 239-242, 1934 A. D)

It would come as a surprise to many to learn that the territory now ruled by the Mahārājā Gāekwār was once under the sway of the Rāstrakūtas of the Deccan and Lāṭa and that its present capital Baroda or the ancient Vaṭapadraka was given in charity by Rāsṭrakūṭa king Kakkarāja of Lāṭa, in A.D. 812, as is evident from his copper plate[1] of Shaka Samvat, 734.

Besides this at the time of the Emperor Muhammadshāh, Mahārājā Abhayasingh of Jodhpur killed Pīlājī, the founder of the present Gāekwār dynasty, and captured the fort of Baroda.

The events connected with the capture of Baroda are related as follows :—

The author of 'Sehrulmutākharīn'[2] writes :—

" When the Emperor Muhammadshāh became displeased with Raushanuddaulā (on account of the numerous complaints of bribery received against him), Samsāmuddaulā gained influence at the Mughal Court of Delhi. The latter soon appointed Mahārājā Abhayasingh as the Governor of Gujrat, and wrote to him to take charge of that province as early as possible and send back the previous governor, Sarbulandkhān, to Delhi. The Mahārājā, taking it as an ordinary task, sent his representative with the contingent of an army to

1. *Indian Antiquary*, Vol. XII, page 160. 2. Volume II, pages 462-463.

carry out the order, but Sarbuland refused to hand over the province. Thereupon another representative was dispatched with a larger army to enforce the compliance of the order by the obstinate governor. But when he too failed, Mahārājā Abhayasingh himself proceeded towards Gujrat (as he was being repeatedly pressed by the emperor to do so at once[1]). Though, at first, on his arrival at Ahmedabad, with his brave Rāthōr army, a fierce battle was fought between him and the governor, the obdurate Sarbuland was soon compelled to yield ; he arrived in person with some of his followers to see the Mahārājā at his camp and to settle the terms of peace. During the discussion Sarbuland took a very submissive attitude and informed the Mahārājā that he considered him as his nephew, denied having any personal animosity and added that the battle had been fought simply to save his honour."

Soon after, when arrangements for money and transport were made, Sarbuland left Ahmedabad, and the Mahārājā took over charge of the province. This event took place in 1787 V.S. (1730 A.D.).

Mr. William Irwin and Sir Jadunāth Sarkār write in the 'Later Mughals'[2] that the aforesaid battle was fought on the 20th October, 1730 A.D., that Sarbuland went to see the Mahārājā on the 22nd October, and that he left for Delhi a few days later when necessary arrangements had been made for money and transport. But the mention of these events in a letter, dated the 4th day of the bright half of Kārtika, 1787 V.S. (19th October, 1730 A.D.) of Mahārajā Abhayasingh, sent to his agent at Mughal Court, shows that all these incidents took place before this date.

The weakness of Sarbuland had given chance to Pīlājī the representative of Khāndē Rāo Dābhādē, who was the commander of the ruler of Satara, to establish considerable sway over Baroda and its adjoining territories. This led Mahārājā Abhayasingh, soon after his possession of Ahmedabad, to march against Pīlājī.

1. This fact is proved by the letters of Kārtika Sudi 4th and Māngasir Badi 2nd 1782 V.S, sent by Savāī Rājā Jayasingh of Jaipur to Mahārājā Abhayasingh of Jodhpur.

2. Volume II, pages 207-213.

A letter dated the 14th day of the bright half of Chaitra, 1787[1] (Chaitradi, 1788) V.S. (10th April. 1731 A.D.) of Mahārājā Abhayasingh to his agent at the Mughal Court states :—

" Our armies, together with those of Bājī Rāo, attacked the garrison of Tryambak Rāo Dābhādé and killed Panvār Mūlājī and the Mughal Momīnyārkhān, the officers of Tryambāk Rāo and the Nizām respectively. We also captured the son of Pīlū along with Panvār Ūdā, Chimnā and Pandit. Thus a victory has been gained over the enemy and the armies of Pīlū, Kanthā, and Ānand Rāo have been driven from the field. Pīlū himself has sought shelter in the fort of Dabhoi. The fort of Baroda is being defended by his (Pīlū's) brother. But our armies have reached both the places and will soon compel the enemies to surrender. Kanthā too has fled to the Nizām. "

Another letter of the same Mahārājā, dated the 11th day of the bright half of Chaitra, 1788 (Chaitrādi, 1789) V.S. (26th March, 1732 A.D.) addressed to his agent, relates the latter events as below :—

" On Pīlū's crossing the Māhī river, our army also advanced from Chandūlā, whereupon Pīlū sent his envoys to our camp. We advised them to evacuate Baroda and Dabhoi and swear allegiance to the emperor. But Pīlū replied that he would not humiliate himself, for not only had he preserved his independence during the time of the last three Mughal Governors but had even forced Sarbuland, who had invaded Baroda, to pay him Chauth (the fourth part of the revenue). "

" These people, instead of giving a straight battle van to van, take the enemy by surprise. As soon as the vanguard of our army advanced about five miles, Pīlū fled towards Dākōr. Apprehending that our further advance would simply mean an indecisive chase, we contrived to fix them on the spot. We sent some emissaries to negotiate with them and then dispatched a column of 2,000 cavalry on the 9th day of the bright half of Chaitra (23rd March). The emissaries killed Pīlū, and the cavalry too reached there at the appointed

1. This is the year commencing from Srāvana

time. Pīlū's brother Memā and a number of his men were (also) put to death. Seven hundred horses and a number of "Janjāls" (long rifles fired from forts) were captured along with many other articles. We are soon reaching Baroda to get it evacuated."

These facts are further proved by a letter, dated the 13th day of the bright half of Vaishākha, 1788 (Chaitrādi, 1789) V.S. (26th April, 1732 A.D.), written by Mahārājā Abhayasingh to his said agent. It records that at that time Pīlū had 1,500 cavalry and 5,000 infantry with him, and that the Mahārājā got 800 horses as the booty.

It further states :—

"After this engagement we reached Baroda on the 8th day of the bright half of Vaisākha (21st April). The enemy was compelled to evacuate the fortresses of Kandālī, etc. Now they have gathered, in large numbers at Kōral, a village on the Narbadā and in the fort of Dabhoi. It is reported that Tryambak Rāo's mother Umā and Panvār Ūdā are coming to their aid, but they too on their arrival will not be spared. We intend to leave Baroda to-morrow to march towards the Narbadā. Up to this day we have captured 24 fortresses and those that are yet under the enemy will soon be taken possession of."

Another letter of the Mahārājā, dated the 11th day of the bright half of Āshādha, 1788 (Chaitrādi, 1789) V.S. (7th June, 1732 A.D.) written to his agent contains :—

"We have conquerred the forts of Baroda and Jambūsar and now the siege of the fort of Dabhoi is in progress."

But owing to the approach of the rainy season the Mahārājā was obliged to raise the siege. And soon after Umābāī, the widow of the late Khāndē Rāo Dābhādē, along with Pīlūji's son Dāmājī, Gāekwār, invaded Ahmedabad to avenge the death of Pīlūji. Owing however to the constant warfare, Gujrāt was suffering from a severe famine[1] at that time ; a treaty was, consequently, concluded between

1. A letter of Mahārājā Abhayasingh, dated the 1st day of the dark half of Bhādaun, 1789 V.S. (27th July, 1732 A.D.) addressed to his agent, shows that at that time, owing to the famine in Gujrāt, grain was not available even at the rate of one rupee a seer,

both the parties, and in 1790 V.S. (1733 A.D.), Mahārājā Abhayasingh, after appointing his representative at Ahmedabad, returned to Jodhpur.

Thus the history of Mahārājā Abhayasingh's capture of Baroda has been collected from his own original letters, which, except one, are now preserved in the Jodhpur State Museum.

19. Maharaja Abhayasingh of Jodhpur and Maharaja Sujansingh of Bikaner.

(Read at the seventeenth session of the Historical Records Commission held at Baroda in December 1940, and Published in its proceedings, pp 202-03).

We give here a letter[1] (along with its English translation) of Mahārājā Abhayasingh, the ruler of Jodhpur, written from Nāgaur, the headquarter of the district adjoining Bikaner, and addressed to his ambassador at the Mughal Court.

A dispute arose, in August 1733 A. D., about the demarcation of the boundary of their respective territories, between Mahārāj Bakhatsingh[2], the Chief of Nāgaur and Mahārājā Sujānsingh, the ruler of Bikaner. Consequently the former invaded Bikaner and later on Mahārajā Abhayasingh also joined him. Mahārājā Sujānsingh though for sometime bravely defended his capital, yet by the end of February 1734 A. D. he was obliged to enter into a treaty with the ruler of Jodhpur on the terms mentioned in the aforesaid letter.

On the other hand at that time the Maharattās were devastating a large part of India and a batch of these marauders, under the leadership of Bājī Rāo, plundered Malwa, while another, crossing Hādōtī, devastated the districts of Jaipur. Mahārājā Jaisingh, the ruler of Jaipur and the Governor of Malwa, being unable to defend the provinces under his care, sought help of Mahārājā Abhayasingh of Jodhpur.

---

(1) It was discovered at the house of the descendant of the person to whom it was written and is now preserved in the Sardār Museum, Jodhpur

(2) He was the younger brother of Mahārājā Abhayasingh of Jodhpur and held the province of Nāgaur as his Jāgīr.

Moreover the conditions in the country became so threatening that Nawāb Khān Daurān, the minister of Emperor Muhammad Shāh, himself decided to march against the enemy but could not succeed in his attempt.

A detachment of these marauders also invaded Ahmedabad but was repulsed by the Jodhpur forces as is evident from the letter, under reference, dated the 3rd March 1734 A. D.

In conclusion, we may add that this letter, besides giving the terms on which a treaty was concluded between the rulers of Jodhpur and Bikaner, exposes the weakness of the Mughal Court and the invasion of the Maharattās on Gujrat, Malwa and Rajputana.

(स्वयं महाराजा के हस्ताक्षरों में लिखी पंक्तियां।)

। श्री परमेसुरजी सायछै

। तथा हकीकत आगै ली (खी) .....

। नागोर पधारीया छां नवाव र वाह ? इणरी ख-
। वर उपर सगलो छोड ने दरकुच पधारीया छां
। नै फेर जैसींघजी रा समाचार आया म्हांरी म-
। दत कीजो तीण उपर पीण ताकीद सुं पधारां छा
। नै जमीत कनै ज्यादा छै तीण सुं अवै नवाव नु
। पुछ जो नवाव कैसो करनै खरची री खवर सनाव
। लेवै तो जमीत रै तीण सुं वीग (त वा) र समाचार
। सगले मनरूप नु फुरमाया छै ती (ण मा) फक नवाव रो
कोल लीजै नै खरची पूजती लीजे नै — — — तो नवाव ने
कैने गाढा रजावंद कीजे नै गाढी नीसां कीजे ने देखां
थारो मुजरो छै कीस ही तरै कर छै सगला समाचार
मनरूप लीखीया सु जाणसी थारै वाच नीचाजम छै
तिण कर सदा खुस्याल रेजे हुकम छै।
तथा खरची सताव मेलाजे म्हाकने खरची कीं न छै
खरची सुं लाग रैसी हुकम छै।

(मुहर में का लेख।)

महामाया श्री हिंगुलाज प्रसादात छत्रपति श्री राजराजेश्वर
महाराजाधिराज महाराजा श्री अभैःसिंहदेवः विजयते
भानुतेजस्वरूपेण महीमध्येषु राजते
हरि अंबा शिव सूर विनायक ये सुरपंच सदा फल
दायक।

(महाराजा की सही)

हुकम छै

(पत्र ।)

॥:॥ स्वारूप श्री श्री राजराजेश्वर माहा-
राजधिराज माहाराजा श्री अभेसिंघजी
माहाराज कंवार श्री रांमसिंघजी देव वच-
नात साहजहांनावाद मां॥ अमरसिंघ दी-
से सु प्रसाद् वांचजे

। तथा अरजदासत थारी आई हकीकत त-
मांम श्री हजुर मालुम हुई ते लिखियो थो
जु नवाव रो कुच गनीम रा हंगांमा उपर डेरि-
यो छै सो गनीम मालवो हाडोती लांघ ढुं-
ढाड आयो नै आंबेर जैपुर रा परगनां वी-
गाडीया तरै नवाव रो कुच सांभल नै आ स-
लाह ठहराई जु उठी नै गनीमांरी तंवीह सा-
रु पोहचीयो जोई जै तरै ईणा कांम उपर नीज-
र न राखणी नै बीकानेर वाला अरज करता
था सो ईणां श्री दरबार री बंदगी कबुल क-
री तरै रुपीया बारै लाख पेसकस रा ठहराया
तिण में आठ लाख रो तो भरणो ने च्यार लाख
रोक खरखुजी सारुंडा री पटी २ दरबार ताल-
क राखणी नै आगा सुं ईणा रो साथ चोकी री
चोकी श्री हजुर में बंदगी करणी ठहराई छै ही-
में अठासुं कुच गनीमांरी तंवी सारु फरमां-
यां जां हीमार जैसींघजी री ताकीद कुमक
सारु ज्यादे लीखी आई नै फेर नवाव रो कुच
सांभलीयो तरै म्हांसुं अठै कुंकर अटकीयो
जाय सो हीमैं नवाव सुं जाहर करजै कहो तां
अेहमदावाद सुं कुच करां फरमावै तो अज-
मेर आंबेर री तरफ गनीम आयो छै तीणरो
जावतो करां खरची नैं तईनातीयांरै वासतै न-
वाव सुं वजीद होय ने खरची २५०००००) पुरकस
कढावजे सारो मुदार खरची सुं छै नै अजमेर
रा सोबा रो तलास करजे और अेहमदावाद री
तरफ गनीम आया छै जिणांनै खारज कीया रा

समाचार तो परवाहरा पोहताहीज होसी फेर
दस हजार असवार फोज सिताब मेलां छां
तिण सुं खरची रो पुरकस जतन करजै नै अज-
मेर रा सोबा रो तलास करजे ईण बात में त-
माम थारो मुजरो छै और समचार भां॥ म-
नरुप दोला नै फरमाया छै सो लिखसी तिण बा-
त रो पुरकस जतन करजे ईण बात में हरगीज
तफावत न होसी हुकम छै
। सं॥ १७९० रा फागुण सुद १० रउ

Translation.

Top and marginal lines written with Maharaja's own pen.

Almighty is our protector

We have already written about the events. We have come back to Nāgaur. As we heard of the march of the Nawāb we leaving all other affairs, have returned here immediately. We also received the request of Jaisinghjī for help and therefore we are coming in haste. As we have with us a large contingent, you would ask the Nawāb about our further movements so that we may act according to it. Further you would arrange for the expenses so that the contingent may be retained. For this we have given detailed instructions to Manrūp and according to which you would take the promise of the Nawāb. You would also obtain sufficient money from him. Further if..........you would tell the Nawāb and get his full approval and convince him fully. In this task your services and the way you proceed will be appreciated. You would note everything written by Manrūp. You would keep yourself always hearty by our favour, which we have for you. It is our command. Arrange to send the money immediately as we are in dire need of it. Pay particular attention towards obtaining money. It is our command.

Inscription of the Royal seal.

By the grace of Almighty (Goddess) Hingulāj, glory be to the sovereign, king of kings, paramount sovereign, Mahārājā Shrī Abhayasingh Dēva, who shines like the sun on the earth.

Hari, Ambā, Shiva, Soor (Sun) and Vināyaka, may these five deities always bestow favours.

Approval of the letter by Maharaja in his own calligraphy

It is our command.

Letter.

By command of the illustrious, king of kings, paramount sovereign, Mahārājā Shrī Abhayasinghji and his heir-apparent Shrī Rāmsinghjī, Bhandārī Amarsingh, at Shahjahānābād (Delhi), would note their favours.

We have received your letter and noted all its contents. You had written that the Nawāb will march against the forces of the invaders, as the enemy, crossing Malwa and Hādōtī, has arrived at Ḍhūndhār and has devastated the districts of Āmbēr-Jaipur. Thereon, hearing the march of the Nawāb, we decided to reach there in order to punish the invaders and not to pay any more attention to this affair (of ours). Further as the Bikaner ruler was also suing for peace and has accepted the allegiance of the Darbār (us), we fixed rupees twelve lacs as indemnity. Out of which he would pay rupees eight lacs in cash and for the remaining four lacs he would cede the districts of Kharbūjī and Sārūndā to Darbār (us). He also promised to serve ourselves, in future, with his full contingent and every available force under him. Now we are marching from this place to chastise the invaders. We have just received an urgent request from Jaisinghjī for the early despatch of a helping force to him, and we have also heard about the march of the Nawāb, therefore how could we delay here any more.

Now you would enquire from the Nawāb whether we are to go to Ahmedabad or march towards Ajmer and Āmbēr to face the enemy, who is reported to have arrived there. As for the expenses and deputies you would personally see the Nawāb and get rupees 25,00,000 at least. Everything depends on money. Also enquire about the Governorship of the province of Ajmer. The news about the repulse of the enemy, who invaded the province of Ahmedabad, might have reached there directly. Further we are despatching there ten thousand horse very shortly. Hence you would arrange for the money and enquire about the Governorship of Ajmer. Your services will be fully appreciated for these efforts. Moreover, we have given orders to Bhaṇḍārī Manrūp Daulā, who will write you and you would also try your best for that. There ought to be no negligence in it. It is our command.

Sunday the 10th of the bright half of Phāgun 1790 V.S. (3rd March 1734 A.D.)

20. Marwar's Timely Services to Mewar.

Published in Dr S. Krishnaswami Aiyangar Commemoration Volume (1936 A D pp 111-115)

Though the magnanimity of the Mahārānās of Mēwār has been widely known all over India, yet the timely help they received from the rulers and the nobility of Mārwār has remained obscure for want of relevant historical facts. Some evidence lending full support to the above statement is being furnished below:—

(1) In his old age Mahārānā Lākhā cherished a keen desire to marry Hansābāī, the daughter of Rāo Chūndā of Mārwār. At the time of the betrothal, however, her brother, Prince Ranmall (Rinmul of Tod), laid down the condition precedent to the marriage that, in case a son were born to his sister, he was to be declared the heir-apparent to the throne of Mēwār even though he might be the youngest of all the sons of the Mahārānā. As Mahārānā Lākhā was very keen on this marriage, his eldest son, Prince Chūndā (Chonda of Tod), partly in concession to the wishes of his father, and partly in consideration of the remoteness of the possibility of the birth of a son to the Mahārānā in his old age, agreed to the condition.[1] Accordingly, on the death of Mahārānā Lākhā,[2] between Samvats 1476 and 1478 (1419-1421 A.D.), Prince Chūndā had to forego his right of succession; and Mōkal (Mokul of Tod), the son of Hansābāī, at the age of eleven, was installed on the throne of Mēwār. But the activities of Chūndā, who had been entrusted with the administration of the country,

---

1 For quite a different version of the motives and circumstances of the marriage see Tod's *Rajasthan*, 1899 Edn. I, pp 290 ff.

2 Tod places this event in A.D. 1398,

aroused Hansābāī's suspicions. So he had to leave Mēwār, and to seek selter with the Sultān of Māṇḍū, a natural enemy of the Mēwār house.

In this state of affairs, Hansābāī called in the assistance of her brother, Rāo Raṇmall. For seven years he carried on the administration of Mēwār, and then returned to Maṇḍōr, his ancestral capital, in V.S. 1485 (1428 A.D.).

(2) In V. S. 1490 (1433 A.D.), Chāchā and Mērā, the half-brothers of Mahārānā Lākhā, as a part of their deep-laid plot,[1] killed Mahārānā Mōkal, their nephew and besieged the famous fort of Chitōr. As at that time Kumbhā, the eldest son of Mahārānā Mōkal, was only seven years of age, and no one among the nobility was forthcoming to avenge the death of their ruler or to rescue Chitōr, the situation grew very critical. Hansābāī, the grandmother of Mahārānā Kumbhā, again looked up to her brother, Rāo Raṇmall for help. On his arrival at Mēwār, with a band of 500 Rāthōrs, Chāchā and Mērā fled towards the hills of Pāikōṭrā. Rāo Ranmall gave chase to them, and, after six months' strenuous efforts, in the course of which he had once even to risk his life while procuring the help of the Bheels, he succeeded in avenging the death of Mōkul, and in suppressing the revolt. Only, Parmār Mahapā, one of the ring-leaders, who escaped in disguise and reached Māṇḍū, was helped by Rāo Chunḍā in getting refuge with the Sultān.

After this, Rāo Ranmall set right[2] the machinery of the administration of Mēwār, and attacked with success Sultān Mahmūd of Māṇḍū, for having sheltered Parmār

1. (Tod assigns this event to A.D 1419). "Though the murder of Mokal is related to have no other cause than the sarcasm alluded to, the precautions taken by the young prince Kumbha ('Koombho'), his successor, would induce a belief that this was but the opening of a deep-laid conspiracy. The traitors returned to the stronghold near Madri, and Kumbha trusted to the friendship and good feeling of the prince of Marwar in this emergency. His confidence was well repaid." (*Annals and Antiquities of Rajasthan*, Vol. I, pp. 332.) (The sarcasm alluded to is described in Tod, Vol. I, p 334)

2 (The bardic historians, says Tod "do as much honour to the Marwar prince, who had made common cause with their sovereign in revenging the death of his father, as if it had involved the security of his crown. But this was a precautionary measure of the prince, who was induced thus to act from several motives, and above all, in accordance with usage, which stigmatises the refusal of aid when demanded. besides Kumbha was the nephew of Marwar".)

Mahapā. Though Rāo Ranmall was treacherously murdered[1], in V.S. 1495 (1438 A.D.) by the conspirators led by Parmār Mahapā and Ēkā, the son of Chāchā, yet the inscription dated V.S. 1496 (1439 A.D.) of Rāṇpur is an incontestible proof of the honesty and valour with which he discharged his duties as a regent.

In V.S. 1496 (1439 A.D.) Mahārānā Kumbhā was only thirteen years of age[2], and therefore the credit for the conquests of Sārangpur (Mālwā), Nāgpur, Gāgraun, Narānā (Jaipur), Ajmēr, Māndalgarh, Būndī, Khātū and Chātsū (Jaipur), mentioned in the above inscription, goes undoubtedly to the regent, Rāo Rānmall, who led the armies of Mēwār against those districts.

(3-4) In V.S. 1577 (1520 A.D.), when Mahārānā Sāngā went against Muzaffar Shāh of Gujrāt[3], and in V. S. 1584 (1527 A.D.), when he himself was attacked by Bābar[4], he received a substantial military help from Rāo Gānga of Mārwār.

(5) In V.S. 1624 (1567 A.D.), when Emperor Akbar attacked Chitōr, Mahārānā Udayasingh, along with his family, was obliged to retire among the mountains for shelter, and the charge of defending the fort against such a formidable

---

1. The historians of Mēwār, being ashamed of this heinous crime, the treacherous murder of Rāo Rānmall, have tried their level best to conceal this unholy sin by accusing Rāo Ranmall of the idea of usurping the throne of Mēwār. But they could not achieve success Had Rānmall really such an idea, he would have neither allowed Mahārānā Mōkal nor Kumbhā to grow in age and power as is evident from the history This is also corroborated by the following lines of the 'vīrvinōd', the official history of Mēwār —

" After the murder of Rāo Ranmall, Hansābāī called her grandson Kumbhā and told him that, though, Rānmall had killed his father's assassins Chāchā and Mērā, defeated the Mohmmedans and raised the name of Mēwār, yet he has also been murdered "

This shows that Rāo Ranmall never had any bad motive in helping Mēwār.

2 According to the old chronicles. on the birth of Kānbā in V.S. 1465 (1408 A D) Prince Ranmall, being asked by his father Rāo Chūṇḍā of Mārwār, abdicated his right to the Gaddi and went towards Mēwār. Soon after this Mahārānā Lākhā married his sister Hansabāi, the mother of Mōkal born in V S. 1466 (1409 A.D) This proves that Mōkal could neither have been more than 11 years of age when his father Mahārānā Lākhā died in about V. S 1477 (1420 A D), nor more than 24 years when he was murdered in V. S 1490 (1433 A D) Further, in the same manner if we presume the birth of Mahārānā Kumbhā to have been in V S. 1483 (1426 A D), when his father was 17 years of age, he could neither have been more than 7 years of age when his father Mahārānā Mōkal was murdered in V S 1490 (1433 A D.), nor more than 13 years of age when the Rānpur inscription was engraved in V S 1496 (A D. 1439)

3 Maharana Sanga pp 79.

4, Annals and Antiquities of Rājasthān, Vol. II, p 953,

enemy as Akbar was given to Raṭhōr Jaimal[1] of Mārwār and Pattā of Mēwār. It is evident from the 'Akbarnāmā' that, no sooner was Raṭhōr Jaimal killed, than the fort fell into the hands of the enemy.

(6) In V.S. 1748 (1691 A.D.) Amarsingh, the eldest son of Mahārānā Jayasingh, revolted against his father, and the Mahārānā, being unable to check this trouble from within, sought shelter with Rathōr Gōpīnāth at Ghānērāo, and sent a request to the court of Mahārājā Ajitsingh of Mārwār for help.

No sooner did Rāṭhōr Durgādās and other nobles of Mārwār arrive there, than the prince was obliged to make a compromise with his father, the Mahārānā.[2]

(7) In V.S. 1752 (1695 A.D.), Amarsingh again raised his head, but as the Mahārānā at once called Mahārājā Ajitsingh to marry his niece, the prince could not succeed[3] in his plans.

(8) In V.S. 1827 (1770 A.D.), Mahāṛājā Arisingh, threatened with the internal intrigues, sent an humble-worded petition to Mahārājā Vijayasingh of Mārwār for help, and presented him with the rich district of Gōdwād which is a part of Mārwār to this day.

M.M. G. H. Ojha, in his 'History of Rājapūtānā,[4] writes that the Mahārānā addressed a letter to Vijayasingh, the Rājā of Jōdhpur, in which he asked him to keep a cavalry force, 300 strong, at Nāthadwārā for suppressing Ratnasingh, and in return allowed him to take the income of Gōḍwād for the maintenance of the garrison so long as it was stationed there. But at the same time he pointed out that the nobles of the district would remain under the direct control of the Mahārānā.

---

१. राजपूतानेका इतिहास जिल्द २, पृ० ७२४-२५

२. अजितोदय, सर्ग १५, श्लोक १—१७, और वीरविनोदमें का मारवाड़ का इतिहास।

३. अजितोदय, सर्ग १५ श्लो. २८—३५. और राजरूपक, पृ० १४१

४. जिल्द २, पृ० ९७०

How far this version is correct will be seen from the letter reproduced below :—

Obverse

१. श्रीमाहाराज बीजेसिंघजी ह-
२. जूर राणा अडसीरो मुजरो मा-
३. लम वे अप्रंच आप मासु कि-
४. रपा करी जोदपुर उदेपुर इक
५. कीदो मारो भलो हुवे जो विचारो
६. जी ऊपर मे आपरी नजर गोडवा-
७. ड नजर कीदी हे सो हु मारो बेटो
८. मारा वंसरो बेसी सो ई वातमे
९. तफावद् पाडसी तीन पर एक-
१०. लिंगजी री आण हे मारी मारा रा-
११. ज री सरम आपने हे जादा कां-
१२. ही लखा परमेसर उपरे कामना
१३. नमत परांग करे जाही कामना वे
१४. ने ईसवर हेयारथ जप नाम पु-
१५. न करे हे तो ईसवर सारी काम-
१६. ना मनोरथ सारो पूरवे हे जु मे
१७. आप ऊपर आगता राख ओराज मे
१८. आपरा खोलाह आछी जाण जू क-
१९. रे पण ढील न वे अवार मारा राज रो

Reverse

२०. हाल सरुप हे जो मालम हु-
२१. सी आप करता सो आसान हे
२२. सारो मीठाय देसी मारे भ-
२३. रोसो आपरो हे समत १८२७ रा वे-
२४. साख वद् ११

Translation

Shrī Mahārājā Vijaisinghjī may accept the compliments of Rānā Adsī. You have been good enough to identify the cause of Jōdhpur and Udaipur. Find out a way of my welfare, for which I have presented you district of Gōdwād and if I, my son, or any one else of my family repudiates this, the curse of Ēkalingjī may fall upon him. My dignity as well as the dignity of my kingdom (state) lies with you. What more shall I write ? One who performs a ceremony with a certain object keeping faith in God gets his desired object. And one who repeats the name of God and bestows charity in his name, the Almighty fulfills all his desires. Similarly, keeping faith in you, I havé placed this kingdom (state) in your lap. Do what you think proper, but do not be slack. You might be knowing the present condition of my kingdom. For you, everything is easy, and therefore you will remove all my difficulties. I am depending on you.

(Shrāvanādi Vikram) Samvat 1827, Vaishākh Vadi 11 (10th April 1771 A. D).

These are some of the broad facts. Besides these, there is some more documentary evidence which proves that, for certain reasons, Mārwār rulers were always alert in defending the cause of the Mahārānā of Mēwār against the Mughal influence.

21. An Old Imperial "Sanad" relating to Raisina or New Delhi

(Read at the thirteenth meeting of the Indian Historical Records Commission held at Patna in December 1930 and published in its proceedings, (pp. 145-149) as well as in the Journal of the Royal Asiatic Society, London, (July 1931 A. D. Part III) (pp. 515-525.)

This "Sanad"[1] had been issued in favour of Mahārājā Bijayasingh of Mārwār by the Mughal Emperor Shāh 'Ālam II of Delhi on the 9th Jumādī-ul-ākhir of the 17th year of his reign.

Emperor Shāh 'Ālam II, whose original name was 'Ālīgauhar, was son of Emperor 'Ālamgīr II.

On 29th November, A. D. 1759 (8th Rabī-us-sānī, A. H. 1173, or Mārgshīrsh Sudī 10, V. S. 1816) when 'Ālamgīr II was murdered, 'Ālīgauhar was in Bihār, where, on hearing of the event, he ascended the throne[2] with the title Shāh 'Ālam II on the 24th December of the same year (4th Jamādī-ul-avval, A. H. 1173, or Paush Sudī 5, V. S. 1816). In the meantime his father's assassin Vazīr 'Imād-ul-mulk Ghāzī-ud-dīn Khān had declared Muhī-us-sunnat as king of Delhi with the title Shāh Jahān II; but he could not remain on the throne even for a year as Sadāshiv Rāo Bhāū had replaced him by Mirzā Jawān Bakht, son of Shāh 'Ālam II. Later, in A. D. 1761 (A. H. 1174 or V. S. 1817), when Ahmad Shāh Abdālī having defeated the Maharaṭṭās at Pānīpat came to Delhi, he announced[3] Shāh 'Ālam II as Emperor, appointed Mirzā Jawān Bakht as heir apparent, and Shujā'-ud-dāula[4] as Vazīr.

1. Its length is about 3 feet, and breadth about 22 inches. It is mounted on a cloth to keep it preserved from decay, leaving the endorsements and the seals on its back open to view.
2. This ceremony had been performed at village Kathaulī in Azīmābād district
3. After this event Ahmad Shāh returned to Qandhār leaving a deputy at Lahore.
4. He was Nawāb of Oudh.

But as Shāh 'Ālam[1] II had adopted his regnal year from the 24th December, A. D. 1759 (4th Jumāda-ul-avval, A. H. 1173, or Paush Sudī 5, V.S. 1816), his seventeenth regnal year commenced from the 3rd July, A. D. 1775 (4th Jumāda-ul-avval, A. H. 1189 or Āshādh Sudī 5, V.S. 1832). Accordingly the corresponding date of the "Sanad" which was written on the 9th Jumāda-us-sānī of the seventeenth regnal year, falls on the 7th August, A. D. 1775 (Shrāvan Sudī 11, V. S. 1832).

Besides the text of the Farmān the "Sanad" contains one imperial "Tughrā" and one imperial seal on the obverse, and two official seals and four endorsements on the reverse. Before dealing with the text of the Sanad I think it proper to examine, in detail, these particulars of the Sanad:—

The "Tughrā": Written in bold arabic characters in gold, occupying a rectangular space, reads: "Farmān vālā Shān Abul Muzaffar Jalāluddīn Shāh 'Ālam Bādshāh Ghāzī." Some scribblings in red occur in the blank spaces and at the top of the "Tughrā" according to custom of the age. This "Tughrā" is placed at the top of the Sanad towards the left.

---

1 On the 12th August, 1765 (24th Safar, A. H. 1179, or Bhādon Badī 11, V. S. 1822), the same king Shāh 'Ālam II had granted the "Sanad of Dīwānī" of the three provinces of Bengal, Bihār, and Orisa to the East India Company in lieu of Rs. 24 lacs (26 lacs as stated elsewhere) per annum. For some time he had also kept his residence at Allahabad, but in A. D 1771 (V. S 1828), being displeased with the English, he returned to Delhi and resumed the reins of the government personally. In A. D 1788 (V. S. 1845) Ghulām Qādir, grandson of Najīb-ud-daulā (whom perhaps Ahmad Shāh Abdālī had appointed, "Amīr-ul-umrā" of the Emperor), came to Delhi and deprived the king of his vision. But he was soon after restored to the throne by Mādhō Rāo Sindhiā, who put Ghulām Qādir to death. For this timely help Shāh 'Ālam conferred on Sindhiā the title of "Farzand-i-'Ālijāh" and has suitably given vent to his sentiment of the occasion in the following couplet —

مادھو جي سندھيا فرزند جگر بند من
هست مصروف به تلافی ستمگاري ما—

i. e. Mādhōjī Sindhiā the affectionate son of mine is engaged in the removal of our distresses.

The title mentioned above still goes with the names of the Mahārājās of Gwālior.

It is evident from history that in the well-known impeachment of Warren Hastings in the British Parliament, one of the charges brought against him was that he had conspired with Mādhō Rāo Sindhiā against the Emperor Shāh 'Ālam II This shows that Mādhō Rāo Sindhiā having reached Delhi might have overpowered the Emperor Shāh 'Ālam II at the instigation of Warren Hastings. Yet, however, the Sindhiā's treatment of the Emperor was not bad.

Later in A. D. 1803 (V. S. 1860) Lord Lake came to Delhi and having pensioned off the king on Rs. 12 lacs per annum, assumed the government of the Empire. Shāh 'Ālam II died in A. D. 1806 (A. H. 1221, or V. S 1863).

The imperial seal: At its top is written "Hāulghālib", i. e. the omnipotent. In fourteen small circles around the seal are written names of the Emperor's fourteen predecessors, as follows: (1) Sāhib Qirān[1] Bin Fīrōz; (2) Ibn Mīrānshāh; (3) Ibn Sultān Muhammad Shāh; (4) Ibn Abū Saīd Shāh; (5) Ibn 'Umar Shēkh Shāh; (6) Ibn Bābar Bādshāh; (7) Ibn Humāyūn Bādshāh; (8) Ibn Akbar Bādshāh; (9) Ibn Jahāngīr Bādshāh; (10) Ibn Shāhjahān Bādshāh; (11) Ibn 'Ālamgīr Bādshāh; (12) Ibn Shāh 'Ālam Bādshāh; (13) Ibn Jahāndārshāh; (14) Ibn 'Ālamgīr Bādshāh.

The words "Bin" and "Ibn" show that the above-named rulers bore the relation of father and son in order. In the inner big circle is written "Abul Muzaffar Jalāluddīn Shāh 'Ālam Bādshāh Ghāzī" as also the "Hijri" year 1173 and the regnal year one. This seal is placed towards the, right above the text.

The Vazīr's seal: The writing in the seal reads: "Shāh 'Ālam Bādshāh Ghāzī, yār vafādār, Sipahsālār, Rustam-i-Hind, Fidvī-i-Qadīm, Yāhyākhān Asaf-ud-daulā.. Shujā-ud-daulā, Abul Mansūrkhān Safdarjang I'timād-ud-daulā Āsafjāh Burhān-ul-mumālik, Jamdeh madārul mahām." It also contains the "Hijrī" year 1190, and the regnal year seventeenth. This shows that this seal is of the time of Āsaf-ud-daulā, the eldest son of Shujā'-ud-daulā, who had died on the 26th January, A. D 1775 (24th-ZīQa'd, A. H. 1188, or Māgh Badī 10, V. S. 1831). This seal is placed on the back of the Sanad towards the left lower corner.

The third seal: Its contents are: "(Shāh 'Ālam)[2] Bādshāh Ghāzī, Fidvī Khānāzād Khān Bahādur." The regnal year given in it is sixteenth. This seal stands near the Vazīr's seal to the right. Just below this seal there is an endorsement, as follows:—

سنه ۱۷ جلوس والا بتاریخ دوم ۲ شهر رجب المرجب نقل شد

i.e. the copy[3] of the Sanad was taken on the 2nd Rajab of the seventeenth regnal year (29th August, A. D. 1775, or Bhādaun Sudī 3, V. S. 1832).

---

1 This was an after death title of Tīmūr (Read Ibn Amīr Tīmūr Sāhib Qirān —Ed.)

2 This portion is torn.

3 (The word is not clear. Probably we should read نقش and the reference is to affixation of the seal.—Ed.)

The second endorsement on the back on the right corner runs as follows:—

بتاریخ دویم شهر رجب المرجب سنه ۱۷ جلوس، والا مطابق سنه ۱۱۸۹ داخل
سیاهه نموده سد مطابق ۷ شهر یورماه نقل بدفتر صاحب نوشته شد [1] ···· بوهانند—

Just near the above there is a third endorsement, as below:

سنه ۱۷ جلوس والا بتاریخ دویم رجب المرجب نقل.... مستوفی ائمه عظام رسید—

The purport of the second endorsement is "Entered in the siyāhā (register) on the 2nd of the month of Rajab of the regnal year seventeenth, corresponding to Hijrī 1189 (29th August, A. D. 1775, or Bhādaun Sudī 3, V. S. 1832). Copy taken in the office of the "Sāhib" on the 7th of "Shahar yūr".[2] May be handed over.

Purport of the third endorsement:—

Copy taken in the office of the "Aiyamā Izām" (high priest)[3] on the 2nd Rajab of the seventeenth regnal year.

The fourth endorsement called "Zimn"[4] on the back of the Sanad, runs as follows:—

Line (1) مقدمه شرح ضمن به رجب سیاهه دفتر باشد حکم صادر شد موضع رای سینا
درنست عمله پرگنه حویلی دارالخلافه شاهجهان آباد بادست محال قدیم····

Line (2) [5] مهاراجه بخت سنگه که در آلتمغا محمد مرادخان شده بود—تاسنا در سنه ۲
پروانه تعالی بنام مهاراجه بجے سنگه عطا گشته بود , من بعد آن (بجا گیردار ·· بعرانهاراے
امان عرف رشند (امان درجاگیر خود[6]····) در خالصه جدید قرار یافته···ربیع قرایل
پیشین Line (3) محال قدیم آلتمغا , زمین داری از محال مالکه شریفه درصیغه انعام
آلتمغا····بجے سنگه بهادر باورندان نسلاً بعد نسلاً····واقع ۲۶ جمادی الاخر

---

1 Here there is some one's signature which is undecipherable.

2 This is the 6th of the Persian months commencing from the "Sankrānti", i. e. sun's zodiacal change.

3 (Should be mustaufī a'-imma-i-'izām = the controller of the great grants.—Ed.)

4 In this endorsement, the following words being copied on a separate slip from the original, the slip is pasted instead at the time of repairing the Sanad —

Line (1) ارالخلافه شاهجهان آباد بادست محال—
Line (2) ارانهاراے امان عرف رشند امان درجاگیر
Line (3) سنگه بهادر باورزندان نسلاً بعد نسلاً—

The cross letters visible in the photo between the 2nd and the 3rd line do not belong to the text of the endorsement, but are superfluous contents of the slips pasted to preserve the paper.

5 The following matter being covered under the cloth mount did not appear in the photo.—

Of the first line.—شده بود تاینا در سنه ۲

Of the second line—ایل پیشین

6 The writing within this bracket being distorted conveys no sense

Its purport:—

The details of the case may be entered according to the Register of the office. Orders issued. Village Rāisīnā situated in the "Havēlī" (Suburban) district of the capital Shāhjahānābād, in view of old "Jāgīr"....of Mahārājā Bakht-Singh, which had passed on to Muhammad Murādkhān as a "Jāgīr" for generations, was for the second time restored to Mahārājā Bijayasingh in regnal year 2, i. e. A. D. 1760 or V. S. 1817; but after this it (having remained in the "Jāgīr" of Rāi Amān alias Rashīd Amān....) had recently lapsed to "Khālsā". (The same Rāisinā) due to its being his ancestral Jāgīr (is granted) from "Khālsā" to Mahārājā Bijayasingh Bahādur and his descendants, generation after generation, by way of reward from the "Rabi" Crop of the "Quīl" year. Dated 26 Jumāda-ul-ākhir (24th August, A. D. 1775, or Bhādaun Badī 13, V. S. 1832).

TEXT OF THE SANAD

(۱) در وقت میمنت اقتران فرمان والا شان—

(۲) واجب الاذعان صادر شد که مبلغ هشتاد هزار دام—

(۳) موضع رایسینه در دستور عمله پرگنه حویلی دارالخلافه شاهجهان آباد که مبلغ
هفتصد روپیه حاصل آن است بابت محال قدیم که در خالصه شریفه قرار یافته بود در وجه انعام—

(۴) التمغا ... زبده راجهای هندوستان راج راجیشر مهاراجه دهراج بجی سنگه بهادر با فرزندان
معافی تصدیق و یادداشت

(۵) بر جمع آن بیفزاید از ابتدای ربیع قوئیل حسب الضمن مقرر داشت—باشد که فرزندان
نامدار کامگار والا تبار و وزرای ذوی الاقتدار و امرای اعلی مقدار و حکام کرام و عمال

(۶) کفایت فرجام و متصدیان مهمات دیوانی و متکفلان معاملات سلطانی و جاگیرداران
و کروریان حال و استقبال ابداً و مؤبداً در استقرار و استمرار این حکم—

(۷) محلی کوشیده داماهی مرقومه را نسلاً بعد نسل و بطناً بعد بطن حالاً و مستقبلاً
متصرف آنها واگذارند و از مرادم تغیر و تبدیل مصون و محروس دانسته بعلت پیشکش
صوبه داری—

(۸) و فوجداری و مال وجهات و سایر اخراجات مثل ... نگارده ... مقدم صدد ...
قانون گوی—مزاحم و متعرض نشوند و از کل تکلیفات دیوانی

(۹) و مطالبات سلطانی معاف و مرفوع القلم شمارند درین باب تاکید اکید و قدغن
مزید دانسته هر سال سند مجدد طلب ندارند و از فرموده تخلف و انحراف نورزند
بتاریخ نهم شهر جمادی الثانی سال هفدهم از جلوس والا زیب تحریر یافت—

Translation: In this auspicious time the sublime command worthy of being obeyed is issued that village Rāisīnā of 80,000 "dāms" in the "Havēlī" (suburban) Parganā of the capital Shāhjahānābād (Delhi), the rental value of which is Rs. 700/-, may be settled as "Inām" (gift) for generations, in view of his old "Jāgīr" that had lapsed to "khālsā", upon Rāj Rājēshvar Mahārājādhirāj Bijayasingh Bahādur, the predominant of the Rājās of India, and his descendants (having been verified as rent free and duly registered, that its revenue may increase) from the third part of the "Rabī" crop (i.e. from the time of the crop being ready) of the "Quīl" (Turkish eighth year) as mentioned in the "Zimn" (Register). Our distinguished, fortunate, and dignified descendants, ministers of high rank, noble grandees, eminent officers, economical revenue collectors, administrators of civil matters, trustees of Royal affairs, "Jāgīrdārs" and "karōrīs" of the present and future, having ever and anon tried to maintain and perpetuate this esteemed order, ought always to leave the above-mentioned "dāms" in their (grantees') possession, generation after generation, and individual after individual. And treating this (grant) as safe and protected from consequences of changes and fluctuations, may not exercise pressure or raise objection about payment of "Sūbedārī", "Faujdārī", "Māl", "Jahāt," and all other cesses like.... "Begār", "Dehnīmī" (½/10), "Muqaddamī" "Sadzuī" (2/100), "Qānūngōī", and should treat (the grant) as free from all civil obligations and Royal demands. Treat this as strict and very urgent, do not demand new "Sanad" every year, and never disobey or act contrary to this grand order. Written on the 9th Jumādi-us-sānī, seventeenth year of the reign (i e. on the 7th August, A.D. 1775, or Shrāvan Sudī 11, V.S. 1832).

From this Sanad it is apparent that the village Rāisīnā, on the site of which the present New Delhi stands, had been during the Mughal period the ancestral "Jāgīr" of the rulers of Mârwār and had regularly remained under their sway up to the reign[1] of Mahārājā Bakhtsingh A.D. 1751-52

1 Mahārājā Bakhtsingh had ascended the throne of Mārwār on the 29th June, A. D. 1751 (Shrāvan Sudī 2, v s 1808), having deposed his nephew Mahārājā Rāmsingh. He died on 21st September, A. D. 1752 (Bhādaun Sudī 13, v. s. 1809), and was succeeded by his son Mahārājā Bijayasingh.

(v.s. 1808-09). But at this time, as dissensions[1] broke out in the royal house of Jōdhpur, the Emperor having confiscated it from Mahārājā Bijayasingh conferred it on Muhammad Murād Khān at the instigation of hostile parties[2]. Later, when the family feud had ended, it was restored again to Mahārājā Bijayasingh in A.D. 1760 (V.S. 1817). But sometime after, when the administration of Mārwār had relaxed due to Maharattā inraids, the Emperor Shāh 'Ālam II, again yielding to hostile influence, confiscated the village from the Mahārājā. Lastly on suppression of all the main risings in Mārwār, it is probable that the Mahārājā might have put forward his claim to this, his ancestral "Jāgīr" village, in the Emperor's court (as is evident from the central endorsement on the back of the Sanad) and the Emperor having seen proofs of this village being the ancestral "Jāgīr" of the Mahārājās of Mārwār and finding no other rightful claimant to it, might have issued this "Sanad" in A. D. 1775 (V.S. 1832) in his favour. We cannot say when and under what circumstances this "Jāgīr" went out of the possession of the rulers of Mārwār, but two conclusions are derived clearly from it:—

Firstly, that this Rāisīnā was an ancestral "Jāgīr" of the Mahārājās of Mārwār, and that, up to, at the most, 155 years hence, it was in their possession.

Secondly, that the titles "Zubdah[3] Rājhā-i-Hindustān, Rāj Rājēshvar, Mahârājā Dhirāj" were used with the names of the Mahārājās of Mārwār up to the end of the Mughal Empire.

---

1 Warfare continued up to A.D. 1756 (v.s. 1813) between the two cousins Mahārājās Bijayasingh and Rāmsingh for the sovereignty of Mārwār. Later through the intervention of the Maharattās peace was concluded and Mahārājā Rām Singh was given eleven districts of Mārwār. Though the internal feud had mostly subsided by this action, yet the government of Mārwār had grown slack through the inraids of the Maharattās. This gave rise to a fresh revolt of the 'sardārs' of Mārwār which was also suppressed to a great extent in A.D. 1760 (v.s. 1816). But in A.D. 1765 (v.s. 1822) due to Mādhōrāo Sindhiā's invasion, the state affairs were again confused. In A.D. 1772 (v.s. 1829) Mahārājā Rāmsingh the root cause of all troubles, breathed his last, and the eleven districts of his 'Jāgīr' reverted to the state. This event broke the hearts of the internal enemies of Mārwār. Further the murder of Thākur Jaisingh of Āuwā, the premier noble of Mārwār, in A.D. 1774 (v.s. 1831) struck terror in the hearts of the rebel sardārs, and brought them round to reason and peace.

2 Mahārājā Īshvarī Singh of Jaipur, being father-in-law of Mahārājā Rāmsingh had sided with him. His influence also must have worked with the Emperor against Mahārājā Bijayasingh.

3 The word "Sarāmad" in place of "Zubdah" has also been used in the titles of the rulers of Mārwār, as is evident from Kharītās, dated 29th May, 1820 (Jyesht Badī 12, Shrāvanādī, v. s. 1877), and 12th June, 1829 (Jyesht Sudī 10, Shrāvanādī, v. s. 1886), from Hon. Richard Cavendish Agent, Ajmer to the address of Mahārājā Mānsingh of Mārwār, as well as from a "Farmān" dated 7th Jamādī-ul-awwal A. H. 1217 (Bhādaun Sudī 8, v. s. 1859 = 5th September, A. D. 1802), from the King of Kabul to the address of Mahārājā Bhīmsingh of Mārwār.

22. Maharaja Mansingh of Jodhpur and Maharaja Suratsingh of Bikaner.

(Bond published in the Report on the administration of the Archaeological Department and Sumer Public Library Jodhpur 1938 A.D., p. 9)

In this paper we are giving copy of a bond[1] (with its English translation) signed by Mahārājā Sūratsingh of Bikaner to pay rupees four lacs and one[2] as indemnity, to Mahārājā Mānsingh of Jodhpur.

It may also help to give an idea of the system of hostage and surety prevalent among the Indian rulers. But before doing so it seems necessary to give the events in brief, which compelled the Mahārājā of Bikaner to sign it.

In 1804 A. D. there arose a dispute in Marwar between Mahārājā Mānsingh and Ṭhākur Savāīsingh of Pōkaran—his feudatory—regarding Dhōnkalsingh an alleged posthumous son of the late Mahārājā Bhīmsingh of Jodhpur.

The relations of the rulers of Jodhpur and Jaipur at that time were strained in connection with the betrothal of Krishna Kunvarī, the daughter of Mahārānā Bhīmsingh of Udaipur. Ṭhākur Savāīsingh took advantage of the situation and in 1807 A. D. succeeded in persuading Mahārājā Jagatsingh of Jaipur to invade Jodhpur. He also induced Mahārājā Sūratsingh of Bikaner to join the campaign. These combined forces attacked Jodhpur but the seige fizzled out due to the ingenuity of Singhī Indrarāj etc., who with the help of some nobles and Mīrkhan, planned an attack on Jaipur at the same time and thus diverted the attention of the Jaipur army.

1. Though we wanted to re-produce a photograph of the document, yet could not succeed

2. In Rājpūtānā putting a cipher at the end of the numerical item is considered inauspicious.

When Mahārājā Mānsingh of Jodhpur regained his power and assassinated the hostile leaders with the help of Amīrkhān the founder of the ruling dynasty of Ṭōnk — he sent an army to invade Bikaner and avenge the wrong done to him by its ruler in joining hands with Jaipur. This compelled the Mahārāja of Bikaner to sign the aforesaid bond.

The bond

कबुलायत १ महाराजाधिराज श्री सुरतसिघजी लिखदीवी तथा श्री जोधपुर दरबार री फौज़ खरच रा रुपीया च्यार लाख ने एक ४,००,००१ ठेहरीया तिणमें छुट रुपीया ४०,००० चालीस हजार बाकी रुपीया तीन लाख साठ हजार एक ३,६०,००१

मतु राठोड सुरतसिंघ उपर लिखियो सु सही
मतु रा दसकत आचारज पुरसोतम
स्हा ॥ अमरचंद रा छै

श्री हुकम सुं १८६५ रा मीती मीगसर वद ५ तिणरी किसतां वसुलायत री विगत १, ४५, ००० ओल में जणां ५ सुराणो रामचंद वगेरे रा आया सु एक लाख रो रुको दे- रासरी आचारज परसोतम, पैतालीस हजार स्हा ॥ अमरचंद दरबारी सवाईराम फागुणी १५ पुनम देणा रो

सा॥ ५०,००० कंपु तालके मेमदसा तालके री हुंडीयां सकराई, पंचोली जसकरण दरबारी ७२,००० सकराई

२,६७,०००

बाकी रुपीया ९३,००१ मधे आया रुपीया ८४,९४५॥-)॥ चोरासी हजार नव सौ पैतालीस साडा नव आना सु पोते दाखल

Translation.

This bond is written by Mahārājādhirāj Shrī Sūratsinghjī that an agreement has been reached to pay, to meet the expenses of his (expeditionary) forces, to the Jodhpur Darbār rupees four lacs and one (Rs. 4,00,001) out of which rupees forty thousand (Rs. 40,000) have been foregone and the balance remains rupees three lacs sixty thousand and one (Rs. 3,60,001).

Signed by Rāṭhōr Sūratsingh, whatever written above is correct.

Signed by Āchāraj (priest) Pursōtam

Signed by Shāh Amarchand

By order of the Darbār, dated 5th day of the dark half of Mangsir 1865 V. S. (8th November 1808 A. D.)

Later details.

The details regarding the payment of instalments are as follows :—

Out of 5 persons including Surānā Rāmchand etc. given as hostage for Rs. 1,45,000,—Dērāsarī Āchāraj Pursōtam has given a written promise for the payment of rupees one lac and Shāh Amarchand and Darbārī Savāīrām for rupees forty five thousand on the 15th day of the bright half of Phāgun.

The Hundīs (Cheques) for Rs. 50,000 regarding the camp, were encashed through Memadshāh and Hundīs (Cheques) for Rs. 72,000 were encashed by Panchōlī Jaskaran Darbārī. Total 2,67,000.

Out of the balance of rupees 93,001 received rupees Rs, 84,945-9-6 (rupees eighty four thousand nine hundred forty five, annas nine and pies six) which have been remitted to the treasury.[1]

1. No mention of the payment of remaining Rs. 8055-6-6 is available in the copy.

23. A letter[1] of Maharaja Ranjitsingh of the Punjab addressed to the Maharaja Mansingh of Marwar.

(Read at the Ranjitsingh centenary held at Cawnpore in June 1939 A.D and published in its proceedings pp 126-128)

This letter was written by Mahārājā Ranjīt Singh, the well-known Sikkh ruler of the Punjab to Mahārājā Mān Singh of Mārwār, who was famous for his religious trend and sagacity.

Though at the time, this letter was written the power of the glorious Mahārājā Ranjītsingh was ascending day to day, yet the English East India Company was gradually gaining ground. The company dethroned Pēshwā Bājīrāo II in 1818 A.D. and threatened the Rājā of Bharatpur, both of whom therefore sought help from the Mahārājā of the Punjab. But he, in his turn, before complying with their request, thought it proper to get the advice and help of Mahārājā of Mārwār whom he considered most eminent ruler of the time among the Princes of India.

The letter gives a number of historical facts and the condition of the then rulers of Hindustān. Brief footnotes have also been added, wherever required, to make the letter more comprehensive.

(श्रीनाथजी)

लाहोर का राजा रणजीतसिंहजी रो खरीतो आयो जिणमें समाचारः—
अप्रंच घणादिन हुवा राज मीजाज के खैर आफीयत व दील के इरादे के
समाचार लिखण सुं परसन किया नहीं सुं जाणवा में आयो कंवरजी का वाका
सुं राजके ताईं कदुरत है सु श्री जी जाणता मालुम है। इण वाका सुणाया सुं
इस्यो सोच फिकर हुवो सु लिखण में आवे नहीं सु श्री जी इच्छा उपर संतोष
कर उणारा फजल का उमेदवार रहसी सु श्री जी राजके दौलतखाना में

1. I came across the copy in Mārwārī of this letter, prepared by Kachardās, a courtier of Mahārājā Mānsingh, in the old records office of the Jodhpur State, and am thankful to Mr. P. P. Kōthāwālā for supplying me with a copy of it.

कंवर वेगो प्रकट करसी। अठारो अहवाल इणभांत है। मुलतान कसमीर को सूबो भखर मनकरा को फीतो वगैरे तो खालसाजी के नीचे आय गया है ने इण वरस खालसाजी को फौज रो इरादो काबुल रो सूबो लेण उपर हुवो थो ने फौज पेशावर नजदीक पहुंची जठे वजीर फतेखां रो भाई अजीमखां नवाव को छोटो भाई समंदखां खालसाजी की हजूर में आयो ने सोगात गुजरात अरज करी। नवाव अजीमखां सिरकार की नौकरी वंदगी में हाजिर रेहण में छे सु तीस हजार सवार वहादुर की महांसुं चाकरी लेवो अर वादस्या कामरा सुं म्हाके भाई फतेखां रा खून वावत दील की दुशमन पडी है ने स्युजाऊ मुलक स्याजमान म्हारा तदारुक वास्ते अगरेजां कने वैठा है जिण सूं म्हे तो म्हाकी सरणो खालसाजी ने सोंपीयो है ने सीर सुध नौकरी में हाजर छां सु काबुल म्हाने फौज खरच में माफ राखो जितरा में ही पेसवा को ने भरतपुर का राजा को वकील आयो ने कहयो कूच रा लाख लाख रुपीया देवां। सिरकार की फौज को कूच दिल्ली कानी करो। सु राज आछी तरे जाणो हो हिन्दुस्तान की अवतरीनी केवल उमरावांरी बे इत्तफ़ाकी सुं है--आपस में संप नहीं सो राज री जान सिवाय दूजो हिन्दुस्तान में धरम व जुवांन की कायमी वालो जाणीयो नहीं जिण सुं चोपदार छड़ो इण कागद समेत मेल्यो है। सु हिन्दुस्तान रा मुल्क रा जावता मुदे जो कुछ नेक सला राज जाणो सु लिखसी सूं उण मुजब करण में आवे। तेथां कोई मातवर समझवार अठे मेलावसी। आपस में कितराक समाचार लिखण में आवे नहीं वो सौगात भेजणी आवे नहीं सु यांही रहवै। चोपदार जुवानी अर्ज करे सु कवूल करसी।

(मालुम हुवो १८७६ रा मिगसर सुद १२
द॥ व्यास कचरदास)

(*Translation of the letter.*)

Though since long we have not been favoured with the news of your welfare and intentions, yet we had come to know that you were much grieved by the untimely demise of the heir apparent[1]. We too felt it so much that we can not express our feelings in writing.

We have to leave such things to the wishes of the Almighty and pray for His Mercy so that he may favour your illustrious house soon with another son.

---

1. Mahārāj Kumār Chhatarsingh died on 26th March 1818 A.D.

The news of our court is as under:—

Multān[1], the province of Kāshmīr[2], Bhakkar, the belt of Mānkērā[3], etc., have already come under Khālsājī (Sikkh-regime).

This year the Khālsā-army intended to annex the province of Kābul and accordingly reached near Pēshāwar. But Samad Khān, the younger brother of Nawāb Azīm[4] Khān, who is the brother of Fateh Khān[5], the Vazīr (minister), presented himself there at the court of Khālsājī and after offering valuable presents declared:—

"Nawāb Azīmkhān is prepared to serve the Khālsā court and you may demand the services of our thirty thousand brave cavalry."

"We have a blood feud with king Kāmrān[6] for the slaughter of our brother Fateh Khān, and Shujā-ul-mulk[7] and Shāh Zaman[8] are staying with the English[9] to get us punished."

"Under these circumstances, we have left ourselves under the protection of Khālsājī and are ready to die in its service. Therefore we hope that Kābūl be kindly left to us to maintain the said cavalry".

In the meantime, the envoys of the Pēshwā[10] and the Rājā of Bharatpur[11] arrived and stated that if the army of Khālsā is sent towards Delhi, they each will pay rupees one lac for it.

---

1. Multān was taken in 1818 A D.

2. This province was conquered in 1819 A.D.

3. Mānkērā, a town situated in the desert and surrounded by a cordon of a dozen fortresses, was captured in 1821 A D

4. Muhammad Azīm was first appointed the governor of Kāshmīr by his brother Fateh Khān and when the army of Mahārājā Ranjīt Singh reached near Pēshāwar he was holding Kābūl.

5. Fateh Khān, the King—Maker, was the son of Pāyandā Khān of Barakzaī tribe and minister of Mahmud Shāh, whom he helped in usurping the throne of Kābūl in 1800 A.D But in 1818 A D i.e (Fateh Khān) was made blind and slaughtered by Kāmrān Shāh, the son of Mahmūd Shāh.

6. He was the son of Mahmūd Shāh, ,the king of Kābūl

7. He was the brother of Zaman Shāh (Shāh Zamān) of Kābūl and was first appointed as governor of Pēshāwar by his brother He proclaimed his independence in 1800 A D, took Afghānistān in 1803 A.D, was defeated at Nimulā, near Gandumak, in 1809 A.D and afterwards was obliged to come to Hindustān in search of help.

8. He was the fifth son of Taimūr and ascended the throne of Afghānistān with the help of Pāyandā Khān He first bestowed the title of Rājā upon Ranjitsingh and gave the city of Lahore in 1799 A.D. Afterwards he was blinded at the instigation of Fatehkhān the son of Pāyandā Khān, and was obliged to live in Hindustān for many years

9. East India Company Officers.

10. Bājī Rāo II.

11. Randhīr Singh son of Ranjītsingh.

You yourself know well that the condition of Hindustān has worsened owing to the enmity among its rulers. There is no cordiality among them.

We do not know any one else in Hindustān except your noble-self, who can stand for his religion and words and for this sake we have sent this special messenger with the letter.

We hope you will give us best advice for the protection of Hindustān which will be followed upon.

Please send one of your trust-worthy and sagacious man here as there are some facts which can not be put on paper and the presents too can not be sent. Therefore the man should remain here.

Please also accept the verbal requests of the messenger.

Submitted on the 12th day of the bright half of Māngsir, Vikram Samvat 1879 (25th December 1822).

24 The First Ray of Social Reform in Rajputana

(Published in the Harbilas Sarda commemoration volume 1937 A.D., pp. 522-523.)

In the Nineteenth century of the Vikrama era, there prevailed some social customs among the people of Rājputānā, and specially Rājpūts which were ruinous. But as soon as the Maharattā peril was over and the country came in contact with the Britishers, a ray of reform gleamed in the hearts of the people. Marwar also took advantage of this change, and in October, 1839 A.D. some rules were framed by the combined efforts of Mahārājā Mānsingh, the British officers, the Jāgīrdārs and officials of the State.

In October, 1843 A.D. some important items of these rules, specially relating to Rājpūts, were inscribed on marble slabs and they were fixed at the district head-quarters of the State.

We give here the transcript and the translation of the rules found inscribed on such slabs, for the information of the readers of this volume, dedicated to a well-known social reformer of Rājpūtānā:

श्री जलंधरनाथजी सहाय छे।

संवत् १८९६ रा कार्तिक में श्री महाराजा साहब वा बड़ा साहब बहादुर वा साहब अजंट बहादुर सिरदार मुतसद्दी सारां ही रे रोबरू रजपूत बेटी रा व्याव में चारण भाट ढोली वगैरे ने देणा रो आइन में इण मुजब लिखीजियो है।

रजपूत बेटी मारे नहीं।

कलम ३६॥ चारण ने इण मुजब देसीः—

१—पटायत हजार री रेख लारे रुपीया पचीस।

२—भोमियो रुपीया दश।

३—घर रो धणी विना जमीवालो रुपीया पांच।

कलम ४६ १—भाटा ने रेख हजार लार रुपीया नव देसी। २—रुपीया पांच सांसण भाटां ने। ३—रुपीया चार पचाड़ीया तथा बालद लदे जिण वगैरे ने।

कलम ५६॥ ढोलीं राणां ने ब्याव में रेख हजार लार रुपीया पांच।

आ नजवीज सारां ही री सलाहसूं ठैरी है सो रजपूत कोई इण सिवाय देसी तथा बेटी मारसी तो राजरो तकसीरवार होसी ने चारण भाट ढोली इण सिवाय उजर करसी तो राजरा गुनैहगार होसी, इणमें तफावत पड़सी नहीं श्री हजूररो हुकम है संवत् १६०० कार्तिक बदि १३ शनी।

Translation.

The following rules regarding the payments to be made to Chārans, Bhāts (bards) and drummers etc., at the time of the marriages of the daughters of Rājpūts have been framed in the month of Kārtik, Vikram Samvat 1896 (October 1839 A.D.), in the presence of His Highness, the Agent to the Governor-General for Rājpūtānā, the Political Agent, Sardārs (nobles) and officials.

That the Rājpūts shall not kill their daughters.

Rule 36: The Jāgīrdār with an annual income of Rs. 1,000/- shall give Rs. 25/-, the Bhōmiyā (holding land in lieu of service) Rs. 10/- and ordinary Rājpūt (having no land) Rs. 5/- to Chārans.

Rule 49: The Jāgīrdār with an annual income of Rs. 1,000/- shall give Rs. 9/-, the Bhōmiyā Rs. 5/- and the ordinary Rājpūt Rs. 4/- to Bhāṭs, Pāvādiyās and Bāladiyās, etc.

Rule 56: The Jāgīrdār with an annual income of Rs. 1,000/- shall give Rs. 5/- to drummers.

These rules have been framed with the consent of all persons, therefore if a Rājpūt pays more than the above-noted amounts or kills his daughter, he will be liable to punishment by the State.

Further, if a Chāran, Bhāṭ or drummer demands more he will also be liable to punishment.

It, being the command of His Highness, shall not be disobeyed.

Dated Saturday, the 13th day of the dark-half of Kārtik, V. S. 1900 (21st October 1843).

APPENDIX C.

1. Ropi Plates of Paramara Devaraja; Vikrama-Samvat 1059.

(Published in the Epigraphia Indica Vol. XXII, (pp. 196-198), (January 1934 A.D.)

This grant of Dēvarāja is in the possession of Audīchya Brāhmanas of Ropsi or Ropi, a village 6 miles south-west of Bhīnmāl in the Jaswantpura District of Mārwār. While touring in that District in 1920, I came across the grant and got it photographed for the Sardar Museum, Jodhpur. It has already been noticed by Prof. D. R. Bhandarkar.[1]

The grant contains two copper-plates inscribed on one side only. The plates, as far as I remember, measure about 9″×8″ and have two holes through which are passed two plain rings. The first plate contains 11 and the second 12 lines of writing.

The characters of the grant are Nāgarī, similar to those used in northern India in the tenth or eleventh century A.D. The language is Sanskrit and the clerical errors are remarkably few. The text is in prose throughout with the exception of one verse in ll. 21-23. At the end is found the signature of the donor. The orthography presents no special features.

The object of the plates is to record the grant of a field situated to the south of the city-wall *(kotta)* of Srīmāla, the modern Bhīnmāl by the *Mahārājādhirāja*, the illustrious Dēvarāja residing at Srīmāla, to one Āurakāchārya, the son of Chaṇḍasivāchārya and the head of the temple of Siddhēshvara Mahādēva at Kshamēmāthuna (Kshatmamāthuka?) on the occasion of a lunar eclipse. The boundaries of the land

1. *See* his *List of Inscriptions of Northern India*, No 103, where he reads the year as Samvat 1060.

granted were as follows: to the east the land of the Brāhmaṇa Gōvinda, to the south the land of Vāmana, the son of Durlabha, to the west the village belonging to the *Mahasamanta* Pūrnachanda and to the north the land of the Brāhmana Shrīdhara. The date of the record is the 15th day of the bright half of Māgha (Vikrama) Samvat 1059 (=1002 A.D.).[1]

The witnesses were Matvāka, the preceptor of Dēvarāja and Pūrṇachaṇḍa. The grant was written by Sūryaravi, the son of Nyāsa.

Though no mention of the clan of donor Dēvarāja is found in the grant, yet on the basis of the year and the place given in it, we may assume that he was a Paramāra[2] ruler of Ābū whose second name was Mahīpāla and who succeeded his father Dharanīvarāha, a ruler famous in the chronicle of Rājasthān. We give here a *chhoppaya* often recited by the bards in honour of Dharanīvarāha:

मंडोवर सामंत हुवो अजमेर सिद्धसुव ।
गढ पूंगल गजमल्ल हुवो लोद्रवै भांण भुव ॥
अल्हपल्ह अरबद्द भोजराजा जालंधर ।
जोगराज धरधाट हुवौ हंसू पारक्कर ॥
नवकोटि किराड्ड संजुगत थिर पंवारहर थप्पिया ।
धरणीवराह धर भाइयां कोट बांट जू जू किया ॥

According to this, Dharnīvarāha distributed the nine provinces of Mandōr, Ajmēr, Pūngal, Lōdravā, Ābū, Jālōr, Dhāt, Pārkar and Kirādū among his nine brothers. It is also said that owing to these nine chiefships, Mārwār has come to be known as "Navakōti Mārwār." But there is very little truth in the above *chhappaya*[3].

Dēvarāja's (Mahīpāla's) son and successor was Dhandhuka who was obliged to accept the allegiance of Sōlankī (Chālukya) Kumārapāla I, the ruler of Gujrāt.

1 (The date is irregular The full moon of Māgha fell on Thursday the 21st January when there was no lunar eclipse The nearest lunar eclipse occurred on the full moon of Phālguna corresponding to Friday the 19th February It is also not verifiable for Samvat 1059 current or Samvat 1069 —Ed.)

2. For the history of Paramāra rulers please refer to my *Bharata ke Prachina Rajavmsha*, Vol. I, and *Raja Bhoja* (both in Hindi).

3. *See* also *Ind. Ant.*, Vol. XL, pp. 238 f.

TEXT.

First Plate.

1 सिद्धम्[1] [॥*] ॐ नमः शिवाय ॥ संवत् १[०]५६ मा
2 घ शु (सु) दि १५ अस्यां संवत्सरमासपक्षदि-
3 वसपूर्व्वायां श्री२[2]मालावस्थितमहाराजा-
4 धिराजश्रीदेवराजः स्वभुज्यमानविषये
5 धर्म्मदायेन क्षेत्रशासन(नं) प्रयच्छति ॥ यदिहै-
6 व श्री२[2]मालीयकोट्टाद्दक्षिणदिग्भागे क्षेत्रं
7 यस्याघाटनानि ॥ पूर्व्वतो गोविन्दब्रा(ब्रा)ह्मण-
8 सत्का भूसीमा । दक्षिणतो वामनदुर्लभसु-
9 तसत्का भूसीमा । पश्चिमतो महासामन्तश्री-
10 पूर्णचण्डसत्क [ग्रा]मेण सह भूसीमा ।
11 उत्तरतः श्रीधरब्रा(ब्रा)ह्मणक्षे[त्रे*]ण भूसीमा [।*]

Second Plate.

12 एवमेतच्चतुराघ(घा) टनाभ्यंतरक्षेत्रं ।[3]
13 अस्माभिः सोमग्रहणे स्नात्वा त्रिलोकी गुरुं शंकर-
14 मभ्यर्च्य मातापित्रोरात्मनश्च पुण्ययशोभिवृद्धय(ये)
15 शासनेतो(नो)दकपूर्व्वमाचंद्रार्क्ककालीनतया प्रति-
16 पादितं [।*]! [आ]उरकाचार्याय ।[4] चण्डशिवाचार्यपुत्रा-
17 य .. ..[5] श्रीसिद्धेश्वरदेवस्याराधीशाय
18 प्रदत्तं न केनापि परिपंथनीयं ॥ अस्मद्वंशजैरन्यै-
19 श्च भाविभोक्तृभिः । अत्र साक्षी श्रीदेवराजगुरुर्म्मत्वा-
20 कः । अत्र साक्षी श्रीपूर्णचण्डः । लिखितं सूर्यरवि-
21 णा न्याससुतेन । यो यः पृथिव्यां राजा हि ममा
22 तोर्द्ध[6] भविष्यति । तस्याहं करलग्नस्तु शासनं सा(मा)
23 व्यतिक्र(क्रा)मे (मे)त् । स्वहस्त[:*] श्रीदेवराजस्य ।

---

1. Expressed by a symbol.
2. The figure 2 is used to denote the repetition of *shri*.
3. *Danda* unnecessary
4. *Danda* unnecessary.
5. The reading seems to be *Kshamemathune* but its meaning is not clear. (To me the reading appears to be *Kshatmamathuke* and may mean 'at Kshatmamāthuka' where the temple of the Mahādēva Siddhēśvara seems to have been situated.—Ed)
6. Read *mad-urdhvam cha* or *mama gotre*.

2. Jalor inscription of the time of Paramara Visala, dated V. S. 1174.

(Published in the Indian Antiquary, Vol. LXII, (p. 41)(March 1933 A. D.)

This inscription was fixed in the inner side of the northern wall of the building called "Tōpkhānā" at Jalor (Mārwāṛ). It was first noticed by Professor D. R. Bhandarkar in *PRASI. W. C.*, 1908-9, p. 54, and summarised by him in No. 194 of his *List of Inscr. N. I.* During my recent visit to the place I found it fixed in the wall upside down and brought it to the Sardar Museum, Jodhpur, for preservation.

The inscription is engraved on a bulky white stone slab, which measures 2′ 3½″×1′ 10″. But on reading the contents it was found that when this stone was removed from its original place to be fixed in the Tōpkhānā (sometimes used as a mosque) it was damaged a bit on one side. This is inferred from the fact that the last two letters of the 4th and the 5th lines are missing.

The inscription contains 13 lines. The language is Sanskrit, and the characters belong to the northern type of the twelfth century of the Vikrama era. As regards orthography, the consonant following *r* is doubled, except in one case.

The date given in this inscription is Samvat 1174, Āsāḍha Sudi 5 Bhaumē, corresponding to Tuesday the 25th June 1118 A. D. The Samvat given in it is Shrāvaṇādi and not Chaitrādi.

The importance of this inscription lies in the fact that this is the only inscription hitherto found which gives the genealogy of the branch of the Paramāras who ruled over Jalor. Vākpatirāja, the first Paramāra ruler mentioned in this inscription, is quite different from Vākpatirāja, the Paramāra ruler of Mālwā. for the latter had no male issue and therefore adopted his nephew Bhojā, while the one mentioned in this inscription had a son named Chandana.

As the inscription is dated V. S. 1174, the time of this Vakpatirāja would be about V. S. 1150. It is therefore probable that the founder of the Paramāra branch of Jalor might have had some connection with Dharaṇī Varāha, the Paramāra ruler of Ābu.

Text.

1. ॐ जेतुं विश्वामित्रं वशिष्ठमुनिनातिकोपपूर्णेन
2. परमारणाय जनित [:] कुंडे तेनैव परमार [:]
3. आसीद्वाक्पतिराजनामनृपति : श्रीपारमारा [न्वये]
4. तत्पुत्रोजनि चन्दना (नो) वनिपतिः तन्नंदनो देव [राट्]
5. तत्पुत्रस्त्वपराजित [:] समभवत्प्रौढप्रताप [: स्वयं]
6. पुत्रोभूदपराजितस्य विजयी श्रीविज्जलो भूपतिः
7. सेनानीरिवशंभो प्रद्युम्न इवाथवा हरे [र्न्नूनं?]
8. दत्ते (त्तो) वाम्बुजसूतेर्धारावर्षो नराधिपतिः ॥
9. धारावर्षस्य पुत्रोयं जातो वीसलभूपतिः
10. येन भूमंडलीकानां धर्ममार्गोत्र दर्शितः ॥
11. राज्ञी मेलरदेव्या (वी) तु पत्नी वीसलभूपतेः ॥
12. सौवर्णं कलसं मूर्द्धनि सिंधुराजेश्वरेत्र (कृ) तं ॥
13. [सं] वत् ११७४ आषाढ सुदि ५ भौमे ॥

Translation.

Ls. 1-2. The enraged Vashishtha created the Paramāra from (his) fire altar to conquer Vishvāmitra and to kill his enemies.

Ls. 3-6. There was a king named Vākpatirāja in the dynasty of Paramāra. His son was Chandana, who got a son named Dēvarāja. Dēvarāja had a son named Aparājita, whose son was Vijjala.

Ls. 7-8. His son, like Kārtikēya to Shiva, Pradyumna to Kṛṣṇa and Daksha Prajāpati to Brahmā was Dhārāvarsha.

Ls. 9-10. Dhārāvarsha's son was Vīsala, who enlightened all the petty chiefs with religious knowledge.

Ls. 11-12. Mēlaradēvī, the queen of this king Vīsala got this golden *kalasa* put here on the steeple of the temple of Sindhu Rājēshvara[1].

L. 13. Saṁvat 1174 Āshāḍha Sudi 5 Tuesday.

---

1. This temple was probably built by Sindhurāja, the founder of the Paramâra dynasty of Âbu, as is evident from the inscription dated 1218 V.S. found at Kirâdu.—

' सिंधुराजो महाराज: समभून्मरुमण्डले '

This temple is not in existence now.

3. Kiradu inscription of the time of Chaulukya Kumarapala and his Feudatory Paramara Someshvara dated V.S. 1218.

[Published in the Indian Antiquary, Vol LXI (pp. 135-136), (July 1932 A. D.)]

This inscription is engraved on a pillar at the entrance of a dilapidated temple of Shiva at Kirādu, a ruined town situated about 16 miles north-west of Bādmēr (in Jodhpur State). It was transcribed by Mr. Puran Chand Nahar in his *Jaina Inscr.*, Pt. I, p. 251 f. A summary of the inscription has also been published by Dr. D. R. Bhandarkar in his List of the Inscriptions of Northern India, No. 312.

The epigraph measures 17″×17″ and contains 26 lines. As the middle portion of the stone from the third line to the twentieth has peeled off, some names, etc. are destroyed. The language is Sanskrit, and the whole of the record except a portion of the last line is in verse. As regards orthography, it is worth noting that, in some places, the consonant following 'r' is doubled, व is used for ब and र्श for श. The importance of the inscription lies in the fact that this is the only record which contains the genealogy of the Paramāra branch of Kirādu and the name of the Paramāra king Sindhurāja of Mārwār, the father of Utpalarāja, the first known Paramāra king of Ābu.

It is dated Samvat 1218 Āshvina Sudi I, Gurau= Thursday, the 21st September 1161 A. D.

The purport of the inscription is as follows:—

In the dynasty of the Paramāras, who sprang from the fire altar of Vashishṭha at Ābu, there was born a king named

Sindhurāja, who ruled over Marumaṇḍala (Mārwāṛ). His son was Ūsala (Utpala[1]). The names of Utpala's son and grandson have peeled off. Then is mentioned Dharaṇīdhara (Dharaṇīvarāha),[2] and his son was Dēvarāja[3], who perhaps built a temple of Dēvarājēshvara. Then is mentioned Dhandhuka[4] who ruled over Maru maṇḍala (Mārwāṛ) through the favour of Durlabharāja (1066-1078 V. S.) (the Chaulukya king). Krishṇarāja[5] (II) was the son of Dhandhuka, and his son was Sochharāja,[6] whose son Udayarāja, being a feudatory of (Chaulukya) Jayasimha (1150-1199 V. S.), conquered Chōḍa, Gauḍa, Karaṇāta, and Mālava. Sōmēshvara (name peeled off here, but appears in line 23), the son of Udayarāja, regained his lost kingdom of Sindhurājapur[7] through the favour of (Chaulukya) Jayasimha Siddharāja (perhaps in 1198 V.S.), became firmly established in 1205 V. S. in the reign of (Chaulukya) Kumārapāla, and protected for a long time his Kirāṭakupa (Kiradu) along with Shivakupa. He also exacted 1700 horses (including 1 five-nailed and 8 peacock-breasted horses) and took two forts, one of Tanukōtta[8] and the other of Navasara[9] from prince Jajjaka on Tuesday, the first day of the bright half of Ashvina 1218 V. S. at 4½ hours after sunrise. But on his (Jajjaka's) acknowledging his allegiance to the Chaulukya king (Kumārapāla), he (Sōmēshvara) reinstated him in the possession of those places.

By the order of the king this *prashasti* was composed by Narasiṁha, was written by Yashodēva and was engraved by Jasōdhara.

---

1. This is the first name of the Paramāra branch of Ābu found in the inscription of Vasantgarh, dated V. S. 1099 (*Ep. Ind.*, vol. IX, p. 10 ff.).

2. *Supra* vol. XL, p. 289: When Sōlankī (Chaulukya) Mūlarāja (998-1052 V. S) attacked him he was obliged to seek the help of the Rāshṭrakūṭa Dhavala of Hastikundi (Hathūṇḍī) in Mārwāṛ (*Epigraphia India*, vol. X, p. 21).

3. He was also named Mahīpāla A copper grant of his, dated V S. 1059 (A. D. 1002), has been found. (See pp 205-207.)

4. He refused allegiance to Chāulukya Bhīmadēva I (1078-1120 V. S.) and was driven away from Ābu, but afterwards Vimala, the new 'Daṇḍapati,' of Ābu settled the dispute and brought him back from Chitor, where he (Dhandhuka) lived for some days with king Bhōja of Mālwā.

5. He was the younger brother of Pūrnapāla (Bhandarkar's *List of Inscriptions of Northern India*, Nos. 135 and 139.)

6. He was the founder of the Paramāra branch of Kirādu.

7. This might have been founded by Sindhurāja himself or by his descendants after the name of founder of the Paramāra branch of Mārwāṛ and Ābu.

8. Tanaut in the Jaisalmer State.

9. Nausar in the Jodhpur State.

The inscription ends with the date: Vikrama-Saṁvat 1218 Ashvina sudi 1 Gurau.

Text.

१. [ॐ नमः] सर्व्वज्ञाय ॥ नमोनंताय सूक्ष्माय ज्ञानगम्याय वेधसे ॥ विश्वरूपाय शुद्धाय देवदेवाय शंभवे ॥ [१]

२. देवस्य तस्य चरितानि जयंति शंभोः सस्व (श्व) त्कपालवि [शुभ] स्म विभूषणस्य। गर्व्वः सकोपि हृदि यस्य प-

३. दं करोति गौरीनितंव (ब) चिरवल्कल—प्रदर्शात् ॥ २ [वशिष्ट]— — — — — [भूपिते] र्व्बु (र्बु) दभूधरे । सुरभ्या :

४. परमाराणां वंशोस्त्यनजकुंडतः : ॥ ३ तत्रानेकम [हीपाल]— — — — — — — — —। [सिं] धुराजो महाराज :

५. समभून्मरुमंडले ॥ ४ निरर्ग्गल मिलद्वैरि — — — — — — — — — —। — — — — — — — —प्रतापोज्वलदूस —

६. लः ॥ ५ शंभुवद्भूरिभूमीशाभ्यर्च्चनीयो [भ]— — —। — — — — — — — — — — — — — — — — — सूः ॥ ६ रणे

७. खड्गरण[त्का]र रावणोल्वणवै [भव :]। — — — — — — — — — — — — — — — — — [॥ ७] सिंधुराजधरा —

८. धारधरणीधरधामवान् । [मा] — — — — — — — — — — — — — [॥ ८] [देवरा] जोभवत्तस्मात्

९. सुरराजो हराज्ञया । देवराजेश्वर — — — — — — — — — — — — — [॥ ९] — — — — — — — — — [म] पहाय महीमि —

१०. मां । मन्ये कल्पद्रुमः प्रायाद्दृश्य [क] — — — — — — — — — — — — — [॥ १०] — — — — — — — — — — — — — — — — — — दारणात् । श्रीम —

११. दुर्ल्लभराजोपि राजेंद्रो रंजितो — — [॥ ११] — — — — — — — — — — — — — — — — तै : । येन दुर्व्वार —

१२. वीर्येण भूपितं मरुमंडलं ॥ १२ ध [र्म्माकरो व (ब) भू]— — — — — — — — — —। — — — — — [कृष्ण] राजो महा —

१३. शब्दविभूषितः ॥ १३ तत्पुत्रः सोछराजाख्य : — — — — — — — — —। — — — — — — — — — — — [कल्प —]

१४. द्रुमो भवत् ॥ १४ तस्मादुदयराजाख्यो महाराज — — — —। — — — — — — — — — — [ऽ मी] कपदाधि —

१५. क : ॥ १५ श्राचो(चौ)डगौडकर्णाटमालवोत्तरपश्चिमं । — — — — — — — — — — — — — — राजं ॥ १६

१६. प्रा (श्री) सिंधुराजभूपालात्पितृ(ता)पुत्रक्रमात्पुन : तस्मादुदयरा — — — — — — — — — ॥ १७ उत्कीर्णा —

१७. मपि योराज्यमुद्दध्रे भुजवीर्यतः। जयसिंहमहीपाला — — — — — — — —[॥ १८]
— — — — — ष्पम (?) — — वर्षे

१८. विक्रमभूपतेः। प्रसादाज्जयसिंहस्य सिद्धराजस्य भूभुजः [॥ १९ — — — — . . —
जेन सिंधुराजपुरो —

१९. द्ध्वं । भूयो निर्व्याज सौ (शौ) र्येण राज्यमेतत्समुद्धृतं ॥ २० पुनर्द्वा [दशसंख्येषु पं]
चाधिकशतेष्ट (ष्व) लं। कु —

२०. मारपालभूपालात् सप्रतिष्ठमिदं कृतं ॥ २१ [कि] रा [ट] कूपमात्मीयं — — — —
— समन्वितं। निजेन त्त (त्ता) त्र —

२१. धर्म्मेण पालयामास यश्चिरं ॥ २२ अष्टाद [शाधिके] चास्मिन् शतद्वादशकेऽश्विने।
प्रतिपद्गुरुसंयो —

२२. गे सार्द्ध [या] मे गते दि [ना] त् ॥ २३ दंडं सप्तदशशतान्यश्वानां नृपजज्जकात्। सह
पंचनखा —

२३. श्वेन मयूरादिभिरष्टभिः ॥ २४ तणुकोट्टं नवसरो दुर्गौ सोमेश्वरोग्रहीत्। उच्चां [ग]
वर [हा] —

२४. साढ्यांत्रके चैवात्मसादा (द) सौ ॥ २५ व (ब) हुशः [सेव] कीकृत्य चौलुक्य-
जगतीपतेः। पुनः संस्थापया —

२५. मास तेषु देशेषु जज्जकं ॥ २६ प्रशस्तिमकरोदेतां नरसिंहो नृपाज्ञया। लेखकोत्र य [शो]—

२६. देवः सूत्रधारोस्तु (०) जसोधरः ॥ २७ विक्रम [संव] त् १२१८ अ (आ) श्विन
शुदि १ गुरौ ॥ मगलं म [हाश्री]: ॥

4 Kiradu inscription of the time of Chaulukya Bhimadeva II and his feudatory Chauhana Madanabrahmadeva, dated V.S. 1235.

(Published in the Indian Antiquary, Vol LXII (p 42). (March 1933 A.D.)

This inscription is engraved on a pillar at the entrance of a Shiva temple at Kirādu, a ruined village near Hātmā about 16 miles north-west of Bādmēr in the Mallānī district (Mārwār). It was first noticed by Prof. D. R. Bhandarkar in *PRASI W. C.*, 1906-07, page 42, and is summarised in No. 381 of his *List of Inscriptions of Northern India.*

It contains 16 lines and covers a space of 17½"×9½". The language is Sanskrit. Except three couplets, one in the beginning and two at the end, the whole is in prose. The middle portion, from the 5th to the 14th line, as also the 16th line, has peeled off. As regards orthography it is to be noted that at some places the consonant following *r* is doubled, at one place *s* is used for *sh* and at others *sh* for *s*.

The record, after paying reverence to Shiva in prose and poetry, gives the date as V. S. 1235, Kārtika Sudi 13 Gurau (Thursday the 26th October 1178 A.D.) when in the reign of Bhīmadēva (II) (V.S. 1235-1298) his feudatory Shākambarī (Chauhāna) *Maharajaputra* Madanabrahmadēva was ruling at Kirātakūpa (Kirādu), and Tējapāla was carrying on the administration. It also tells us that the latter's (Tējapāla's) wife, seeing the old image of the temple broken by Turushkas, installed a new image on the aforesaid date ; and, making a request to the ruler (Madanabrahmadēva), provided two gifts for the gods.

TEXT.

१. ॐ ॐ नमः शिवायः (य) सधूर्जटि [र्जयत्यद्य] जयिनां (?) विजया इव[1] यस्यैकपलित-भ्रांतिं क—

२. रोत्यद्यापि या (जा) ह्नवी । संवत् १२३५ कार्तिक [शुदि] १३ गुरावद्येह श्रीमदणहिलपाटकाधिष्ठितमहाराजाधिराज-

३. परमेश्वर परमभट्टारक रिपुवंशाप्ररोह [रामावतार ?] श्रीमद्भीमदेवकल्याणविजयराज्ये तत्प्रभुप्रसादावास श्री-

४. किराटकूपे रविरिवसप्रतापः हिम [कर [रुचिर] कराभिरामः मेरुरिव] सुवर्णश्रिया-मनोरमो अनेक समरसंघ—

५. ट्टवैरिकरिघटापीठदारुणकरवाल [शा] कंभरीभूपा [ल] — — — — — [महा] राज-पुत्रश्रीमदनब्रह्मदेवराज्ये तस्य स —

६. दाज्ञाभिधायी लब्धमहापंचशब्दादिसर्व्वालंकारो — — — — — — — — [सर्व्वा] धिकार सकलव्यापारचिंतांत (भ) र स (श) कट-

७. धुराधौरेयकल्पमहं० श्रीतेजपाल [देव] सुपत्नीव [मानस ?] — — — — — — — [श्री] राजहंसीमिव ललितपदमार्गा सुरसुंद —

८. रीमिवसत (सतत) मनिमेषावलोक [न] — — — — — — — धल देवा (?) — — — — — — — — जललवतरलतरं जीवितव्यं चाकलय्य ऐ —

९. हिकाऽमुष्मिक [फ] लं चांगीक्व [त्य] — र देवभवा[2] मूर्तिरासीत् सातुष्कै (ष्कै) र्भग्ना

१०. तां च निरीक्ष्य तस्मिन्न्य (न्न) पि — सकलसुरासुरमुकुटमणिकिरि (र) ण —

११. संघट्टघर्षितपादपद्मयु [गलं] — कारयित्वाऽस्मिन् दिने प्रतिष्ठिता ॥

१२. तया च चतुर्द (श) महानदी — [वि] चिंत्य स्व राजानं प्रशा (सा) दं याचयित्वा

१३. श्रीकिराटकूपीय शु — दिनं दत्त [मिदं] विंशोपकद्वयं ॥

१४. तथा दीपार्थ च दत्त (त्तं) तैल — — — — — — — — — — — — — — — — — — — न्यैरपिभूपालैश्चाचंद्रार्क

१५. यावत् पालनीयं ॥ बहुभिर्व्वसुधा भुक्ता राजभिः सगरादिभिः । [यस्ययस्य यदा] भूमी तस्य तस्य तदाफलं ॥ १

१६. स्वदत्तां परदत्तां वा — [फ] ल [म्] ॥२ मंगलं महाश्रीः ॥

---

1. The orignal seems to have °र्जजटाजूटो जयताद्व विजयाइ (य) वः[।]—D. R. B.

2. Perhaps °देवतना (belonging to the god) has to be read.

5. The Sambhar inscription of Chaulukya Jayasimha's time.

[Published in the Indian Antiquary, Vol LVIII (pp. 234-236), (December 1929 A.D.)]

This inscription was fixed in a well known as Umar Shāh-kā-kūān at Sāmbhar, and was first examined by me in 1925.

Afterwards I requested the Jodhpur State authorities to have the inscription removed from the well and sent to the Sardar Museum for completion of its reading, and for its preservation. It was accordingly taken out of the well and sent to the Museum in 1926.

The inscription is engraved on two black stone slabs, which were fixed with lime, one below the other horizontally. The surface of each slab measures 16"×14¾", which is nearly all covered with writing. The inscription contains 28 lines, of which 14 are written on the one and the rest on the other slab, which are more weathered and damaged. The first two lines are in somewhat bigger characters than the rest. The engraving on both the slabs is filled with *chunam*. The language of the inscription is Sanskrit, and the characters are of the Northern type of the twelfth century of the Vikrama era.

As regards orthography, the letter ब at one place stands for व, and the dental स for the palatal श.

Through the date of the inscription is not traceable, yet the following words in lines 13 and 14 show that it was written in the reign of Jayasimha after the birth of his sons Mahipala

Kīrtipāla and Kumārapāla, *i.e.*, towards the end of the third quarter of the twelfth century of the Vikrama era.

जय (जै) सिंह [दे]
नरमौलिभाः जाता......गुणैर्युता

The special historical importance of the inscription lies in the date given in it for the establishment of the Anhilwāḍā kingdom by the Solankī Mūlarāja. The year assigned, hitherto, for the latter event by V. A. Smith was 961 A.D. (V.S. 1018); while Mahāmahopādhyāya G. H. Ojhā has suggested V.S. 1017 to 1052. But this inscription carries Mūlarāja back to Samvat 998, or A.D. 941 as would appear from the following verse :—

वसुनन्दनिधौवर्षे व्यतीते विक्रमार्कतः
मूलदेव नरेशस्तु [चूडाम] णिरभूद्भुवि ॥ ६ ॥

which means that after the expiry of 998 years from Vikrama Mūladēva came as the crest of the earth.

The Gujrāt chronicles also assign the same date to Mūlarāja, and they further tell us that he was the son of Rājī, as is also evident from Mūlarāja's copper-plate grant of V.S. 1043 (A.D. 987).

According to V. A. Smith, Rājī was probably one of the many designations of king Mahīpāla, who reigned from about A.D. 910 to about 940. Smith also adds that presumably Mūlarāja was his viceroy and, finding an opportunity, became independent.

It is stated in the *Prabandha-chintamani* and in the *Kumarapala-prabandha* that the marriage of Rāja, son of Munjāldēva, king of Kalyān Katak of Kanauj, was performed with the sister of the Chaora king Bhūyadadēva, and that Mūlarāja was the issue of this connection. It is also stated that Mūlarāja, on attaining maturity, killed his maternal uncle and usurped his kingdom: but no mention is found of the Solankīs having ever ruled over Kanauj. No doubt they held sway over Kalyāṇi in the Deccan and they had been feudatories also of the Pratihāra kings of Kanauj.

As regards Mūlarāja's death, V. A. Smith says that he was killed by the Chauhān Vigraharāja II, but in the *Prithvirajavijaya-mahakavya* it is stated that Mūlarāja was only defeated and driven towards Kanth-kōt (in Kachh) by Vigraharāja. This fact is also borne out by Mērutunga's *Prabandha-chintamani*, which further informs us that when the king of Sapādalaksha attacked Mūlarāja, Bārap, the general of king Tailapa, also attacked him simultaneously, and that Bārap was killed in the action. There is mention of Bārap in *Kirti-kaumudi* also. In the *Sukrit-sankirtan* Bārap is stated to be a general of the king of Kanauj, but this does not seem to be correct.

In the *Dvyashraya-kavya* king Dvārapa of Lāta is stated to have been killed by Chāmunda Rāja, son of Mūlarāja.

The mention of Mūlarāja's name in the inscription of Rāshtrakūta Dhaval of V. S. 1053 (A.D. 997) as a contemporary also goes to show that he was reigning in that year. The Gujrāt chronicles also mention that his death occurred in V. S. 1053.

Only three copper grants of Mūlarāja have been found as follows :—

1. of V. S. 1030 Bhādrapada *sudi* 5 (Monday the 24th August 974 A.D.) found at Pātan (Baroda State).
2. of V. S. 1043 Māgh *badi* 15 (Sunday the 2nd January 987 A.D.) found at Kadi (Baroda State).
3. of V. S. 1051 Māgh *sudi* 15 (19th January 995 A.D.) found at Baroda.

The second of these plates speaks of a grant made on the occasion of a solar eclipse. But according to Kielhorn this eclipse had not been visible in India. Kielhorn further adds that if the month mentioned in the plate is *amant* then there was no eclipse at all, but that if the month is *purnimant* then there had been a total eclipse, but it was not visible in India.

In this plate the king's *vamsha* is mentioned as Chaulukik, and his and his father's titles as Mahārājādhirāja. It also adds that Mūlarāja conquered the Sārasvat *mandala* by the force of his own arm.

TEXT.

१—[॥ओं॥*] श्रीगणेशाय नमः ॥ श्रुतांबुधौ पोत इव प्रसिद्धा (।) [सदैव] ब्र (ब्र) ह्मादिभिरीडिता

२ पुरा । सानंददा जाड्यहरा तु भूतले । रक्षां [सदा] मे विदधातु भारती ॥ १ ॥ ब्रह्म-

३ स्वभूशंकरपर्शुपाणयः (।) क्रियासुरेते भुवि स्वोवसीयसं । केशेंदि [रागर्वगजा] भियुक्ता [:*] सनातनं वो विबुधाः क्ष (दि) ती—

४ शाः ॥ २ ॥ सिद्धयोष्टौ च सिद्धयंति यस्य स्मरणमात्रतः । सर्वकार्याणि विघ्नेशो (श ?) पनादव ? नुमः सदा ॥ ३ ॥ सर्व्वसंप—

५ [त्क] रो लोके सर्व्वविघ्नप्रणास (श) कः । युष्माकं त्रिदशेशस्तु रविर्यच्छतुमंगलं ॥ ४ ॥ चौलक्यनामा जगति प्र—

६ सिद्धो बभूव वंशोनररत्नयुक्तः । विपक्षमातंगहरिस्तु सूर्यो दारिद्र (द्र्य) ध्वांत (ते) विमलः प्रभाकृत् ॥ ५ ॥ यथा देवेषु

७ देवेशो ग्रहेषु रोहिणीपतिः । सर्व्वाचलेषु मेरुश्च । यथा लोकेषु भूधरः ॥ ६ ॥ तथा चान्येषु वंशेषु पुर्णाशो (शु) रि—

८ व मेदिनी ? । चौलक्यपतिवंशस्तु जातः को (टीर) वद्भूवि ॥ ७ युग्मम् ॥ तस्मिन् कुले मूलनृपो बभूव । वयोनि—

९ [पात]स्तु इति प्रसिद्धः । धर्म्मार्थिकामाक्षरसाधकस्तु (कानि)। चैत्यादिकार्याणि कृतानि येन ॥८॥ वसुनंदनिधौ वर्षे । व्यती—

१० ते विक्रमार्कतः । मूलदेवनरेशस्तु [चूडाम] णिरभूद्भुवि ॥ ९ ॥ सूनुश्चामुंडराजःसमजनि मतिमान् [सर्वसिद्धा]—

११ र्थमल्लः । जातस्तल्लभाख्यः (ख्यो) विपुलगुण [गणै] र्दुर्लभाख्यःक्ष (क्षि) तीशः । तत्सूनुर्भीमदे [वोतिबलत्रल] ◡ — — ◡ —

१२ द्भूतले भू [व । श्रा] सीत (त्त) त्पुत्ररम्यः [स] कलक्ष (क्षि) तिधरो (रः) कर्णदेवो [नरेंद्रः] ॥ १० ॥ जात ◡ — — ◡ ◡ — ◡ — — । — —

१३ जनाधार इति प्रसिद्धः । जय (जे) सिंह [दे] — ◡ ◡ — ◡ सिंहो । — — ◡ नाना ◡ ◡ — ◡ [मौलिः] ॥ — — — — ◡

१४ — — भ । — — — नेरमौलिभाः । जाता — — ◡ — — — । — — — — गुणर्युताः ॥

१५ — — चौलक्यनामनि । प्रसन्नः सुकृतीलोको (कः) कूपादेः कृत्यकार [कः] । — — — — [वो] भवत्तत्र भक्त ◡ । कुम—

१६ — — नरा गु [णैः*] । [वि] ष्णा [वे] ◡ रतोनित्यं । दानीसत्पात्रपोपकः ॥ १४ — — — — ◡ यः शूरा

१७ — — ⌣ — — [आ] तो । वालाग्वघ्नाकुरस्तथा ॥ १ ॥ [५*] — — — — ⌣ — — — — — दंता वि —

१८ — — — — — वकुलमंडनः ॥ १६ ॥ वप्रद्वयीस — — — — — — — — — — — — — — गृहै

१९ — — — — — [पि] यैश्च । शाकंभरीमात्यम — — — — — — — — — — — — — — मस्तु

२० — — — — — — — — द नरेश्वरः ॥ तस्यश्रीन — — — — — — — — — — — — — — स्तनया

२१ — — — — — — — — गरश्चैव हेमाख्यो हरये — — — — — — — — समुद्भवा

२२ — — — — — नाम [मि] का डूंगर [सी] — — — — — — — — — — — — त्र

२३ — — — — — नगराजपु [त्र] — — — — — — — — — — — — — — व

२४ — — — — — — का । जिणर — — — — — — — — — — — — —

२५ — — — — — — — चंद्रेच । — — — — — — — — — — — — —

२६ —

२७ — — — — — [द] राज्य — — — — — पुत्र । च उ — — — — — — — —

२८ — — — — — — — कु [डूं] — — — [व] नमालीनाथ [सू] — — — — —

Abstract of the Contents

This inscription opens with an invocation addressed to the goddess Sarasvatī and then to some other gods (down to verse 4). After that the poet in three verses praises the powerful Chālukya dynasty. From the 8th verse it goes to show that after the expiry of 998 years from Vikrama, Rājā Mūladēva came as crest of the earth in this dynasty, and that his son was Chāmundarāja, whose son was Vallabharāja, after whom came Durlabharāja. Durlabharāja had a son named Bhīmadēva, Bhīmadēva's son was Karṇadēva, after whom came Jayasimha. Here ends the 11th verse, beyond which the inscription discloses no historical fact, though here and there some names are discernible. The name Shākambharī[1] also appears at one place, most probably to denote the site where this inscription had been set up.

1. We learn from history that this Jayasimha was the first Chāulukya king who conquered Sāmbhar (Shākambbarī) from the Chauhāns.

APPENDIX D.

1. Jhalrapatan Stone Inscription of Udayaditya [Vikrama] Samvat 1143 (1086 A. D.)

[Published in the Journal & proceedings of the (Royal) Asiatic Society of Bengal, Calcutta, (New series), Vol. X, No 6, 1914 A D., PP 241-243]

This stone inscription lies in Sarvasukhiyā Kothi at Jhālrāpātān. It contains ten lines of writing which cover a space of 8″ (in breadth) by 6½″ (in height). It is well preserved. The characters are Nāgarī. The letters in the first seven lines are bigger than those in the last three[1]. The language is Sanskrit and the whole of the inscription is in prose.

The inscription is dated the 10th of the bright half of Vaishākha in the [Vikrama] year 1143. It is mentioned in this inscription that Janna a Teli Patel built a temple of Shīva and dug a Vāpi (tank) in the reign of Udayāditya. Two prashastis (eulogies) of Udayāditya, dated Vikrama Samvat 1116 and 1137, have already been published. From this inscription it appears that Udayāditya Paramāra reigned till 1143. How this prince was related to Paramāra Bhōja has not yet been known. But his inscriptions show that he was related to Bhōja. A copper-plate of Paramāra Jayasimha I, dated Vikrama Samvat 1112 (A.D. 1055), published in Epigraphia Indica, vol. III, page 48, shows that Bhōja was succeeded by Jayasimha and afterwards by Udayāditya. A detailed account of these has been published by me in the issue of January 1914 of the Saraswati Magazine.

1. It is probable that the last lines may have been engraved afterwards.

TEXT. [1]

1 ओं[2] नमः शिवाय ॥ संवत् ११४३ वैसाख[3]शु(सु)दि १० अ-
2 द्येह श्रीमदुदयादित्यदेवकल्याणविजयराज्ये । तै-
3 लिकान्वए(ये) पट्टकिल[4]चाहिलसुतपट्टकिल[5]जन्न [के]-
4 न शंभोः प्रासादमिदं कारितं[6] । तथा चिरिहिल्लतले चा-
5 डाघोषकूपिकावुवासकयोः अंतराले वापी च ॥
6 उत्कीर्णेयं पडित[7]हर्षुकेने[8]ति ॥ * ॥ जानासत्कमा-
7 ता धाइणिः प्रणमति ॥ श्रीलोलिगस्वामिदेवस्स[9] केरिं[10]
8 तैलका[11]न्वयपट्टकिल[12]चाहिलसुतपट्टकिल[13]जंनकेन ॥ श्रीसेंधवदेवपर-
9 वनिमित्यं[14]दीपतैल्य[15]चतुःप(ष्प)लंमेकं मुदकं क्रीत्वा[16] तथा वरिषं[17] प्रति स(ं)विज्ञा-
10 ७ तं ॥ ॥ मंगलं महाश्री ॥ ६

TEXT.[18]

1. Oṁ[19] namah Shīvāya ‖ saṁvat 1143 Vaisa (shā) kha Shudi 10 a-
2. dyēha Shrīmad-udayādityadēvakalyāṇavijayarājye Tai-
3. likānvayē Pattakila Chāhilasuta Paṭṭakila Janna-[kē]-
4. na Shaṁbhoh prāsādamīdam[20] kāritam[21] । Tathā Chirihil-latalēchā.
5. dā-ghausha-kūpikāvruvāsakayoh aṇtarālē vāpīcha ‖
6. utkīrṇn-ēyam Padita[22] Harshukēnēti[23] ‖*‖ Jānāsatkamā-
7. tā Dhāiṇih praṇamati ‖ Shrī Lōligasvāmidēvassa[24] kērim[25]
8. Tailakānvaē[26] PattakilaChāhilasutaPaṭṭakilaJanṇakena ‖ Shrī Sēndhavadēvapara
9. -va[27] nimityam [28] dīpatailya[29] chatuhpalam-ēkam mudakam[30] krītvā tathā varisham[31] prati savi-[jnā]-
10. tam[32] ‖ ‖ Maṇgalam Mahāshrī ‖ ६

---

1 From an impression kindly supplied by Mr G. H. Ojha.

2 Denoted by a symbol.

3 Read, वैशाख । 4 Read, पट्टकिल ।

5 Read, पट्टकिल । 6 Read, प्रासादोऽयं कारितः ।

7 Read, पण्डित । 8 Read, हर्षुकेणे° । 9 Read, °देवस्य ।

10 The meaning is not clear perhaps कृते is meant.

11 Read, तैलिका° । 12 Read, पट्टकिल ।

13 Read, पट्टकिल । 14 Read, पर्वनिमित्तं । 15 Read तैल° ।

16 The meaning is not clear perhaps मोदकं क्रीत्वा is meant.

17 Read, वर्षं ।

18 From an ink impression kindly supplied by Mr. G. H. Ojha.

19 Denoted by a symbol 20 Read prāsādoyam.

21 Read karitah. 22 Read Paṇḍita 23 Read Harshukeṇēti.

24 Read Dēvasya. 25 Read kritē 26 Read Tailikānvayē.

27 Read parva 28 Read nimittam 29 Read taila.

30 Read Mōdakaṁ. 31 Read varsham. 32 Read Saṁvijnātaṁ.

TRANSLATION.

1 Om! Reverence to Shiva.

In Sanvat 1143 on the 10th of the bright half of the month Vaishākha,

2 to-day in the prosperous reign of Udayādityadēva,

3 Tēli Patēla Chahila's son Patēla-Janna

4 erected this temple of the god Shiva and also in Chirihilla,

5 between Chādāghausha Kūpikā and Vruvasaka, (dug) a Vāpī (tank).

6 This inscription is engraved by Pandita Harshuka. The mother of Janna,

7 Dhāini, bows. For Shrī Loligasvāmidēva,

8 Tēli Patēla Chāhila's son Patēla-Janna at the ceremony of Sēndhavadēva

9 Promises four pala (a measure) oil and a ball of sweet to be offered every year.

10 prosperity! Great fortune!

2. Hathal Plates[1] of (Paramara) Dharavarsha [Vikrama] Samvat 1237 (1180 A. D.).

[Published in the Indian Antiquary, vol XLIII, (September 1941) (pp. 193—194)]

THIS inscription was found in the Hāthal village in the Sirohi State about 3 miles North-West of Mount Ābū. It is engraved on two copper plates, each of which measures about $6\frac{1}{2}''$ broad by $5\frac{1}{2}''$ high and contains a ring hole but the ring has been lost.

Each plate is engraved on one side only. One of these plates contains 10 lines and the other 11. But the 11th line seems to be a post script, for the letters in this line differ widely from the others.

The characters are Nāgarī of the 12th century. The language is very incorrect Sanskrit. This may be due to the fault of the engraver. It is written in prose throughout except the three imprecatory verses (lines 15 to 20 of the second plate). In respect of orthography the letters *b* and *v* are both denoted by the sign for *v*.

This inscription is dated Thursday, the 11th of the bright half of Kārtika in the (Vikrama) year 1237, and refers to the reign of Dhārāvarsha, who, in this inscription, is styled the descendant of Dhūmarājadeva, Rājā of Ābū who is described in the inscriptions of Ābū[2] and

1 The ink impressions of these plates were kindly given to me by Rai Bahadur Pandit Gauri Shankar H. Ojha, Superintendent, Rajputana Museum, Ajmer.

2 तत्राथ मैत्रावरुणस्य जुह्वतश्चंडोग्निकुंडात्पुरुषः पुराभवत् ॥
मत्वा मुनीन्द्रः परमारणक्षम स व्याहरत्तं परमारसंज्ञया ॥ ११ ॥
पुरा तस्यान्वये राजा धूमराजाह्वयो भवत् ॥
येन धूमध्वजेनेव दग्धा वंशाःक्ष्माभृताम् ॥ १२ ॥
(Unpublished Inscription in the Achaleshvara temple at Abu).

Girvar[1] as the founder of the Paramāra clan.[2]

The minister, at that time, was Kovidāsa. The day of the charter specified in the inscription is *Devottham Ekadashi*; and it says the following with regard to the donee Bhattāraka Vīsala Ugradamaka, *acharya* of Shiva-dharma: (1) That he be granted....in Sāhilvādā. (2) That he be permitted to graze his cattle on the pasture grounds free of charge. (3) That a pasture land be granted to him in Kumbhāranulī. (4) That he be granted an area of land which can be tilled with two ploughs in a day. (5) In the 11th line of the second plate, which is supposed to be a postscript it is mentioned that the pastures of Māgavadi and Hāthaladi villages also be granted to him.

Lines 5-10 of the second plate contain curses on those princes who would deprive him of these privileges.

Of the localities mentioned here Hāthaladi is obviously Hāthal where the plates were found. In the 15th century inscriptions, this village bears the name of Brahmasthāna. This name must have been given to it either because it was granted to Brāhmanas by Paramāra princes, or because there was a temple of Brahmā near it which is now in ruins.

Text.

First Plate.

१ ॐ[3] संवत् १२३७ वर्षे कार्तिक सुदि ११ गुरौ वद्ये[4]—
२ ह चाह्मापत्नं[5] ॥ समस्तराजावलीसमलंकृ [त] श्रीमदर्वुदा[6]—
३ धिपतिश्रीधुमराज[7]देवकुलकमलोषो (द्यो) तनमान्त [र्त] ड—
४ मा [ं] डलिकेसुर[8] शंभुश्रीधारावर्षदेवकल्याणविज—

---

1 जयतु निखिलतीर्थैः सेव्यमानस्समन्तान्मुनिसुरसुरपत्नीसंयुतैरर्वुदाद्रिः ।
विलसदनलगर्भाद्भूत श्रीवशिष्ठः कमपि सुभटमेकं सृष्टवान् यत्र मंत्रैः ॥ ३ ॥
आनीत धेन्वे (न्वै) परनिर्जयेन मुनिःस्वगोत्रं परमारजातिम् ।
तस्मैद द वद्भुतभूरिभाग्य तं धौमराजं च चकार नाम्ना ॥ ४ ॥
(Pātnārayān Inscription of Girvar) I shall edit this inscription also as soon as possible.

2 श्रीधूमराजः प्रथम बभूव भूव सवस्तत्र नरेन्द्रवंशे ।
भूमीभृतो यः कृतवानभिज्ञान् पक्षद्वयोच्छेदनवेदनासु ॥

3 Expressed by a Sign,

4 Read गुरावद्ये[0]

5 Read चाज्ञापत्नं

6 Read [0]दर्वुदा[0]

7 Read धूमरा[0]

8 Read [0]का सुरशंभु[0]

५ यराज्ये तत्पादपद्मोपजीविनमहं[1] श्रीकाविदे[2] स-
६ मस्तमुद्राव्यापारान य (प) रिगंथयतीत्येव[3] काले प्रवर्त्त-
७ माने श [।] सनान्तराणि लिख्यते[4] यथा। अद्य संजा-
८ त देवोष्ठनीएकादस्यां[5] महापव्वीणि[6] नलिनीदल-
९ गतजललवतरलतरं जीवितव्यासिद्[7] विधाय[8]
१० परमषैवा[9]चार्यभट्टारकवीसलउग्रदमके-

Second Plate.

११ स्य[10]साहिलवाडाग्रामे ... मुक्ति [:] ॥ तथा एतदीयध-
१२ षोः[11]गोचरे चरणीया[12] तथा कुंभारनुलिग्रामे सुरभिम-
१३ र्यादापर्यंत भूमी दत्त[13] हल २ हलद्वयभूमी[14] शासने-
१४ नोदकपूर्व्वं [ं] प्रदत्ताः[15] ॥ द्यूतेऽत्रमहं[16] श्रीकोविद[17] से-
१५ ठि° जाल्हणौ ॥ मतै ॥ श्रीः ॥ बहुभिर्व्वसुधा भुक्ता रा-
१६ जभिः सगरादिभिः यस्य यस्य यदा भूमी तस्य[18] तस्य त-
१७ दा फल [ं] ॥ १ ॥ स्वदतां[19] परदत्तां वा यो हरेद्वसुंधरां[20] । षष्ठि-
१८ र्वर्षसहस्राणि[21] वलमाया [ं][22] जायते कृमि [ः] ॥ २ ॥ ममवंश-
१९ क्षये क्षीणे[23] अन्योहन्नृपतिर्भवेत् । तस्याहं करल-
२० ग्नोस्मि[24] मम दत्तं न लोपयेन्[25] ॥ ३ ॥ शुभं भवतू[26] ॥ छ ॥
२१ मागवाडीग्रामग्रासभूमी दत्ता[27] हातडलीग्रामग्रासभूमी दत्त[28] [।]

---

1 Read °जीव्यह

2 Read कोविद.

3 Read °पारान् परिपन्थयामीत्येव

4 Read लिख्यन्ते°

5 Read °देवोत्थान्येकादश्या

6 Read °पर्व्वणि

7 Read जीवितव्यमिद

8 Read विधाय

9 Read °मशैवा°

10 Read °दमकाय

11 Read °धेनवो

12 Read चारणीयाः

13 Read °पर्यन्ता भूमिर्दत्ता

14 Read °भुमिः शा°

15 Read प्रदत्ता

16 Read दूतकोऽत्राह

17 Read कोविद·

18 Read भूमिस्तस्य

19 Read स्वदत्ता

20 Read हरेत वसुंधराम्

21 Read षष्टिवर्षसहस्राणि

22 Read विष्ठायां

23 Read °क्षये जाते

24 Read °लग्नोस्मि

25 Read लोपयेत्

26 Read भवतु

27 Read °भूमिर्दत्ता

28 Read °भुमिर्दत्ता

3. Patanarayana stone inscription of Paramara Pratapsimha. [Vikrama] Samvat 1344 (1287 A. D.).

[Published in the Indian Antiquary, Vol XLV, (May 1916) (pp. 77—80]

I edit this inscription from an excellent impression kindly given to me by Rai Bahadur Pandit Gaurishankar H. Ojha, Superintendent, Rājputānā Museum, Ajmer. The original inscription was found in the Pātanārāyana temple near Girvar about 4 miles west of Madhusūdana in Sirohi State.

This inscription consists of 39 lines covering a space of 2 ft. 6 inches broad by 1 ft. 11 inches high. The inscription is well preserved. The **Characters** are Nāgarī. The **Language** is Sanskrit. Lines 1-35 are written in verses numbering 46. Lines from 35 to the end are in prose. With regard to **Orthography** it must be noted that a consonant following *r* is sometimes doubled, and sometimes not. As regards **Lexicography**, the following words deserve to be noticed.

(1) *Devada* employed in 1.36, denotes a line of Chāhamānas: the present rulers of Sirohi also belong to this line. (2) *Donakari*, 1.36, the appropriate meaning of which can not be explained: it may denote a Mārwārī word *doli*; if it is a Sanskrit word, it is composed of two words *drona* and *khari*, the respective meaning of which are 32 and 96 seers. (3) *Dhībadau*, 1.36, means *dhimada*, (a well), well-known in Mārwār. (4) *Arahatta*, 1.37, means a Persian wheel. (5) *Dhikada*, *dhikaa* are also used for *dhimada*. (6) *Gohil-utra* stands for the Sanskrit word *Gohila-putra*.

The inscription is of great importance in connection with Paramāra history. It contains the genealogy of the Paramārās as follows:—

Vāshishṭha created Dhūmarāja Paramāra, by means of *mantras* from the *agni-kunda* at Ābū. Dhārāvarsha was born in his family. In the 15th *shloka* it is mentioned that this Dhārāvarsha pierced three buffaloes with one arrow. This is supported by the fact that on the Mandākinī tank outside the temple of Achalēshvara on Ābū there is a statue of Dhārāvarsha, about 5 ft. in height with a bow in his hand and three buffaloes standing before him with a hole running through their belies. Dhārāvarsha had a son Sōmasimha by name who had a son named Krishṇarāja. The son of the latter was Pratāpasimha, who defeated Jaitrakarna and regained Chandrāvatī. Perhaps this Jaitrakarna may be Jaitrasimha of Mewār, who was the grandson of Rāula Mathanasimha and son of Padmasimha. Pratāpsimha's Brāhmaṇa minister Dēlhana re-built the temple of Pātanārāyana in [Vikrama] Samvat 1344 (1287 A. D.)

1 ॥ॐ॥ ॐ नमः पुरुषोत्तमाय ॥ श्रीरामेण विजित्य रावणमथ स्वीकृत्य सीतां किल व्यावृत्तेन
पुरीं पुराऽर्बुदतटे कृत्वाऽथ देवार्च्चनां विप्रस्थानसमं सुमं-
2 गलपदं यः स्थापितोऽसौ विभुर्भूयाद्भूरिविभूतये स भवतां श्रीपट्टनारायणः ॥ १ ॥
देवस्या[द्भु]तविक्रमस्य भवतो रामस्य धर्म्मक्रमं वाशिष्ठं च तथार्बुदं च चरितं किं-
3 चित्प्रमारोद्भवं । चक्रे देल्हणमंत्रिणोद्धृतिरथ श्रीपट्टविष्णोर्यथा विप्रः सर्वमिदं व्यनक्ति
विजयादित्यः कविग्रामणीः ॥ २ ॥ जयतु निखिलतीर्थैः सेव्यमानः समं-
4 तान्मुनिसुरसुरपत्नीसंयुतैरर्बुदाद्रिः विलसद [न] लगर्भादद्भुतं श्रीवशिष्ठः कमपि
सुभटमेकं सृष्टवान् यत्र मंत्रैः ॥ ३ ॥ आनीतधेन्वे (न्वै) पर निर्जयेन मुनिः स्वगो-
5 त्रं परमारजातिं । तस्मै ददावुद्धतभूरिभाग्यं तं धौमराजं च चकार नाम्ना ॥ ४ ॥
वशिष्ठगोत्रोज्ज्वल एष लोके ख्यातस्तदादौ परमारवंशः । स्वस्त्यस्तु तस्मै क्रमसंकथा-
6 यां विधास्यते तस्य विभावनापि ॥ ५ किलैकदा निर्हुतरावणः श्रीरामोऽर्बुदोपांतनिविष्ट-
सैन्यः वह्नौ विशुद्धामिह वीक्ष्य सीतां शुद्धेश्वरं स्थापयति स्म देवं ॥ ६ स्था-
7 नं तथाग्रे ग्रिविडं च नाम्ना साम्नायविप्रैरभिनंद्यमानं। निवेश्य पट्टे प्रकृताभिषेकः श्रीमद्वशिष्ठेन
तदा मुदा च ॥ ७ श्रीमद्वशिष्ठस्य च गौतमस्य पुण्याश्रमोत्तीर्णसुरश्र (स्र)-
8 वंत्याः । इह प्रवाहद्वयसंगमार्णाः पूर्णापगापट्टनदोपकंठे ॥ ८ श्रीपट्टनारायणमेनमुच्चैः
प्रकल्प्य तत्रैव च लक्ष्मणेशं,। सौमित्रिसीतापरिचर्यमाणस्ततः प्रतस्थे स्वपु-
9 रीमयोध्यां ॥ ९ तदादि गंगाह्वयवारिपूर्णः ख्यातः स्फुटं पट्टनदोयमुच्चैः । कृष्णोपकंठे ननु
मुक्तिहेतुं यं गुह्यतीर्थं प्रवदंति तज्ञाः (ज्ञाः) ॥ १० किं ब्रूमहे वैभवमर्बुदाद्रेः सम-

10 स्नतीर्थैः समलंकृतस्य । च्छा (छा)यापि यस्यातनुते मनूनां तनुत्यजां दुर्गतिनाशमुच्चैः ॥११
स्थाने ततस्तत्स विधोर्वरायां वराणि तीर्थान्यतनोत्स रामः अथोज्ज्वलं स्थानमपि प्र-
11 सिद्धं सद्धेद्विद्विप्रवरोपरुद्धं ॥ १२ श्रीरामशासनमहो किमु वर्णयामः किंवा प्रमार-
पृथिवीपतिसच्चरित्रं । ये राममुख्यपृथिवीपतिदत्तभूमिरापालयंत प्रतिपदं विनिरस्त-
12 लौल्यैः ॥ १३ तस्मिन् किलार्बुदधरावलये स धारावर्षो बभूव नृपतिर्गुरुवीररत्नं । यस्य
प्रभापरिकरोऽद्यदिनानि यावत् यस्मिन्नसत्यपि जलध (द्धु) तिरद्भुतं तत् ॥ १४ एकबा-
13 णनिहतत्रिलल्लायुं[1] यं निरीक्ष्य कुरुयोधसदृक्षं । चंडिकाकृततदेककपाला लज्जितासिमधुना
न धुनाति ॥ १५ श्रीसोमसिंहोजनि भूमिपालस्ततोरिभूपालनिबद्धकालः ।
14 यः शौर्यदानाधिकयोगभावात्संगीयते राम इवाभिरामः ॥ १६ श्रीकृष्णदेवस्तनयस्ततो-
भूद्बुद्ध्यापि शौर्येण च कृष्णकल्पः । प्रद्युम्नकल्पोऽजनि येन स श्रीप्रतापसिंहोरिकरीं-
15 द्रसिंहः ॥ [१७] कामं प्रमथ्य समरे जगदेकवीरस्तं जैत्रकर्णमिह कर्णमिवेंद्रसूनुः ।
चंद्रावतीं परकुलोदधिदूरमग्नामुर्व्वीं वराह इव यः सहसोद्दधार ॥ १८ अथालमेषामनु-
16 संकथाभिरेतन्महीमुख्यनयाहृताभिः । वि (वी) च्या (त्ता) महे संप्रति पट्टविष्णुप्रासादजी-
र्णोद्धरणक्रमं तं ॥ १९ कालः किलास्ति दुरतिक्रम एव योसौ तान् निर्जरानपि
जराविधुरा-
17 न् करोति । चेन्नेति निर्जरपतेः किमनेन चक्रे प्रासाद एष ननु जर्जरिताश्मबंधः ॥ २०
इति ननु कतिचिद्भिर्वा-(कतिभिश्चिद्वा) सरैः शीर्णसंधौ शिथिलितशिखराग्रे
निर्गलद्वृष्टिबिंदौ । बत रु-
18 दितवतीव स्वाश्रयेस्मिन्हरिस्तत्पटुतरकरणार्थं देल्हणं व्यादिदेश ॥ २१ ततः पटुतरं मंत्री
देल्हणो ब्राह्मणो व्यधात्[2] । श्रीपट्टविष्णुप्रासादं जीर्णं वित्तरसायनैः ॥ २२ व्यापारधौ-
रेयतये-
19 षमंत्रीऽऽऽऽऽ[3] किं नेति तर्त्कि ननु मंत्रयोगात् । यो मंत्रयित्वा हृदि रामराजं धर्मेण
साहाय्यमहो चकार ॥ २३ इतश्चोपमन्योर्मुनेः (ने) रम्यगोत्रे स वींका-
20 क इत्याविरासीद्वि (द्द्वि) जेंद्रः । यतः संप्रसूता चरूपी ति नाम्नी सुता चंद्रिकावत्सुरूपातिशुद्धा
॥ २४ तया संगमासाद्य सादाकनाम्ना द्विजेनोज्ज्वलेनेंदुकांतोपमेन । सुताः पं-
21 चयशोपमाः पंच जाताः सुधापंचनिस्यंदसंदोहकल्पाः ॥ २५ लक्ष्मणकेल्हणवाल्हणसंज्ञास्तु-
र्यस्तु देल्ह (ण) स्तेषु । ख्यातो भास्करनामा पंचमकः श्रुतिविदः सर्वे ॥
22 २६ निजं गर्गमुपि (नि)गोत्रं शाखां माध्यंदिनीमथ । प्रवरान् त्रीन् यजुर्वेदं स्वस्थानं त्रिवर्द्धि
तथा ॥ २७ आवस‥‥‥ लावेतौ वानादेदाकसंज्ञकौ । केशवो महमूणश्च मा-
23 ल्हासाभिधानकौ ॥ २८ आत्मना सह तान् सप्त पूर्वजानिति च क्रमात् ॥ लक्ष्मणादीनथ
भ्रातॄनन्यानपि च पूर्वजान् ॥ २९ उद्दधार स धर्मात्मा देल्हणो सुमहामतिः । स्वकीर्त्ये-
24 व सुधाधौतं विष्णुप्रासादमुद्धरन् ॥ ३० तुर्योपि धुर्यस्तु गुणैरुदारैः स देल्हणो वित्तरसा-
यनेन । यः कालजीर्णं ननु पट्टविष्णुप्रासादमेनं नवमेव चक्रे ॥ ३१ जीर्णो-
25 द्धाराद्प्रतिष्ठादिनं च भक्त्या विष्णावेकवेलाशनोऽभूत् । कर्मस्था ये यश्चपूर्णे तितूर्णा
मेने म(मा)नी स्वं ततःपूर्णकामं ॥ ३२ हैमे पट्टं भूषणं भालमूले चक्रे वैकुंठस्य कं-

---

1 Read लुलायं

2 By a mistake the engraver has left the word ब्राह्मणो out of the 18th line and engraved it in the 19th line.

3 These five signs ऽऽऽऽऽ are redundant.

26 ठे च रौप्यं । हैमेनासीन्मुक्तिलोकोऽन्वयोस्य रौप्येणानंदो महीयान् पितॄणां ॥ ३३ प्रायशः
कलिमलाकुलितानां शुद्धये हि शरणं हरिरेकः । सर्वपातकनिराकृ-

27 तिहेतुर्यस्ततः शरणमेनमयासीत् ॥ ३४ जीवितं तरुणताथ धनं वा कस्यचित्कचन न
स्थिरमास्ते । इत्यव (वे)त्य सुकृतैरिति तैर्यस्तानि सुस्थिरतमानि वितेने ॥ ३५ संवत्

28 त्रयोदशशते त्रिचत्वारिंशद्राख्यया । ख्याते संवत्सरे शुक्लदशम्याम (मा)श्विनस्य च ॥ ३६
जीर्णोद्धारसमारंभं कारयामास देल्हणः । आगामिनि चतुश्चत्वारिंशदाख्येथ वत्सरे ।

29 ३७ ज्येष्ठस्य सितपंचम्यां प्रतिष्ठां च ध्वजोच्छ्रयं । समापय्य च तत्कृत्यं सर्वं शांतिक-
(प्र) पूर्वकं ॥ ३८ ततो यदृच्छयाभोज्यवस्त्रदानैर्द्विजोत्तमान् यथापात्रं तथा लोकान्

30 प्रीणयामास तद्दिने ॥ ३९ विप्रः किल ग्राहकपात्रमेव प्रायः कलौ यो विदधे वृथेति ।
न्यायार्जितैः स्थानविभागवृत्तिः धनैनि (र्नि) जैरीदृशधर्मकर्त्ता ॥ ४० गंगाप्रवाहप-

31 यसोः (सः) स्तवकः किमुच्चैः किंवाऽस्य सा(शा)व इव सांग इहास्ति शुद्धः । आभात्यलं
धवलितः सुधया विदूरात्प्रासाद एष जनलोचनकर्म्मण [:] श्रीः ॥ ४१ श्रीमालवाधिपति
(तु) रु-

32 ष्कवर्जैकजैत्रश्रीमाददेवसुतवीसलरम्यराज्ये । सर्वैर्द्विजैरनुमतादिमदेवदायैः जीर्णोद्धृ-
तिर्व्यजनि दत्व (त्त)चतुःशतीकैः ॥ ४२ धरणीधरपण्डितस्य पुत्रो जननी य-

33 स्य च चांपलेति साध्वी । द्विजयोगिबुधाग्रणीः स तेने वइजादित्यकविः प्रशस्तिमेतां
॥ ४३ ॥ रोहेडास्थानवास्तव्य मूंमदेवात्मजः सुधीः । गांगदेवः सूत्रधारः प्रशस्ति (स्तिं)
कीर्णवानिमां ॥ ४४ ॥

34 ये शब्दविद्यानिरवद्यभावाः साहित्यसौहित्यमुपेयिवांसः । येषां मना (नो) मत्स-
रमुक्तमेषा समूह्यता (तां) तैर्विजयार्कवाणी ॥ ४५ ॥ श्रीमद्वशिष्ठभवभूपगुरूत्तमोयं
मूकावभासिपद-

35 वाक्यविदा (दां) वरेण्यः । आल्हादनस्य तनयोजनि सथिरदेव[1] मोहनाख्यः संकीर्त्यते स
इह तत्कवितातमित्रं ॥ ४६ ॥ देवस्य नैवेद्यहेतोर्दत्तायपदव्यक्तिर्यथा ॥

36 महाराजकुलसो (शो) भितपुत्रदेवड़ामेलाकेन कनारे ग्रामे दोणकारी क्षेत्रु १ उभयं दत्तं ॥
षीमाउलीग्रामे वीहलरा० वीरपाजेन ढीबडउ १ दत्तं । आडलिग्रामे ।

37 ग्रामेयकैः अरहट्टंप्रति से ८ ढीकडा ढीकआ प्रति सेः २ दत्तं ॥ काल्हणवाडग्रामे हलं
प्रति सेः १ गोहिलउअनुडिमल (ले) न प्रतिग्रामपाद्रं दत्त द्र० १० तथा

38 मडाउलीग्रामे रा० गांगू कर्मसीहाभ्यां द्वादशएकादशीषु चोलापिका आयपदं दत्तं ।
चंद्रावतीमंडपिकायां विसार

39 अंकतोऽपि ॥ सं. १३४४ ज्येष्ठशुदि ५ शुक्रे जीर्णोद्धारप्रतिष्ठा

Brief sketch of the Text.

The inscription opens with obeisance to Purushōttama.

Verse 1 invokes the blessings of Shrī Paṭṭanārāyana, who, we are told, was established on Mt. Ābū by Rāma on his way back to his capital with Sitā after defeating Rāvana. Vijayāditya the author of this *prashasti* (v. 2) promises to give a short account of Rāmachandra, Vashishṭha,

[1] The letters सथिरदेव are in excess of the metre.

Mount Ābū, the Paramāras and of repairs to Pātanārāyana temple by Dēlhana, minister of the Paramāras.

Verse 3 relates that Vashishtha created a warrior from his *agnikunda* on Mount Ābū. The sage conferred the title of Paramāra and named him Dhūmarāja for defeating his enemies, who had stolen away the sage's cow (v. 4). From that day the Paramāras became of Vashishtha *gotra* (v. 5).

The sixth verse shows that Rāmachandra, after examining Sitā's piety by means of *agni*, established Shuddhēshvaradēva near Ābū.

Verses 7 to 9 show that Rāmachandra, being installed by Vashishtha, and having established Pattanārāyana and Lakshmanēsha on the bank of Pattanada, the source of which lies near the *ashramas* of Vashishtha and Gautama, left for his capital, accompanied by Sitā and Lakshmanā.

(Verse 10)—From that day the said Pattanada has become a famous holy place known as Guhyatīrtha.

Verses 11 and 12 contain words in praise of Mount Ābu.

Verses from 13 to 18 give the genealogy of the Paramāras as has been mentioned above.

Verses from 19 to 23 describe the repairs of the temple by Brāhmana Dēlhana, the minister of Paramāras.

Verses 24 to 26 give a genealogy of Dēlhana as follows:—In the line of Upamanyu Muni was born a Brāhmaṇa Vīnkāka, whose daughter Charūpī was married to Sādāka, by whom five sons were born namely Lakshmana, Kēlhana Vālaṇa, Dēlhana, and Bhāskara.

Verses 27 to 31 show that the fourth son Dēlhana, by repairing the temple, made known his Garga Gōtra, Mādhyandini Shākhā, three Pravaras, Yajurvēda, his village Grivida, and seven ancestors namely Āvasa...lā, Vānā, Dēdāk, Kēshava, Mahamūṇa, Malha, Sāsā, including himself and his five brothers Lakshmana, etc., in this world.

Verses 32 to 35—Dēlhana is praised for his conduct during the time the temple was being re-built.

Verses 36 to 40—show that the work of repairing the temple was commenced on the 10th of the bright half of the Āshvina, Vīkrama Samvat 1343 and finished on the 5th of the bright half of the Jyēshtha, Vikrama Samvat 1344.

Verse 41 speaks of the beauty of the temple.

Verse 42 shows that the repairs were carried on during the reign of king Vīsala, son of the king Bhādadēva, victor of the Turushkas and the king of Malwa.

Verse 43 tells us that the author of this *Prashasti* was Vijayāditya, whose parents were Dharanīdhara and Chāmpalā.

Verse 44 shows that this inscription was engraved by Gāngadēva, son of Mūmadēva, resident of Rōhēdā.

Verse 45 speaks of the ability of the author.

Verse 46 refers to the author's father as a friend of Mōhana, the son of Ālhādana, perhaps one of the seven forefathers of Dēlhana.

For the maintenance of this temple the following grant and offerings were made by neighbouring persons.

L. 36. Dēvadā Mēlāka son of Sōbhita: one *donakari* and a field in the village of Chhanāra. Rājaputra Vīrapāla son of Vihala: a *dhimada* in the village of Khīmāulī.

L. 36-37 The villagers of Āulī: 8 seers of corn from each *arahatta* and 2 seers from each *dhimadu*. In village Kālhaṇavādā: one seer of grain at each plough. Nuḍimala son of Guhila: 10 *drammas* from each of his villages.

L. 38 Rājaputra Gāngū and Karmasimha: for twelve *ekadashis* the revenue of the Chōlapikā, in the village of Madāulī and export duty of Chandrāvatī.

L. 39 on Friday the 5th of the bright half of Jyēshtha, [Vikrama] Samvat 1344, the Pratishṭhā ceremony was performed.

4. The Caste System and Religion Among Hindus.

[Published in the Indian Culture, Calcutta, Vol IV., No. 3, (January 1938 A. D.) pp. 366-371].

In a chapter of Rigvēda, known as 'Purusha Sūkta' the Brāhmanas are said to have been born from the mouth, the Kshatriyas from the arms, the Vaishyas from the thighs and the Shūdras from the feet of the 'Virāta Purusha' (Omnipotent).

Though owing to the mention of the names of three 'Vēdas' this chapter may be supposed to be a later addition,[1] yet the real motive which the old sages had adopted in it, to avoid the struggle of life by separating all the main occupations in four branches, has totally been ignored.

It is quite clear that by allotting the different parts of the body of the Omnipotent as the sources of Brāhmaṇas, Kshatriyas, Vaishyas and Shūdras they have pointed out the duties of these 'Varnas' as learning, protection, trade and service respectively.

But in spite of all this people were at liberty to change their Varna by proving their fitness to other occupations.

The following hymn of the 5th Mandala of Rigvēda states:--

अग्ने सहन्तमाभर द्युम्नस्य प्रासहा रयिं ।
विश्वा यश्चर्षणीरभ्या ३ सा वाजेषु सासहत ॥

(Sūkta 23, hymn 1)

i. e, O sacrificial fire! grant me thy sage a son, who may be a destroyer of enemies and who being well versed in hymns may defeat all the enemies, who dare face him in the field.

---

1 It is supposed that previously there was only one 'Vēda' but Vēda Vyāsa assorted the hymns and named their collections as Rig, Sāma and Yajurvēda,

The hymn next to it also asks:—

तमग्ने पृतनाषहं रयिं सहस्व आभर ।
त्वं हि सत्यो अद्भुतो दाता वाजस्य गोमतः ॥

(Sūkta 23, hymn 2)

i.e., O sacred fire! thou art an emblem of the truth and giver of cows and corn. Give me a son, who can defeat the armies of opponents.

These hymns show that at that time even Brāhmaṇas did not hesitate to have their sons profess the characteristic of Kshatriyas.

The following hymn of the 6th 'Maṇdala' of Rigvēda mentions:—

गावो भगो गाव इन्द्रो मे अच्छान् गावः सोमस्य प्रथमस्य भक्षः ।
इमा या गावः स जनास इन्द्र इच्छामीद्धृदा मनसाचिदिन्द्रम् ॥

(Sūkta 28, hymn 5)

i.e; Cows are my wealth. May Lord Indra give me cows. Cows are helpers of Soma, O people: such cows are equal to Lord Indra and I wish to worship this Lord Indra devotedly.

The following hymn of 9th 'Mandala' of Rigvēda tells:

आ नः पवस्व वसुमद्धिरण्यवदश्वावद्गोमद्यवमत्सुवीर्यम् ।
यूयं हि सोम पितरो मम स्थन दिवो मूर्धानः प्रस्थिता वयस्कृतः ॥

(Sūkta 69, hymn 8)

i. e., O Soma! give us prosperity which may comprise money, gold, horses, cows, corn, and power.

O Soma! you being the crown of heaven and grower of corn be my ancestor.

These two hymns point out that Brāhmanas at time were willing to adopt the life of Vaishyas.

Another hymn of the same 'Mandala' of Rigvēda narrates—

कारुरहं ततो भिषगुपलप्रक्षिणी नना ।
नानाधियो वसूयवोऽनुगा इव तस्थिमेन्द्रायेन्दो परिस्रव ॥

(Sūkta 112, hymn 3)

i. e., I am a compiler of hymns, my father is a physician and my mother a corn grinder. Like cows in pasture we live in this world pursuing different occupations for the sake of wealth. Therefore O Soma! flow thy juice for Lord Indra.

This hymn shows that at that time even the members of one and the same family were at liberty to adopt different occupations.

Further there are so many instances of changing the Varṇa by elevating or lowering one's character.

It is stated in 'Aitarēya Brāhmana':—

तस्य ह विश्वामित्रस्यैकशतं पुत्रा आसुः, पञ्चाशदेव ज्यायांसो मधुच्छन्दसः पञ्चाशत् कनीयांसः । तद्ये ज्यायांसो न ते कुशलं मेनिरे ।ताननुव्याजहारान् तान्वः प्रजाभक्षीष्टेति । त एतेऽन्ध्राः पुण्ड्राः शबराः पुलिन्दा मूतिबा इत्युदन्त्या बहवो भवन्ति वैश्वामित्रा दस्यूनां भूयिष्ठाः । (सप्तपञ्चमिका, अध्याय ३, खण्ड ६, म १८)

i. e., out of one hundred sons of Vishvāmitra (who by his own efforts raised himself from a Rājarshi to Brahmarshi) first fifty degraded themselves and were thrown into the category of the 'Dasyūs' like Āndhras, Puṇḍras, Shabaras, Pulindas and Mūtibas.

Gītā also supports the division of 'Varṇa' according to the quality and occupation:—

चातुर्वर्ण्यं मया सृष्टं गुणकर्मविभागशः । (अध्याय ४, श्लोक १३)

The famous and learned king Bhōja, who flourished in the 1st half of the 11th century A. D. also supports this theory. He writes in his book named 'Samarāṅgana Sūtradhāra'[1]:—

एकोऽग्रजन्मा वर्णोऽस्मिन् वेदोऽभूदेक एव च ।
ऋतुर्वसन्त एवैकः कुसुमायुधबान्धवः ॥ १२ ॥

i. e., there was only one 'Varṇa' called Brāhmana, one 'Vēda' and one season known as spring to keep the people happy.

But in course of time when vices began to victimise the people God Brahmā, to protect his creation, made Prithu as the first king on the Earth.

After that—

ततःस चतुरो वर्णानाश्रमांश्च व्यभाजयत् ।

i. e., he (Prithu) divided them (the people) in four 'Varṇas' and the period of their life in four 'Āshramas.'

तेषु ये देवनिरताः स्वाचाराः संयतेन्द्रियाः ॥ ९ ॥
सूरयश्चावदाताश्च ब्राह्मणास्तेऽभवंस्तदा ।
यजनाध्ययने दानं याजनाध्यापनार्थिताः ॥ १० ॥
धर्मस्तेषां विमुच्यान्त्यां स्त्रीं तुल्याः क्षत्रवैश्ययोः ।

[1] महदेवाधिकार (अध्याय ६) and वर्णाश्रमविभाग (अध्याय ७) ।

i. e. among those who are devotees, of excellent character, pious, scholars, and virtuous were named Brāhmaṇas and were entrusted with the task of performing sacrifices for themselves as well as for others, acquiring knowledge and imparting it to others and giving and accepting charities. They were permitted to marry the daughters of first three Varṇas.

ये तु शूरा महोत्साहाः शरणया रक्षणक्षमाः ॥ ११ ॥
दृढव्यायतदेहाश्च क्षत्रियास्त इहाभवन् ।
विक्रमो लोकसंरक्षा विभागो व्यवसायिता ॥ १२ ॥
एतेषामयमप्युक्तो धर्मः शुभफलोदयः ।

i. e., those who were brave, energetic, capable to protect and give shelter to refugees, strong and able-bodied were made Kshatriyas.

In addition to some of the tasks mentioned above they were put in charge of brave acts, protection, justice and enterprise.

निसर्गान्निपुणं येषां रतिर्वित्तार्जनं प्रति ॥ १३ ॥
श्रद्धादाक्ष्यदयावन्ता वैश्यांस्तानकरोदसौ ।
चिकित्सा कृषिवाणिज्ये स्थापत्यं पशुपोषणम् ॥ १४ ॥
वैश्यस्य कथितो धर्मस्तद्वत्कर्म च तज सम् ।

i. e., those who were shrewd, desirous of wealth, honest, skilled and tender-hearted were classed as Vaishyas.

They were put in charge of the work of treatment of diseases, agriculture, commerce, craftsmanship, breeding of cattle and manufacture of metal-articles.

नातिमानभृतो नातिशुचयः पिशुनाश्च ये ॥ १५ ॥
ते शूद्रजातयो जाता नातिधर्मरताश्च ये ।
कलारम्भोपजीवित्वं शिल्पिता पशुपोषणम् ॥ १६ ॥
वर्णत्रितयशुश्रूषा धर्मस्तेषामुदाहृतः ।

i. e., those who were devoid of self-respect, impious, cruel and irreligious were branded as Shudras.

They were allowed to earn their living by performing different physical feats or uttering various sounds, and by craftsmanship, breeding of cattle and the service of the first three Varṇas.

These quotations show that the people previously belonging to one and the same 'Varṇa' in course of time were divided in four 'Varnas' according to their qualities and occupations.

Further the changing of one's 'Varna' was in vogue even in the latter half of the 11th century A.D. as is evident from the poem known as 'Ballālacharitra':—

यदि दाम्भिकान् सुवर्णान् वणिजः शूद्रत्वे न पातयिष्यामि ……
गो-ब्राह्मणघातेन यानि पातकानि तानि मे भविष्यन्तीति ॥ ११ ॥
कार्या लोकहितार्थाय कैवर्त्ता दास्यकर्मसु ॥ १६ ॥
मालाकाराः कुम्भकाराः कर्म्मारास्च ततोऽन्यदा ।
युक्तहस्ता गलेवस्त्राः पुरस्तस्थुर्महीक्षितः ॥ २० ॥
सन्तुष्टः सेवया तेषां व्याजहार वचो नृपः ।
यूयं सच् शूद्रवद् ग्राह्या भवेत वचनान्मम ॥ २१ ॥ (अध्याय २३)

i.e., Ballāla being displeased with goldsmiths degraded them to the standard of 'Sachchhūdra' while to increase the number of domestic servants elevated the position of fishermen, gardeners, potters and black-smiths to the same level.

These events have been quoted by Ānanda Bhatta (the author of the poem) on the authority of previous scholars:—

यद्व्याहृतं भट्टपादैरुक्तं यच्चान्यसूरिभिः ।
तत्तद्राजचरित्रेऽस्मिन् बाल्लाले प्रकटीकृतम् ॥ ६ ॥

(at the end)

i. e., what is said by Bhatta Pāda and other scholars have been included in this 'Ballāla-charitra'.

Thus considering all the above facts it becomes clear that the division of 'Varna' among Hindus was based on the quality and occupation like the modern division known as Bābu, Thākur, Sēth and Mazdūr (labourer).

Before concluding this paper we may also state—that our Hindu religion was not so conservative as it is today. There are several proofs which go to show that even foreigners like Greeks, Turks (Yoe-chis), Shakas and Huns were freely admitted to its fold. Leaving apart the Buddhist records the Bēsnagar pillar inscription of 140 B. C. states that this 'Garudadhvaja' (column) was erected by Heliodorus the Greek, who was a staunch Vaishṇavite.

Kalhaṇa in his 'Rājataraṅgiṇī' writes:—

ते तुरुष्कान्वयोद्भूता अपि पुण्याश्रया नृपाः ।
शुष्कलेत्रादि देशेषु मठचैत्यादि चक्रिरे ॥ १७० ॥ (प्रथमतरङ्ग)

i.e., those pious kings (Hushka, Jushka and Kanishka) though born of Turkish race built monasteries and 'Chaityas' at places like Hukhlētrōṅ, etc.

We conclude from the inscriptions of Ushavadāta, the son-in-law of king Nahapāna, who flourished in the 1st half of the second century A.D., that he was a devotee both of Brāhmanism and Buddhism.

We also learn from 'Rājataraṅginī' that:—

श्रीनगर्यां हि दुर्बुद्धिर्विदधे मिहिरेश्वरम् (३०६) (प्रथमतरङ्ग)

i.e., at Srinagar the cruel king (Mihirakula) got built a temple of Shiva called after his own name.

Moreover in commenting on the Panini's 'Sūtra' 'शूद्राणामनिर्वसितानां' (।२।४।१०) the commentator Pataṅjali has counted Shakas and Yavanas as Shūdras and Kaiyaṭa in his turn has concluded that—

'शूद्राणां पञ्चयज्ञानुष्ठानेऽधिकारोऽस्तीति भावः ।'

i.e., Shūdras are also entitled to perform five sacrifices.

Therefore if, setting aside the conservatism prevailing at present and allowing due margin for the changed conditions, we follow the path chalked out by our ancestors we will be more happy and can pass a more peaceful life in this world.

INDEX TO THE HISTORY.

A

B

C

D

E

F

G

H

K

L

M

N

Q

R

S

Index to the appendices.

A

K

Q

R

S

T

W

Y

Z

ERRATA

Page	Line	Incorrect	Correct
III	30	Nagabhat I	Nagabhat II
VI	18	Trivendrum	Travancore
VII	18	मात्रिभक्तिः	मातृभक्तिः
XVI	5	has.. assassins	had.. .the assassins
XXII	1	address	addresses
XXXIII	24	500	5,000
XXXVII	25	Deccan	the Deccan
XLI	36	in	for
XLIV	1	charge	the charge
LI	3	in	as
LXI	6	The Prince	Prince
LXI	18	Further	(delete)
LXIII	23	sum	a sum
6	16-17	Kshartriyas	Kshatriyas
7	8 & 14	Kannauj	Kanauj
7	44	no ther	another
10	26	Sixth	fourth
34	30	Jayachandra[1]	Jayachandra
34	30	Writes:—	Writes[1]: —
50	1	second	other
56	4	(1173 A. D.)[1]	(1173 A. D.)
56	5	inscription	inscription[1]
67	9	Dundada	Dunada
67	31	Rao	the Rao
71	3	resented	enraged
74	12	Emperor[3]	the Emperor[3]
75	8	in	under
75	16	Maharana	the Maharana
76	11	three	five
81	34	chapter 1	chapter 2
83	41	anmity	enmity
95	33	both in this	both this

Page	Line	Incorrect	Correct
99	13	sow	show
105	10	भुंज्ञां	भुजां
117	15	a great rank	a special flag.
141	1	Fort, occupied	Fort and occupied
149	21	under this head	(delete)
155	25	तीव:मराव	तीरमकराव
155	27	नीमांज	नींजाम
156	29	नीजुं—	नीजां—
160	8	willalsobe brought	might also come
170	11	by command	This is our command
173	4	by the	on the
173	27	bright	dark
174	20	latter	later
175	27	Conquerred	Conquered
184	2	selter	shelter
184	25	Rao	Ravat
186	18	Maharaja	Maharana
190	31	Sindhiain	Sindhia
193	24.	داشذ	داید
193	26	یاگر	جاگیر
193	33	تاگیز	تاکید
196	26	Mirkhan	Amirkhan
199	2	the Maharaja	Maharaja
205	2	1059	1069 (Because the lunar eclipse falls in Magh of this year. According to this, the date will be 29th January 1013 A D).
206	31	Kumarapala I	Bhimadeva I
209	25	राज्ञी मेरलदेव्य: (वी) तु पत्नी	राज्ञ्या मेरलदेव्या तु पत्न्या
215	21-22	Shakambari (Chauhana)	Shakambhari-Chauhana
217	25	Through	Though
217	27	after the birth of his son Mahipal,	(delete)

Page	Line	Incorrect	Correct
218	1	Kirtipala and Kumarpala, i. e	(delete)
218	7	by the Solanki	by Solanki
220	9	स्वोवसीयस	श्वोवसीयसं
225	3	Sanvat	Samvat
227	13	Hathaladi	Hatadali
230	12	belies	bellies
234	18	grant	grants
235	8	of three	of the three
238	20	तजसम्	तैजसम्

Page	Column	Line	Incorrect	Correct
243	II	18-19	XXXVIII XLIII	XXXVIII-XLIII
243	II	33	LX	LXIV
246	I	26-27	XLV,I-XLVIII, XLIX-LXIV	XLVI-LXIV,
246	II	12	Kambaksh	Kambakhsh
255	II	27	Chara	Chaora
255	II	48	1,56	156
257	II	29	Govind Das	Goyand Das
258	I	17	104	140
260	II	12	Khsatriyas	Kshatriyas
261	II	37	62	66
262	II	19	158-174	158,174